gap years for GROWN UPS

gap years
for
GROWN
UPS

Susan Griffith

VACATION WORK
The Gap Year Experts

This edition published in Great Britain 2008 by
Crimson Publishing, a division of Crimson Business Ltd
Westminster House
Kew Road
Richmond
Surrey
TW9 2ND

First published 2004

Third edition 2008

A catalogue record for this book is available from the British library.

ISBN 978 1 85458 441 0

Printed and bound by Mega Printing, Turkey

CONTENTS

PREFACE

As an enthusiastic traveller, I vividly remember my 26th birthday as a low point. Transalpino, for those too young to remember, was at one time the student and youth discount on European rail travel available to anyone under 26. For me, turning 26 marked the end of carefree youth as symbolised by the overnight doubling of rail fares. This of course was in the era before £37 no-frills flights to Berlin and Barcelona were accessible to everyone aged 2–99.

That dreaded watershed has been eroded in many other ways too. It may not yet be routine for ordinary people to disappear from their homes and jobs for extended periods, but the numbers are dramatically increasing. Just the other day, a 31 year old hospital doctor from Surrey, T.M. Brabants, won a gold medal in canoeing at the Beijing Olympics, having 'put his career on hold to pursue Olympic glory'. Few career breaks will result in such record-breaking feats, but it is enough that individuals achieve their personal best even if it is simply to prove that they can flourish outside their comfort zone. No longer is it the unique privilege of the young and of students to be able to contemplate taking time off to travel in search of adventure. The idea of leaving it all behind, of temporarily shedding responsibilities at home and at work, has become almost mainstream and has ever been championed by the likes of *Saga* magazine. A whole new market has suddenly materialised – among those not in the first flush of youth – for extended adventures and a chance to contribute something worthwhile abroad. Furthermore, more and more firms are introducing a sabbatical policy.

Several decades ago, a commonplace vision of the future was one of vast quantities of leisure time. I am not sure what happened to that dream, but it certainly hasn't come true for the majority of us in hot pursuit of our careers. Rather than liberating us from the servitude of the office, the new technology seems to have enslaved us even further so that we are expected to be within email reach of the boss wherever we are. The answer to this patently unhealthy state of affairs is to absent ourselves properly for a life-enriching period of time.

The rising popularity among professionals and freelancers of taking three, six or 12 months out to travel, volunteer or study has prompted a corresponding increase in the number of programmes and schemes offered by specialist companies. These target not only the school leaver but the grown-up gapper as well. The path leading to exciting and memorable gap year experiences whether teaching in Mongolia, enjoying the café life of Buenos Aires or doing conservation in New Zeland may be smoother than you think.

This book aims to canvas the possibilities as comprehensively as possible, and covers a wealth of both mainstream and obscure options. Enterprising and energetic grown-ups from all walks of life are beginning to realise that the opportunity to take time out is open to them, whether to join a project in some exotic part of the world, to enhance their CVs through improving a foreign language, or simply to see the world through fresh eyes.

In addition to providing practical and realistic advice about where and how to spend your gap year, these 342 pages aim to spark the imagination of anyone trying to decide whether or not to take time out.

Susan Griffith
Cambridge
September 2008

ACKNOWLEDGMENTS

This third edition of *Gap Years for Grown-ups* owes a substantial debt to all the kind folk (some of them personal friends) who have told me how they finally came to bite the bullet and head off into the unknown. I never get tired of meeting and hearing from those intrepid (and sometimes not-so-intrepid) grown-ups who have set the work-a-day world to one side long enough to explore places and test dreams.

This new revised edition would not have been possible without the help and inspiration of grown-ups from all walks of life including a lorry driver and a Conservative party worker, all of whom have generously shared their information. Their insights and experiences have been enthusiastically received and have been distilled into the pages that follow. I won't list all the scores of people here who are included in the next section, called *Dramatis Personae*, and whose stories are quoted throughout the book.

I am also grateful to the many directors and PR staff of the specialist year out organisations who patiently rooted round in their client files to put me in touch with grown-ups who have had some amazing experiences on their various gap years.

The photographs for the colour section between pages 176 and 177 have been supplied by Mondo-Challenge of Malsor House, Gayton Road, Milton Malsor, Northampton NN7 3AB (☎ 01604 858225; www.mondochallenge.org). MondoChallenge is a UK based non-profit organisation, sending volunteers to work on teaching and business development in Africa, Asia and South America. The average age of a MondoChallenge volunteer is 35, 50% are non-UK based and couples/families are welcome.

DRAMATIS PERSONAE

All of these individuals, couples and families have generously shared their memories, insights and pearls of travelling and volunteering wisdom since the first two editions of this book were published, most recently in 2006. Turn to the Personal Case Histories dotted throughout the book for more detailed accounts from some of these and other enterprising grown-ups.

Ness and Stefan Aalten-Voogd were leading the frantic lives of London urbanities, when a restructuring at Deloitte resulted in redundancy for Stefan. With an injection of cash in the bank, Ness negotiated unpaid leave from her job in financial services and serious travel plans started to brew. They spent 16 months travelling on five continents.

Lisa Bass had a generous employer in Yorkshire who granted her three months unpaid leave to join a conservation project in Madagascar with Azafady. There she came down with a serious case of the 'Africa Bug' so within a month of returning to England gave in her notice and returned to Madagascar for a year to work on policy development for Azafady.

John and Susan Battye from New Hampshire were undaunted in their determination to take six months off to volunteer and travel, despite having four children aged between 3 and 13. After much research they found a small education charity in Thailand where they all found a role at a school and were welcomed to the hearts of the family with whom they stayed and the rest of the village of Rasi Salaic.

Beth Buffam has taken two separate five/six-month breaks in Vietnam. On the first occasion she knew she was going to be laid off from her job in computer programming and decided to spend an extended time in Vietnam. Having made inroads on the language as well as good friends, she returned four years later to a full-time paid job as an English teacher. She was given free accommodation and lived so frugally that she was able to save $800 a month to cover her bills at home.

Sue Burns summoned the courage to leave her home, family, career and dog to chase a dream normally the preserve of energetic, bullet-proof 18-year-olds, i.e. to teach in Nepal. An unprecedented twist of fate saw her arrive on the day the Peace Talks between the Maoists, the Government and the Monarchy of Nepal irreconcilably broke down. Undaunted, she lived in a rebel stronghold during a turbulent time in the country's history, and realised that you are never too old for an adventure.

Virginia Burton describes herself as 'the daughter of refugees and a care survivor, a social worker, civil servant, magistrate and trainee florist'. She spent time in Nicaragua at La Mariposa Spanish School and Eco-hotel (www.spanishschoolnica.com) founded by an old friend from England, Paulette Goudge, which was 'one of the most life affirming and positive things I have done in my life'.

Gosbert Chagula knew that the firm employing him as a mortgage adviser would not allow a three-month break, so he handed in his notice before joining a human rights project in Kumasi,Ghana, arranged by Changing Worlds. Now Gosbert is more sure than ever that he wants to qualify as a solicitor.

Katy Chan wanted to leave behind the corporate dog-eat-dog world for a bit and realised that this also meant leaving her familiar comfort zone. She chose a three-month placement in Costa Rica with Cross Cultural Solutions which had the right balance of volunteering in the mornings and cultural and recreational activities in the afternoons. While she was there she tried surfing, white water rafting and held dance workshops (since she had been a dance teacher).

Bryony Close, her husband and two teenage daughters joined a Blue Ventures volunteer expedition in Madagascar. She felt that the children had their eyes opened not only to the poverty in the developing world but to the differing value system which meant the people were not dissatisfied with their lot.

Kathy Cooper is an American grandmother who suddenly decided to live in Europe. Immediately after obtaining a Trinity Certificate in TESOL (Teaching English to Speakers of other Languages), she was offered a job in southern Poland and has fallen in love with her life there, the chemical-free foods, the teaching and the culture.

Joanna Elgar teaches reception at a school in Derby and was lucky enough to be permitted a luxurious whole year off to teach in Tanzania for six months through a worthwhile charity Village Africa (www.villageafrica.org.uk) and to spend the rest of the year travelling round the world.

Tina Freeman works in business consultancy, but she had always wanted to teach abroad. She was going through a difficult time after losing her son, and thought if she planned to volunteer in Africa, it would give her something positive to focus on and look forward to. She grew so attached to the mountain community of Yamba in her first two-month stint of volunteering in Tanzania (again through Village Africa) that she went back for a longer period in 2008 and now volunteers as the UK administrator.

Peter and Deby Hardy had treated their stint of volunteer teaching in Thailand as soon as their last child left home in 2006 as a taster before a four-month trip to Nicaragua from September 2007. They stumbled across a volunteer-run project in beautiful Granada to refurbish the Armonia School and workshop for disabled people which they were welcome to join. Their main expense was the £125 a month for good accommodation in the volunteer house.

Margaret Hollamby had been prevented from fulfilling her travel ambitions by having a sick husband and two sons to care for. But her chance came last year and she took herself off to volunteer in a women's prison in Quito, to explore the national parks and cloud forests in the region and to visit the Galapagos.

Bradwell Jackson gave up his job as a youth counsellor in the USA to work and travel the world at whim. So far he has taught English in Mexico, Mauritania and now China, where he has been delighted with his reception.

Paul Jones had already given up an IT job in his native Australia and decided to look for similar work in Bristol which he uses as a springboard for various volunteering forays such as in Tanzania and most recently at a summer camp in Russia.

Raheel Khan was becoming disillusioned with his job as a corporate lawyer. He found that there were placements in Belize via Challenges Worldwide that would not only use but challenge his legal background, so he spent three months writing a legal summary for public consumption of the new Domestic Violence Act. He came home clear in his mind that he wanted to change his speciality to international development law.

Maddie Kilgour felt time leaking away and decided to take five months off to go to South America with VentureCo. Although old enough to be the mother of many of the young volunteers at the eco-reserves where she worked, she enjoyed the company and the work (apart from all the mud when it rained). Trekking to isolated spots overlooking the ocean in the Galapagos was a highlight.

Jeffrey Lawson, an American who retired early, has an interest in joinery and traditional sailing ships. He tracked down a volunteering opportunity at a boatyard in Sweden which involved hard work but was very rewarding.

Tara Leaver had enjoyed a summer volunteer placement at a Mexican school so much that she decided to use an inheritance to fund a whole year off starting with a project in Costa Rica.

Tessa Mills decided to take to the road after her 30-year marriage came to an end. She found her nine months of travelling around the world so empowering that she moved to London to create a new business – The Gap Year Guru – to offer advice and support tailored to older people.

Fiona Passey had just obtained her MBA and had a high level banking job before deciding to spend three months teaching in Inida with VESL. Her Husband was totally supporting and is determind to accompany her next time.

Carol Peden found herself widowed prematurely and knew that she had to get away. She negotiated a six-month break from her job as a consultant anaesthetist. She pursued an interest in alternative medicine in both India and China, joined two small group trips with Intrepid Travel in China and Southeast Asia and spent her final month studying Italian and art history in Florence.

Nigel Pegler is a school caretaker and a cycling enthusiast who wanted to go to Africa to help people less fortunate than himself. After speaking to People and Places and ascertaining that it was an ethically sound company, he accepted a placement on a cycling project in South Africa.

Howard Peters enrolled to join a small band of 10 volunteers and a team of professionals at a newly established marine conservation base in Fiji through Coral Cay Conservation. At nearly 60, he was older than the other volunteers but he was already a qualified diver. His experiences in the marine environment had such as profound effect on him that he went on to complete an MSc in the field and is proceeding to do a doctorate.

Barbara Plane, a former primary school teacher, was inspired by the friendliness of the Nepali people. Despite having so little, they just get on with family and life. Her teaching placement in Nepal was arranged by POD.

Marie Purdy was made redundant from her council job when she was just 50, prompting her and her partner Howard to take five months off to travel round Australia, New Zealand, the South Pacific, and finally to visit friends in Montana.

Jane Reddaway had previously enjoyed several short conservation holidays with BTCV (in Iceland, Namibia and China) so much that she decided to take a gap year to put together a series of eco-projects. Her intended route was to include the Italian Dolomites, Iceland and possibly Greenland, Peru south to Patagonia, Easter Island to join an archaeological team setting up a museum, the Galapagos for a month's volunteering and up through Central America including conservation work in the rainforests of Belize. The finale was to be crossing the Rio Grande on horseback.

Tim Rhodes Jones is a young physiotherapist from the Isle of Man who wanted to extend his practical skills by volunteering in Ghana through Changing Worlds in partnership with Africa Sabbatical.

Karen Rich has had a career working on cruise ships and as airline cabin crew. After a serious car accident prompted her to reassess her life, she decided to obtain a TEFL (Teaching English as a Foreign Language) certificate and teach in the country that took her fancy, which turned out to be Latvia. She enjoyed her three-month placement with Changing Worlds so much that she extended it and stayed for a full year.

Dave Sands has taken scores of very cheap air courier flights over the years but now that that option has all but disappeared he still finds amazing bargains, often in pursuit of his hobby which is the tango. He and his wife have recently had extended tango-themed trips to Switzerland, France, Italy, Croatia and China and Cuba.

Ralph Stone from Melbourne believes that unless you see for yourself, you don't really know how the majority of people really live, and how the world works. He has made several trips to Ghana to volunteer through Ikando in Accra and in 2008 was involved with planning a new school in Liberia.

Helen Tirebuck had moved from Edinburgh to London but realised the big city did not suit her. Because she had worked in the office of a volunteer-sending charity, she knew what options were open to her. She had always enjoyed scuba diving on holiday so decided to do an internship on the Pacific coast of Costa Rica to qualify as an instructor with a view to pursuing this as a full-time job.

Rupert Tubbs wanted more than a holiday experience of Africa for his family. The Tubbs family joined a dolphin-monitoring volunteer project in Kenya through The Leap, which was a huge success (even if 10-year-old Felix had to wait until near the end to rival his little sister in the number of dolphins spotted).

Gemma Whitehouse had achieved a lot for someone under 30. She had a position of responsibility with KPMG and had completed a part-time MA in Marketing. Still feeling unfulfilled she set off to volunteer in Africa, with the blessing of her husband. Her experiences there led to her setting up her own agency to send conservation volunteers to Africa. The company is named Amanzi; after an orphaned lion cub she nursed to health on her gap year.

INTRODUCTION

The rise and rise of the gap year has become one of the travel sensations of the past 15 years. Now that the concept is firmly embedded in the consciousness of school leavers, grown-ups are beginning to catch on too. Statistics in this area are difficult to establish but, according to research published by www.gapadvice.org, an estimated 90,000 Britons take career breaks every year, compared with 230,000 young people and 200,000 people in retirement. The respected market analyst Mintel is preparing one of its influential reports on Adult Gap Years in 2008, to unpick changing and emerging trends in the UK and globally.

A recent article in *The Times* identified the biggest trend in travel as the number of '*28–40-year-old career breakers who are opting out of the rat race in search of a better work-life balance.*' A staggering 40% of the population under 35 in full-time employment claim that they have considered trading a high-pressured life for a simpler and better quality of life, which very often includes travel, adventure and volunteering. Just as adults and young people have swapped the teacher/learner roles when it comes to using new technologies, so the 18-year-olds have introduced to an older generation the notion that taking time away can cure all sorts of ills, primarily stress and burn-out – just as likely to be suffered by a teacher, IT contract worker or accountant as by a pre-university student examined within an inch of his or her life.

The concept of a break is central to the natural world. We spend a third of our life sleeping at night to rejuvenate ourselves for the day. Why then should it be considered self-indulgent or lazy to take a chunk of time out of our working life to pursue a different agenda? When work becomes onerous, stressful or dull and begins to swamp other interests, it might be time to reclaim our life by taking a break.

GAP YEARS FOR GROWN-UPS

A gap year can embrace anything from a period of rest and relaxation to an opportunity for reassessing goals and reconnecting with our real values. For some it is simply a case of itchy feet; for others it is a chance to test an alternative vocation or spend time with loved ones. Taking stock periodically allows us to look beyond the details to the bigger picture. The sound of the ticking clock can be silenced when pursuing adventures, and worries about work, children and everything else that have become second nature can be left behind. The individuals who have shared their experiences during the research for this book each illustrates how liberating and important a gap year can be.

The gap year between leaving school and attending higher education is now a well-established transition between childhood dependence and adult maturity. A new trend is for the parents of these teenagers and their contemporaries to follow suit. A desire to trek in distant mountain ranges, volunteer in an African village, or take a cookery course in Italy is not unique to youth.

In response to the sometimes overwhelming demands of our jobs and the news that we may be expected to work until well past the current retirement age, the notion of a career break is becoming more attractive. One more week dealing with a broken photocopier or waking in the night with your head spinning with office tasks and politics may force your hand. Setting a boundary between the personal and the professional is essential for maintaining good mental health.

The stories in this book establish that taking a gap year can be a choice for everyone, not just people with authority and wealth nor those who want to drop out. Now that institutions such as National Health Trusts, large supermarket chains and multinational companies recognise the value of breaks for their employees, they are establishing the principle that time out from work is more than just an eccentric and nostalgic hankering for freedom from responsibility. The idea is gradually gaining legitimacy in the corporate world. Government too is pushing the concept of a work–life balance so that family life will not be sacrificed on the altar of Mammon. When people step back and do the calculations, they often conclude that the balance needs to be shifted a little bit more in favour of life.

Gap years have nearly become part of the *zeitgeist*, the spirit of the age we live in. Every week it is possible to find references in the media to adventurous grown-ups taking off as individuals, couples or families, such as the article in the *Daily Telegraph* 'Aviva boss leaves for gap year he never had' about 56-year-old Richard Harvey who was inspired to spend some time in Africa in the wake of his daughter's gap year. A prime illustration of media interest in this kind of thing was the airing on BBC2 a couple of years ago of a mainstream observational documentary *Grown-up Gappers* which featured eight individuals who had temporarily packed in their everyday lives to explore the world. At the time of writing Channel 4 had commissioned a production company to work on a documentary series with the working title 'Family Gap Year' which will follow parents who take an extended break abroad with their children. Not long ago, a TV network in the USA carried a series titled *Radical Sabbatical* which focused on '*the extraordinary stories of people who risked it all to pursue their passions*'.

As the number of people pioneering this choice increases and in a society where the span of working life is stretching well beyond 40 years, taking breaks may eventually become routine.

Trawling the Internet will lead you to the 'blogs' of any number of heroes and eccentrics who have thrown over safe secure jobs to do something fresh and inspiring. For example the Fleming family whose 'Family Tale of a Global Adventure' can be read at www.rfleming.net/aboutus.htm completed a round-the-world trip a few years ago. A typical catchphrase is attached to the blog of a Canadian couple: '*Sold the house, got rid of the crap, travelling the globe with no exact plans. Follow us on our 15-month journey through Africa, South-East Asia, China, Tibet, Europe and Mexico*' (www.travelpod.com/travel-blog/audreyandjack/worldtrip-2005/tpod.html).

The media has shown huge interest in the phenomenon of older people kicking over the traces. For example *The Times* published regular reports from the Tims family (starting with 'The Rats Can Race Without Us') who were away for 17 months with their children aged 4, 6 and 8.

The *Independent* published an article called 'Gap Years for All' with the sub-head 'Gap years are too important to be the sole preserve of the young'. An online BBC debate on the topic 'Are gap years a waste of time?' attracted a number of adults who waxed enthusiastic: one wrote '*My wife and I decided to take two years out to travel, read and hang out, which was the best, most liberating 24 months we've ever had. We're better people – mentally, physically and socially. Gap years are the best thing anyone could do.*'

A large expanse of time can be the ideal opportunity to stretch yourself or to act on a long-held ambition whether it be to navigate the Amazon, help to rescue orangutans in Borneo or perform music. Striving for different experiences is a way of feeling that we have done something with our lives, and it could be something as simple as exploring a temple complex or mountain range seen on a television documentary. This trend also complements another recent travel phenomenon, the growing interest in ethical or responsible travel.

One of the most ardent advocates of pursuing a dream has been the journalist Matthew Parris. Having turned 50, he felt stuck in a rut and in need of a change so he went to live on the bleak and remote Kerguelen Island close to Antarctica for four months, which he had hoped to visit once in his lifetime since first finding it on a map as a boy. His articles in *The Times* chronicled how he gradually adjusted

Life changing time out in over 35 countries from 2 weeks to 2 years

Hundreds of programmes from volunteering and teaching to adventure experiences and learning new skills

"Making the decision to go was the hardest thing, but once I'd told everyone it was plain sailing and the most amazing experience"

CATHERINE, 46, BIRMINGHAM

Visit **www.gapyearforgrownups.co.uk** for our full range of programmes
If you need help choosing, call **01892 701 881** and chat to one of our advisors

to the loss of all that was familiar. Writing of his decision to go, he summed up the common fantasy of escape that many feel at some point in their lives:

Everybody, every busy man or woman, must have experienced the urge to drop everything. In moments of fatigue, moments when either the workload or the routine – the sameness of things – get on top of us, who has not offered a silent prayer: 'Beam me up. Pluck me out. Whisk me away. Sweep me off my feet.' Each has an impossible dream about how we might abdicate. For some it would be holy orders in a monastery beneath Mount Sinai; for some, the ascent of Everest, the Foreign Legion or a new life sketching wild flowers on the Isles of Scilly. And for others it might be a glorious slide into as many of the seven deadly sins as it proved possible to embrace.

But a gap year shouldn't be viewed purely as an escape. There's a larger purpose too, which some view as an almost spiritual search for meaning beyond material satisfaction. In the developed world, work has undoubtedly brought great material comforts and technological progress has also suppressed the threat of hunger and mitigated the worst effects of disease. But you may find that you have to look elsewhere for happiness. Some of us have become too fixated on economics and money to be able to gauge the value of experiences.

Try not to view a gap year as a self-indulgence, but simply a period to regain your balance. More ambitiously, it can be a rite of passage like learning to swim again, that moment in childhood of heading out of your depth in the water to learn that instead of sinking, you float. Women in particular can blossom when freed from the habit of always trying to ensure that everything runs smoothly for husband, children, parents and boss. For a stimulating account of just such a gap year, read Alice Steinbach's *Without Reservations: The Travels of an Independent Woman.*

Some accounts of taking time out resemble mythological journeys of self-discovery. **Deborah Howell** eloquently captures the awe-inspiring benefits of a personal odyssey:

In terms of what I actually 'did' during my year out, the answer is everything! I visited monuments and art galleries. I climbed glaciers and went white water rafting. I met hill tribe people and holy men. I swam with dolphins and sharks. I spent an entire day trying to send a parcel in India. I lay on beaches and sailed around desert islands. I climbed pyramids and temples and was awed by the giant Ayers Rock. I panned for opals in an underground Australian town and was offered and declined the chance to get involved in smuggling. I walked away from Las Vegas a winner and flew through the Grand Canyon. I sang karaoke with the locals in China and listened to the voice of Peter Ustinov guide me round the Forbidden City. I played with children in the Vietnamese jungle amidst the ruins of shot down helicopters. I slept in palaces and in squalid, depressing places. I sat on buses and trains for hours and relaxed on deserted white sandy beaches. I snorkelled with exotic fish and found a scorpion snuggled in my shorts! I missed friends and family and met some wonderful people. I fell in love with some countries and cultures and hated others. Like I say, I did everything.

PART 1

TAKING THE PLUNGE

WHAT IS A GAP YEAR?
PURSUING A DREAM
TRIGGERS AND MOTIVES
HOW WILL A BREAK AFFECT MY CAREER?
EMPLOYERS' ATTITUDES
TAKING CHARGE OF YOUR CAREER
WHAT CAN BE ACHIEVED?

MY GROWN UP GAP YEAR:
LISA BASS

In her mid-30s Lisa Bass had just finished doing up her house and had a secure job she loved, managing emergency responses for the British Red Cross in Yorkshire. She had gone straight from school to university to a job, and then had commitments that kept her from realising her ambition to work abroad. But when she found herself with no ties and her employers said they were willing to grant her a three-month career break, she knew she wanted to seize the opportunity 'before life got in the way again', ignoring her friends and family who thought that this wasn't quite career minded enough. But then she was faced with the daunting task of choosing what to do.

In terms of choosing where to go and with which organisation – it was harrowing. Going through all the different websites and seeing all the need that there was in the world for volunteers to go and do at times life-saving work – you did at times feel guilty at just picking one project above the others. The choice was overwhelming, and you had to stay focussed on what you wanted out of the three months as well as what you had to give, so that you made a choice with both your heart and your head. Just because a project working with orphans in rural India touched your heart didn't mean that you were necessarily the right person to go and work there for three months.

I realised that there were just too many variables, and had to start to narrow the choice down a bit. I did this by thinking that taking my three months off was a once-in-a-lifetime opportunity, so, if I could go anywhere in the world, where would it be? Immediately I knew that it would be Madagascar, so then all I needed to pick one that was most suited to my needs and skills. One of the things that really came over from the Azafady website was the straight talking, no nonsense, honest approach to what the scheme was about – warts and all! It was a welcome change from some of the others and I chose it.

There were so many high points. The chief of the village we were first working in met us and told us how he had been praying for our safe arrival so that we could help them build the well. He explained that since the first well had been built in another hamlet, no children under five had died. In a country that has an infant mortality rate of up to one in 10, that really struck us about the difference a couple of weeks of our time actually meant. I don't think any of us doubted from that moment on why we were here. One of my most emotional moments was when we all went down to the well we had just built with the villagers and pumped water for the first time. It was nothing short of a miracle that in that barren, parched landscape, clear drinking water was suddenly appearing and this would enable lives to be saved every day from here on in.

Another highlight was from my time later on in the local Azafady office doing policy work. Gradually I realised how much I was learning and changing as the Malagasy staff worked with me on developing policies that had to marry up international law and Malagasy culture. I felt that I was stretched in a way that I had never been before, and I gained an appreciation and deep understanding of a culture and belief system that was so different to what I had grown up with and really changed for the better my outlook on how I approach work.

I had wanted something that was hard but rewarding and totally different from sitting at a desk job with the pace of life that has become the norm in Britain. And I found it - getting up at 5.30 each day to a fantastic sunrise, working in a brilliant and motivated group of volunteers, living with local guides and villagers who taught you everything about the local culture and history and knowing that every single placement that you worked on made a real difference to the lives of the villagers that you had come to know. Returning back home was a nightmare! I gave myself a month to make sure that this wasn't just a bad case of holiday blues, and then gave in my notice at work, and started fundraising to go back to Madagascar for a year to work for Azafady. My time away was a completely life changing experience. It allowed me the time and freedom to really look at what I wanted from life and showed me a way, with a little determination, that I could have this. I've given up a good job, great social scene and comfortable house back in the UK to live in a place where the electricity and water are sporadic, food is basic to say the least and there is no salary at the end of the month. And yet, I know that I have got the best of the deal! It just goes to show, you should never under-estimate the difference to your life 10 weeks can make.

WHAT IS A GAP YEAR?

In the first place a gap year need not be literally 12 months long. Mini gaps lasting a couple of months can be invigorating and bring with them all the benefits extolled throughout this book. But the expression 'gap quarter-year' is unlikely to catch on (just as a new coinage 'quarter-life crisis' is unlikely to achieve common currency).

The term Gap Year must remain a loose one but, essentially, it means changing the regular pattern of your working life over a period that is longer than just a regular holiday. A short gap 'year' might last six weeks, though the premise of this book is that you will have three, six or 12 months of freedom from professional obligations, a miraculous period of time in which to pursue dreams and create memories.

In academia and the teaching profession, the notion of a sabbatical is established by tradition. A sabbatical leave of absence from duties allows a teacher or lecturer to recharge, refresh their knowledge of a subject, conduct original research or join an exchange programme. Whereas sabbaticals are earned with loyal service and are usually paid, gap years or career breaks tend to be thought of as self-granted and unpaid. But sabbaticals are a version of gap years and the expression 'career sabbatical' is often used by companies that permit them. In business the concept of an earned break is becoming more common as an incentive for staying on with the same employer. Typically, after a fixed period of time, the employee is allowed to take up to a specified number of weeks off, usually without pay but without loss of benefits such as pension contributions. Where there is no formal policy of granting career breaks, employees are negotiating unpaid gap years on a discretionary basis, a concept which is gaining wider acceptance.

For example, at the Nationwide Building Society, employees may apply for up to six months unpaid sabbatical. The tax and auditing firm Deloitte allows unpaid breaks of up to a year for personnel who have been working for at least three years, while one of its rivals, Ernst & Young, permits career breaks of 26 weeks or even longer in other circumstances.

Other firms stipulate that time off must be used for personal development; for example in addition to its offer of unpaid six-month sabbaticals, Avis makes £250 awards available for personal development (study, volunteering) that need not be connected to the employee's role in the company. A gap year may take place as a pause from a specific job to which you fully intend to return. Alternatively it can encompass leaving one job to further your education or take the opportunity to experience an extended period of travel before returning home to look for new employment. In either case your professional life is put on hold.

Going abroad is not an essential component since career breaks at home are perfectly feasible. For some it might simply mean stepping off the treadmill or whatever metaphor you wish to use, to slow down or spend more time with children, immerse yourself in a hobby or do full-time voluntary work. You don't need to leave the country to take a challenging journey. A gap year is more disruptive than a holiday, but that is precisely its appeal. It demands a level of radical change in your normal routine.

A gap year provides a chance to re-connect with former interests and old friends or to acquire new interests and new friends beyond the boundaries of work. Emotionally, your activities during a break may reawaken old loves, introduce new interests and act to inspire your efforts back in the workplace.

A GAP YEAR INVOLVES SIX STAGES:

- The dream – *This might be associated with a specific ambition (e.g. to see the world) or just a longing to get out of your present circumstances*
- The determination – *Achieving the confidence to go ahead and do it*
- Persuading the boss (or delegating your business) – *Employers are increasingly aware that it is in their interests to grant unpaid leave*
- The practicalities – *Organising your life, partner, family, mortgage, finances and so on*
- The break itself – *What you can do with a stint away from work*
- Re-entry – *What differences can a gap year make when it comes to an end?*

MY GROWN UP GAP YEAR:
KAREN RICH

After recovering from a serious car accident, Karen realised how short life really is and decided she wanted to find out what else was waiting for her. She had been flying as airline cabin crew for seven years and discovered that her employer, Thomas Cook Airlines, had a career break policy so her job remains open if she chooses to go back to it. After much thought, she hit on Latvia as her preferred destination and at the same time undertook some TEFL (Teaching English as a Foreign Language) training with i-to-i and Intesol. The gap year company Changing Worlds set up a teaching position in the small town of Tukums, about an hour from Riga, which came to an end in June 2008.

Everyone I know has encouraged my decision to take a career break as they understand how important it was to me. However that's not to say that they weren't surprised and thought I was completely crazy to be setting off on a different path at the age of 36. I worked and saved hard for about a year before leaving, but if it's something you are so motivated by and passionate about, it's easy.

Initially I was supposed to be in Latvia for three months but extended twice (the visa part was easy) and worked at my school for 12 months. It's truly been a life-changing year for me. I changed careers, I moved to a small town where I'm the only English person and I've travelled to many new and exciting countries including Russia, Lithuania and Estonia. Although I didn't notice it at the time, I went from being like a tourist to joining in the local life, living, shopping, working. If I had to choose one highlight it would be travelling independently to St Petersburg by bus. No-one spoke English, only Russian and Latvian, and I did it. It was worth it just to see a performance of Swan Lake at the Hermitage theatre. Wonderful.

As for the teaching, I hadn't expected to have so many students and classes. I had to call a halt at around 50 students and working weeks of 40 hours. I felt so proud that students who had been shy and reserved at the beginning of the year were relaxed and able to chat to me quite openly at the end. When I received leaving cards written in English it was very special.

I don't have to think very hard about what was the low point - loneliness. All your friends, colleagues and family say they'll visit, but Latvia didn't entice them. Plus all my colleagues in the school were Latvian and had their own families, so it was difficult to mix with the local people as the culture was different and it's not acceptable for a single woman to sit in a café and drink coffee. I noticed that the people didn't laugh much. I guess one thing they will always remember about me is my smile, since that was a constant topic of conversation. I have no regrets. I wouldn't change anything. It's all been a learning curve and experience in my life. Now it's time to look back at all that I've done and achieved in the last year and plan my next adventure.

PURSUING A DREAM

Grown-up gap years are for people who don't want to end up saying 'I could have' or 'I should have' instead of 'I did.' The decision is never easy. Some experience a 'Road to Damascus' revelation when suddenly they feel a compulsion to pursue a specific dream or escape an unsatisfactory situation. Others take years of toying with the idea, taking a few tentative steps before they finally discover the wherewithal to carry through the idea. While pursuing a career in the city, 30-something Roz Savage claims to have imagined two possible obituaries for herself: the safe and dull one and the risky and daring one, which is why she found herself giving up her career in order to row across the Atlantic by herself.

There seems to be no end to the original and energetic ways found by working people of all ages to spend two or four, six or 12 scintillating months. Once you have squared taking a break from work, either by sorting something out with your employer or working out the financial implications if you are self-employed, it all gets much easier. After you have explained to your friends and family that you have decided to take a chunk of time off work (they will either be envious or disapproving) and once you have booked your flight, enrolled in a course, contacted some voluntary organisations, put a specific project in motion or embarked on whatever you want to do with your gap year, the rest seems to look after itself.

IS A GAP YEAR RIGHT FOR ME?

Anyone who has uttered the words, 'How I'd love to be a . . .' or 'I'd give anything to see . . .' is a possible candidate for achieving their dream on a career break. People sometimes hide behind an assumption that something they dream of doing is impossible because of the pressures of work and home life. While airing your fantasies, your family or friends might be tempted to say, 'Why don't you just go ahead and do it?' – whatever it is, such as write a play, build a harpsichord, renovate a bothy, climb Kilimanjaro with your children, work for Mother Teresa's charity in Calcutta, explore your genealogy.

Humphrey Walters, an international management training guru (www.humphreywalters.com) believes that the most important element is the simple decision to take a break:

> *Once you make a decision to take a sabbatical, to do something, you don't need to base it on an event or activity. If you wait for something to drop out of the woodwork, it won't happen and a lot of people do. People should simply take the plunge because the payoff is massive. The trick is to create the dream for yourself. Look for a dream. At the outset you don't need to know what it is.*

WHO CAN TAKE A GAP YEAR?

Taking a year off is a luxury, a product of a wealthy society. If you suggested the concept to say a Nepali porter, Brazilian taxi driver or Polish farmer, they would think you were speaking Martian. But in the privileged West, people from many backgrounds, not just an elite few, have the freedom to exercise the choice to withdraw temporarily from work. This is a freedom that should be cherished and not squandered.

The thesis of this book is that ordinary people can entertain extraordinary ambitions and do extraordinary things. An eye-catching ad campaign was run by VSO (Voluntary Service Overseas) to persuade ordinary working people to consider a stint of voluntary work. A flyer read: '*The tanned, toned, blonde*

Australian Ironman Champion who normally hands out these flyers is in Liverpool helping to build a youth centre for disabled children.' Another one was displayed prominently on a truck: '*This truck should have been towed away but the driver is away in Peru rescuing llamas by four-wheel drive.*' People on ordinary wages have managed to save enough money to fund trips to far corners of the world to do amazing things.

When you are wondering whether you are the right sort to take a break from work, do not imagine that your circumstances are peculiarly disadvantageous. Since the last edition of this book, I have heard from:

- A former drugs counsellor who realised how much he enjoyed teaching appreciative Chinese children when he worked in a small city outside Beijing.
- An ad salesman and his new wife who spent a year travelling round South and Central America for their honeymoon.
- A family consisting of two doctors and their two sons who were planning to take a whole year off and spend part of it cycling from Istanbul to Estonia.
- A bored cosmetologist who suddenly decided to move to Europe and ended up teaching in southern Poland where she felt almost instantly at home.
- A nurse married to a former vet practice manager who took Spanish lessons in Nicaragua before stumbling across a volunteer opportunity in Granada to help refurbish a school for disabled children.
- A Toronto journalist who participated in an official work exchange scheme so she could get to know London while temping there.
- A recently bereaved mother who taught knitting to Tanzanian villagers.
- A senior real estate agent who went to Rio to join one of the grassroots volunteer projects supported by Iko Poran (see entry in Part 5 Directory of Specialist Programmes).
- A young woman who after undergoing cancer treatment volunteered at an animal rehabilitation centre on the southern tip of Africa.
- A Scottish administrator who realised in her mid-50s that her work–life balance was all wrong so spent four months in South America, part of which she spent volunteering at a biological station on the Galapagos.
- A post-production TV manager who decided to take six months off to investigate media possibilities in Toronto.
- A woman who qualified as a ski instructor in Whistler (Canada) after having worked in the insurance industry for 25 years.

THE DETERMINATION TO REALISE YOUR DREAM

Deciding to take a period of time off work and then deciding how to spend it may not be as momentous as some other life decisions like choosing a life partner, having babies, choosing or changing careers, but it is as individual. It certainly takes guts and that is an essential ingredient in achieving a break from your career. The hardest step is summoning up the determination simply to get up and leave. No book or even trusted adviser can make the decision for you. All that outsiders can do is set out the possibilities and see if any of them takes your fancy enough to pursue. Do as much research as possible, let the ideas swill around in your head and see what floats up.

There is no doubt that it is far easier to stay on the funicular of employment that chugs along its tracks to the goal of retirement. After all, that is exactly what the majority of working people still do. For many people in work, the decision to treat oneself to a sabbatical is a difficult and complex one. The first question to ask yourself is: does the idea have a strong appeal? Do you get a buzz if you close your eyes and imagine yourself trekking through a Costa Rican rainforest or teaching in a Tanzanian village school or studying in an Italian language class? The next question is, do you have the energy to make the dream actual?

REASONS TO BE TEMPTED

We all fantasise about taking extended time off from work. But acting on this fantasy is a daunting prospect. What are the practical implications for our careers, families and daily responsibilities? Much depends on the complexity of our lives and to what extent we rely on the structures and routines we have built to provide personal security, self-esteem, professional achievement and financial stability. Younger people in their late twenties and early thirties with fewer commitments are better placed to take an extended break. However, individuals in their 40s and 50s will be more likely to have a degree of financial security and better professional qualifications, which may allow a smoother return to professional life.

Sometimes we just need to step back from work to put our lives in perspective or re-evaluate our goals, professional or otherwise. People sometimes feel that their life has become too detached from simple pleasures and the rhythms of nature. Even if the gap year you choose does not specifically focus on the natural world, exposure to beautiful landscapes is often a by-product of travel and volunteering in distant lands, as **David MacKintosh** commented about his MondoChallenge placement teaching in Kalimpong in West Bengal:

> *I had gone from a bustling office (Conservative Party HQ), with people screaming of political scandal and urgent deadlines, to the calm tranquillity of the Himalayas with snow-topped Kanchenjunga in the background and no mobile reception for days!*

Perhaps you have simply become miserable in your job and want a complete change. Sometimes people are pushed into a career break against their wishes (and not just members of the acting profession). Economic recession or an employer's financial misfortunes may force a period of unemployment or under-employment. One of the most common reasons is to be with a partner or spouse who is living and working elsewhere. For example, freelance photographer **Barbara Schick** followed her husband when he was posted to Brazil and had a wonderful time extending her portfolio and volunteering with the Rio charity Nos do Cinema which works with children from the *favelas* (and she was involved with the making of the film *City of God*).

At a deep level some people are dissatisfied with their life, not necessarily because of their job but for reasons unrelated to work. Perhaps your relationship is foundering and it is time to break free for a while. Perhaps you are single and are longing for a shake-up in your social life. Perhaps your children have recently left home and you and your partne r are looking for a new activity to fill the emptiness at home. Perhaps you have come into an inheritance on the death of a relative or found yourself with a windfall. Perhaps you are grieving at the loss of a loved one or for a marriage that has ended. Your personal circumstances may have altered for any number of reasons making it possible in practical terms for the first time to consider a break from work.

Provided you can delegate or shed your responsibilities (see *Nuts and Bolts* in Part 2 for advice), ask yourself 'Why *shouldn't* I take a gap year?'. In all probability you have worked very hard and earned the right to step back temporarily from the demands of your job, to concentrate on yourself for a change and to establish what you really value in your life.

MY GROWN UP GAP YEAR:
TINA FREEMAN

In response to the grief of losing one of her two sons, Tina searched the net for a volunteer teaching programme that would suit her. She liked the personal approach of POD and also the fact that TEFL training was provided on-site in Tanzania. She never dreamed that she would also spearhead a 'knitting revolution' as described in an article for safaritalk.net (which she has given this book permission to quote).

Before I left home I was given a knitting bag with about 14 pairs of knitting needles and a few odd balls of wool. As I was reading up about Yamba, the project and environment I was shocked to learn how cold it gets in the mountains. I heard how children with only the holey clothes on their backs would jump up and down to try and get warm before trying to go to sleep. So I thought with the wool and needles maybe I could show a few of the ladies in Yamba how to knit little squares and to sew them together to make blankets. I thought even though I hadn't knitted anything since I was very young (except a failed attempt to knit my son a scarf) I could manage to teach them how to knit a simple square: knit, knit, knit and maybe even purl. They very soon learnt knit and purl, and it was at this time I realised I had forgotten how to cast off. As the squares took size and shape I had to remember - fast! (I later realised that it wasn't the best way - but it worked).

The lessons were given weekly after school and I was only going to be in the village for seven weeks. They seemed to think that I was going to show them how to make a hat ... a hat!! OK - I like a challenge. I thought - rib to start should be OK to teach, but a hat! I had a few attempts and finally success (of sorts - it was sort of pixie styled - all pointy). I wrote a very simple pattern out 14 times (translated into Swahili) and by the next lesson I was presented with a sea of multi-coloured hats - not just completed, but stripy as well. By this time we were buying wool for them from Tanga (five hours away) to keep up.

And what did I hear they wanted to make next? - A sweater! I thought I could send them a pattern from the UK, maybe simplified, even translated, but it seemed that they really wanted to be shown. I made no promises, but studied the jumpers I had brought with me and attempted to make a sweater myself, before attempting to teach them. All I managed to show them before I had to leave was the V-neck shape and roughly how to achieve it. I heard, via email, long after my departure from Yamba that the ladies were still knitting. On a rather quiet Christmas Eve I received another email - this time with attached photos - of Yamba ladies and their children and their multi-coloured stripy V-neck raglan sweaters. Tears came to my eyes.

TRIGGERS AND MOTIVES

Most of us sail along on our normal work-a-day and domestic course more or less contentedly. But then something happens that throws us off-course and makes us wonder where the meaning lies in our ordinary routines. Why do we have to spend hours every day on crowded tube trains or in boring meetings or placating irate bosses? When was the last time we gasped with amazement at some new sight or laughed out loud at some absurdity?

Sometimes we have no choice in the matter. Women are lucky in this respect. Many have a career break thrust upon them when a baby is born. Few experiences in life so radically change daily routines as the birth of a child. People who are made redundant and are forced to take a career break are less lucky but even this can have a positive outcome. Understandably, people can be thrown into total consternation by redundancy but with luck and determination, this will only last 48 hours. If you have marketable skills, you may find that it will mark a liberation, as it does for many who treat themselves to an exciting break with their redundancy money and then come home to make their way as a freelancer, thereby achieving a more balanced lifestyle.

Sometimes there is an identifiable event or circumstance which prompts a desire to do something a bit mad. It is not unusual for career breaks to follow in the wake of a failed romance, as one 30-year-old gapper described it: '*The main catalyst for going was that I had just had my heart well and truly trampled over and I felt that by far the best way was to go abroad to feel good about life once again*'.

But often it is the culmination of a background urge long suppressed – to do something selfless, to pursue a sport, to swim with dolphins or visit the pyramids before you die, whatever it is. The worst thing about doing the same thing for years on end is how it makes time speed up. Because there is so little to delineate one day from another, the days all collapse in on another and get compacted, as if by a computer programme trying to make more space. But if you do something completely different, suddenly each day and each week stretches to accommodate the range of new experiences.

The impulse to organise a gap year can come from many directions. You may find yourself thinking (obsessively) that if you don't grab the opportunity now you never will. You may have come to the realisation that you need de-stressing or simply been inspired by the travel tales of a sibling, friend or television presenter.

All those who *do* it rather than merely talk about it or dream about it arrive at a point of no psychological return. For **Polly Botsford**, a lawyer who had just turned 30, there was an underlying conviction that *something* was needed to shake up her life. For her it felt a bit like the need to change her bedroom around or try a new hairdresser. She thinks that if she had been younger, she might have been satisfied with a change of job. But once you are entrenched in a career, you cannot nonchalantly walk out of one job and into another. So the solution is to have an extended holiday from your job, which is what she did when she went to work for a small charity in Cambodia.

BURN-OUT

No matter how glamorous and interesting a job may be, it usually has the capacity to lead to boredom or burn-out at some level. No matter how hard you work, you can sometimes never clear the backlog, which can lead to a feeling of defeat and profound weariness. And it is this problem which a gap year can address. American TV documentary maker Holly Morris has a vivid expression for what she felt in a 9–5 job: '*rigor mortis of the soul*'. Her solution was to take a sabbatical in Sumatra to rethink her position. On her return she went half-time as an editor, spending the other half freelancing and working on an idea for a TV series about strong adventurous women around the world. She simply created a more flexible life for herself which allowed her to make a pilot programme in Cuba. She then sold it to PBS and went on to make a TV series called *Adventure Divas*.

AT ABOUT THE AGE OF 50, ANDY MORGAN WAS FEELING BURNT OUT AS A GENERAL PRACTITIONER AND WAS EVEN TOYING WITH THE IDEA OF LEAVING THE NATIONAL HEALTH SERVICE (NHS):

Although he was prepared to take some unpaid leave, he decided to apply for one of the research grants offered (rarely) by the NHS and was successful. On the application he had described as honestly as he could his reasons for wanting the time out and his targets for the year. He was interested in the use of videos to improve doctor–patient interaction and wanted to explore how video training can be used more extensively in medical training. On a more practical level, he wanted to master the skill of touch-typing. Administering a busy medical practice in Twickenham, one of the frustrations of his job was that he was a very slow typist. Although he had had several stabs at teaching himself, he hadn't made much progress and was determined to acquire this time-saving skill.

On a more personal level, he had been coping with grief. He had been widowed quite young and had much more recently lost the elder of his two daughters when she was killed in a road accident on her gap year in Malawi. But life began to look up when he formed an attachment to an Australian woman and decided that he would like to spend his year out with her in Melbourne, which is what he did. In that time he learned to type, he ran successful workshops with Australian doctors in video training, he got married and has since become a father again.

Andy came back to England much more positive about practising medicine and in pursuing video training to help future doctors deal more sensitively with their patients. He feels that the NHS's investment in allowing him a year out was not wasted, not only because of the 30,000-word report he touch-typed for them but because he has decided to remain in the health service for the foreseeable future.

EXCESS AND AFFLUENCE

You have only to read a newspaper or watch the television news about the plight of earthquake victims or the AIDS crisis in Africa or the feelings of hopelessness among Palestinians, to realise the extent to which citizens of Britain, North America and other developed countries are extraordinarily privileged even to be able to contemplate a grown-up gap year. Such a concept would be entirely alien to the vast majority of the inhabitants of the globe for whom it is an unrelenting daily struggle to obtain basic necessities.

Undoubtedly many of us have never been better off or had more opportunities at our disposal. Some might even consider themselves members (reluctant or otherwise) of the 'have-it-all generation'. With apologies to Harold Bloom's famous study of poetry called 'The Anxiety of Influence', the anxiety of *affluence* is (fortunately) not uncommon in our culture. The disparity between what we have and what millions of others lack through no fault of their own can be overwhelming at times. It is an awareness of our amazing good fortune to be born when and where we have been that prompts some people to withdraw temporarily from the good life and try to bring good to others. Many people want to reverse the cash-rich, time-poor equation.

It is no doubt the case that a disincentive to many people in taking a gap year is the loss of income (i.e. buying power) that will ensue, if only temporarily. Depending on your predisposition and background, you may find it easy or well-nigh impossible to come to the view that it is probably not essential for you to earn constantly.

SENSORY OVERLOAD

The choice of goods in the shops, programmes in the media, training courses and possible career paths, travel destinations, information on the Internet, all of these are almost infinite. Many people feel oppressed by the sheer quantity of choice available to us in the 21st century. Their impulse is to seek out a simpler life and one way of achieving this is to put one's job on hold for a while, put one's possessions in storage and remove oneself from the busy crowded world of the materialistic West.

Paradoxically, in the midst of all this profusion of possessions and experiences, we have less time to absorb and reflect on the experiences open to us and often lack the ability to turn them into something of quality. An extended period spent away from the work-a-day treadmill, with all that it implies – the ringing phone, the expectations, the routines – can help to make that possible.

BEREAVEMENT AND DEPRESSION

Who is to say how any of us would react to grief, but some people find it helpful to get away. **Carol Peden**, a consultant anaesthetist just into her 40s, lost her husband unexpectedly. For a while she just wanted to be in a familiar place but after selling the family house, moving five times, suing two sets of lawyers and trying to keep a demanding career going, she was exhausted and wanted a break. She was granted six months of unpaid leave provided she could find a suitable replacement to cover her absence.

Tina Freeman is another woman in her middle years who coped with a tragic loss by going abroad, in her case to a village project in the mountains of Tanzania:

> My motivation was wanting to do something rewarding and meaningful during a terrible period of grief. I'd always wanted to teach abroad, and was going through a difficult time after losing my son, so it gave me something positive to focus on and look forward to. My placement was a particularly amazing experience considering the 'place' I was in my life when I went. The people who have to deal with poverty and child mortality and death in general every day were so joyous, welcoming and fun – it was such a shock. At first I was coy about disclosing my trauma, but the project leader encouraged me to share the details as this might encourage others in my position.

Psychological troubles might also propel some people into taking a period off work. Anyone who is truly depressed is unlikely to be able to summon the energy and initiative necessary to plan a constructive gap year. But many people who feel worn down by their jobs and lives contemplate alternatives that will rescue them from their gloomy state of mind. **Caroline Kippen** is one for whom this worked splendidly:

> I decided to take a gap year because I was finding life quite disheartening and depressing! I made my decision in the depths of winter when the UK has to be one of the most depressing places to be. I guess I was suffering from a severe case of SAD [seasonal affective disorder] and decided to do something proactively to change my situation. I was also dissatisfied with my job (in customer services for

a mortgage endowment company) so decided that the best thing would be to take a break and then start a new career after that. I guess I went away to decide what I wanted to do next – I kind of had the idea of teaching because it is easy to fall into, but luckily my gap year led me away!

Firstly, I went on a two-month round the world trip and was a real tourist seeing places I has always wanted to see and having incredible fun – that has now all blended into one and I have difficulty distinguishing one place from the next. The other part was volunteering in Africa. I chose an organisation called SPW which runs health education programmes in Africa. Teaching about HIV/Aids seemed so much more important than teaching maths. The rewards have been great. I have so many skills now and my life has meaning and order to it! The drawbacks are that I can never go into another mundane boring job because I will always compare it to my experience and it means that I have to constantly challenge myself in new ways – but maybe that isn't a bad thing!

In more than a few cases, the death of an elderly parent is a trigger for someone to decide to take a gap year, especially if they have been heavily responsible for the care of their parents and unable to get away. The death of **Sarah Spiller's** father marked a turning point in her life. Planning a volunteer trip abroad provided a distraction not only to Sarah but also to her mother who was enthusiastic on Sarah's behalf. Because Sarah had inherited some money from her father, she didn't need to worry about the financing of the trip. Her husband was also supportive of her idea to go away and do something different. She settled on Sri Lanka – which had bewitched her on a previous visit – and a turtle protection scheme through Projects Abroad; where she helped escort the turtles safely to their breeding ground, worked in a hatchery for turtle eggs and helped show visiting parties of Sri Lankan children round so as to instil the conservation message in them.

Similarly, teacher **Nigel Hollington** (then age 50) was spurred to action by the death of his father, which freed him from some of his filial responsibilities. His mother was well looked after in sheltered accommodation but, given her age, he was reluctant to go away for long periods of time at a stretch. So he decided to divide up the year out he had been granted by his headteacher into chunks and do a variety of things and come home in between.

Siamak Tannazi was 29 when she decided to apply to her boss at BT for a six-month break, partly because she had been in a serious motorbike accident and partly because the tsunami that happened at the same time made her think about all the charities in the Indian subcontinent dependent on foreign volunteers who would be redirected to tsunami relief. **Neil Munro** (who tells his story on p. 125) had suffered a serious betrayal by a brother, which made Neil fall apart and feel the need to get out of Scotland. Any number of unexpected events can bring you up short and make stepping out of your routine seem a necessity.

Traumatic events occurring in your own life, those close to you or even to strangers (as in natural disasters around the world) can lead to a sudden reassessment of what is important. Two friends of one of our contributors (in her 50s) became seriously ill without ever having done anything in their lives apart from work, and she didn't want to be like them.

THE DANGER AGE

An article entitled 'Quarter life crisis hits UK PLC' appeared in *The Times* several years ago arguing that 30 is the crunch age for wanting more purpose at work. As soon as they can clear their debts, young high fliers who feel caught in a career trap are deserting employers whom they believe to be intolerant of their wider life ambitions.

Alongside the pressures to become a property owner, society (often in the guise of a parent) seems to expect people who have been earning a salary for a few years to 'settle down', find a spouse and reproduce. This might engender panic that it is time to have your last fling with youth. You may therefore derive great pleasure in announcing to all and sundry that in fact you have decided to leave your job for a while to sail across the Atlantic, do marine conservation in the Philippines or ride your bicycle through Chile. That will teach them to pin their assumptions on you! On a more serious note, you will want to avoid causing unnecessary anxiety to ageing parents. However, you can't please all of the people all of the time and if a mother is anxious that her daughter has hit 30 without making her a grandmother, this is not a sufficient reason to stay on the straight and (very) narrow.

Although it is possible to have a gap year after parenthood (see Part 8; *Taking the Family*), the commitment-free gap year is the paradigm. **Jennie Sanders,** at age 26, took nine months off from her job with PricewaterhouseCoopers to do a Yachtmaster sailing course:

> *I will probably spend a lot of the years to come sitting at a desk. To be able to take some time out while I had no commitments such as a family or a mortgage meant that it was an ideal time to seize the opportunity. I wouldn't say that I came back 'a changed person' but it was a fantastic experience and all I have missed out on is a few months sitting in an office! There were other people on our course who had borrowed from friends, given up jobs completely, sold their businesses and left family at home to come on the course, and I don't think anyone regretted taking the time out to do something completely different.*

PROPERTY LADDER PRESSURES

After starting a job, most people are happy to rent property for a few years. But soon the knowledge that hundreds of pounds a month are disappearing into a black hole begins to worry them. Family and friends suddenly seem to be in cahoots with the local estate agent to pressurise full-time earners into getting onto the property ladder at any cost. This pressure can be hard to resist, especially in an economic climate where house prices have risen astronomically so the longer you delay the more you will have to borrow. However, at the time of writing, the Bank of England was predicting that the price of houses was falling prompting some first-time-buyers-to-be to delay the inevitable.

Rob Evans came late to the joys of travel but had greatly enjoyed a one-month backpacking trip round Peru with friends in his late 20s. So he began to toy with the idea of taking leave from work to travel. On the same day that his landlord had told him that he wanted to reclaim the flat, he attended a party to welcome back some other travellers he had met in South America and a couple of choices started to crystallise:

> *On one hand I could make my belated first step onto London's property ladder and scour the suburbs for a grotty flat. On the other I could blow the money I'd been saving for a deposit on doing the thing I'd been threatening and disappear to foreign climes for some time. Given that I was at a party with a large number of people who had been travelling themselves, there was probably only one way this decision was ever going to go.*

There will be time enough for locating a grotty flat in the suburbs.

FREEDOM FROM RESPONSIBILITIES

The last child goes off to university or to a job and all of a sudden, people in their 40s and 50s have a lot more freedom. As their children progressed through adolescence, they may have been taking their first tentative steps to rediscovering the joys of child-free travel: an anniversary weekend in Barcelona or Prague, a week in a country cottage in Ireland. But now parents are at liberty to plan something more ambitious without having to take any account of their children's propensity to travel sickness or their dislike of hotels without swimming pools or of remote villages with no nightlife.

The sudden lifting of parental obligations is often more keenly felt by mothers than fathers. Whether busy career women or not, mothers frequently bear the burden of anxiety on their children's behalf. Not that this vanishes once the children leave home for further education or employment, but many women find that for the first time in many years they have an urge to think about themselves and what they would like. This may not come easily at first and it may take time before they can dust off an old pre-motherhood dream or two. According to lots of volunteer sending agencies, the single biggest demographic group among their volunteers is women in their 50s.

While still headteacher of a girls' school in Surrey, **Marjorie Harris** found herself free of family responsibilities:

The last of my four children had just gone away to university, my husband was working away from home and I decided that I was interested in doing what my three other children had done. I was working long hours, and while still enjoying my job I felt that I was missing out on a real life. Plus my school was due to have an inspection, which was another reason to resign when I did, as I had already done one excellent inspection at the school.

TURNING 50

Mid-life crises are a bit like failing eyesight and greying hair; they can strike at any point between the ages of about 40 and 60. But research for this book revealed that the half-century seems to act frequently as a prompt to appraising the direction and priorities of one's life. People coming up to 50 often begin to panic that they have embarked on the gentle slope to retirement. They want something to wake them up, in the hope that it will extend their life.

Sometimes attending a school or college reunion can instantly reinforce your suspicion that doing the same thing for years on end is not good for you, and this realisation may catapult you into a frenzy of planning on how to make your life take a different course, if only temporarily. After 20 years as an insurance executive **Marcelle Salerno** signed up for various exotic volunteer roles including a dive project in the Seychelles and concludes, '*After all this, if nothing else, I'm more interesting at cocktail parties*'. Similarly 43-year-old **Gillian Drake** enjoyed the attention that her plan to spend 10 weeks teaching in Sri Lanka attracted among her friends and acquaintants. She felt flattered when they told her how brave she was, while also feeling anxious at the prospect of her adventure.

Time stretches when you are doing something outside your routine, for example it always seems that you pack much more into a week's holiday than a week spent at home. You can test this hypothesis over two weekends. In the first, do the usual stuff: hoover the sitting room, go to the supermarket, read a magazine, maybe go to the pub, sleep in, read the Sunday paper, watch television. Then at 7.45 on Monday morning, ask yourself 'How long ago was Friday?' and the answer will be 'it seems no time at all'. The following weekend, leave work a little early to catch a train to Bradford/Wales/Brussels; check in to a B&B/pension/hostel and spend the weekend exploring the local buildings/landscapes/cafés/museums. Then ask yourself the same question at the same time on Monday morning and the answer is guaranteed to be different. The second weekend will inevitably be more memorable, more rewarding and 'longer'. The same applies even more forcefully to the decade between our 50th and 60th birthdays. A recent coinage 'denture venturers' for this age group might bring on a premature mid-life crisis in some. A less depressing label (at least for the parents) is 'SKI-ers' (Spending the Kids' Inheritance).

PAUL EDMUNDS WAS 43 AND WORKING FOR THE BRITISH AIRPORTS AUTHORITY IN A VARIETY OF MANAGERIAL ROLES AT GATWICK AIRPORT, A JOB HE HAD FOR OVER 20 YEARS:

The idea of turning 50 without having done anything apart from work in one field frightened him, and a combination of work and personal reasons led him to consider a change in direction. He realised that for some time he had been finding himself profoundly at odds with the direction that aviation has been taking in the UK, particularly the decision to add more runways at Heathrow and Stansted, which in his view would merely enable more yobs to take £60 flights to Ibiza to urinate on the beaches and generally cause offence.

After deciding to resign and take a gap year, he asked himself many times why it had taken him so long to cut the umbilical cord. He now feels that the world is a place full of possibilities. He had noticed a small ad in The Sunday Times *looking for volunteers over 35 for the BBC documentary* Grown-up Gappers *and was selected to be the subject of one of eight programmes (aired in 2005). He investigated what he might do in his three month trip and decided to travel around Ethiopia for a month to meet the Rastafarian community, and on to Uganda to see the gorillas, then climb Mount Kilimanjaro in Tanzania and relax for a week in Zanzibar and finally join a voluntary cricket-teaching project in Ghana through Travellers Worldwide (the West Sussex gap year agency) for five weeks.*

Even if you don't plump for such an elaborate trip to commemorate turning 50, you might think of a gap-year-cum-party. For her 50th, Jakki from Yorkshire found herself between jobs (in management of a housing association) and decided to rent a large villa with swimming pool in Andalucia for an extended period to which she invited all her friends and family to spend time whenever they could. This seemed to be a good place to be when the invitation to attend the mammogram clinic dropped through her letter box at home and also meant that she couldn't succumb to the temptation of going to Glastonbury alongside all those other wrinkly professionals.

It is not unknown for spouses in middle life (generally the female of the species) to think longingly of packing their life partner off for a period of time. Usually the idea goes no further than giving hubby a copy of this book for Christmas (hint hint) so I will not be taking up a friend's suggestion that I write a book for disgruntled middle-aged couples called 'A Gap Year Apart'.

RETIREMENT

If a change is as good as a rest, then **Ed McFadd** and **Eva Hagen** have the right idea. As soon as they hit retirement, they left home to do something completely different: Ed went from California to Montreal in the dead of winter to take a French course after rediscovering his long dormant love of the language and Eva signed up for a conservation/farming project on a homestead in Australia, having harboured a lifelong dream to live and work there.

With an increasing number of early retired people expressing an interest in volunteering abroad, some organisations have developed programmes specially for the older volunteer. One such is MondoChallenge, which has established a division specially for those who have retired and are looking for something worthwhile and reasonably challenging to do with their time. MondoChallenge Managing Director, Anthony Lunch, feels that the growth of early retired volunteers is a positive trend for projects of the kind the organisation specialises in. '*We have always focused on career break people and older volunteers and our programmes include business development as well as a range of teaching projects. The senior age group, mainly over 50s, has a huge amount to offer, not least life experience. They have a wider variety of skills that can be put to use*'.

One year before his planned retirement, **Paul Kirk** accepted voluntary redundancy from the university where he was an associate dean, and started planning his gap year. He rented out his house, applied to VSO (unsuccessfully) and then lined up several placements through MondoChallenge in Sri Lanka, India and Tanzania. Between placements he came back to the UK and stayed with his children (in his words, 'nice pay-back!'). On his return from Sri Lanka, he reflected on his year of volunteering:

> *The range of placements gave me the opportunity to experience very different cultures. In Tanzania I was able to teach topics in biology that were very relevant to the African situation (e.g. about infectious diseases and their control including malaria, tuberculosis, and HIV) which was a rewarding experience and linked well with some of the work Mondo was doing with the local communities in supporting HIV/Aids patients. In Sri Lanka there was a kind of innocence about the way of life in the community which was charming. In India I learned what life was like without electricity. The history, politics and religion were all absolutely fascinating with a significant legacy from colonial Britain. The people were always appreciative of the work that I did. I have made many friends in the different communities that I shall always remember. There were so many highlights in each of the three places I worked. It was just fantastic to see children so keen to learn, so enthusiastic and so well behaved. The communities I worked in were all relatively poor but the people were wonderfully warm, welcoming, friendly and above all happy – especially in Sri Lanka and India. If you like, it was a practical demonstration of the saying that 'money doesn't buy happiness'.*

OVERCOMING RELUCTANCE

You will almost certainly be assailed by doubts at various points, both in the early stages when you are wondering whether or not to go for it, as well as at the moment that you show your boarding pass at the departure gate. In between, possibly at your farewell party in the pub, you will suffer some pre-departure blues as you contemplate leaving behind the comfortable routines of your working life. But these separation anxieties are usually much worse in anticipation than in retrospect.

No one can avoid confronting the question, 'What if it all goes horribly wrong?'. In the research for this book, I couldn't find anyone who said that they wished they had avoided the hassle of taking off and stayed quietly at home – including those whose gap years included a bout of homesickness or malaria and a finished relationship. Mark Twain is often quoted in this context: '*Twenty years from now you will be more disappointed by the things you didn't do than by the ones you did. So throw off the bowlines. Sail away from the safe harbour. Catch the trade winds in your sails. Explore. Dream. Discover.*'

Once the decision has been made, obstacles fall away or at least become manageable. This is usually the case, however daunting the prospect of taking an extended period off seemed at the outset and however many problems stood in the way.

FOUR MAJOR OBSTACLES TO TAKING A GAP YEAR THAT CAN BE READILY IDENTIFIED

- *It never occurs to people. They do not think outside the box (a jargon term implying that the best employees are those who can look for solutions outside the normal parameters).*
- *Their spouse/partner is not enthusiastic.*
- *They worry that they will slip down the career ladder and when they return will have to start at the bottom again or won't find a job.*
- *They can't afford it – too many financial commitments.*

RELATIONSHIP ISSUES

Being in a relationship with someone who is not keen on joining you in your adventures can be an understandable disincentive. 'Telegamy' (a neologism for marriage over a distance) is invariably problematic over an extended period. It is impossible to generalise or even for the individuals involved to know what the right course of action should be. Frequent writing, emailing and talking on the phone alleviates some of the anxiety. Compromise is one answer, for example to organise a break that might be shorter than otherwise or plan to rendezvous with your partner part way through the gap year. What most people hope is that their relationship will survive a serious separation which is what happened to **Paul Carroll** who had a wonderful six months with VentureCo and then travelled independently in South America:

> *Colleagues, friends and family were very supportive of my plan to go away as they felt I spent too much time working. In fact I had absolute encouragement from everyone except my girlfriend of four years, who was not interested in travelling. I had no choice but to split with my girlfriend to go on the trip that I so wanted. That was difficult, but in the end we are much stronger as a couple than before. Where previously I had not considered taking things further, I now see no barriers.*

But there is no guarantee of a fairy tale ending. **Andrea Martins** found herself having risen as high as she could in an international export firm in London and was keen to take a gap year, possibly in Peru or Russia, though ended up with a teaching placement in Mexico:

> *I had positive feedback about my plan from my family, friends and work colleagues. Everyone knew how much the idea of travelling had been burning on my mind for months if not years. Unfortunately, my boyfriend at the time was not so keen. Due to my gap year (among other problems) we have since split up. This wasn't part of the plan though.*

On the other hand, you may be lucky enough to have a partner who is just as keen as you are to take a big break, but you may be anxious that this will place too much of a strain on your relationship. Before

Ness and her husband **Stef**, both in their late 30s, left to go round the world, they noticed that their families were running a number of books on whether they would still be talking to each other after having been together 24/7/365. **Marie Purdy** and her partner Howard used her redundancy money to go around the world in five months. Things were harmonious between them most of the time, but Marie experienced flashes of homesickness for the company of women. On such a trip you spend far more time with your partner than you do in the normal routines; if you have spent the whole day with someone, there's not much to say in the evening. One solution is occasionally to go your separate ways during the day to pursue individual interests, and then have something to say to each other when you next meet.

SHAKING OUT THE COBWEBS

You don't have to hate your job to want a change. But we all become stale when we conform to the same routine day in day out. You can liven yourself up by small things, take an evening class in botanical drawing or Spanish, join a jazz club or a choir, become involved in Amnesty or any cause close to your heart, choose unusual destinations for your annual holidays. But these will not alter the fundamentals of your life.

When the home routines begin to pall and you find yourself craving a challenge or an opportunity to expose yourself to risk, it is time to give some thought to bringing about a change. As they say, you'll be a long time dead. Few books (with the notable exception of *Diary of a Nobody*) have been written to catalogue everyday working life. But hundreds have been written by people who have had adventures when away from their offices and factories. The titles of some of these evince how precious time away from routines can be, such as Libby Purves' *One Summer's Grace* about sailing around the perimeter of the British Isles with her husband and two pre-school children.

MY GROWN UP GAP YEAR:
TESSA MILLS

After 26 years of marriage and a successful business partnership, 52-year-old Tessa Mills felt sure there was another world waiting for her, and so left the comforts of a sensible life, for a journey that took her on the road less travelled.

I had been going to buy a house but I ended up going round the world instead, which came about through the most innocuous of sentences. When seeking advice about the possible purchase of a property, I was asked 'Do you like this house?' 'It's sensible and practical,' I replied; but as I said it I realised that buying a house wasn't really what I wanted to do. Live a little, throw caution to the wind, do something adventurous, my family urged me.

I had recently waved off and welcomed back two children on their gap years. Why not me? I was at a gap and a new juncture in life. So many places to see, things I wanted to do! This really did seem a much more exciting, life-changing and inspiring option. Then a thousand reasons suddenly occurred as to why I couldn't or shouldn't pack it all in and set off. But from somewhere a voice urged me on and encouraged me to continue to pursue this dream and opportunity.

Where would I go, what would I do? Explore India, do some conservation work in the rainforests of South America or Australia, spend time in south-east Asia - all these appealed. And so I began to plan, and as with anything big, I ate the elephant one bite at a time. Trips to travel agents, voluntary projects to research, luggage to buy, travel books to read, lots of little things to keep me focused and believing that I really was going.

As I now wasn't buying a house, I decided to stop renting my present flat and to use that money along with some other savings from selling my business to fund the adventure. It gave me an allowance of about £37 a day which didn't quite cover everything but gave me a budget to work on. Obviously I spent more in Australia and New Zealand, but the dong, baht and rupees went much further in Asia. Like anyone else, I succumbed to the occasional and very enjoyable extravagance. Jet boating in NZ [New Zealand] the occasional luxury accommodation and one or a few 'souvenirs' that I couldn't resist.

Waved off by my daughters on a cold and snowy November morning, I settled a little apprehensively into my seat. There is something so thrilling about a plane as it hurtles down the runway, forcing you back in your seat. I knew I truly was off and away. The experience had begun.

I had hoped to do some work or a project on this trip, and tried to find out about teaching, environmental projects and voluntary work. In the event I didn't do any. During my nine months away I came to feel that this journey was not about saving others, or even the planet, but about saving me. And in more ways than one this journey certainly did rescue me. It was indeed a wonderful, inspiring, mesmerising adventure. It's not only the different and unique cultures that you become immersed in that are so rewarding, but the people and friends you meet along the way that are the

(continued)

memories you retain. Smells and sounds so different from those that are familiar, initially jar the senses but then become like comfortable companions.

I saw brown bears and Alaskan jade on remote islands off Vancouver, where life is simple, real and peaceful. I stayed with the grandchildren of some of the early European settlers who now check their gold reserves on a computer whose batteries are charged by their own generators. I unexpectedly loved my time in Waikiki where I 'hung loose' and exercised by joining a young Italian as he trained for the Hawaiian half marathon. Re-visiting Australia and New Zealand and catching up with old school friends was a time full of nostalgia and reminiscences. I had spent a year hitch-hiking in NZ as I left my teenage years behind. Despite the many changes and developments that I noticed, the rural idyll still remained, even as the 21st century crept up around this gentle land. And a New Year celebration with old school friends beside the Sydney Harbour Bridge, with a steak on the barbecue and a glass of champagne in your hand takes some beating.

I fell in love with south-east Asia: the smiling faces of the Cambodians as I got lost amongst the ruins of Angkor Wat, and I loved the food of Vietnam so much I took cookery lessons. The love affair continued on into India, despite the fascination and frustrations as I travelled throughout its length. My two months there gave me a great depth and dimension in understanding this colourful and unique country. The dark-skinned southern Indians, with their highly colourful and decorated temples and the buzzing night life in Mumbai where our evening's entertainment was paid for by two admiring Indians who were so impressed by our attempts at karaoke, and then north to the infinitely colourful and bewitching Rajasthan, a sunrise over the sublimely beauti-ful Taj Mahal, and even further north to the foothills of the snowy Himalayas.

Istanbul at the crossroads with Europe and Asia seemed surprisingly un-European, as I danced with the whirling dervishes there and headed west and homeward. It was only in Austria and Holland that I became aware of the effects of the European Union.

After such experiences, I knew life back in England would seem dull. Although inspired, invigorated and empowered by my travels, I feared slipping back into the sensible, safe comfort zone of old. Fortunately a chance encounter with an inspirational busi-nessman changed everything. He reminded me to continue to do in life only what I felt passionate about, and to make a Life and not a Living.

My nine months of travelling had given me a desire to keep pursuing my dream, and I was now thirsty to live life to the full. I began to see for myself a career and a life that I could be excited about. And so I started my new business in the travel industry, offering grown-ups a mentoring service to help them keep their dream alive as they plan their own Grown Up Gap Year. For me it's a chance to give back and share with others my knowledge, enthusiasm and passion for the world and all that it offers us.

And I still haven't bought a house - life is busy, inspiring and fulfilled.

Tessa Mills's advisory business (www.thegapyearguru.com) is described on page 133.

HOW WILL A BREAK AFFECT MY CAREER?

The principal concern about taking a gap year is its potential effects on your professional life. Getting out of the swim and losing touch understandably frightens a lot of people. It's indisputable that single people in their 20s will probably feel less wedded to their jobs and their employers than those in their 40s with responsibilities at a more senior level, and certainly far less bound than individuals who have spent years building up their own businesses.

As a founder of his own successful business, **Humphrey Walters** is an eloquent advocate of sabbaticals for their value in the modern economy and is quick to refute the obvious doubts that will arise:

> *I thought if you slogged your guts out and became indispensable and then went away, your business would go down the drain or your career would suffer. That's absolute rubbish. Quite the reverse. If you do not keep yourself in a learning environment you get left behind because your ability to acquire knowledge is diminished massively. It's essential that everyone should take a break no more than half way through his or her career. It could be going back to university. Just engineer a break.*

The government's championing of lifelong learning is underpinned by an appreciation that the nature of work has become flexible and this meshes nicely with the idea of a gap year. In the modern economy, we are less tied to a career in one field or to employment with one company for the duration of our working lives. Just as the pre-university structured gap year has been endorsed by the Department for Innovation, Universities & Skills and by UCAS (Universities & Colleges Admissions Service), so too the establishment is gradually giving its seal of approval to the idea of grown-up gap years.

IMPROVING CAREER PROSPECTS

Improving career prospects is not or should not be the major motivation for taking a gap year. The break should be self-fulfilling as a unique opportunity to regain the child-like ability just to have fun, and not to measure everything in terms of success and failure. At the same time it allows you to step back and examine your life and lifestyle and to enrich and broaden interests and experiences. However, many people do end up deriving concrete career advantages from their career breaks.

Onlookers may doubt the value of a break and may view it as merely a self-indulgent opportunity to ease off the pressure of working life. But a career break can also be an empowering move in the contemporary workplace, a chance to use your own time to equip yourself with experiences and skills that complement your formal professional training. It can be interpreted positively by employers as a sign of self-sufficiency and initiative. Perhaps most valuably, it will at least illustrate to yourself that you are capable of managing your own time to suit your own ends and that work need not dominate your life to the exclusion of everything else. If you can reinvent yourself once (as a builder of village schools, carer of oil-soaked birds, round-the-world adventurer), you can do it again, and this confidence and flexibility can be highly valued by employers.

Gap years can also propel you into a different field of work. For example the leading youth charity Raleigh accepts staff volunteers of all ages and backgrounds, many of whom find that the experience alters their future course. Recent examples include: a 50-year-old accountant who changed roles and started doing lots of charity fundraising as a result of her time in Namibia; another accountant who volunteered as a project manager in Malaysia and is now working for a regeneration charity in Kabul; a keen amateur photographer volunteering in Malaysia who is now trying to set up his own travel photography business; and a graphic designer who took on a logistics role to learn new skills and is now re-training to become a mountain leader.

Demanding experiences outside the normal workplace will make a beneficial contribution to anyone's career, which can be particularly useful in cases where the individual is unsure about the next career step. **Clare Southwell** cites the experience of one friend who recruited for a large bank. He admitted that he would put former Raleigh volunteers at the top of the pile because he knew that they would never be short of an impressive answer to the question, 'Which difficult situations have you faced?'.

Even rather frivolous ways of spending a career break have proved professionally beneficial as in the case of **Michael Tunison** from Michigan:

Newspaper work was exactly what I thought I was leaving behind by globetrotting. I'd temporarily sacrificed (I believed) my career as a journalist. The last place I thought I'd be working was at a daily paper in Mexico. But things never work out as planned and before I knew it I was the managing editor's assistant and a month or so later the managing editor of the paper's weekend editions. How ironic. By taking a step my newspaper friends believed to be an irresponsible career move, I was soon years ahead of where I'd have been following the old safe route back home.

EMPLOYERS' ATTITUDES

An independent survey of employees for Direct Line Travel Insurance in April 2007 found that around a quarter of respondents work for a company where sabbaticals are a staff perk. Among those in the public sector, finance and insurance industries, that proportion rose to 40%, followed by IT and telecoms at 36%.

More and more large companies have introduced formal schemes for employees, some of which have grown naturally out of their maternity leave policy. For example the BBC has been operating a career break scheme for many years; originally it was designed for staff with caring responsibilities, and was then extended to covering further education breaks, and, more recently, it was expanded to cover travel. Marks & Spencer grants career breaks for up to nine months (unpaid); the John Lewis Partnership offers 26 weeks of paid leave after 25 years of service; Asda allows long-standing employees over 50 to take off three months unpaid (referred to as 'Benidorm Leave'); and even McDonald's gives four weeks paid leave after 10 years of service.

A growing number of companies and government organisations offer career break schemes, including Lloyds TSB, Tesco, American Express, Littlewoods, Prudential, BT and the NHS. Most companies that have signed up to support the work–life balance campaign offer career breaks alongside flexible working hours. These large and important employers have introduced formal schemes in response to a growing interest in the opportunity to travel, live overseas, gain further qualifications or simply have the time to step back from the pressures of work to re-evaluate the direction of one's life. Smaller companies can afford to be more flexible and agree to sabbaticals on a case-by-case basis, though they may have more trouble covering for an absent worker. One of the most attractive examples around is offered by the famous map and travel bookshop, Stanfords in Covent Garden, which keeps open jobs for staff who have worked there for at least one year while they travel for up to three months. When they get back they do a presentation to the rest of the staff about their experiences.

Breaks can range from several weeks to the five years of unpaid leave that the Foreign & Commonwealth Office offers to staff who can return to a job at the same level. A very few companies offer paid leave, but the crucial feature of a formal company scheme is that employment and pension rights are guaranteed. The Post Office is an example of a large organisation that runs an enlightened and long-standing scheme. For more than 30 years it has allowed its workforce to take unpaid extended leave for up to three years. All employees are eligible to apply for the career break scheme provided they have at least two years' service, a good performance record and a good absence and conduct record. Permission is granted by the line manager and pension contributions cease during the break. The Post Office's guidelines stress the importance of maintaining regular contact with the organisation and it makes a point of communicating developments in the company to the employee on a sabbatical. These employees are also required to work a minimum of two weeks every year of the break. The right to return to the former division or business unit on the former grade is guaranteed. Retraining is offered if the employee is given a different job.

TAKING CHARGE OF YOUR CAREER

The substantial economic shift during the past two decades has seen a decline in the notion that a job could be held for life. Once individuals were offered a tight and reliable career structure. But few people can fail to have been touched by significant changes in patterns of employment.

It is possible that a new psychological contract is emerging in the workforce. Managing your own career has become important because your employer no longer looks after your interests as a matter of course. Downsizing is commonplace; final pension schemes are becoming a thing of the past. This new approach stresses the importance of self-motivation, personal responsibility and a willingness to take risks. Employment practices at the BBC illustrate this shift: where once it encouraged lifelong loyalty, employees are now hired on short-term contracts.

One consequence of this perceptible shift is that loyalty to one employer is frequently being re-placed by economic opportunism in which employees with valuable skills are tempted to look for the highest bidder. It is common for an organisation to experience high rates of turnover among the workforce particularly in areas of high growth, such as finance, IT and the Internet. Within the private sector, companies have had to become more creative in devising non-pecuniary rewards for staff they want to keep.

As a consequence of general professional uncertainty, there is a growing perception among individuals that they only live once and they want their lives to have greater value, hence the growing popularity of volunteering. The prediction is for the contemporary sabbatical to evolve and become an important perk among the list of benefits designed to attract and retain good staff.

CONSIDERATIONS FOR THE SELF-EMPLOYED

The sharp rise in the number of people working freelance from home, many in front of com-puter screens all day, means that more people than ever have the freedom to opt out of work at intervals. Every so often it dawns on a freelance worker that he or she has barely stepped outside the house for days at a stretch and he or she will think with longing of the cheerful swirl and hubbub of the outside world. That might be the time for a freelancer to step back and answer the question whether it is really necessary to earn X number of pounds or dollars; etc., 52 weeks a year.

The self-employed can make their own decisions about taking time out from work without recourse to a line manager, but they may have clients who depend on them. In an ideal world, you could pass the business on to a reliable contact, but at least you should give plenty of warning to customers about your intention to withdraw temporarily. Experienced freelancers who are paid sporadically often become adept at careful budgeting. With luck, they might be able to work extra hard for a limited period in order to accumulate enough savings to fund a career break. The downside is that they have no guarantee of work and benefits when they return.

PERSUADING THE BOSS

It is surprising how many forward-thinking companies are at least willing to consider granting a sabbatical to a valued worker. When you bite the bullet and finally ask to have a word with your boss, he or she will probably be quite relieved when you do not announce that you have accepted a better job offer elsewhere but merely want six months unpaid leave to broaden your horizons. You should give some careful thought to how you can put as positive a spin as possible on what you intend to do so that your employer will be persuaded that the gap year will benefit the company as much as it will you. **Siamak Tannazi's** request to her boss was mentioned earlier. Together with citing her personal reasons for wanting to volunteer in Kerala, she described why the timing of her requested break might be beneficial. It was at a time when BT was preparing for a radical network transformation and Tan (as she is known) wanted to take her break before the change really kicked in. She pointed out to her boss that the other members of her team were happy to provide cover and were willing to support her in her efforts. In the end her boss granted three months special leave and that turned out to be about right for her. It turned out that the pitch she made was more than empty rhetoric:

> *As things in India are prone to change ALL the time, you automatically become accustomed to thinking on the spot and expecting the unexpected. For example, half way through the school term in India, I had to help choose the English teacher out of a selection of applicants in an interview. This task was laid upon me at two minutes' notice. It was a situation that I don't have experience in or ever expected to be placed in, yet it seems to happen all the time while I was in India. This has helped me in BT, as I do actually try to look at the bigger picture when I'm working. So changes happening at the moment don't unsettle me as much as they did before I left for India.*

Of course it is much easier to arrange a sabbatical from some jobs than others. The word sabbatical means literally one in seven and a break (roughly) every seven terms or seven years that is built into academic life. Sabbaticals are routinely granted in higher education to allow lecturers to pursue their research, which is as important a part of their job as teaching.

In most branches of the Civil Service, career breaks of up to five years are offered to established employees, especially if they can argue that a break will enhance their ability to contribute in the workplace. **Vicky Waite** was an established civil servant who had been working at the Cabinet Office for four years. Although she found her job challenging and interesting, she was nagged by a suspicion that something was missing. Her department was flexible about giving unpaid leave, and when she was 32, Vicky decided to go to Mongolia to work in an orphanage. Doing voluntary work was viewed favourably by her bosses as potentially broadening her skills and competencies, which would benefit them in the long run.

> *I had always wanted to travel and do voluntary work, but had never had the opportunity. It just seemed like the ideal time and I very much wanted to go to Mongolia as I was fascinated by the nomadic culture. Working with the very young children in the orphanage turned out to be much more rewarding than I expected. Building up relationships with individual children and offering time that the staff did not have was highly rewarding. For example, I looked after quite a sickly 1-year-old child who had been born premature and as a result was very slow to develop. I took him outside into the sunshine every day and encouraged him to explore and play. By the time I left he was nearly crawling and reaching to grasp toys, which he had never done before. I went back to visit the orphanage a month after I'd left, and his face lit up when he saw me. I felt very glad that I'd given him some happiness in what was quite a deprived environment.*

One of the leading placement agencies, Madventurer, has created a specialist website (www. careerbreaker.com) to put forward the arguments for taking an adult gap year. As it rightly points out, big companies spend thousands on team building exercises and leadership courses for middle managers, which in many cases are aiming for the same things as a gap year project. The potential benefits of a volunteer expedition include recharged batteries, new skills outside your traditional skills set, improvement of communication and teamwork skills, a new-found respect for community values, an appreciation for what privileges we often take for granted, incentives to progress your career and an enhanced CV:

No longer does a gap on a CV suggest to an employer that they took time out to 'find themselves'. Increasingly nowadays, employers encourage people to take time out, recognising the importance of motivating key staff and encouraging creativity in the work place. As businesses become globally focused, an understanding of cultures different from our own is considered a huge asset. Not only that, you become interesting. How many interviews are conducted which the candidates can barely be distinguished from one another? Everybody looks the same, everybody has the same qualifications and everybody has the same experience. How many built an orphanage, taught in a school in Africa or climbed a mountain? Employers are looking for evidence of experience beyond the workplace, for the ability to be innovative and creative.

Wendy Burridge considers herself to be lucky in life with a fantastic job insuring art collections. She feels that we in the West have so much that we take for granted, such as fantastic health schemes and job opportunities, and yet there are people across the world who can't even begin to imagine living such a life. With gathering determination she decided she wanted to give something back. The next step was to persuade her employers to allow her to join a Madventurer project in Uganda, helping Aids orphans:

At work I am part of a small team of six so negotiating nine weeks off work for sabbatical leave was rather tricky. I wanted to spend six weeks on the project site and take a further three weeks exploring Uganda, however with work pressures and trying to distribute my accounts this was simply impossible. Relentless in my desire to join the project, I negotiated six weeks, giving me 24 hours from landing back in the UK before stepping back into the office.

Having had to fight with her boss to take a mini-sabbatical, Wendy was promoted on her return. She was also grateful for the support she got from her employer when fundraising since they allowed her the use of office stationery and equipment for her letter-writing campaign.

Everybody's circumstances are different. Many people reading this will feel discouraged, assuming that their present employer would not be prepared to consider granting leave of absence. For example in manufacturing, banking and industry generally, many companies have been down-sizing and might jump at the chance to get rid of one more employee if they stepped out of the usual groove.

Shell, Accenture and PricewaterhouseCoopers are among the companies that have entered into a scheme with Voluntary Service Overseas (VSO) to send skilled volunteers with financial, management and IT skills, to the developing world. Instead of the usual VSO two-year commitment expected of individual volunteers, these corporate employees will be seconded for shorter periods of between six and 12 months. Similarly, VSO has also established a Public Sector Partnership Scheme along similar lines to the Business Scheme for public sector employees (see Part 4; *Doing Something Worthwhile* for more about VSO).

Perhaps your employer has instituted similar opportunities for its workforce. If not, how can you persuade your employer to keep the job open for you? Are you sufficiently confident of your skills and experience to walk away from a job if an employer refuses to grant a sabbatical? Dismissal is seldom the tragedy that it might have been considered a generation or two ago. Of course your employer might surprise you and allow you to take a break. If they don't, maybe they were the wrong kind of employer for you in the first place.

Your chances of success when asking an employer for leave are greater if your contribution is highly valued or is in some way difficult to replace. Timing can be critical here, though again success is not guaranteed, as **Paul Carroll** found out:

> *I started by challenging the two-week maximum single holiday period permitted without CEO [Chief Executive Officer] approval in the software testing company where I had been working. Upon completion of a major new project for our largest client, I requested a one-month holiday for trekking around the Himalayas. This was rejected. I then did the same six months later upon completion of the second phase for this client. Again this was rejected. The third time was four months later and the CEO personally took me aside to explain that if he agreed to my request, others would want a month or more. Although two of the three directors feel flexibility is needed, the CEO (who is responsible to the investors) doesn't believe the company can risk key members being away for longer than a fortnight at a time.*

So Paul had to reconsider his options, and decided to quit altogether. This left him with six months to join a VentureCo expedition and to travel independently round South America. On his return his old employer offered him a consultancy role but he has chosen to change his lifestyle considerably, exchanging the work-hard, play-hard London lifestyle for a more relaxed travelling consultant's job based near the Peak District. Although he still works quite hard, he now feels he is mobile, in control of his career and a lot happier with life in general because he is able to achieve his personal goals outside the working week.

Some companies offer the possibility of sabbaticals in the recruitment process, but may not want to advertise it to current staff. In other organisations a formal policy may actually be in place but is little known or quietly neglected for fear of encouraging a flood of applicants at the same time.

Check with the human resources (HR) department to see whether your company or organisation has established a specific policy on sabbaticals. Even if your employer doesn't have a formal policy, employees should make a case for an unpaid break and its value to the company in the long run. The process should be advantageous to each party. Emphasise the skills you will acquire in an activity outside the boundaries of your normal job. Your departure may give a colleague the opportunity to learn new skills too.

The more people who take a career break, the more the concept will be taken for granted. According to an article in 2008 called 'Accountants and Sabbaticals' in the journal of the Association of Chartered Certified Accountants, the majority of accountancy firms include sabbaticals as part of their employee offering. This is because corporate clients are finding it increasingly difficult to retain talented individuals in financial roles. Rather than face losing the member of staff permanently, they are willing to lose them temporarily.

TAKING THE INITIATIVE

In all but a handful of cases, it is necessary to be proactive about making a grown-up gap year happen. Imagination and determination will be required so you must be strongly committed to the idea before setting out.

Ceri Evans, a senior Sexual Health Counsellor in the NHS, happened to spot a pamphlet in the HR office about a scheme which allowed staff with at least two years service to take up to two years unpaid leave. The policy had not been advertised nor were applications actively encouraged. It seems that it was primarily intended for staff who needed to travel or care for sick relatives. It included the proviso that paid work was not allowed during the break. She later learned that a colleague's application to the scheme had previously been declined because she had wanted to study at university. Undeterred, Ceri decided to use her initiative to make her plan viable.

Ceri had decided to take a complete break from her work in the HIV field but needed to make the case that she wanted to go to Spain to study treatments there. In reality it was not very practical because she didn't speak Spanish and her primary concern was to spend a year in Barcelona with her partner who was working there.

As the manager of her department, Ceri needed to persuade her boss that her absence wouldn't be too disruptive and so she took the initiative to find a replacement within the Trust. She found that a colleague working in another clinic was interested in the experience afforded by her absence and who wouldn't require an extra salary. She also reassured her employers that she fully intended to resume her job on return, being conscious that there was a prevailing anxiety about losing trained staff. However, be cautious about making promises you suspect you may not be able to keep. Dishonesty and maltreatment of employers will only engender distrust of employees who come after you with a request for a chance to take time away from work.

CAREER BREAK CHECKLISTS

Working Families is a UK-based campaigning organisation working towards a healthy work–life balance. It publishes a factsheet entitled 'Breaks from Work' which can be read online (http://workingfamilies.org.uk/asp/family_zone/factsheets/Breaks_from_Work.doc). Its guidance on the subject of negotiating a career break includes some of the points listed below.

NEGOTIATING A BREAK
If you want to negotiate leave with an employer without a formal sabbatical scheme consider the following:

- *What will my employment rights be while on the break?*
- *Will my job be guaranteed on return?*
- *How much responsibility will I have in putting replacement mechanisms in place?*
- *Can I do some work experience while on the break?*
- *Can I take part in training courses or undertake assignments?*
- *What contact can I have with my employer in order to keep in touch with changes at work?*
- *When do I want to return to work?*
- *What other benefits can I keep (e.g. membership of the social club)?*

ESTABLISHING YOUR VALUE
Before approaching an employer, thoroughly identify the skills he or she needs most and think about the following:

- *Your real value to your employer, i.e. how much has your employer invested in your recruitment, training and development?*
- *The skills shortages in your profession or area of work.*
- *Your employer's future developments and planned growth.*
- *What costs will your employer incur in replacing your skills, experience and knowledge?*
- *The value of employment breaks to improving employee relations, recruitment, retention and public image.*

MY GROWN UP GAP YEAR:
MADDIE KILGOUR

Frustrated with her work–life balance and plagued by a feeling that she was wasting her time, Maggie decided to use some personal savings to join a five-month VentureCo programme in South America, which she completed in April 2008. The volunteering phase of the trip was with Jatun Sacha, an Ecuadorean foundation that manages nine biological reserves to protect endangered ecosystems throughout the country, including one in the Galapagos Islands. Although that placement was far more expensive than the landlocked ones, ($770 per month as opposed to $45) she describes the rewards.

The Galapagos Jatun Sacha reserve is on San Cristobal Island and is reached by an hour's taxi ride into the hills. Once you leave the town, the road is muddy with many potholes and you can easily become seasick as the car sways from side to side as it winds its way through some stunning scenery. The accommodation was good. If you are lucky you have your own room - more like a stall in stables - but most of the time you will be sharing and there is certainly no privacy where sound is concerned. Lighting is by candles which are rationed, so it is best to take along a torch, preferably a head torch. The dining area is completely separate, some five minutes walk away from the accommodation, an open area with a large communal table. The whole place is open to the elements, the birds, the flies, the dogs, etc.

Many of the volunteers are young, and come from all corners of the globe. A good number were from the USA and all were good fun while I was there. I am in my mid-50s and was not at all sure how I would fit in with the youngsters, but I had no problems at all. There were several other volunteers in the more 'advanced' age groups and I think the mix worked really well. We oldies mucked in and had just as much fun as the kids. I have a slight disability with very little sight and no hearing on my right side, and some balance problems when climbing and trekking, but once again the younger group was happy to stop for a short rest when necessary to allow me to catch up.

Much of the work being done is in clearing non-native species and reforesting with indigenous trees, but they also have their own vegetable gardens that are used daily to feed the volunteers and live-in staff. The rain can last for days at a time and this turns the whole place into a quagmire making even the easiest of tasks much more difficult. Work parties set off immediately after breakfast, returning for lunch. Be prepared to be eaten alive by mosquitoes! A head net is a must - as are rubber boots which may be provided depending upon your size being available. After a siesta you are out again until dinner. There are various projects ongoing, depending upon the time of year. You will be able to collect coffee beans, see them dry out in the heat of the sun, roast them, grind them, and drink the result!

There are a few treks that can be taken from the station, both up into the hills and out to the cliffs. From the cliffs (a trek of an hour or so from the station, through jaggy bushes and over boulders) you look across a huge expanse of sea. Sitting a vacancy; so I am still using my accountancy qualification but in a field that I am really interested in. During that year in Sudan, I managed to get married to a Sudanese national, and am now pregnant and back in the UK to have the baby.

When I came back from my travels I needed to take out a loan for £10,000 to pay everything off. All in all I think I probably spent about £16,000, which was quite expensive but worth every penny. The biggest expenses were the plane ticket (£1,772), the Greenforce expedition (£2,750) and the Travellers Worldwide fee (£1,710).

My future plans are to start a business buying handicrafts from third world projects and selling to the UK market, and in 2008 to sail around the world the wrong way with the Global Challenge. Luckily my husband is supportive of all this and I just have to work out how it can be done with no money and family responsibilities!

In general my gap year was a mental breakthrough for me. I managed to get out of the need for working for money, the necessity of earning a living and craving for stability with partner, house, etc. I actually went out and did something that I really wanted to do. That gave me the inspiration to do other things that I really wanted to do. I may not now have a house or the latest car but I have managed to find a life partner and I have not regretted the trip one bit. On the contrary, I feel that I did the right thing at the right time and learnt a lot of useful skills, which I am putting into use all the time.

WHAT CAN BE ACHIEVED?

Perhaps you've always dreamed of farming alpacas, playing the harmonium, joining a circus or sailing through the Bermuda Triangle. Alternatively, you might want to stay at home to look after a newborn baby or learn to paint or write a pub guide to your region. You might simply need an extended break from a demanding job or want to assess the direction of your career. Grown-ups will have their own reasons for wanting to take a gap year. The only activity which is prohibited is to sit around doing nothing.

Some will want to do their own thing while others may want a more structured break by volunteering time and knowledge to a charitable organisation at home or overseas. Many possibilities are canvassed in the chapters that follow. To take just one example, MondoChallenge offers career break programmes lasting two to six months for volunteers who want to have an impact on world development at a grass-roots level. In the past few years, MondoChallenge has noted that the number of career break volunteers has more than doubled, mainly high flyers in their 20s and 30s looking for a new challenge in a new environment. MondoChallenge has also recently been involved in a new corporate social responsibility venture with a London based project management company, whereby a team of employees helped set up a media hub in a Maasai vilage in Tanzania. More such projects are being planned. **Andrew Allright** worked in a small school in the Himalayas with his fiancée and commented:

> *It was such a joy to teach these children and to see them developing. We lived with the local teacher and his family and really felt part of the community. People there have so little, yet they help each other in a way we don't see here in the UK. Stepping outside your comfort zone forces you to grow and achieve things you did not think possible. It was an amazing experience where we learnt so much about ourselves. I think I felt I made a difference volunteering, and coming back to work did not feel like that all. I am back in an office job but still think something is missing.*

Shirley Graham, a 38-year-old communications manager for Unilever, was impressed by the same spirit of community when she spent two months through the same agency working at the Niketan School for orphans and street children. The positive adjectives tumble out when she describes her time in Nepal as '*illuminating, fascinating, fun, challenging, emotional, fulfilling and deeply satisfying*' and she concluded that the loving and inclusive community way of life was much more real than the stressful existence most people endure in London.

It is important to strike a good balance between slavishly following a predetermined programme and starting off with no idea of what you're hoping to achieve. Sometimes, a gap year can lead you in unexpected directions. Unpredictability is part of the adventure. During travel or time spent living in a foreign city, difficulties and frustrations are bound to crop up when dealing with different languages, customs, laws and hazards such as theft or illness. Research and planning in advance are absolutely essential. **Fiona Carroll,** a software engineer and IT manager who took time off from her job in Switzerland to concentrate on her love of painting while winding down from stress, warns that '*planning is important or the time just goes.*'

Be prepared for unfamiliar challenges. However well planned your break, chance events can blow it off course. A real break will assist your appreciation of your personal gifts and understanding of your weaknesses. You should be aware in advance that project funding can run out, a security situation may suddenly deteriorate or a crisis at home may require your presence. All of these will require far more flexibility than your normal life does.

Taking a career break affords a unique opportunity to experience an aspect of life that would otherwise be inaccessible to you in the course of your professional life. For some, taking a career break has had a profound effect on their values in life and on their futures.

PART 2

NUTS AND BOLTS:
PREPARING TO TAKE OFF

INTRODUCTION
HOW TO AFFORD A GAP YEAR
THE FINANCIAL IMPLICATIONS
ACCOMMODATION MATTERS

MY GROWN UP GAP YEAR:
CAROL PEDEN

Finding herself a widow in her mid-40s, Carol Peden knew that she wanted to get away, and took six months unpaid leave, which was granted once she found someone to cover for her post as a Consultant in Anaesthesia and Intensive Care Medicine in Bristol. Partly by making use of an earlier edition of this book, she pieced together a remarkable variety of experiences.

I started with two months in India, with the aim of relaxing but also of experiencing some alternative medicine and yoga practice. Next the plan was to spend one month in south-east Asia, followed by two months in China; the first in Xian arranged by Cross Cultural Solutions - again I wanted to experience some traditional Chinese Medicine - the second on a small group tour with Intrepid Travel. Finally I booked one month in Florence at the British Institute studying Italian and Art History.

One of the highlights was living in the centre of a Chinese city, going to the park in the morning to do Tai Chi, wandering through the streets on my own with my camera, making friends with the Chinese doctors - wonderful. I did some travelling with an Australian based company called Intrepid. Their southern India trip was fantastic, great food, wonderful Indian experiences and fun travelling companions (a group of 12, and 10 of us were singles and we all got on really well).

The low point probably should have been breaking my foot (à la Wayne Rooney) six weeks into the trip in India and having to spend six weeks in plaster and another four on crutches. It did force me to change my plans - I had to abandon Laos. The worst part however was that it made me travel very expensively because I could not manage on my own. I stayed in the Raffles hotel in Siem Reap at Angkor Wat in Cambodia, and was studiously ignored by the rich package tourists as otherwise they might have to speak to the mad woman travelling on her own on crutches! That was a very lonely time.

In Florence I was advised to rent a room in a widowed lady's apartment. Perhaps someone younger without my personal experience would have found it easier, but I was acutely aware I was invading her space and wished I'd rented my own place or even shared with some of the younger students.

The time away was fantastic - a great life experience. I spent too much money and was quite lonely at times but the good bits were some of the best experiences of my life.

INTRODUCTION

Having made a commitment to negotiate a sabbatical or even having resolved to leave your job altogether, the next step is to clarify your position financially and personally. Everything can fall into place with the right preparations. How are you going to finance your leave? What are the implications for long-term financial security? How can you look after the house if you are going to be away for many months or even a year or more? Will your mortgage lender permit you to rent out your house to tenants? What can be done with the dog, cat or goldfish if you plan to be away from home? These are some of the many considerations any individual or family needs to consider before stepping away from their work and regular income.

All the improving talk of renewal and rejuvenation during a gap year must be balanced with an unflinching look at the downside. Organising the mechanics of a long stay abroad will take scores of hours. A family spending a year's sabbatical in Paris estimated that even eight months into their stay, one of them was having to spend at least an hour a day on what they termed 'administration'.

HOW TO AFFORD A GAP YEAR

Financial resources may prove to be a stumbling block. But have you truly explored all the options to take that dreamed-of break? Have you set out a rigorous budget for yourself to increase your level of savings? If you intend to do something charitable during your break, have you thought about fundraising activities such as those described below?

Everyone's circumstances and responsibilities will vary. Being younger with fewer financial obligations is naturally going to be an advantage, but you will probably have fewer savings and no income-generating property to finance the break. As this book illustrates, people take gap years at different points in their life depending on what their priorities are.

It is crucial to recognise that taking a gap year is probably easier in practical terms than you imagine. It may sound glib to claim that there are ways round most potential obstacles, but others who have gone before have found solutions and you can learn from their experiences. As you start to prepare to take your leave, make an audit of all your responsibilities outside work that will need to be sorted out or put into mothballs. Your life is poised to change from your usual routine and this will have an impact on all aspects of your life.

Inevitably, funding a period of time in your life without a salary is going to be expensive, especially if this time includes extensive travel or voluntary work abroad. It would be misleading to gloss over the considerable costs involved, although you have to bear in mind that the cost of living in a developing country might end up being less than it would be if you just stayed at home. Before deciding on his gap year projects, long-time teacher **Nigel Hollington** calculated that his average monthly spending at home left not much change from £1,000. So he was quite content to pay the required fees to join a series of interesting projects, starting with a 10-week conservation project in Zambia with Greenforce. He did not begrudge the cost since he knew that some of his fee would be used to support a worthwhile conservation cause.

Tempted as you might be by the idea of a gap year, you might be deterred by the assumption that a period of time without a salary would be out of the question in your circumstances. But before you put the idea out of your head or procrastinate yet again, you should be aware that there are many ways of keeping the cost down. This might involve working for a charity abroad that pays a stipend sufficient to support you in, say, the local economy of India. It might mean you could concentrate your energies on finding paid work abroad even if it was only pocket money. This might involve taking a job in a bar or using your fluency in English to teach the language (see Part 6, *Working and Living Abroad,* for more details).

Beth Buffam fell in love with Vietnam on a six-month gap year in 2002. When she returned home to the USA she found jobs in her profession (computer troubleshooter) in short supply. She then began teaching English as a second language, a skill she took back to Hanoi a few years later, where she was able to save $800 a month to cover the part of her mortgage that early social security didn't cover. Beth's breakdown of her monthly expenses on top of the free accommodation provided by the school are remarkable – $30 for food, $50 for local transport, $50 for gifts and occasional expenses and $20 for school expenses – proving that gap years need not break the bank. When she told her brother that with the air ticket her total expenditure was less than $2,000, he replied, '*Wow, I spend that much in one day when my family travels*'.

Perhaps it will be possible to obtain a grant or loan to help you obtain another qualification that might increase your earning powers when you return to work. Alternatively, you may want to use some savings you have accumulated or you might be able to take advantage of capital growth in your property by increasing your mortgage. If you are in rented accommodation, think how much you would save if you gave it up and maybe moved in with your partner (as Jane O'Beirne did in anticipation of their six-month round-the-world trip) or even into your mother's attic (as Paul Edmunds did after renting out his house to a young couple in order to pay for his trip to Africa).

If you can't afford the agency fees, consider finding a low-cost grassroots volunteer project on your own. As experienced and adventurous travellers, **Deby and Peter Hardy** (aged 49 and 53) decided to go to Nicaragua and see what turned up:

> *We never organised anything before we went, as we wanted to see things for ourselves before we committed. When we visited the old colonial city of Granada, we loved it and knew that was where we would work. We went out the second night there to find a restaurant, and stumbled across a place which Deby said we must go into. It turned out to be the opening night of a restaurant run by ex-street kids and supervised by an American. We were introduced to another American who was involved in a project to refurbish a school and workshop for learning disability and physically disabled artisans. We agreed to work for them there and then, and they even sorted out accommodation for us in a volunteer house! Of course we had to pay rent for the volunteer house which was £125 per month – slightly expensive for Nicaragua, but good accommodation.*

If you have a young child in full-time childcare, think of saving that huge expense every month. If you gave up smoking, drinking, the gym, whatever other vice, think how much richer you would be after six or 12 months. If you are a property owner, imagine renting it out for a sum that would cover the monthly mortgage payments with some to spare for your spending money.

> **SOME PEOPLE ARE LUCKY ENOUGH TO BENEFIT FROM A WINDFALL. THE WHITLOCK FAMILY, WHO TOOK A YEAR OUT TO GO ROUND THE WORLD, MADE THEIRS STRETCH AS FAR AS POSSIBLE:**
>
> *My grandmother died about a year and a half before we left. She left me £25,000 in her will, and this prompted us to plan the trip. At first we couldn't believe it. It seemed such a lot of money, but really, given the fact that a decent, large, family car can cost that much in itself, we couldn't work out how best to spend it. We wanted it to change our lives for the better in some way. The plans for the trip began as dream-talk, but grew and grew, until it would have been a let-down (not least to Gran's memory) not to have gone ahead with it . . . Some colleagues thought it was rather a reckless thing to do, but most of their concerns seemed to centre on our policy of selling/chucking away all of our possessions. Frankly, to me, that was the least traumatic thing of all.*
>
> *We were strict throughout the trip from the point of view of budget, everything from long-distance bus journeys and accommodation to loose change given to beggars being tapped into a calculator memory and added to the 'books' at the end of each day. This was boring and a constant drag, but it was necessary and it worked. The whole trip in fact fitted into our £25,000 overall budget, with the flights for the four of us costing about £8,000, and a daily spend of £42, after buying insurance, rucksacks, immunisations and other essentials. At the end of the trip, it was a source of pride to us how well we felt we'd handled the finances. There were relatively few occasions when we had to compromise on excursions/activities (a notable one being the Galapagos Islands, which Nick would love to have visited). On the whole, by 'roughing it' in cheap accommodation, etc., we balanced the books without missing out.*

DOS AND DON'TS WHEN TAKING A CAREER BREAK

According to Anthony Lunch, Managing Director of non-profit volunteer sending agency Mondo Challenge, the following practical considerations will help to ensure a smooth and rewarding gap year:

- *Research your destination thoroughly before you go and buy a good guidebook and maps. Also look at the advice given by the Foreign Office (www.fco.gov.uk).*
- *Be aware of the laws, customs and dress code for the country. Your guidebook should provide all this information.*
- *If you wish to return to your job on your return, contact your employer as early as possible about the opportunities for taking a sabbatical. Your company may offer paid or unpaid sabbaticals. Emphasise the positive benefits your career break will bring to your company, e.g. you will return to work more motivated and energised having learned new skills and gained more confidence.*
- *Online banking is a great way to manage your finances while you are away. But many Internet cafés are slow and access may not always be easy so don't leave important transactions until the last minute. Set up standing orders for key items (e.g. household utilities, credit card minimum payments).*
- *Calculate how much money you will need for your trip and make sure you have some extra. Find out if you can use a credit or debit card to withdraw money at your destination. It's best to have a combination of credit/debit card, travellers cheques, sterling and some US dollars.*
- *Visit your doctor for advice on vaccinations and medication needed.*
- *Contact the relevant embassy or consulate for advice on obtaining a visa. Many have online forms. And often visas can be obtained on arrival although having one in your passport ahead of time can be comforting. If you plan to visit lots of countries, make sure your passport has plenty of blank pages, or get a new one well before you leave.*
- *Shop around for travel insurance and make sure you are covered for everything you intend to do, e.g. white water rafting.*

- *Make photocopies of your passport (including visa pages), insurance details and plane tickets. Leave copies with family/friends and take copies with you.*
- *Make sure your family or friends at home are aware of your travel itinerary.*
- *If you intend to use your mobile phone, contact your operator to check whether you will have coverage. If not you will need to take it into a shop to have the phone 'unlocked'. Warn friends not to call your UK mobile while you are away; you will be paying for all incoming calls from abroad (but see below for alternatives).*
- *Take a good international plug adaptor (or two).*
- *If you are volunteering through an organisation, ask for the contact details of the most recent volunteers on your project. They will be able to give you the best advice about what to expect on the project.*
- *Register your details with your embassy on arrival. This can simply mean sending them an email to inform them that you are in the country.*
- *If you are volunteering with an organisation ensure that local managers are aware of your plans, e.g. if you decide to go away for the weekend.*
- *Keep your photocopies of important documents (passport, insurance information, plane tickets) in separate bags from the original copies.*
- *Take advice from your local manager about your personal safety and where best to keep your valuables.*
- *Keep your valuables out of sight. Combination locks are useful for your bags.*
- *Ensure you respect local customs in regard to dress code, personal relationships, smoking and drinking alcohol. It is important for you, the organisation you are with and the other volunteers that you do not cause offence.*
- *If you are staying in one country for several weeks, consider getting either a cheap local mobile phone or a local SIM card for your UK mobile. Don't forget to alert friends back home to the new number. Local texts and calls tend to be very cheap and incoming calls from abroad are free, which avoids the massive charges when using your UK mobile. Even better, ensure your UK contacts have the special access codes available for low cost dialling to your country (try Telediscount or Just Abroad).*

MY GROWN UP GAP YEAR:
MARIE PURDY

On being made redundant after a restructuring at Cambridge County Council, Marie (who is Irish) and her partner Howard travelled round the world over five months.

With the extra redundancy money and rental money from a home she inherited from her mother in Ireland, Marie and her partner Howard decided to take a long trip to Australia and NZ. When Marie began to do the research with a travel agency she discovered that for only a couple of hundred pounds more they could buy a Star Alliance round-the-world ticket. Because they did not want to be pinned down to a fixed timetable, they paid a premium so that dates could be changed without penalty, a facility they made use of several times.

Marie tried to anticipate all the logistical problems. She pre-booked accommodation in their stopover destinations (Vienna, Dubai and Singapore) and Perth. She rented the Dublin house out through an agent. She made sure her mobile phone was unlocked so that she could buy Australian and New Zealand SIM cards. She re-directed her mail in both Ireland and England to friends who reported to her anything that looked important.

In Australia, they did a huge amount of motoring, first from Perth to the south-west corner, then from Cairns all the way to the Blue Mountains, Sydney and Melbourne (4,000km in five weeks). In general they would stay in hotels or motels if they were staying in a place for just one night, but try to find self-catering accommodation if they were staying for longer. Marie admits she is an anxious person and thinks she took her responsibility to choose the perfect places to stay too seriously.

Their week in Cairns was a highlight. They stayed in a lovely place, visited the coral reef, took the Skyrail to Kuranda, visited a bird sanctuary and so on. This was late November, so out of season (ie not the school holidays) so travel was very easy. They did a sailing trip in the Whitsunday Islands, and stopped at Surfer's Paradise. They were a bit sniffy about the idea but it was great fun in this quiet season. The beaches were gorgeous and the theme parks good fun. The key to a successful trip is building in lots of variety, and this coast of Southern Queensland offered something different.

They continued their journey in New Zealand (six weeks), Fiji and the Cook Islands (where Marie suffered from the heat) and on to Vancouver which they both loved. They had to time their stay in the US carefully because the only affordable insurance policy they could find to cover Howard (who has had major heart surgery) was for a maximum of 21 days. They spent this whole time in Montana where old friends (the wife is from the Blackfeet tribe) run a restaurant in Glacier National Park.

Marie concludes that five months is perhaps a little too long for travelling from place to place and thinks that three months would be ideal. She thinks that the key is to visit fewer places and stay longer. The endless need to make decisions (where to go, where to stay, where to eat) becomes wearing.

But they have further plans to travel, perhaps to South America, and with this in mind, Marie spent June 2008 obtaining a CELTA certificate to qualify her to teach English if the opportunity arises.

THE FINANCIAL IMPLICATIONS

Taking a career break will have substantial implications for your personal finances. Whatever the purpose of your career break, it means that your financial affairs will be undergoing a period of flux that requires some planning. If you own your home, you are likely to have a mortgage to maintain. Other financial concerns may include a pension, insurance policies, standing orders and direct debits from your bank account to cover regular household costs such as utilities or personal activities such as club memberships, charitable donations and journal subscriptions. Some of these financial commitments will need readjusting if you are going away. Even if you are staying at home, you might need to make financial provisions for the loss of income.

Usually, a career break effectively means living without a salary for the duration unless you're taking maternity leave, in a job with paid sabbaticals or you've been awarded an academic grant or scholarship for a course or research. When evaluating how much money you will need to pursue your ambition, you might consider cashing in those premium bonds your grandparents bought for you as a child or some shares that have risen in value. Perhaps a relative has left you a bequest.

Other ways to raise revenue include selling assets such as cars or a valuable painting you once inherited but never really liked. A sensible option for homeowners who wish to travel is to make use of the empty property to generate income (see detailed section later in this chapter). This may be possible even if you are not going away for your career break; you could think about taking in a lodger to defray expenses. If you live in a town which has English language schools, contact them to see if they are looking for rooms for their foreign language students. You can increase your income by as much as £100 a week if you're prepared to have halting conversations in English over breakfast.

MANAGING YOUR AFFAIRS

If you are planning to be away for some time, it is useful to set up direct debit arrangements on the television licence, the water rates and all the other bills that might arrive in your absence. Find out how much flexibility is built in to your mortgage and pension since the regulations allow some leeway (see below).

You'll need to leave enough money in the relevant accounts to cover expenses plus an extra stash for unforeseen emergencies, e.g. a tree blowing on your roof, a flood in the basement or a defaulting tenant.

Make an audit of all your additional regular expenses and decide which ones to pay and which to cancel. Unless you have very few ties, shifting your life for a career break will take some military-style planning to ensure your departure is smooth. Note that some organisations such as private insurers and gyms might allow members to suspend payments until they return home without losing the initial joining fee.

It cannot be denied that clearing the financial decks can involve a certain amount of tedium and drudgery. But a personal dream to accomplish a goal outside a career should not be set aside just because some of the preparations might be considered tiresome. When the list of obligations is drawn up, the task may seem somewhat overwhelming. But if you leave plenty of time and tackle one at a time you will soon have dealt with them all and be able to chime in with the breezy departure of Sir Cedric (from Roy Gerrard's charming children's stories):

There was rushing and fussing and bustling and packing,
And cancelling the milk the last day.
Then the cat was put out and they all gave a shout
For at last they were off on their way.

MONEY MATTERS

One of many advantages of the Internet is online banking. All the major banks and building societies have encrypted websites whereby you can access your personal account and check your balance, make financial transactions and payments and set up direct debits. Furthermore, online banks such as Smile (www.smile.co.uk) and Egg (http://new.egg.com) give favourable rates of interest. Nowadays you can also correspond with most institutions by email to sort out the inevitable glitches. Technological and human errors will happen at some point to delay payment of bills and cause aggravation, usually while you're crossing Mali or Mexico.

Paul Edmundo knew that he did not have enough savings to cover his six-month break, the first three months of which he spent travelling and volunteering in Africa. He had no intention of returning to the workplace he had left after more than 20 years (Gatwick Airport) and was prepared to take a cut in income, even after he returned to work in a freelance consultant capacity. He therefore talked to his bank manager who arranged an overdraft for him so that he could avoid paying expensive interest charges.

Consider consulting a financial adviser if you don't already use one, to help you prepare a financial strategy for your career break so that the time away from paid work can have minimal impact on your long-term financial security. Arguably, the most important aspect of taking a gap year from any corporate employment is to research how a break will affect your benefits. Companies often offer a pension, private health insurance, life assurance and income protection for their employees. Will these be affected by a break? If you're taking a sabbatical as an employee with a job being held open for you it's important to understand whether these in-house benefits will be affected. In all probability your company benefits will not be diminished during your absence, particularly if the company has a formal sabbatical scheme, though you'll certainly have to hand back the company car. Typically a career break of more than 12 months may require you to resign from your current position with the promise of a job at the same level being available to you on your return, and this can affect your entitlement to important benefits such as redundancy payments.

HOW WILL MY PLANS AFFECT MY MORTGAGE?

For a homeowner, a mortgage is probably the greatest financial obligation during their working life. Maintaining monthly payments is a crucial feature of financial planning. The good news is that mortgage policies are becoming increasingly flexible, precisely because the banks and building societies recognise that the working population needs greater choices to reflect greater competition and changes in the nature of employment.

Many of the leading mortgage companies now offer flexible mortgages, allowing suspension of payments for a few months, colloquially known as a 'payment holiday'. Specific options vary according to each policy and you will need to check with your mortgage lender.

Mortgage specialist David Hollingworth, of London and Country Mortgages (www.lcplc.co.uk), recommends thinking about this question a long way in advance to give you a chance to change your mortgage before taking a gap year:

It's important to look at the small print of your agreement and to be very upfront with your lender about your plans. Try to contact the lender as soon as you have made a decision to take a break or least before you actually leave work.

Your mortgage conditions must count as the major financial factor in evaluating whether you can afford to suspend your regular salary. A logical and simple solution is to find a paying tenant for the duration of your absence (see *Renting Out Your Property* below). Remember though that if you decide to rent out the property the payments may increase depending on your mortgage rate (explained below).

If in the past few years you have taken out a flexible mortgage, it might give you the opportunity to take back capital you have put in above the mandatory interest payments. For example, if every year you pay in an extra £1,000 to decrease the total loan, you might be able to take some of that money back in cash. Every policy will offer different benefits and detailed enquiries will have to be made before reaching any decisions about altering the terms of your mortgage. Setting up an offset mortgage – which lets you take money out of your mortgage account without penalty – may be the best course of action.

Another option for raising capital is by taking advantage of your home's increased value to extend your mortgage. If for instance you have a £100,000 loan, you may after five years of ownership be able to increase that loan to £120,000 which would cover any mortgage payments during a break and provide cash for travel or educational expenses in the time off work. Most lenders will allow you to increase the mortgage up to 75% of the current market value. But don't just renegotiate the mortgage with your current lender. Now might be the right time to shop around and switch your mortgage to take advantage of a lower rate or a more flexible policy to assist your gap year finances. Visit a broker and take a good look at the various deals available in the mortgage marketplace. Each borrower will have unique requirements and the challenge is to find a policy that besides suiting you during your career break will also accommodate any foreseeable career plans after your return.

Paul Edmunds had problems with his mortgage lender, Abbey National, which was reluctant to let him continue paying a low rate of interest under his flexible mortgage arrangement as he was sub-letting to tenants while he went to Africa. Although he persuaded the building society to let him keep paying at the low interest rate for a limited time, the society told him that after a certain period it would double the rate. With hindsight, he wishes that he had given three months notice and moved his mortgage to a different kind of account or to a different building society before his gap year started when he gave up his income.

Unfortunately, flexibility may not apply to older mortgage policies. Certainly endowment mortgage payments must be maintained regardless of circumstances. Effectively, you are locked into regular payments until the policy matures. The only alternative is to close the policy but this will incur heavy penalties. Endowments are best left until they mature because, at least in theory, the fund proportionately gains most value during the final years. Similarly, traditional repayment mortgages will require that you maintain regular contributions. Remember that life assurance payments must be kept up especially if they are attached to a mortgage.

PENSIONS

Pension funding is another important feature of any plan to take a gap year from employment. Until 2001, taking a career break had a deleterious effect on your pension because only earned income put into a pension would qualify for the government's tax relief. With the introduction of stakeholder pensions, it is possible for anyone whether in employment or not to contribute up to a ceiling of £3,600 gross (i.e. £2,880 from you, the rest from the government in tax relief) per year. This contribution is not a great amount but is better than relying on the state pension. According to Anna Bowes of Chase De Vere's (now AWD) Financial Planning department:

> *The stakeholder pension is helpful for non-working mothers or fathers and likewise for people on a career break because they don't need to forgo the government's contribution while they have no earned income. It's common for the newer pensions to allow for a break in contributions, allowing the holder to take premium holidays for up to a year. Unfortunately, some older policies may not grant this period of suspension.*

For clear background information, the personal finance website www.moneyextra.com (click on *Pensions*) is helpful.

Charles Bailey of Jelf Financial Planning Ltd (www.jelfgroup.com) has helped several clients prepare for a gap year or career break. He advises anyone contemplating a substantial break to investigate how the employer's final salary pension scheme might be affected. Ask the HR department during any negotiations if a long absence from contributions will reduce the total number of years' service with the company, which is used to calculate the pension when you retire or leave the company. The worst situation is if your employer treats you as having left the scheme. So many final salary schemes are being abolished that it might disappear in your absence. But ideally there will be no break in benefits, especially regarding pensions.

Other individuals may work freelance or for companies that are too small to offer pension schemes. In this case you'll probably be contributing to a private money purchase scheme. Once again, you'll need to check whether there are any penalties if you wish to suspend contributions until you return to regular employment. Many pension companies have introduced flexible pensions with provisions for 'premium holidays', a period each year when you might want to halt contributions without paying a penalty. If your pension predates this change, you will probably have to maintain payments or face some extra charges.

If taking a break of a year or more, some employers expect you officially to resign while promising to re-employ you on your return. Make sure that benefits that have been accrued are merely frozen temporarily rather than suspended.

NATIONAL INSURANCE

Another factor to consider is the possible effect of a break on your state pension. Projections for the state pension are dispiriting and all but a few have stopped relying on it to provide for retirement. Nevertheless it's still a benefit you're contributing to through compulsory National Insurance contributions. If you fail to make National Insurance contributions while you are out of the UK, you will forfeit entitlement to benefits on your return. You can decide to pay voluntary contributions at regular intervals or in a lump sum in order to retain your rights to certain benefits.

The normal projected figure is calculated to represent contributions from 90% of your working life. A career break will have implications although it is likely to be marginal. But you will need to check first to see how the state pension will be altered by any suspension of National Insurance contributions. If you are out of the country for an extended period, you are not obliged to continue paying National Insurance contributions, however you might choose to make voluntary contributions all the same if you want to maintain your rights to a state pension and other benefits (though this won't entitle you to sickness or unemployment benefit). Voluntary (Class 3) contributions currently stand at £8.10 per week (2009). Check HM Revenue & Customs' website for further information (www.hmrc.gov.uk/nic) or if you are self-employed and want to pay Class 2 National Insurance contributions, call 0845 915 4655.

As in many important choices in life these decisions all depend on individual preferences and priorities. Achieving a balance between the imperatives of living a full life right now and making sacrifices for retirement should be the aim. One source of valuable information on pension allowances, stakeholder pensions and the state pension is the government's public service portal www.direct.gov.uk. The website enables you to access bodies that regulate taxation and personal finance.

RED TAPE IN THE EUROPEAN UNION

If you are a national of the European Economic Area and will be living or working in another member state, you will be covered by European Social Security regulations. The information leaflet SA29 'Your Social Security Insurance, Benefits & Health Care Rights in the European Economic Area' was last updated January 2006 and can be read online at www.dwp.gov.uk/international/sa29 or obtained from HMRC, Residency the Centre for Non Residents, Room BP1301, Benton Park View, Newcastle-upon-Tyne NE98 1ZZ (☎ 0845 915 4811; www.hmrc.gov.uk/cnr). The booklet *The Community Provisions on Social Security* can be read on the European Union website (http://europa.eu.int/comm/employment_social/soc-prot/schemes/guide_en.pdf).

TAXATION

Taxation is probably the most complex area of personal finance to be affected by any prolonged absence from the UK. As anyone faintly familiar with taxation knows, there's a professional industry dedicated to helping the individual navigate the murky waters of tax. It must be expected that your taxation will be different if you take a gap from full-time employment, since your earnings are likely to drop substantially. Because tax calculations are based on previous earnings, it may be that after your break you will be eligible for a rebate.

Calculating your liability to tax when working or living outside your home country is notoriously complicated so, if possible, check your position with an accountant or financial planner. Everything depends on whether you fall into the category of 'resident', 'ordinarily resident' or 'domiciled' in the UK. Career breakers are usually considered domiciled in the UK even if they are away for more than a year. Formerly it was possible to claim a 'foreign earnings deduction' (i.e. pay no tax) if you were out of the country for a full 365 days. However the legislation has changed so that you are eligible for this only if you have been out of the country for a complete tax year (6 April to 5 April) though you are allowed to spend up to 62 days (i.e. one-sixth) of the tax-year back in England without it affecting your tax position. Anyone who is present in the UK for more than 182 days during a particular tax year will be treated as resident with no exceptions.

One HM Revenue & Customs leaflet which you might find useful is IR20 'Residents and Non-Residents: Liability to Tax in the UK' (www.hmrc.gov.uk/pdfs/ir20.pdf, updated 2008). Any profit from rented property is subject to income tax. Note that there is no penalty for stopping contributions to your existing ISAs (Individual Savings Account) and Unit Trusts. You can put in as little as you like. Halting contributions will only affect your fund's rate of growth.

If you decide to stay for a prolonged period of time in another country you will need to check out the requirements for establishing residency. For example, in Spain any person who spends more than 183 days a year in Spain is considered a resident and is liable to pay Spanish tax, although Spain has a double taxation treaty with the UK. Almost all countries have double taxation agreements with Britain so it is most unlikely that you will be taxed twice; but it is a wise precaution to keep all receipts and financial documents in case problems arise.

If you plan to live and possibly work in another country, contact the consulate and ask for the relevant dossier of information. The financial planning company the Fry Group (☎ 01903 231545; www.the-frygroup.co.uk) specialises in advising UK expatriates and can offer expert tax advice on questions of residency. The big five accountancy firms in the UK all have international offices across the world giving you the advantage of drawing on both UK and foreign expertise:

Accenture – www.accenture.com
Deloitte – www.deloitte.com
Ernst & Young – www.ey.com
KPMG – www.kpmg.co.uk
PricewaterhouseCoopers – www.pwcglobal.com

BANKING

Advice on how to carry your money while travelling and how to transfer funds in an emergency is included later in this chapter. One way of getting money which will not inconvenience the folks back home works best for those who know in advance where they will be when their funds will run low. Before setting off, you open an account at a large bank in your destination city, which may have a branch in London. Most won't allow you to open a chequing account so instant overdrafts are not a possibility. But knowing you have a fund safely stashed away in Sydney, San Francisco or Singapore is a great morale booster. It can also assist with other red tape problems such as obtaining a reference to be a tenant.

If you are planning to spend your sabbatical away from home, you should prepare the ground with your bank. If you are asking family or friends to conduct business on your behalf while you're away, it might make it easier to arrange power of attorney so that your signature is not required. Even something as simple as cancelling a lost or stolen credit card can be tricky for a third party to do. **Stef and Ness Aalten-Voogd**, who used their redundancy money to go around the world for 12 months, nominated Ness's sister Caroline to act as Power of Attorney; although she claimed she did very little for them, it was reassuring to the wanderers to know that there was an anchor of stability at home.

And while you're at it, update or draw up a will. If you die intestate the government takes an automatic 40% of your estate in inheritance tax and lawyers will get much of the rest as they apportion your wealth according to fixed rules. Do-it-yourself will-writing kits are readily available though you may feel happier paying for the services of a professional will writer (not legally trained) or a solicitor.

FUNDRAISING IDEAS

Once you have resolved to meet a particular target, say £2,500, it is surprising how single-mindedly you can pursue it. The ingenuity which adult gappers have demonstrated in organising money-making events, etc., is impressive, for example one guy got everybody he knew to sponsor him to stay up a tree for a week. You may choose to shave your head, jump out of an aeroplane, organise a fancy dress pub crawl or think of a thousand other ways to raise money. Publicise your plans and your need of funds wherever you can. Local papers and radio stations will usually carry details of your planned expedition, which may prompt a few local readers/listeners to support you. Ask family and friends to give cash instead of birthday and Christmas presents. Consider possibilities for organising a fundraising event such as a concert or a ceilidh, a quiz night, wine tasting or auction of promises. (If you have ever been active in your children's school, you may have previous experience of some of these.)

Target organisations and companies with which you have some links, such as your old school or college, for sponsorship. Local businesses are usually inundated with requests for donations and raffle prizes and are unlikely to give cash but some might donate some useful items of equipment. Keep track of all the individuals and businesses who have helped you and be sure to send them a thank you note later on describing the success of your fundraising trip.

Sarah Elengorn's most lucrative event, held a few weeks before her departure for Mexico to work with street kids, was a netball tournament organised through her club at home in Middlesex (which gave her use of the premises free of charge). Twelve teams paid £40 to enter. The event was on a Mexican theme with a bar, raffle, etc. Sarah had been hoping to raise £500 but instead made £800.

Wendy Burridge who went to Uganda with Madventurer also organised two raffles, one in her home town and another for brokers on the London art market with whom she had dealings through her job in art insurance. The raffles generated support from many companies who donated excellent prizes such as a £100 hamper, a gym membership and an evening of drinks. As the support grew so did her fundraising ambitions. She wrote to every Premiership football team asking for signed photographs and had fantastic support from Liverpool, the FA, Everton, Tottenham and Arsenal. The raffle raised nearly £1,000.

If you want to go down the route of applying to trusts and charitable bodies, consult a library copy of the *Directory of Grant Making Trusts* or check the website of the Association of Charitable Foundations (www.acf.org.uk) which links to a document 'Applying to a Charitable Trust or Foundation'. Another possible source of useful information is the Funderfinder website (www.funderfinder.org.uk/advice_pack.php). Also check the National Charities Database (www.charitiesdirect.com). Not many are willing to support individuals and you may be mostly met with rejections. (One enterprising fundraiser got his friends and family to sponsor him for every rejection.) If you are going through a registered charity, always include the charity number in your letter of request since this may be needed by their accountant.

The Winston Churchill Memorial Trust (www.wcmt.org.uk) awards about 100 four-to-eight week travelling fellowships to UK citizens of any age or background who wish to undertake a specific project or study related to their personal interests, job or community. The deadline for applications falls in October. Past winners are listed on the website with their ages and diverse topics of study; for example in 2008 a man in his 50s was funded to go to the USA to examine the role of volunteers in botanical gardens and a 42-year-old was funded to go on a Congo River expedition.

ACCOMMODATION MATTERS

Younger individuals may decide to break their careers before taking on the large financial commitment of a mortgage. Going away for them may simply involve giving up rented accommodation. The only major logistical hurdle is finding a place to store your possessions. Disposing of furniture is difficult but even if your worldly goods consist only of clothes, books, CDs, photographs and letters, you'll have to find a place for them. It will be a time of shedding superfluous possessions (think of car boot sales, eBay and so on) and will feel like a symbolic counterpart to putting work to one side as you prepare to head off into the unknown. With luck you'll find a willing parent or friends with spare space in a garage or attic for your clobber. Otherwise you will have to shop around for the cheapest storage facilities; a sample price for storing the contents of a one-bedroom flat might be £125 a month, and up to £200 for the contents of a three-bedroom house.

For many people in their 30s, 40s and 50s, travelling or living abroad will entail serious plans for the care of their homes. Just as making the arrangements to put a job on hold or to leave an employer is a major hurdle, so is solving the problem of what to do with your abode while you're taking a sabbatical abroad. The process of making the necessary arrangements to rent out the property or in a more radical move to sell it will take many months so it is essential to plan a long way in advance.

Five solutions can be considered: leaving the property unoccupied; finding a friend to stay in it rent-free but keeping an eye on it; finding a tenant either independently or through a letting agency; registering with a house-swapping agency; and using the services of a housesitting agency. The latter is so expensive as to be of interest mainly to the seriously wealthy (see below). Not everyone is comfortable with the idea of strangers living in their house, whether paying tenants or house-swappers. In the end it will be a personal decision, but be assured that tens of thousands of people have been delighted with the ease with which it can be accomplished.

RENTING OUT YOUR PROPERTY

Assuming you are a property owner, your house or flat is probably your greatest financial asset. It is also your home, a place of emotional and physical security which you will not want to hand over to strangers lightly. However, if you want to spend all or part of your gap year travelling or living overseas, renting out your home can go a long way to covering your costs and is usually worth the bother. Renting to tenants also neatly solves the problem of security and makes use of the home to provide a revenue stream at a time when you may not be drawing an income. If you are lucky you will find a tenant through the 'mates network' (which can be accessed very simply through your email address book) as Mike Bleazard did when he wanted to leave home for six months. Mike was very happy to rent his flat to the colleague of a friend at somewhat below the market rate for Cambridge, i.e. at £800 a month including all the bills apart from council tax and telephone. This worked out easier all round because it meant that Mike didn't have to worry about meter readings or disconnections when he left and returned.

The 1960s and 1970s were notorious for sitting tenants who refused to leave at the end of the rental period. The Housing Act of 1988 and a subsequent amendment have virtually solved this abuse, ensuring that a contract between landlord and tenant explicitly sets out terms for the rental, for example the prohibition of pets, and makes the time limit legally binding.

Try to avoid switching to a buy-to-let mortgage (as some lenders may try to impose on you) which is almost always more expensive and will force you to pay all the costs of remortgaging (legal fees, valuations, etc.). Make sure your lender knows that you will be returning to occupy the property within a specified period. They should give you a 'permission to let' for which there may be a fee (usually under £100) but will allow you to carry on with the same mortgage terms.

Above all, it is essential to notify both your mortgage lender and your insurance company that you intend to rent out your home before agreeing to any tenancy. Any changes to the normal habitation must be cleared first. Most insurance companies are amenable to making provision for your time abroad but they may want to reassess risk if there is a change of occupancy. Mike Bleazard was glad that he had topped up his contents insurance before renting out his flat, making sure the policy would cover tenants, because the flat was burgled while he was on his gap year.

If you put many valuable items such as furniture or pictures into storage for the duration of a tenancy this might actually lower the cost of contents insurance. Your insurer will prefer and occasionally even insist that you use a registered agency or at least delegate responsibility for keeping a regular check on the property to a trustworthy person close by.

When notifying the mortgage lender, you need to know whether you have a 'residential mortgage rate' and if so whether you can retain these preferable terms while you're renting the property instead of becoming liable for the more expensive 'standard variable rate'. You will be permitted to maintain your mortgage status if you sign a form stating that you are renting to a private individual on an 'Assured Shorthold Tenancy'. With hindsight **Paul Edmunds** realises that he made an error in accepting his tenants' suggestion of paying six months' rent in a lump sum at the beginning of their tenancy. This meant that he had to declare the rental income for tax purposes in that tax year, whereas if their payments had been staggered or paid later, in the next tax year when his income was much lower, he would have had to pay considerably less tax.

Three publications that may be worth consulting are *The Complete Guide to Letting Property* (Liz Hodgkinson, Kogan Page, 2008, £10.99), *Renting and Letting* (Which guides, 2006, £10.99) and *Renting Out Your Property for Dummies* (2006, £15.99) which tackles all the common problems that arise between landlord and tenant, and explains how the law operates to help avoid most of them.

USING A RENTAL AGENCY

Putting your home into the hands of professionals often imparts peace of mind even if it cuts into your financial gain. Most agencies charge a fee of at least 10% of the rent plus VAT (value added tax). The Association of Residential Letting Agents or ARLA (www.arla.co.uk) advises – and of course it is in their members' interests to do so – that you use a professional agency to manage the tenancy while you are away. Homeowners often find comfort in knowing that any problems that arise over money or maintenance can be delegated to an impartial intermediary. Also agency fees are an allowable expense that can be offset against tax.

A letting agency will screen potential tenants according to particular criteria to ensure that you let your home to responsible people. They may for example have regular company customers who rent property on behalf of company employees, diminishing the likelihood of any disputes over unpaid rent. A company let is safer because the company in question becomes legally responsible for any transgressions by the tenant.

Letting agencies are increasingly experienced at working with private homes being placed on the rental market for a set period of time. Short lets are possible to arrange if you are intending to be away for less than six months. Even if renting out your home is a novelty and feels rather risky, there is plenty of professional help available to make it a viable proposition, allowing you to benefit from the property's intrinsic value while maintaining all your legal rights to possession.

If you are using an agency, find out if it is one of the 1,800 members of ARLA and therefore obliged to follow a professional code of conduct. These registered agents are bonded which ensures that any misuse of your rental income or of the tenant's deposits is guaranteed by the Association's special fund. If there are any financial irregularities you can go straight to ARLA for compensation. You can ring ARLA (☎ 01926 496800) for information about where to find a local agent or with specific questions about letting your home. Most questions should be answered in the 'Information for Landlords' section on its website.

RENTING INDEPENDENTLY

Of course it is possible to take the independent course and organise the rental yourself and thereby save a substantial sum of money. Managing your own rental will be more difficult if you plan on being abroad. However, with the rise of the Internet it is easier to locate suitable tenants, and with advances in communications, it is possible to keep tabs on a tenant via email.

The tried and tested method of finding a tenant is to advertise in the local newspaper or to target a magazine read by the kind of people you want as tenants (ramblers, stamp collectors, vegetarians, alumnae of your old university, etc.) Even people who do not happen to live in prime tourist locations can often rent out their houses to people who have come to work at the local hospital, or been transferred by their employer and are renting for a time while they look around to buy. A 57-year-old kitchen fitter from the small Midlands town of Measham, who was planning a long break in New Zealand, realised that there was not much of a rental market in his town. However, he discovered that the local Council was looking for properties to rent out for a minimum of a year. The rent of about £250 was low but they guaranteed to find tenants.

Always ask prospective tenants to supply references from their current employer, bank and previous landlord and follow them up because dodgy tenants have been known to fabricate references. Holding one month's rent as a deposit is standard practice. This can be used to pay outstanding bills at the end of the tenancy and to cover any potential damage, and then the difference is returned. Depending on the nature and duration of the tenancy, you can consider putting the utilities in the tenant's name (which is a major hassle) and asking them to pay the council tax. Together, you and your tenant should also draw up an inventory of all the items in the property, which you should both sign in front of a witness. You will want to ask a neighbour (preferably a nosy one) to contact you in the event of problems especially in an emergency such as theft or fire.

Philip Hardie was due a sabbatical term and decided to take it away from Cambridge. His twin sons were in their last year of primary school and this seemed like a good opportunity for a change. Although Australia is not the first destination to spring to mind when classicists plan a sabbatical, he had several friends at the University of Sydney who assured him that the welcome would be warm and the library resources adequate for the book he wanted to research.

The family's first thought was to arrange a house swap for their four-month trip since there is plenty of sabbatical traffic in the other direction, Sydney to Cambridge. However, matching dates was going to present problems and it seemed simpler to rent out the family house in central Cambridge and find a place to rent in Sydney. Universities often have an accommodation office that caters to visiting academics and Cambridge is no exception. The rather grandly titled Society for Visiting Scholars tries to match accommodation requests from abroad with furnished houses and flats for rent. It is simply an introduction service rather than an agent and charges no commission, though it welcomes donations if its services are appreciated. Usefully, the office gives its clients a template of a letting contract.

ALWAYS CONSIDER THESE PRACTICAL STEPS WHEN RENTING OUT YOUR HOUSE INDEPENDENTLY AND GOING AWAY FOR AN EXTENDED PERIOD:

- *Notify your mortgage lender that you intend to let the property. Your lender will want you to sign a form stating that you are renting to a private individual on an Assured Shorthold Tenancy.*
- *Remember you will be liable for tax on the rental income minus the mortgage payments, letting fees and other expenses.*
- *Agree a method of rent payment with the tenant, possibly asking for evidence that a standing order into your account has been set up or asking for a set of post-dated cheques which you (or a trusted proxy) can pay into your account.*
- *Read the utility meters at the last minute before departure. If they are not accessible, request the electricity and gas supplier to take interim readings.*
- *Telephone the phone company for an interim reading. You can leave a cheque made payable to the phone company to cover your share of monthly or quarterly calls and leave the tenant in charge of paying the phone bill.*
- *Put away valuables such as computers and paintings plus any items you would not want damaged. It may be that you can store such items in the smallest room which can be declared off-limits (assuming this has been agreed with the tenant beforehand).*
- *Prepare a file with all relevant instruction manuals, guarantees or insurance cover for appliances.*
- *If tenants are new to the area, a few tips on local shops, services, pubs and restaurants, doctor's surgeries, etc. would be appreciated.*
- *Ask a friend or neighbour to keep an eye on the property and ask them to contact you by phone or email if anything seems amiss.*
- *Obtain a mail forwarding application form from any post office; the current fees within the UK are £7.35 for one month, £16.15 for three, £24.90 for six and £37.40 for 12; fees for forwarding mail abroad are double. These fees apply per surname.*
- *Cancel subscriptions to newspapers, book clubs, the cleaner, window washing services, etc. after ascertaining that the tenant does not want to retain them.*

The family house was registered early in the year for a September departure with an expectation that expressions of interest would roll in. By July, the family had had just one enquiry that had come to nothing, and the university office could guarantee nothing. With their departure less than eight weeks away, Philip began to panic and discovered a local website for Cambridge accommodation on which he posted (free of charge) brief house details. Within 48 hours he had had three replies, one coincidentally from Sydney, two others from people already in Cambridge and therefore available to come to see the property. One took it for precisely the dates it would be empty. The family appreciated the chance to meet the tenant in the flesh, especially when they discovered that she was the daughter of a family friend of a neighbour. References (one work, one personal, one bank) were requested and produced, an Assured Shorthold Tenancy Agreement was signed in the presence of witnesses and all went ahead smoothly.

On the family's return, they found their house not only in one piece but mostly unchanged from when they had left it. Inevitably a few dishes had been broken, a saucepan ruined, a lampshade torn, a wall gouged (the tenant had a 2-year-old daughter), but they felt that this was fair wear and tear from tenants paying £700 a month and thereby covering all their rental expenses in Sydney.

As for organising the paying of bills, the Hardies had continued to pay the electricity and gas bills by standing order. On their return they read both meters themselves then calculated the number of units used over the whole rental period and added the pro-rated standing charge.

The telephone bills had been slightly more problematic. Rather than change the billing name, the bills were forwarded to the owners (since they had organised all mail to be forwarded by the post office). After marvelling at how high their tenants' phone bills were, they sent them on to the tenant and trusted her to pay them. If for some reason she had not paid them, she is the one who would have suffered the inconvenience of having the service cut off. As soon as they returned home, they contacted the telephone company for an interim reading and were told the amount owing at that time was a whopping £300. This amount together with the total amount owed for utilities came in at about £50 less than the deposit of a month's rent, so there was no need to extract extra money from the tenants after they had gone.

To satisfy Health & Safety regulations, you should make sure that furnishings show labels that prove that they qualify under the Furniture and Furnishings (Fire & Safety) Regulations (amended 1993), that all gas appliances meet the Gas Safety regulations, and that you have a valid safety certificate supplied within the previous 12 months by a CORGI-registered engineer.

HOUSE SWAPPING

Another option to explore is swapping your home and sometimes also your car with an individual, couple or family from the city or country you want to visit. Exchanging houses with a homeowner abroad will not only save accommodation costs, but also immediately take you off the tourist trail and set you down in a real neighbourhood. The two main requirements are that you be willing to spend at least a few weeks in one place and that you have a decent house in a potentially desirable location. You also have to be someone who can plan ahead since most swaps are arranged six months in advance. And of course you must be prepared to bring your housekeeping up to an acceptable standard.

Many home exchange agencies are in the business of trying to match up compatible swappers. Swaps are usually arranged for short holiday breaks up to about a month in the summer (especially popular with school teachers) but longer ones are possible too. The great advantage of a home swap is that this is not a commercial transaction, so the costs are minimal. The more desirable your home location is, the easier it will be to attract interested swappers. People who live in central London, Sydney or New York or in a Cotswold village or near a Californian beach will certainly have an advantage. But there will be people looking not just for historic or culturally interesting destinations but for a specific university town or a home with easy access to the countryside. Even if you don't live in a popular destination, it is worth registering since you might just happen to find someone who is looking for a property just like yours in your particular area of the country.

It is easy to register with an agency online. You simply complete a questionnaire describing your home and its location and pay a registration fee. Most agencies have stopped distributing printed directories because of the enormous cost and operate totally in cyberspace, which has brought annual membership down in most cases to around £30. Once you have subscribed, you can search the company's listings and make direct contact with the owners of properties that interest you. The vast bulk of this communication now happens by email. The final stage is an exchange of formal letters of agreement.

Green Theme International (www.gti-home-exchange.com) is one of the pioneering companies in this field and has an environmental motivation. By encouraging house swaps it is hoping to limit the demand for package destinations and the appeal of second homes. The founder, Kathy Botterill, says success in finding a suitable match is often due to good luck, particularly if you have your heart set on a particular destination. The modest fee for a one-year online listing is £25/$50. As home swapping is a form of bartering, it's entirely possible to swap your home for an extended stay, provided you can find someone willing to live in your home for that length of time. The cost will be exactly the same as if you swapped for a fortnight. In the past, Green Theme has helped residents of Australia and New Zealand swap homes for periods of one and even two years.

Homelink International (www.homelink.org.uk) is one of the largest agencies with more than 13,500 properties worldwide on its website. They send out two directories per year as well as maintaining web listings; the annual membership fee is £115. The longest established company is Intervac (www.inter-vac.com) whose list includes 8,000 properties in 50 countries, and who has emailable contacts in many countries of the world. California-based HomeExchange (www.homeexchange.com) has a purported 10,000 listings in 85 countries ($100 membership). Another to consider is Home Base Holidays (www.homebase-hols.com) which charges £29 for an annual listing. The main organisations can arrange travel insurance specifically tailored for home swaps, covering such problems as cancellation owing to illness, marital collapse, etc. A free house swap website is www.digsville.com.

If you are taking the children, you will obviously check whether the house you're going to live in is safe or suitable for them. Likewise, if a family with children is coming to stay in your home try to check if it meets safety standards. If possible, swap with another family or couple who mirror your life to some extent, for example, if they have children of a similar age.

It's a wise precaution to notify your insurance company too. Check to see if your home contents and building insurance covers any potential damage. Legally, people on a house swap are classified as guests not tenants. It is also sensible to put into storage your most valuable possessions to avoid accidental damage or breakage. If a car is included in the swap the guests will need to be added to the policy and details given of their driving licences.

LEAVING YOUR PROPERTY EMPTY

You will need to make careful preparations to ensure that your home is well cared for and protected in your absence. Assuming you have decided against renting or lending it out to a lodger or student, can you arrange for a neighbour, relative or friend to make regular visits? How important is it for the garden to be cared for in your absence if only to have the grass mown so it looks occupied? Preventing burglary and guarding against burst pipes in winter are real considerations.

Naturally, friends or relatives may not be able or willing to commit the same amount of time or apply the same degree of professional expertise as an agency. Appointing a friend as agent can strain good relations if anything goes wrong. A bottle of wine and box of chocolates are probably not enough compensation for the anxiety the job may have caused them.

CARS

If you own a vehicle that you do not intend to sell, you can either take it off the road for the duration of your absence or lend it to a friend/tenant. Motor insurance in the UK is less flexible than in many countries (such as the USA and Australia) since it covers named drivers rather than the vehicle. It can be expensive adding one or more names to the car insurance for an extended period, an expense which should be passed on to the borrower. If you have a no-claims bonus, try to find out if it can be protected in the event of another driver having an accident.

If you are taking your car off the road, you will obviously want to store it in a safe place, perhaps a friend's unused garage or driveway. Some homeowners prefer to leave their vehicle in their own drive to disguise the fact the property is empty.

If a vehicle is off the road for more than a calendar month, it is possible to reclaim the unused months of road tax by declaring SORN (Statutory Off Road Notification). You can get the required from from a post office (form V14). Send it to the Driver and Vehicle Licensing Agency in Swansea (Refunds Section, DVLA, Swansea SA99 1AL). Alternatively apply online at www.taxdisc.direct.gov.uk.

PETS

Taking a gap year abroad will pose a special challenge for pet owners. Most pets are well-loved friends, especially for children. Your dog or cat is virtually a member of the family and it will be very hard to imagine leaving them behind. The Passport For Pets scheme is now well established and allows you to take a dog or cat (or rodent, rabbit, reptile or ornamental tropical fish) abroad to a number of approved countries, without subjecting the animal to six months' quarantine when you return. Check to see whether your destination is included in the scheme.

If you plan to take a dog or cat abroad, give yourself plenty of time to make the necessary preparations to comply with the regulations of the pet passport scheme. A dog or a cat will need to be vaccinated against rabies and have a microchip implanted by the local vet which gives the animal a unique number, procedures which will run to several hundred pounds. Essentially, you have to prove that an animal is clear of rabies for the six months following the blood test after the vaccination It's a slightly convoluted process but nevertheless is a great improvement on the previous rules which made quarantine compulsory for six months. You can obtain an information pack by calling the Department for Environment, Food and Rural Affairs (Defra; ☎ 0870 241 1710) or by consulting its website (www.defra. gov.uk/animalh/quarantine/index.htm), which lists all the approved countries in the passport scheme.

On some journeys, like a walking pilgrimage over the Pyrenees to Santiago de Compostella in Spain, it might be wholly appropriate to take your dog for company. You'll never be far from shops or veterinary care in Europe. On other trips, such as driving across Africa, it would be impractical. If you are renting or swapping your house, you can hold out for a tenant who is willing to take on the care of your animal. Another option is to put the pet into a boarding kennel. To find one, ask your vet for a recommendation and then check if it is licensed by the local council. An alternative would be to find a foster family, perhaps a good friend or a relative willing to take on the care.

HOUSESITTING

Ideally you might hear of someone via the grapevine who is looking for temporary accommodation and who would be willing to look after your house, pet and garden in exchange for a rent-free stay. Graduate colleges and teaching hospitals are just two places with a mobile population and potential housesitters. If you do not know the person beforehand, ask for references just as you would of a rent-paying tenant.

You might want to investigate other possibilities. A journal called *The Caretaker Gazette* (www.caretaker.org) published in the USA has been listing properties that need live-in caretakers and housesitters since 1983. An annual subscription to the newsletter costs $29.95 and an advert for a housesitter costs 65 cents a word. A UK equivalent which operates only online (www.HouseCarers.com) maintains a housesitting database; annual membership costs $45. A final solution is to hire a housesitter, who will take care of the pets and provide a range of light domestic support such as simple cleaning and gardening, all for a large fee. Effectively you'll be hiring an individual or a couple to act as housekeepers. But if you can afford it and if you own a home that requires special care owing to age or an outstanding garden or a menagerie of animals, this might be the best solution.

Hiring housesitters is certainly not a cheap option and can cost £500 a fortnight plus expenses. In return the companies will guarantee that the employee will care for your animals according to any instructions you leave. Companies include Animal Aunts (☎ 01703 821529; www.animalaunts.co.uk), Home & Pet Care Ltd (☎ 016974 78515; www.homeandpetcare.co.uk) and Homesitters (☎ 01296 630 730; www.homesitters.co.uk).

STAYING IN PRIVATE HOMES

If you are not in a position to swap your own accommodation for someone else's, you might like to consider a homestay or some variation on that theme. A number of worthy organisations dedicated to promoting world peace and understanding match up people interested in hosting foreign travellers with those on the move. Socially it can be a gamble but financially it is brilliant since expenses are minimal.

Servas International is an organisation begun by an American Quaker, which runs a worldwide programme of free hospitality exchanges for travellers, to further world peace and understanding. Normally you don't stay with one host for more than a couple of days. To become a Servas traveller or host in the UK, contact Servas Britain, 68 Cadley Road, Collingbourne Ducis, Marlborough, Wiltshire SN8 3EB (☎ 020 8444 7778; www.servasbritain.u-net.com), which will forward your enquiry to your area coordinator. Before a traveller can be given a list of hosts (which are drawn up every autumn), he or she must pay a fee of £25 (£35 for couples) and be interviewed by a coordinator (rates are less if you are also willing to be a host). Servas US is at 11 John Street, Suite 505, New York, NY 10038 (☎ +1 212 267 0252; www.usservas.org). There is a joining fee of US$85 and a refundable deposit of $25 for host lists in up to five countries.

Hospitality exchange organisations can make travel both interesting and cheap. **Bradwell Jackson** had been mulling over the possibility of travelling the world for about a decade before he finally gave up his drug misuse counselling job in the USA to take off for an indeterminate period of time to see the world. On his earlier travels he had discovered the benefits of joining Servas and two other hospitality exchange programmes Global Freeloaders (www.globalfreeloaders.com) and the Hospitality Club (www.hospitalityclub.org). His first destination was Mexico, where to his amazement he found English teaching work at the first place he happened to enquire in Mexico City:

> *I really must say right away that Servas is not simply for freeloading in people's homes. However, once you take the plunge and commit to wandering the earth, things just start to fall into place. If you belong to clubs such as Global Freeloaders, Hospitality Club, or any of the other homestay organisations, don't be surprised if the family you stay with invites you for an extended stay. The first such family I stayed with in Mexico invited me to stay for six months. All they asked is that I help with the costs of the food they prepared for me and hot water I used.*

Bradwell is continuing his couchsurfing travels in some unlikely locations. He left Mauritania at the beginning of 2008 and stayed with a host in Bamako, Mali, who offered to let him stay for two months in exchange for two hours of English lessons a day. He was a wealthy man who gave Bradwell all his meals, Internet access, laundry and so on. He commented that '*once one lands into a dream situation like this, you are apt to feel a bit guilty, and such hospitality takes time to get used to. Still, I am certainly not complaining*'. More recently he stayed with a host in Hong Kong who kindly gave him a copy of a book called *How to Find Happiness* by the Dalai Lama, which inadvertently got him into hot water when he tried to cross into China with it.

When you register with the Hospitality Club, Global Freeloaders or the Couchsurfing Project (www.couchsurfing.com), all of which are completely free, you agree to host the occasional visitor in your home in order to earn the right to stay with other members worldwide. Another possibility is the Hospitality Exchange (www.hospex.net) which charges $20 for a year's membership.

Members of the Globetrotters Club are often willing to extend hospitality to other globetrotters. Annual membership of this travel club costs £15/$29; contact the Globetrotters via their postal address (BCM/Roving, London WC1N 3XX) or on the web (www.globetrotters.co.uk). Members receive a bimonthly travel newsletter and a list of members, indicating whether or not they encourage other members to stay with them.

Other hospitality clubs and exchanges are worth investigating. Women Welcome Women World Wide (☎ 01 104 405441, www.womenwelcomewomen.org.uk) enables women of different countries to visit one another. There is no set subscription, but the minimum donation requested is £35/$67, which covers the cost of the membership list and three newsletters in which members may publish announcements. There are currently 2,500 members (aged 16–80+) in 70 countries.

Language courses abroad often arrange for clients to live with local families as paying guests which is a great way to improve a language in the context of family life. This is commonplace throughout Latin America but can also be arranged in France, Germany, Spain and so on. And many volunteering programmes include homestay accommodation. Not all grown-ups relish the prospect of becoming a temporary family member. When **Katy Chan** (aged 36) was choosing her programme, she realised it was important to her not to stay with a local family but to be with other volunteers so she could meet new people from different countries and share experiences. '*I felt that staying with a family would isolate me, especially in a country like Costa Rica where there were language barriers.*' Forty-something **Paul Edwards** found living with a family in suburban Accra Ghana during a cricket coaching placement was not ideal and regretted that he wasn't able to live independently, kind and welcoming as his host family was. He found his situation slightly claustrophobic and he struggled with the Ghanaian diet, yet it was awkward going out to find a more palatable alternative.

FINDING ACCOMMODATION ABROAD

As if it weren't enough trying to work out what to do with your property while you're away, you will have to worry about where you can afford to stay while you're abroad. If you intend to spend your gap year travelling, see Part 7, *Travel and Adventure,* for information about where to stay on the road.

If you have organised a house swap, your accommodation has already been taken care of. Renting a flat or house abroad will be miles cheaper than staying in hotels or other travellers' accommodation but it is sure to be more complicated (unless you are lucky enough to find something through a personal contact). Property agencies usually charge steep fees and are legalistic about checking the inventory, etc. Numerous online rental agencies offer properties in Europe and worldwide for short or longer-term lets, and their fees tend to be lower and in a few cases non-existent. Try tapping 'self-catering' and your destination into Google.

Agency fees can be avoided by answering advertisements in local newspapers, though this can be discouraging in an unfamiliar city. You can end up wasting a lot of time going to see flats in areas you might deem too seedy or unsafe to live in. Furthermore, competition for accommodation advertised in daily papers will be fierce. To stand any chance you might have to buy a morning paper as soon as it goes on sale the night before and act quickly first thing in the morning.

If you are willing to consider student-style accommodation, it is worth contacting the student housing office or checking notice boards in student unions, preferably one aimed at graduate students and therefore with notices of accommodation a little more grown-up than undergraduate digs.

One of the main drawbacks of renting is that you will be expected to sign a lease, typically for a minimum of six months which locks you into staying in one place for longer than you might have chosen. You will probably be required to pay a sizeable bond, usually at least one month's rent, which will be held back if you leave before the lease expires or if you leave the property in less than immaculate condition. Some flat-letting agents will give shorter leases for higher rents. You may be asked to provide a bank reference or evidence of a reliable income.

MY GROWN UP GAP YEAR:
DEBBIE RISBOROUGH

Although Debbie Risborough at age 38 was enjoying her job as accountant for a small friendly company, she was bored and decided she wanted to travel and try something completely different. Like everyone in this position, the idea of abandoning everything to get on a plane left her nerves in tatters, especially with her mother treating her as though she had gone mad and would never return. The year out was to be funded initially by savings, although she knew eventually she would have to make use of the £4,000 credit limit on each of her four credit cards and her overdraft facility of £1,400.

In total I was away about 14 months. I decided to do voluntary work as I am not a very good tourist, and I also needed things to be planned upfront so that I would not worry about what would happen next. I made a list of all the countries that I wanted to visit and looked for voluntary work in them. Three months was a good length of time in most countries, as tourist visas last that long. My trip included India for six weeks (three weeks with Indian Volunteers for Community Service and three weeks travelling); South Africa for three months with Sneewitje Creche; Australia for one month of holiday (since I had nothing planned, a month was enough for me); Fiji (nine weeks with Greenforce on a marine expedition and about 10 days travelling); Argentina for three months teaching English with Travellers Worldwide, while taking a Spanish course at the University of Buenos Aires, and finally two months of holiday in Canada, where I liked it so much I stayed on until my ticket was due to expire.

The India stay was quite a short time as I wasn't sure how I would cope with the change in culture. I chose the Greenforce expedition because I had always wanted to learn to dive, and that was an opportunity to do that. The Travellers programme in Argentina seemed good value for money. In fact Argentina turned out to be the high point, as everything just worked and I loved it all. The low point was the last few weeks of the Greenforce placement. The weather was not good, I was stuck on an island with 15-18-year-olds for company (it really didn't matter how nice they all were) and I knew I had another three weeks to go!

In general the reality far exceeded my expectations, as I didn't really know what to expect so was really nervous. The only part of the trip I had built up in advance was the Fiji expedition, so it was not surprising that reality kicked in here. I am still amazed that I managed to effectively travel around the world on my own and nothing bad happened. I didn't lose anything, get anything stolen or have any nasty stories to tell. I am truly thankful for that.

When I returned I was totally amazed at how life continued. When I got back I was on a mission to work in the NGO field, and temp in the meantime. I managed to get a temporary job after 10 days back in the UK, and obtained a year's contract with an NGO in Sudan within four months by consulting the website of MANGO which matches accountants with overseas aid agencies. The job was as Finance Officer for Concern Worldwide in Darfur, which progressed to Country Accountant due to a vacancy; so I am still using my accountancy qualification but in a field that I am really interested in. During that year in Sudan, I managed to get married to a Sudanese national, and am now pregnant and back in the UK to have the baby.

When I came back from my travels I needed to take out a loan for £10,000 to pay everything off. All in all I think I probably spent about £16,000, which was quite expensive but worth every penny. The biggest expenses were the plane ticket (£1,772), the Greenforce expedition (£2,750) and the Travellers Worldwide fee (£1,710).

My future plans are to start a business buying handicrafts from third world projects and selling to the UK market, and in 2008 to sail around the world the wrong way with the Global Challenge. Luckily my husband is supportive of all this and I just have to work out how it can be done with no money and family responsibilities!

In general my gap year was a mental breakthrough for me. I managed to get out of the need for working for money, the necessity of earning a living and craving for stability with partner, house, etc. I actually went out and did something that I really wanted to do. That gave me the inspiration to do other things that I really wanted to do. I may not now have a house or the latest car but I have managed to find a life partner and I have not regretted the trip one bit. On the contrary, I feel that I did the right thing at the right time and learnt a lot of useful skills, which I am putting into use all the time.

PART 3

PRACTICAL ADVICE FOR TRAVELLERS

INTRODUCTION

The best advice comes from other people who've done it first. They've learnt the hard way, so talk to your friends, colleagues and acquaintances who have hit the road or volunteered abroad, and make use of the Internet to locate travellers who have gone before. Try searching message boards such as Lonely Planet's Thorntree or www.travellersconnected.com, an online community site for travellers that is free to use. You can register your profile and contact travellers around the world to seek insider tips or put you on your way to connecting up with a like-minded companion. Of course you don't always have to act on advice shared on the Internet, some of which will be too cautious or too daring for your tastes, may conflict with other reports and even be downright wrong. Be prepared to cherry pick what makes sense to you.

While travelling, be open to meeting the locals and other travellers because they are a valuable source of information and of course companionship. But the same limitations apply to their advice. You may meet an educated professional in Islamabad who warns you against going up the Karakoram Highway on the grounds that it is populated by bandits. The same day you might meet a hardened traveller who encourages you to wander at will in the hills of the Hunza Valley on that same highway. You will have to choose your own course between these extremes and try to filter out advice based on prejudice on the one hand or bravado on the other. All the information and contacts in the world are useless unless you make a personal approach to every particular situation. If you have elected for a placement with a local non-governmental organisation (NGO), you will be able to benefit immediately from local advice.

It is amazing how far the English language can take you in even remote corners of the world. But it is a gesture of respect to learn at least a few local phrases and words. In some cases, it may be essential, for example in finding the local toilet or if you're vegetarian and want to avoid eating meat. At least carry a relevant phrase book or mini-dictionary.

Many single women would love to take a gap year travelling but are intimidated by perceived danger. Statistically the chances of serious mishap are negligible but it still takes courage to organise a solo trip, especially without prior experience. Of course women should only undertake to travel in a way with which they're comfortable. Travelling in Islamic countries where women are barely seen in public presents special problems. The respected independent travel agency in Bristol Marco Polo Travel (☎ 0117 929 4123; www.marcopolotravel.co.uk/pages/women.html) offers a one-hour consultancy to up to four women (cost £40) to offer inspiration and build confidence before a major trip.

Thelma and Louise www.thelmaandlouise.com is an online community of women worldwide which enables members to find travel companions (among other things). Registration is free and enables members to contact other members and use the messageboard. The membership includes women who are interested in gap years and career breaks; members can post plans to join an expedition or project on the website. Another source of possible travelling companions is www.someone2travelwith.com, which operates a bit like a dating agency. Interested parties register the details of their proposed trips on the site and then are matched with other members. When a match is accepted, the fee is £30. If contemplating an ambitious trip, it might be worth trying a taster trip closer to home or of shorter duration to see if you can enjoy your own company and the delights of choosing an itinerary with reference to no one but yourself. As mentioned earlier, many suitable companions will be met along the route.

Both women and men who remain unconvinced that they could enjoy travelling alone might prefer to travel with an organised expedition (see the section *Adventure Travel* in Part 7, *Travel and Adventure*).

However there are no guarantees of finding someone with whom to team up. **Tara Leaver** had easily found congenial company on a summer volunteer project in Mexico she had joined in the long summer vacation when she was a teacher. She had enjoyed it so much that she decided to use an inheritance to fund a whole year off, starting the following spring with a volunteer project in Costa Rica. In this case, she found that most of the other volunteers – on what turned out to be a disorganised and unsatisfactory project – were 10 years younger than her and she did not to find any potential travelling companions among them. She travelled on by herself to Panama, Nicaragua and Guatemala where she had some brilliant times but ultimately found it quite lonely. An illness that had dogged her in the past reared its ugly head again and, with no one to look after her, she was forced to cut her gap year short.

MY GROWN UP GAP YEAR: PAUL JONES

Australian Paul Jones spent the summer in Russia as a gap within a gap since he was already on a working holiday in the UK to fund trips to Europe and beyond.

I worked as a counsellor in a summer camp near the city of Perm. When I first arrived, my heart sank because it looked like a gulag (for which the area around Perm is famous!) But you soon forget the physical conditions, mostly anyway. If I didn't like the food at the start, I definitely learnt to like it by the end and now reminisce about the worst of it! My job, as with American summer camps for kids, was to help lead a group of up to 30 children for their three weeks stay at the camp. Because I did not speak the language, I was placed with two other leaders so my services weren't really necessary. However, this region of Russia doesn't exactly get many international visitors so the role I played at camp sometimes felt more like being a rock star!

The types of activities the kids did ranged from football, basketball and swimming (the colour of the pool was scary) to singing, dancing and crafts. But while I tried as best I could to lead my group of kids in their daily activities, every single kid in the camp wants a piece of you because you're the foreigner! So a lot of the job is to just be there and share a different culture with the kids (and their parents sometimes), other Russian counsellors and the Camp Director. In return, they also shared their culture. I've actually stayed in contact with a number of the local counsellors. The ones that don't speak English very well make up for it with sign language and friendliness. I found that a few words in Russian go a long way to bridging the culture gap. And if possible take some souvenirs for the kids. Even a pack of cards with the British flag on them provides 52 little gifts.

RED TAPE

PASSPORTS

A 10-year UK passport costs £51 for 32 pages and £62.50 for 48 pages, and should be processed by the Identity and Passport Service within three weeks. The one-week fast track application procedure costs £77.50 and an existing passport can be renewed in person at a passport office but only if you have made a prior appointment with the Passport Agency (☎ 0870 521 0410), and are willing to pay £96.50 (£104.50 for 48 pages). Passport office addresses are listed on passport application forms available from main post offices. All relevant information can be found on the website (www.passport.gov.uk).

VISAS

Outside the Schengen Area of Europe, in which border controls have been largely abolished for EU nationals, you can't continue in one direction for very long before you are impeded by border guards demanding to see your papers. Post September 11th, immigration and security checks are tighter than ever before and many countries have imposed visa restrictions, particularly on North Americans in retaliation for all the new restrictions the USA has implemented. Embassy websites are the best source of information or you can check online information posted by visa agencies. For example CIBT Global Visas (incorporating Thames Consular Services) in London (☎ 020 7802 1091; www.uk.cibt.com) allows you to log on as a guest and search visa requirements and costs for UK nationals visiting any country. An equivalent source of visa information in the USA is Travisa (www.travisa.com) with offices in Washington, New York, Chicago, San Francisco, Miami and London. Travel Document Express in the USA (www.traveldocument.com) provides visa application forms that can be downloaded, and can process visa and passport applications; or try Travel Document Systems in Washington, New York and San Francisco (www.traveldocs.com).

Getting visas is a headache anywhere, and most travellers feel happier obtaining them in their home country. Set aside a chunk of your travel budget to cover the costs; to give just a few examples of charges for tourist visas for UK citizens applying in London: £30 for India, £30 for China, £11 for Jordan, £38 for Vietnam, £30 for Armenia, £55 for Pakistan, £55 for Sudan, £76.20 for Nigeria, £38 for Sri Lanka (if staying more than 30 days) and so on. Last-minute applications often incur a much higher fee, for example a Russian visa costs £45 if applied for 10 days in advance, but £95 for same-day processing. If you do not want to pin yourself down to entry dates, you may decide to apply for visas as you travel for example from a neighbouring country, which in many cases is cheaper, though may cause delays.

If you are short of time or live a long way from the embassies in London, private visa agencies can undertake the footwork for you, at a price. CIBT, mentioned above, charges £37 handling fee plus £6.17 recorded delivery on top of the consular fee. Other visa agencies include Global Visas (☎ 0808 109 9110; www.globalvisas.com). If you intend to cross a great many borders, especially on an overland trip through Africa, ensure that you have all the relevant documentation and that your passport contains as many blank pages as frontiers which you intend to cross. Travellers have been turned back purely because the border guard refused to use a page with another stamp on it. **Stefan and Nessa Aalten-Voogd**, who had to cross dozens of borders on their 12-month round-the-world trip, believe that being smartly presented and suitably respectful eased the process and although it is impossible to quantify, they are sure that '*being older than the typical backpacker made a difference when dealing with officials*'.

Information about documents needed for working abroad can be found in Part 6, *Working and Living Abroad.*

ACCESSING MONEY ABROAD

Once you are resolved to save for your gap year, set a realistic target and then go for it whole-heartedly. If you are participating in a scheme through a recognised charity, you will be able to fund raise (see Part 4, *Doing Something Worthwhile*). Estimate how long it will take you to raise the desired amount, set some interim deadlines and stick to them. If you are lucky enough to be in a position to rent out property while you're away, you will have to make arrangements for transferring the income abroad (covered earlier in this chapter).

The cost of a trip varies tremendously, depending on modes of transport chosen, your willingness to sleep and eat modestly and to deny yourself souvenirs. People used to splashing out on one or two an-nual holidays sometimes take time on a gap year to realise that spending patterns have to be different. It is always a good idea to have an emergency fund in reserve or at least access to money from home in addition to a return ticket, should you run into difficulties. To estimate daily expenses, it might be helpful to know that the average budget of a travelling student is roughly £25–£35 a day, though older more affluent gap year travellers can easily spend much more.

Whatever the size of your travelling fund, you should plan to access your money from three sources: cash, credit cards and travellers' cheques. Travellers' cheques are falling out of favour and banks able to encash them are not always near to hand, even in Europe. But it is a sensible precaution to keep one or two cheques at the bottom of your luggage for an emergency. They might also be a useful standby if you happen to find yourself stranded in a place without an ATM. The best way to find out where you can change American Express cheques in advance is to log on to www.americanexpress.co.uk/travel-lerscheques, where the contact details of fee-free exchange partners are listed. For Visa cheques, see www.cashmycheques.com.

The most straightforward way to access money abroad is by using your bank debit card in ATMs. There is usually a minimum fee for a withdrawal so you should get larger amounts out at one time than you would at home. Read the fine print on those leaflets that come with your debit card because it may be that your bank has various loading fees, withdrawal fees and transaction fees. For example, the transaction fee for withdrawing foreign currency abroad, or paying at point-of-sale with a standard Maestro card, is 2.65%, in addition to the ordinary exchange rate disadvantage. Cash machine with-drawals cost 2.25% of the sterling transaction up to a maximum of £4 (no minimum). The point-of-sale charge is a more reasonable £0.75. If you are going to be abroad for a considerable period, drawing on funds in your home account, it would be worth shopping around for the best deal. At present Nation-wide's FlexAccount debit card is the only one that can be used abroad for free (www.nationwide.co.uk). The website www.moneyfacts.co.uk carries a comparative list of commission charged by the main providers (search for 'Travel Money').

The ICE Travellers Cashcard (www.iceplc.com) is a pre-paid Mastercard which can be loaded up before your departure and then reloaded online or by someone at home if necessary. Similarly Travelex markets a Travel Currency card (www.travelex.co.uk). It is advisable also to keep a small amount of cash handy. Sterling is fine for most countries but US dollars are preferred in much of the world such as Latin

America, eastern Europe and Israel. The easiest way to look up the exchange rate of any world currency when planning your travels is to check on the Internet (eg www.xe.net/ucc) or to look at the Monday edition of the *Financial Times*. Most banks require a few days' notice to obtain a foreign currency for you. Marks & Spencer's Travel Money offers favourable exchange rates with no commission or handling charges on currency or travellers' cheques. Furthermore, these can be ordered online.

A credit card is useful for many purposes, provided you will not be tempted to misuse it. For example it could be invaluable in an emergency. Few people think of crediting their Visa, Mastercard, etc., account before leaving and then withdrawing cash on the credit card without incurring interest charges (since the money is not being borrowed). Even in remote countries such as Niger in West Africa, it is possible to draw money on them. The international banking network is limited in Africa and parts of Asia, so some banks and businesses will only accept American Express and/or Visa cards. Check the respective websites or your card issuer to see where your card is accepted abroad.

For information on what to do if you need to have money sent to you in an emergency, see the section below, *Theft*.

MY GROWN UP GAP YEAR:
HOWARD PETERS

Having just seen in an unwelcome 58th birthday, Howard thought it was a time for reflection 'when middle-age shows signs of losing its middle'. He had been running a small business importing fashion accessories from the Andean countries of South America, which involved lots of long journeys to remote places, but he had decided it was time to wind down. He had come across a Coral Cay Conservation project in Belize some years earlier and so thought it was time to investigate what they had on offer.

Around the world, coral reefs are under relentless pressure from over-fishing, pollution and other human impacts. My time around the Amazon and the primary forests of Central America had shown me first hand the widescale destruction being inflicted on the terrestrial world. CCC were attempting to address issues of equal or even greater severity in the tropical marine environment. Supported by the government of the host country, their reef assessments were leading directly to the establishment of marine protected areas to conserve fish and protect their habitats. It was a cause with which I could relate.

And so it was I enrolled to join a small band of 10 volunteers and a team of professionals - expedition leader, science officer, scuba instructor and medical officer - as the pioneer group in the inauguration of a new base in the Mamanuca group of islands in Fiji in the western Pacific. It was an eclectic mix of individuals: mostly young and waiting to go on to university, but with a few mature volunteers in their 30s and 40s and with me approaching 59, soon to be celebrated on a remote and largely uninhabited island. Although I was a qualified diver albeit with limited experience, the majority of volunteers were novices who first underwent on-site training to a level that would give them the capability to dive to the 30m survey depths. Dive certification out of the way, the next two weeks involved comprehensive education in species identification held in the classroom and on practicals diving the reefs. Only then could the volunteers be formed into survey teams and return reliable statistics. Later, my dive training would be taken by CCC to divemaster level.

Almost all the volunteers had no previous experience in marine environmental sciences. The older members in particular had come from occupations as diverse as a furniture maker from Canada to an oil driller from the North Sea. But it would be wrong to imply it would suit everyone. Volunteers need to have the time available, a reasonable level of fitness and an affinity with the water. They must be prepared to leave behind many daily comforts and accept basic living conditions, and they should expect to work intensively especially during the training period. Most importantly they must enjoy being part of a team. But the rewards are substantial for those willing to accept the challenge, whatever the age.

WHAT TO TAKE

BACKPACKING EQUIPMENT

Outdoor equipment shops carry an enticing range of shiny new products though if you are operating on a tight budget, you should first check out eBay or the small advertisements in the online or paper version of the free-ads paper *LOOT* (www.loot.com), or scour army surplus and charity shops. Tents are sold very cheaply by Asda (e.g. £20–£30) and other discount stores though they are not built for harsh weather conditions. For your main luggage, Paul Goodyear of the excellent Nomad Travel Store (www.nomadtravel.co.uk) recommends the new travel sack over the traditional rucksack, which he compares to a tunnel you have to push everything into. By contrast the 50 litre or 65 litre travel sack can be slung over the shoulder and immediately offers the advantage of making you look less like other backpackers. The travel sack can also be opened at the back for easy access and is designed to be more comfortable for your back during long walks. Another advantage is that it includes a daypack which can be zipped off to carry essential items like passports and money for a day trip.

Packing for travelling as a backpacker will always entail compromises because you will be limited in the amount of clothes and equipment you can take with you. When you're buying a backpack/rucksack in a shop try to place a significant weight in it so you can feel how comfortable it might be to carry on your back, otherwise you'll be misled by lifting something usually filled with foam.

Another important consideration is what you take for sleeping. Paul Goodyear recommends a tropical quilt for equatorial areas instead of a sleeping bag. It can be spread out as a bed to sleep on, folded to create a lightweight sleeping bag or used as a shawl in chilly weather. The other advantage is that it is much lighter to carry and takes up less room in your luggage. *The Telegraph* journalist Rosemary Behan who reported back to the paper throughout her gap travels allowed herself the luxury of taking a silk sleeping bag liner which she used in dodgy hotels throughout Asia. Other handy equipment includes a travel towel which can be used to dry or wash yourself. Unlike a conventional towel which occupies space and turns smelly in the heat and damp of the tropics, this one will dry very quickly after it has been wrung out.

In the heat of the tropics you should carry at least 2 litres of water in order to prevent dehydration. The best water bottles are soft-sided bladder-style ones (look for the Platypus brand); some have small separate compartments for a purifying agent such as chlorine or iodine (mentioned below).

Belts with a zipped compartment worn under a shirt are handy for carrying money unobtrusively. A bandana in the tropics will keep the sun off your head, and you can use it to mop up sweat or put round your face in windy desert conditions. Some bandanas even have backgammon and chess sets printed on them to provide portable entertainment.

When packing it's best to roll rather than fold clothes to save space and put the heaviest objects at the bottom of the pack. Always carry liquids (such as shampoo or water) inside a plastic bag in case they leak.

Try to do some research about the shopping facilities at your destination before weighing down your luggage. Prior to leaving for her voluntary placement in a law office in Belize, **Sara Ellis-Owen** emptied the shelves of Boots and also stocked up on favourite foodstuffs such as marmite and Earl Grey tea. She later realised that Belize City already had everything that she needed; the local supermarket even stocked Waitrose supplies.

Other specialist travel merchandisers include the award-winning Itchy Feet in Bath (4 Bartlett Street, Bath; ☎ 01225 337987) and London (162 Wardour Street; ☎ 020 7292 9750; www.itchyfeet.com), and the mail order Catch 22 in Lancashire (☎ 01942 511820; www.catch22products.co.uk).

HANDY TRAVEL TIPS FOR BACKPACKERS

- *Keep a record of vital travel documents such as passport numbers, driving licences, travellers' cheque serial numbers, insurance policy, tickets, emergency number for cancelling credit cards, etc. Make two copies: stow one away in your luggage and give the other to a friend or relation at home. An even shrewder method is to take a scan of your passport and store it digitally in your email account so that you can access it in an emergency.*
- *Make sure your passport will remain valid for at least three months beyond the expected duration of your trip; some countries require six months' worth of validity.*
- *Carry valuable items (such as your passport, essential medicines, digital cameras and of course money) on your person rather than relegating them to a piece of luggage which might be lost or stolen.*
- *Only take items you are prepared to lose.*
- *When deciding on clothes to take, start at your feet and work your way up the body; then try to shed up to half. If you find that you need some missing item of clothing, you can always buy it en route.*
- *Take waterproof and dustproof luggage.*
- *Remember to ask permission before taking photographs of individuals or groups. In some cultures it can be insulting.*
- *Take advantage of the toilets in expensive hotels and fast food chains.*
- *Take a list of consular addresses in the countries you intend to visit in case of emergency.*

MAPS AND GUIDES

Good maps and guides always enhance one's enjoyment of a trip. If you are going to be based in a major city, buy a map ahead of time. If you are in London, visit the famous map shop Edward Stanford (12–14 Long Acre, Covent Garden, WC2E 9LP; ☎ 020 7836 1321), whose searchable catalogue is now online (www.stanfords.co.uk), and Daunt Books for Travellers (83 Marylebone High Street, W1M 4DE; ☎ 020 7224 2295). The Map Shop in Worcestershire (☎ 0800 085 4080; ☎ 01684 593146; www.themapshop.co.uk) and Maps Worldwide in Wiltshire (☎ 01225 707004; www.mapsworldwide. co.uk) both run a mail order business in specialised maps and guide books.

Phrase books, dictionaries and teach-yourself language courses can be more useful once you arrive in a country than at home.

ELECTRONIC ITEMS

Few serious travellers will want to leave home without a decent camera. These days most people prefer digital cameras though traditionalists still prefer 35mm single lens reflex (SLR) technology.

Try to minimise the gadgets you are carrying. If you can't live without your hair dryer or travel iron, find out what the voltage and frequency are in the countries you intend to visit and invest in an earthed adaptor. Plug adaptors suitable for North American, British and European plugs can be bought from major electrical stores. For converting voltage (e.g. between European and North American equipment) you need a transformer.

The miniaturisation of gadgetry these days means that travellers will not be weighed down too much if they load up their iPod with music before leaving home (which along with a pair of sunglasses can prove useful in protecting you from unwanted attention). You may want to consider travelling with a laptop or palmtop computer. If you are going to be based in one place and are fairly comfortable with the idea of doing some troubleshooting, it is probably a good idea. It may be necessary to find someone to plumb it in, i.e. take apart a wall socket or telephone. Once you're connected, you simply sign up with a local or international internet service provider (ISP). For technical details about getting hooked up from far-flung places, see the online manual at www.roadnews.com.

MEDICATIONS

Prescribed drugs (except contraceptives) that you take with you should be accompanied by a doctor's letter explaining why you need them. Do not carry non-prescribed drugs stronger than aspirin or anti-malarials, and then only in the original packs. Customs officers are highly sensitive about drugs of all kinds, and can be suspicious of some available over the counter in Britain but that are available only on prescription in other countries.

If you are planning a long trip, take a prescription from your doctor. It can be endorsed by a doctor abroad and used to obtain drugs.

GIFTS

When you encounter the kindness of strangers it is sometimes appropriate to bestow a small gift to acknowledge your appreciation. In developing countries, a supply of postcards from your hometown or stamps to give to children as a memento of your visit are often appreciated. Symbols of American culture such as T-shirts and baseball caps are highly prized by many.

After spending some months working as a volunteer in Cambodia, **Polly Botsford** knew what she would do differently another time:

> When I go back I will take a lot more presents from England. Ask your host country contacts if there is anything which is particularly expensive/unobtainable where you are going and bring bucket loads of whatever it is.

Choosing what to take for friends or relations, or to ingratiate yourself with friends-of-friends on whom you wish to impose, is an art. If your beneficiaries are British expats, then virtually anything British might be appreciated, from a copy of *Private Eye* to Marmite to Scotch whisky.

Scott Burke, founder of a volunteer placement organisation in the USA called Cosmic Volunteers, has a good suggestion, especially for anyone who is going to be working with children in a school or orphanage. When suffering acute culture shock in Nepal and in danger of abandoning his plan to become a volunteer English teacher, he found the solution:

> What ended up saving me was . . . Mr. Bubbles. That's right, a four-ounce bottle of bubbles I had brought with me to Nepal on the advice of a friend. A great icebreaker with kids, she had said. I took the bottle, walked outside and started blowing bubbles alone in my front yard. Sure enough, in a few minutes several children appeared, seemingly from nowhere. Without exchanging even one word for the next two hours, the children and I blew bubbles and laughed and ran around. Back in my room, I sat back down on that bed, took a deep breath and thought to myself: maybe I can do this.

All sorts of obscure items can come in handy though few are likely to follow Hannah Stevens's example and remember to pack a nit comb.

STAYING IN TOUCH

The revolution in communication technology means that you are never far from home. Internet cafés can be found in almost every corner of the world where, for a greater or lesser fee, you can access your email, keep in touch with friends via Facebook, check relevant information on the web or upload and distribute digital photos. Internet cafés can easily be located on arrival in virtually any place in the world simply by asking around. For updated listings and prices, check www.world66.com/netcaféguide, which has a searchable database of Internet cafés worldwide, or the revealingly named www.cybercaptive.com, whose database at the time of writing included 5,763 cybercafés, public Internet access points and kiosks in 161 countries (although these numbers never seem to change, so it seems that the site is not updated).

Sending photos home electronically has become a piece of cake as is setting up your own website or blog (i.e. web log) to share travel tales with family and friends. Lots of companies will help you create your own blog, for example:

- **www.blogger.com/start** – this is free
- **http://realtravel.com**
- **www.getjealous.com** – which allows a maximum of 40 photos
- **http://community.webshots.com** – free for storing up to 240 photos.

If you do decide to keep a blog, remember that less is more: the folks back home probably don't have the time to read all the ins and outs of your long bus journeys and negotiations with hoteliers. Try to record the most interesting highlights.

To avoid floating off into a news vacuum, some people subscribe to the BBC daily email service, which sends out a selection of news stories according to the interests you register (http://newsvote.bbc.co.uk/email). Others relish the prospect of no longer having a clue about who is who in the Cabinet or what scandal has befallen footballers and their wives.

EMAIL

Fixing yourself up with a web-based email account before leaving home is now virtually compulsory. Not only does it allow you to keep in touch with home and with friends met on the road, it is also very handy for managing your finances and staying in touch with professional resources. The most heavily subscribed service for travellers is still hotmail (www.hotmail.com; www.hotmail.co.uk) though its popularity occasionally places strains on the system. A popular alternative, also free, is provided by Google (www.gmail.com).

The danger for people who rely too heavily on the new technology is that they spend so much time on Facebook in cybercafés that they end up not having the encounters and adventures they might have otherwise. Just as the texting generation is finding it harder to cut ties with home knowing that a parent or a school friend is only a few digits away wherever they are, so too travellers who spend an inordinate amount of time online risk failing to look round the destination country in depth and missing out on meeting locals in the old-fashioned, strike-up-a-conversation, getting-in-and-out-of-scrapes way. They will also be deprived of another old-fashioned treat: arriving at a poste restante address and experiencing the pleasure (sweeter because deferred) of reading their mail.

TELEPHONE

To avoid paying extortionate charges on your mobile, you should investigate global SIM cards. Lonely Planet, the travel publisher, has an easy-to-use communications card called ekit which offers low cost calls; the website (www.ekit.com) attempts to explain the options for using your mobile abroad as clearly as possible. If you are going to be mainly in one country, you should be able to buy a SIM card locally for use in that country, provided your phone has been unblocked. Fortunately the cost of making and receiving calls within Europe was brought down to more reasonably levels in 2007; a typical call might cost £0.38 per minute or £0.19 to receive.

Companies selling global SIM cards worth considering are Oneroam (www.oneroam.co.uk), www.globalsim.net, and www.united-mobile.com. The costs of setting up with Oneroam, for example, are about £16 for the card including UK delivery and €5 credit and the cost of unlocking your phone if necessary (£10–£15). If you are not sure whether your phone needs unlocking just swap SIM cards and see if you can make a call. Call charges depend on the country and whether to a landline or mobile and consist of call set-up charge plus charge per minute and possible small loss on the exchange rate. Credit can be topped up online or you can sign up for an automatic top-up option. If you do opt for this kind of deal, you will have to inform all your contacts of your new number and of the access number for the service.

The best alternative to the mobile phone is the pre-paid calling card sold by a plethora of companies in the UK and USA, intended to simplify international phoning. You credit your card account with an amount of your choice (usually starting at £10 or £20), or buy a card for $10 or $20. You are given a multi-digit access code which can be used from any phone. Friends and family at home may wish to investigate the companies that offer low cost dialling to overseas numbers. For example with an access code from Telediscount (www.telediscount.co.uk) you can call landlines or mobiles in Ghana for as little as £0.08–£0.09 per minute.

**THESE ARE THE STEPS STEPHAINE FUCCIO FOLLOWED IN VAGUELY CHRONOLO-
GICAL ORDER, IN PREPARATION FOR A BIG TRIP TO GUATEMALA.**

1 Followed gut feeling and decided it was time to head down to Guatemala.
2 Researched volunteer opportunities and Spanish schools.
3 Bought plane ticket.
4 Sub-let my rented San Francisco apartment through Craigslist.com. Created a three-page sublet agreement that would make my lawyer boss from a decade ago proud. I will be a long way away, and don't want to think about my SF life when I am down there.
5 Looked for travel partners, for parts of the trip via Lonely Planet Thorntree, Bootsnall, and an ad on Craigslist SF community page.
6 Started to contact locals and expats who live in Guatemala.
7 Gave notice at present job.
8 Spent time going over my budget with a fine tooth comb. My usual method of travel is to save money then travel or, if planning a long period of travel, work along the way to finance, come home and work more. This time I am not travelling on savings so much as travelling on rent money.
9 For peace of mind I am paying May and June bills before I go, since I may not be working right away when I return. I hope I do, but you never know with temping.

10 Set up this blog.

11 Researched necessary immunisations and travel advisory warnings.

12 Downloaded all music into iTunes, in case I do break down and take an iPod. I prefer to listen to local music/radio when I am in a place, but I have also noticed that familiar sounds are settling during times of strong culture shock or stress.

13 Sorted through tons of papers lying around my apartment, sorting out what projects I can realistically complete before leaving in two weeks, and what needs to be postponed until my return. Breaking down projects no matter how big or small and assigning a day to work on them has helped a lot in the past few months. I also noticed that if there is a project that I keep putting off, then it tends to go into the 'better off as an idea than reality' pile.

14 Made a packing checklist that included travel towel, earplugs (essential), sunblock and other things I might forget.

15 Researched travel insurance. So many choices, and prices vary a lot. Used Google and followed links from respectable travel websites such as Lonely Planet, Rough Guides, Bootsnall and Budget Travel Magazine. Will probably reject the one you can't extend once you are on the trip. My main concerns this time are health (since I will be doing some hiking) and theft protection (since I am taking my digital camera and iPod).

TRAVEL ARRANGEMENTS

Those who are joining an organised voluntary or expeditionary scheme will no doubt receive plenty of advice on how to book their flights and travel. Independent travellers should be looking at discounted tickets, last minute bargains and no-frills airlines (see Part 7, *Travel and Adventure,* for detailed advice).

ACCOMMODATION

Places where travellers tend to congregate always have a good selection of reasonably priced accommodation. In many parts of the world, the status of backpacking is rising, and the growing range of facilities pitched at this important sector of the more mature backpacking market is impressive.

Joining the Youth Hostels Association (☎ 0870 770 8868; www.yha.org.uk) is highly recommended even if you do not imagine yourself the type. Those who haven't stayed at a hostel since their student days will be surprised at the revolution that has taken place. Hostels generally offer higher standards of comfort than a generation ago and have become far more attractive to older travellers (not least because they have abolished the dreaded compulsory chore). Nowadays many hostels offer single, double and family rooms in addition to the standard dormitories. In major cities, youth hostels often represent the cheapest accommodation and in remote areas, they often represent the most beautiful. Many are located in prime sites and some are in beautifully restored old buildings. A growing number of privately owned hostels is providing lively competition. Check the websites for links to thousands of hostels worldwide (www.hostels.com; www.hostelworld.com; www.hostels.net). VIP Backpacker hostel group (www.vipbackpackers.com) includes hundreds of hostels in Australia, New Zealand, South Africa and Europe; a membership card costs £18.

For many travellers, hostels are the key to an excellent holiday. Not only do they provide an affordable place to sleep (typically £10–£15+ in developed countries and much less in developing countries), they provide access to a valuable range of information about what to see, how to get there and whom to go with. Additional services are often provided such as bicycle hire or canoeing and trekking trips.

The cheapest accommodation of all is a tent, an attractive option if you're travelling into remote areas such as national parks where accommodation is in short supply or if you are ever caught at dark without a roof over your head. The drawback of course is the extra weight of a tent and sleeping bag. Discretion is always recommended when camping by the side of the road. If you are camping on private land, always seek permission from the local farmer or enquire locally. Finding a supply of water may present problems. Never be tempted to camp in a dried-up river bed, since a flash flood can wash you away.

MY GROWN UP GAP YEAR:
BEV WOOD

Bev Wood from Hamilton New Zealand took on travel with a difference when she became a volunteer in Vietnam and then wrote about it for the local Waikato Times magazine in April 2008 (quoted with permission).

Travel has long been a passion of mine. I love the preparation, reading about new places, when to go, where and for how long. I love the sights, the sounds, the smells, the people, the food, getting a glimpse of an unfamiliar way of life and the excitement of new experiences. There seems there is a revolution in travel circles - ethical travel or responsible travel seems to be the new way to go - and I wanted a part of it. So when I saw an advert for a different way of travel, I decided to investigate further. Five months later I was in Vietnam via the New Zealand-based Global Volunteer Network...

What appealed to me was the chance to try a stint of volunteer work for a short time, in my case the month of March 2008, to see whether I had anything to offer and whether I could cope with the demands of the task. Having recently trained as a home tutor with the Refugee & Migrant Centre, my interest had been stimulated in helping people from different ethnic backgrounds. But to work with babies and toddlers in an orphanage, helping in centres for the disabled and doing a bit of English teaching seemed a real challenge.

The age limit given for volunteers was 18-65, but when I queried the upper limit, the helpful GVN staff suggested I provide a medical certificate to prove that I was fit and able. The day after I provided the magical piece of paper, my application was accepted.

One of the highlights for me was teaching English at a local university. Initially I thought it would be too much of a challenge, but as the students wanted conversational English (and I'm very experienced at that, as my friends and family will tell you) it worked really well... I spent two sessions a week in a local technical college where I was told I would be working with groups of tourism students and to prepare lessons about service in restaurants, hotels, how to greet an English-speaking person, how to give directions, how to ask what type of room required, etc. One day I explained the difference between twin rooms and double rooms, about en suites, tariffs, services available, etc, only to learn that I was speaking to an economics class! They were just as interested in talking and asking questions as the tourism classes.

People were intrigued to see older foreign women living and working in their community ... If you think you can help - regardless of how little - do it. It mightn't seem much but donating your time can make a difference. Volunteering is so rewarding. And it's a great way to see the world.

TRAVEL INSURANCE

European nationals are eligible for reciprocal emergency healthcare. However outside Europe a good insurance policy is absolutely essential. Increased competition among travel insurers has brought costs down over the past few years, though it will still be necessary to set aside a chunk of your travel fund. Travel policies do not automatically cover certain activities deemed to be dangerous such as winter sports and manual work (e.g. on a volunteer project). Anyone wanting to engage in adventure or extreme sports such as bungee jumping, scuba diving or sky diving should do some comparison shopping, since by studying the fine print they may find a company that will cover their preferred activity without the need of investing in special cover. You are expected to inform your insurer ahead of time if you plan to indulge in any potentially risky activities.

The UK has reciprocal health agreements with more than 40 countries worldwide that entitle you to emergency care, though it is still recommended to have your own comprehensive private cover which will cover extras such as loss of baggage and, more importantly, emergency repatriation. Many countries in Africa, Asia and Latin America and the USA do not provide any reciprocal cover. Travelling without travel insurance can literally break the bank. Medical care in an emergency might cost an individual tens of thousands of pounds.

All travellers must face the possibility of an accident befalling them abroad. In countries such as India, Turkey and Venezuela, the rate of road traffic accidents can be as much as 20 times greater than in the UK. Certain activities obviously entail more risk. For example, broken bones are common on ski treks and evacuation can be difficult in mountainous areas where trekking is popular. If you are thinking of travelling with a tour group, ask the company how they deal with medical emergencies and whether repatriation is included in their group policy.

If you're travelling independently, you will find that almost every enterprise in the travel business will be delighted to sell you insurance because of the commission earned. Ring several insurance companies with your specifications and compare prices. Europ-Assistance (☎ 0870 737 5720; www.europe-assistance.co.uk) is the world's largest assistance organisation with a network of doctors, air ambulances, agents and vehicle rescue services managed by more than 200 offices worldwide offering (at a price) emergency assistance abroad 24 hours a day. Many companies charge lower premiums, though you will have to decide whether you are satisfied with their level of cover. Most offer a no-frills rate which covers medical emergencies and a premium rate which covers extras that might be considered non-essential, such as loss of personal baggage. If you are not planning to visit North America, the premiums will be much less expensive. Note that if the Foreign and Commonwealth Office (FCO) advises against travelling to a certain country, your travel insurance will be invalidated if you ignore this advice.

Some companies to consider are listed here with a rough idea of their premiums for 12 months of worldwide cover (including the USA). Expect to pay in the region of £25 per month for basic cover and £35 for more extensive cover.

USEFUL CONTACTS

Age Concern – ☎ 0845 600 3348; www.ageconcern.org.uk/AgeConcern/travel_insurance.asp. Specialises in travel insurance for over 60s and over 70s (no upper age limit), with policies provided by Fortis Insurance Ltd. Pre-existing medical conditions can be covered. Sample price of £82.50 covers one month of volunteering in India or Kenya.

Austravel – ☎ 0870 166 2020; www.austravel.com/travel-info/insurance. Specialist in travel to Australia and New Zealand sells a range of competitively priced insurance policies for the budget travellers and families. Cover for adventure sports is available too.

Club Direct – ☎ 0800 083 2466; www.clubdirect.com. Provides year-long cover for £310; back-packer cover for £220.

Columbus Direct – ☎ 0870 033 9988; www.columbusdirect.com. Globetrotter policy with basic cover costs £232 for one year. More extensive cover is offered for £330.

Direct Line Insurance – ☎ 0845 246 8704; www.directline.com. One year of backpacker cover for £275. No upper age limit on single trip cover but maximum duration of 42 days for clients over 60.

Downunder Worldwide Travel Insurance – ☎ 0800 393908; www.duinsure.com. Backpacker policy starts at £214. Adventurer policy covering adventure sports costs £347.

Europ-Assistance Ltd – ☎ 0844 338 5555; www.europ-assistance.co.uk. Maximum duration of 91 days costs £283 for worldwide cover.

gosure.com – ☎ 0845 222 0020; www.gosure.com. Explorer one-year policies for 18–34-year-olds cost £216 with no baggage cover, £240 with.

Lockton International (formerly Alexander Forbes World Service) – 6 Bevis Marks, London EC3A 7AF; ☎ 020 7933 0000; www.lockton.com. Providers of International loss/damage vehicle insurance for people of any nationality living or working outside their country of origin, including travellers on expedition, diplomats, expatriates, teachers, aid workers and journalists, in their key markets of Africa, South America, Asia, the Middle East and eastern Europe.

MRL Insurance – ☎ 0845 676 0691; www.mrlinsurance.co.uk. Policies for £139 for 4 months, £239 for 12 months. Also offer policies to travellers up to age 90.

Travel Insurance Agency – ☎ 0844 482 3300; www.travelinsurers.com. Policies for £275.

Emergency medical claims are usually processed efficiently but if you have to make a claim for lost or stolen baggage, you may be unpleasantly surprised by the amount of the settlement eventually paid, especially if you have opted for a discount insurer. Loss adjusters have ways of making calculations which prove that you are entitled to less than you think. The golden rule is to amass as much documentation as possible to support your application, most importantly medical receipts and a police report in the case of an accident or theft.

HEALTH AND SAFETY

Travel inevitably involves balancing risks and navigating through hazards real or imagined. But with common sense and advice from experts, you can minimise potential problems. In addition to issues involving red tape, another major area of concern is health and if you are planning to travel outside the developed world, you will have to research what precautions are possible. You will also have to consider how to minimise loss or theft of money and belongings, something to be considered when you are deciding what to pack.

The FCO runs a regular and updated service; you can call the Travel Advice Unit on 0870 606 0290 or check the FCO website (www.fco.gov.uk/travel). This site gives frequently updated and detailed risk assessments of any trouble spots, including civil unrest, terrorism and crime. The webpage www.fco. gov.uk/en/travelling-and-living-overseas has useful links including to the FCO 'Know Before You Go' campaign, run in alliance with many partners in the travel industry, to raise awareness among independent travellers of potential risks and dangers and how to guard against them, principally by taking out a water-tight insurance policy. The same emphasis can be detected on the FCO site launched in 2005 aimed at young travellers (www.gogapyear.co.uk). Adult gap year travellers will be reassured (unless they are parents of gappers) by the MORI poll statistic that the younger the traveller the more likely (up to 50% more likely) they are to get ill, hurt or become caught up in a civil disturbance. In the USA, the State Department publishes its warnings and advisories on its website (www.travel.state.gov).

General advice on minimising the risks of independent travel is contained in the book *Passport to Safer Travel* published by Thomas Cook in association with the Suzy Lamplugh Trust. The 50-page leaflet *World Wise* prepared by Lonely Planet for the FCO and available to read online (www.fco.gov.uk/resources/en/pdf/2855621/world-wise) might raise some travel issues you hadn't thought of. Arguably much health and safety advice is over cautious, advising travellers never to ride a motorbike or accept an invitation to a private house. Adult travellers will have to decide for themselves when to ignore advice and trust their instincts. A couple of specialist organisations in the UK run courses to prepare clients for potential dangers and problems on a gap year. Needless to say, these are usually aimed at naïve 18-year-olds whose parents are paying for the course.

Managing director John Cummings of provider Safetrek (East Culme, Cullompton, Devon EX15 1NX; ☎ 01884 839704; www.safetrek.co.uk) notes that more grown-ups have been requesting personal safety and awareness training. The over-40s are interested not just in what to do when abroad but how to leave their homes secure. He acknowledges that a lot of it is common sense but not necessarily common practice. People in the older age group are undoubtedly more confident than their gap year counterparts straight out of school but more worried about things going wrong at home in their absence. John Cummings also suspects that older men are more inclined to react too quickly to an incident thereby making matters worse; he thinks that they could benefit from the training which urges them to remain calm and walk away. The one-day courses are offered in Exeter or Bristol and cost £140.

Another training provider in this area is Planet Wise (10 Swan Street, Eynsham, Oxfordshire OX29 4HU; ☎ 0870 2000 220; www.PlanetWise.net) which runs one-day travel safety and awareness courses (£160) which can be tailored to an older age group (55+). Travellers of whatever age might feel reassured by rehearsing what to do in a crisis, such as the best course of action when getting out of a burning building or what to do if drugs are planted on you. It also offers a three-day course (£445) which includes a first-aid course. News of tragedies affecting travellers crop up in the news from time to time, most recently the tragic death of four young women on their gap year plus their British leader in a traffic accident in Ecuador in April 2008. Occasionally these stories are about more mature travellers as in the case of 50-year-old nurse Jennifer Pope from Greater Manchester who stopped making contact with her family after four happy months of working and travelling in South America; nine months after she went missing, probably in Ecuador, a man was arrested for her abduction and murder. All that can be said by way of reassurance is that these events are exceedingly rare.

TRAVELLERS' HEALTH

No matter what country you are heading for, you should obtain the Department of Health leaflet T7.1 *Health Advice for Travellers* (updated May 2006). This leaflet should be available from any post office or doctor's surgery. Alternatively you can request a free copy on the Health Literature Line (☎ 0870 155 5455) or read it online (www.dh.gov.uk), where you can also find country-by-country details.

Increasingly, people are carrying out their own health research on the Internet; check sites such as the NHS's www.fitfortravel.scot.nhs.uk and www.travelhealth.co.uk. The website of the World Health Organization (www.who.int/ith) has valuable country-by-country information and a listing of the countries in which a yellow fever certificate is a requirement of entry.

The old E111 certificate of entitlement to medical treatment within Europe has been superseded by the free European Health Insurance Card (EHIC). This entitles you to the same free healthcare that the state provides to nationals of that country. It does not cover repatriation, so many travellers choose to obtain private travel insurance as well. You can pick up an EHIC application form from main post offices, or request one by phone (☎ 0845 606 2030) or you can apply online (www.ehic.org.uk).

If you have a pre-existing medical condition it's important to anticipate what you might require in a crisis. Ask your GP or specialist support group for advice before you leave. If you're travelling with a tour operator let the company know about your condition in advance. Under extreme climatic conditions, chronic or pre-existing conditions can be aggravated. Try to ascertain how easy it will be to access medicines on your trip, whether you'll be able to carry emergency supplies with you and how far you will be from specialist help. Always carry medications in their original containers and as a precaution you might carry a note from your doctor with an explanation of the drugs you're carrying and the relevant facts of your medical history. This could also include details of any allergies, for example an intolerance of antibiotics. This might be of use if you are involved in an accident or medical emergency.

In an age of mass communication it is usually possible to manage a medical condition while travelling. If you plan to travel to an area with poor medical standards and unreliable blood screening, you might want to consider equipping yourself with sterile syringes and needles. The Department of Travel Medicine at the Hospital for Tropical Diseases recommends that you should carry a specially prepared sterile needle kit in case local emergency treatment requires injections; Travelpharm (see below) sells these for about £15.

Any visits beyond the developed world, particularly to tropical climates, require careful preparation. You will face the risk of contracting malaria or water-borne diseases such as typhoid and cholera. You will need to provide your medical practitioner with precise details about where you intend to travel. Visit a medical centre at least a month before departure because some immunisations (such as those for yellow fever) must be given well in advance.

Some of the advice given below may seem intimidating. While preparing for travelling in the developing world, you might begin to feel as if you're joining an SAS induction course. Expert medical advice is widely available on how to avoid tropical illness, so you should take advantage of modern medicine to protect yourself. And be prepared to pay for the necessary inoculations which are not covered by the NHS (apart from typhus and anything you can get in the UK). It is always worth asking at your surgery as the injections may be considerably cheaper there than at a private specialist clinic (the Internet has made it possible for any doctor or practice nurse to access this information). As an example of how high the costs can be, check the price list on the MASTA website (see next section) where immunisations against hepatitis A with typhoid cost £84, Japanese encephalitis costs £43, cholera costs £59 and so on.

INOCULATIONS AND PROPHYLAXIS

Depending on where you live, it is possible that your GP is not up to date with all the complexities of tropical medicine particularly malaria prevention for different areas of the world, etc. The only disease for which a vaccination certificate may be legally required is yellow fever. Many countries insist on seeing one if you are arriving from an infected country, though it is a good idea to get protection if you are planning to travel to a yellow fever zone (much of Africa and almost all of Latin America).

A company that has become one of the most authoritative sources of travellers' health information in Britain is MASTA (enquiries@masta.org; www.masta.org). Calls to the Travellers' Health Line (☎ 0906 822 4100) are charged at £0.60 per minute (average cost of call £2–£3) or you can purchase a health brief tailored to your proposed journey for £3.99. MASTA maintains a database of the latest information on the prevention of tropical and other diseases, from which it dispenses practical advice on its website and helpline. It can provide personalised advice depending on your destinations, and these can be either emailed or posted to you. Here you can find explanations about protection against malaria, guidelines on what to eat and drink, and how to avoid motion sickness, jet lag and sunburn. MASTA's network of travel clinics administer inoculations and, like its online shop, sell medical kits and other specialist equipment (such as water purifiers and survival tools). MASTA also cooperates with the Blood Care Foundation (www.bloodcare.org.uk), a charity that aims to deliver properly screened blood and sterile transfusion equipment to members in an emergency.

Private specialist clinics abound in London but are thin on the ground elsewhere. A worldwide searchable listing of specialist travel clinics is maintained by the International Society of Travel Medicine (www.istm.org), although its listings are not comprehensive.

The Hospital for Tropical Diseases in central London (Mortimer Market Building, Capper Street, Tottenham Court Road, WC1E 6AU) offers appointments at its travel clinic (☎ 020 7388 9600) and operates an automated travellers healthline advisory service (☎ 020 7950 7799; www.thehtd.org) which charges £0.50 a minute (an average phone call lasts about seven minutes).

Other travel clinics include Nomad Travel Clinics in several London locations including Victoria (☎ 020 7823 5823; www.nomadtravel.co.uk) and also in Bristol, Manchester and Southampton. These clinics offer walk-in appointments and 10-minute consultations that cost £5 (which can be deducted from the cost of vaccinations). The Royal Free Travel Health Centre at the Royal Free Hospital on Pond Street in London (☎ 020 7830 2885; www.travelclinicroyalfree.com) is a well-regarded private clinic, and the Trailfinders Travel Clinic (194 Kensington High Street; ☎ 020 7983 3999; www.trailfinders.com/clinic.htm) is long established. The Fleet Street Travel Clinic (☎ 020 7353 5678; www.fleetstreetclinic.com) charges £45 for a 15-minute consultation. Several online shops compete for travellers' custom, among them Travelpharm (☎ 01395 233771; www.travelpharm.com), which carries an extensive range of mosquito nets, anti-malaria drugs, water purification equipment and travel accessories at keen prices. Note that if you want to buy medications online you will have to send a prescription with your order; GPs usually charge £15 for this service.

For routine travellers' complaints, it is worth looking at a general guide to travel medicine such as *Bugs, Bites and Bowels* (Dr. Jane Wilson Howarth, Cadogan, 2006, £9.99). Americans seeking general travel health advice should ring the Centers for Disease Control and Prevention (CDC) Hotline in Atlanta (+1 877 394 8747; www.cdc.gov). The CDC issues travel announcements for international travellers rated from mild to extreme, i.e. minimal risk to a recommendation that non-essential travel not take place.

For advice on protecting your sexual health, Marie Stopes International (☎ 020 7574 7400; www.mariestopes.org.uk) is helpful; it has published a free guide to travellers' sexual health called the *Back Pocket Guide*. It also sells for £15, a special safe sex kit for women which comprises one pack of emergency contraception, condoms, glo-in-the-dark Spikeys (to prevent drinks from being spiked with a 'date rape' drug), and a copy of the *Back Pocket Guide to Sexual Health Around the World*.

MALARIA

Malaria is undoubtedly the greatest danger posed by visits to many tropical areas. The disease has been making a comeback in many parts of the world, due to the resistance of certain strains of mosquito to the pesticides and preventative medications that have been so extensively relied upon in the past. Because of increasing resistance, it is important to consult a specialist service as above. You can become better informed by looking at specialist websites such as www.hpa.org.uk/infections/topics_az/malaria/default.htm or www.preventingmalaria.info. You need to obtain the best information available to help you devise the most appropriate strategy for protection in the areas you intend to visit. Research indicates that, for example, the statistical chance of being bitten by a malarial mosquito in Thailand is once a year, but in Sierra Leone it rises to once a night. Start your research early since some courses of malaria prophylaxis need to be started up to three weeks before departure. It is always a good idea to find out in advance if you are going to have any side effects as well.

Falciparum malaria is potentially fatal. On average between 1,500 and 2,000 travellers return to the UK with malaria every year (the number has been declining in recent years), and last year five people died from the disease, although in the past it has been as many as between 10 and 20. The two main drugs can be obtained over the counter: chloroquine and proguanil (brand name Paludrine). Doxycycline is by far the cheapest drug but has a higher incidence of side effects and is not so effective in some areas. In regions resistant to these drugs, you will have to take both or a third line of defence such as maloprim or mefloquine (or Lariam) available only on prescription. Because of possible side effects it is important that your doctor be able to vary the level of toxicity to match the risks prevalent in your destination. A relatively new (and expensive) drug called malarone is used as an alternative to mefloquine or doxycycline, and is recommended for short trips to highly chloroquine-resistant areas.

Lisa Bass spent three months volunteering in Madagascar at the end of 2007 and has gone back for a complete gap year in May 2008. She shared her thinking about how to protect yourself when malaria is so prevalent and recommends Coartem (trade name for artemether–lumefantrine):

> *People do get malaria down in Fort Dauphin but it is very effectively treated using Coartem a drug that can be bought without a prescription in the towns. Apparently there is another variant of this drug now which is also very good. The type of malaria you tend to get down here isn't too bad— although obviously you want to avoid it if you can. However, once diagnosed the people reported starting to feel much better after just six hours after taking the drug. Then it is just a matter of lots of rest and building yourself back up over about the next few days. I took Lariam when I was here last time, which made me very disorientated on waking up in the morning and sent me a bit weird when I drank coffee (so I didn't). I'm out here for a year now and was going to take doxy for the first couple of months but this really didn't suit me at all. So I'm currently on nothing at all. I use lots of DEET and cover up at night. Although I still get bitten a bit I would rather take my chances than feel permanently ill.*

Unfortunately these prophylactic medications are not foolproof, and even those who have scrupulously swallowed their pills before and after their trip as well as during it have been known to contract the disease. For example **Tom Grundy** virtuously took his Lariam on a gap year placement in Uganda – enduring the discomfort of taking this powerful drug on an empty stomach and anxiety about possible side effects such as brain damage and depression – and also used repellent coil burners, impregnated mosquito nets, 'Doom' room spray and repellent gel. And he still succumbed to the disease 10 months after returning to Britain.

Gosbert Chagula, who spent his gap year working in the field of human rights legislation, was also unlucky with the mosquitoes that bit him:

> *The low point was catching acute malaria. That was probably the worst illness I've ever experienced, it wasn't just the fact I had malaria, it was the fact it kept on returning. I estimate I went to the hospital in Kumasi on at least eight separate occasions and at some points it seemed that the doctors didn't know what was wrong with me. They knew it was malaria, yet they had no answers as to why it kept returning with a vengeance. With hindsight, I would not have compromised on malaria tablets. I chose to take the cheaper doxycycline, instead of the far more expensive (and effective) Lariam.*

It is essential to take mechanical precautions against mosquitoes. If possible, screen the windows and sleep under a permethrin- or DEET-impregnated mosquito net since the offending mosquitoes feed between dusk and dawn. (Practise putting your mosquito net up before leaving home since some are tricky to assemble.) Some travellers have improvised with some netting intended for prams which takes up virtually no luggage space. If you don't have a net, cover your limbs at nightfall with light-coloured garments, apply insect repellent with the active ingredient DEET and sleep with a fan on to keep the air moving. Try to keep your room free of the insects too by using mosquito coils, vaporisers, etc. DEET is strong enough to last many hours. Wrist and ankle bands impregnated with the chemical are available and easy to use.

Prevention is vastly preferable to cure. It is a difficult disease to treat, particularly in its advanced stages. If you have a fever up to 12 months after returning home from a malarial zone, visit your doctor and mention your travels, even if you suspect it might just be flu.

Paula Donahue is a doctor in Canada as well as an inveterate traveller, with a cautionary tale. She and her 13-year-old son decided to take an extended trip to Madagascar, partly because Gabriel was attracted to the exotic name and partly because they had met some charming Madagascan musicians at the annual jazz festival in New Orleans earlier that year. Naturally she was more familiar with the health risks than most and researched them thoroughly. Given the worrying side effects of anti-malarials, especially in children, and the care with which she intended to prevent mosquito bites, she decided not to take anti-malarial drugs. They came back from a wonderful month in Madagascar unscathed. Gabriel felt a bit feverish a couple of days after returning to Ontario but it was assumed that he had caught the same flu that his stay-at-home sister and her friends all had. Four days later he was hooked up to every high-tech machine in the hospital and was fighting for his life. Six months later he had regained the 25 pounds he lost and returned to full strength and vigour but it was a horrible experience and, as his mother admits, forced her to give back the Mother-of-the-Year award she had received for organising their Madagascar trip. Paula now thinks she knows the occasion on which their defences were penetrated: on a day when they went for a walk to spot lemurs in the bush, Gabriel had forgotten his long trousers, refused to borrow a pair because of the heat and as a consequence got bitten. Paula says that the next time she takes her children to a malarial zone she will steel herself to the possible side effects and prescribe the recommended anti-malarials.

FOOD AND WATER

Tap water throughout the developing world is unsafe for travellers to drink because there is always a chance that it contains disease organisms to which the Westerner has had no chance to develop immunity. Do not assume that you can get by with substitute beverages such as tea or beer or even bottled soda water. In hot climates, it is imperative to drink large quantities of water to avoid dehydration, possibly as much as six pints a day. The most effective method of water purification is boiling it for at least five minutes. However this is seldom convenient and in hot weather the water never gets cooler than lukewarm.

A more manageable method of water sterilisation is to use chemical purifiers. Simply pick up the appropriate chlorine tablets or tincture of iodine from a chemist before departure, checking how long they take to become effective (10 minutes is preferable to 30 in a hot climate when you're gasping for a cold drink). You can buy a product that neutralises the unpleasant taste of iodine. Remember that ice cubes – however tempting – should be avoided. Drinking water can also be purified by filtering. MASTA and Nomad market various water purifiers; among the best are the 'Aquapure Traveller' (£40+) and the 'Trekker Well Purifier' (£70).

Deciding what food is safe to eat is not always easy. You should aim to eat only freshly cooked food and avoid raw vegetables unless they have been peeled or washed thoroughly in purified water. Many people are nervous to eat street food in developing countries. In fact, food served in such places is usually safe provided it has been thoroughly cooked and does not look as though it has been hanging around in a fly-invested environment. A vegetarian diet is less likely to give trouble than meat or fish. Try to eat lots of yoghurt, since the bacteria help to combat the bugs in the stomach.

DIARRHOEA

Up to 50% of travellers will suffer the trots or 'Delhi belly', and a mild case of diarrhoea is virtually inevitable for travellers outside the developed world. Doctors warn that however many precautions with food and water you take, it is simply impossible to guard against it completely. If left to its own devices, most bouts clear up within two or three days, although in an extreme case the fluid loss may leave you weak and tired. You should keep drinking to avoid dehydration. This is particularly important for the young or the elderly. Rehydration tablets, which replace lost salt and sugar in the right proportions, are a possible item for your first-aid kit.

Diarrhoea will clear up more quickly if you can get a lot of rest and stop eating altogether. When you begin eating again, stick to as simple a diet as possible, e.g. boiled rice and tea (without milk). If the problem persists, try a recommended medication such as kaolin and morphine or codeine phosphate. The antibiotic ciprofloxacin can speed up recovery, but you'll need to obtain a prescription from a doctor before you leave.

CULTURE SHOCK

Not all travellers' ailments are as straightforward to treat as mild diarrhoea. Enjoying yourself won't be easy if you are suffering the adverse psychological effects of culture shock. Adult gappers who elect to spend time in a developing country are invariably shocked to some degree by the levels of poverty and deprivation. Shock implies something which happens suddenly, but cultural disorientation more often creeps up on you. Adrenaline usually sees you through the first few weeks as you find the novelty exhilarating and challenging. You will be amazed and charmed by the odd gestures people use or the antiquated way that things work. As time goes on, practical irritations intrude and the constant misunderstanding caused by those charming gestures – such as a nod in Greece meaning 'no' or in Japan meaning 'yes, I understand, but don't agree' – and the discomfort of those impossibly crowded buses may begin to get on your nerves.

However, most mature gappers who have researched their destination or volunteer situation beforehand learn to cope with the cultural differences even if they sometimes find them exasperating. While teaching and living in Vietnam, **Beth Buffam** felt that her life had been taken over by her minder:

> My main problem during the six months I was in Hanoi with the Ministry of Trade was communication. Very few people spoke any English. I had a delightful liaison person, Hue, who unfortunately didn't speak much English. Since I knew quite a bit of Vietnamese and wanted to learn more, at first this was a plus. But eventually it became a huge problem. Most requests I made to Hue were answered with a smile and a sigh. Although Hue couldn't or didn't solve my problems, she loved to spend time with me, hand in hand, arm tightly in arm, walking around. It felt controlling and uncomfortable, and unpleasant given the fact that eventually I didn't feel very close to her.
>
> People were **very** respectful, but almost too much so. For meals, it was extremely difficult for me ever to pay for my own or everyone's food. I really wanted to be 'one of the guys', but it was always: 'It's our custom, we pay for our guests'. Even after six months? And I got tired of the fact that although I'm strong and carried a lot of heavy books most of the time, when Hue and I had some work to do (like moving tables), she rushed to make sure I didn't lift a finger.
>
> I also felt like a puppet, pushed and pulled. People were always telling me what to do, never asking, and inviting me to their homes on minimal notice ('but my wife is cooking right now . . .'). So many invitations which all assumed a Yes answer. Finally, after four months there, I realised the existence and value of the word 'No'. Another irritant was invariably being introduced as: 'This is Beth. She is 59 years old. She has one son but no husband. Her son is 36 years old.' So much for keeping personal matters personal!

When **Nikki D'Arcy** from Watford volunteered in a home for the elderly in Peru with Cross-Cultural Solutions, she only gradually overcame her fears that she wouldn't be able to cope. Like so many other Westerners who have immersed themselves in a developing community, she was left full of admiration:

> Despite considering myself an independent, confident person, the thought of completely immersing myself in another culture was still slightly daunting. I won't lie. During my time there, I saw some things that saddened and shocked me, I didn't realise that people could live in such poverty. But I also got to know those people and saw such amazing strength in them. They were so happy to invite me into their lives, to share their stories and were so full of life, it put me to shame for moaning about the tiny problems we have. Even after a few days, I felt my attitudes and perceptions changing. I began to really understand what is important in life. Not the material things that so many of us seem to become obsessed with, but family and friends and enjoying life. Don't get me wrong, I already knew that, but I don't think you can fully understand it until you see people who have nothing, and I mean literally nothing, sometimes not even a roof, but yet they meet up with their friends and dance and sing and laugh like they don't have a care in the world. They are truly inspirational.

THEFT

From London to La Paz crooks lurk, ready to pounce upon the unsuspecting traveller. Theft takes many forms, from the highly trained gangs of children who artfully pick pockets all over Europe to violent attacks on the streets of American cities. It is also not unknown to be robbed by fellow-travellers from hostels, beaches, etc., or by corrupt airport officials in cahoots with baggage handlers.

How to carry your money and valuables should be given careful consideration. The first rule is not to keep all your wealth in one place. A money belt worn inside your clothing is good for the peace of mind it bestows. When choosing a money belt avoid anything too bulky and therefore indiscreet. In fact, a simple money belt can easily be manufactured at home by any handy seamstress from a left-over length of cotton or silk (preferable to synthetic fibres). Just cut a strip of cloth several inches longer than your waist with a six inch (15cm) bulge in the middle large enough to accommodate bank notes and traveller's cheques folded lengthwise. If heavy rain is a possibility, put the money in a plastic bag first. Use Velcro to close the flap over your money and also to fasten the belt round your waist under your clothes. It is a good idea to wear your belt for a few days before departure to make sure that it is comfortable and to prove to yourself that it won't fall off. Keep large denomination travellers' cheques and any hard currency cash there plus a large note of the local currency. Then if your wallet or purse is stolen, you will not be stranded.

To reduce the possibility of theft, steer clear of seedy or crowded areas and moderate your intake of alcohol. If you are mugged, and have an insurance policy which covers cash, you must obtain a police report (sometimes for a fee) to stand any chance of recouping part of your loss.

If you end up in dire financial straits without a cash or credit card, you will have to contact someone at home to send you money urgently. You can contact your bank at home (usually online but possible by telephone or fax) and ask them to wire money to you. This will be easier if you have set up a telephone or Internet bank account before leaving home, since they will then have the correct security checks in place to authorise a transfer without having to receive something from you in writing with your signature. You can request that the necessary sum be transferred from your bank to a named bank in the town you are in – something you have to arrange with your own bank, so you know where to pick the money up.

If a private individual has kindly agreed to bale you out, they can transfer money in several ways. Western Union offers an international money transfer service whereby cash deposited at one branch by your benefactor can be withdrawn by you from any other branch or agency, which the sender need not specify. Western Union agents – there are 90,000 of them in 200 countries – come in all shapes and sizes (e.g. travel agencies, stationers, chemists). Unfortunately it is not well represented outside the developed world. The person sending money to you simply turns up at a Western Union counter, pays in the desired sum plus the fee, which is £14 for up to £100 transferred, £21 for £100–£200, £37 for £500 and so on. For an extra £7 your benefactor can do this over the phone with a credit card. In the UK, call 0800 833833 for further details, a list of outlets and a complete rate schedule. The website www.westernunion.com allows you to search for the nearest outlet.

Thomas Cook and the UK Post Office offer a similar service called MoneyGram (www.moneygram.com). Cash deposited at one of their foreign exchange counters is available within 10 minutes at the named destination or can be collected up to 45 days later at one of thousands of cooperating agents in 180 countries. The fee is £12 for sending £100, £18 for up to £200, £24 for up to £300, £46 for between £750 and £1,000 and so on. Check the Post Office website (www.postoffice.co.uk). In an emergency, your consulate can help you get in touch with friends and relations, usually by arranging a reverse charge call. British Consulates have the authority to cash a personal cheque to the value of £100 supported by a valid banker's card.

CONSULAR HELP IN EMERGENCIES

Widespread confusion persists concerning the help available from the UK government to its citizens in a crisis. In the first place it is the consulate or consular services department which is responsible for looking after UK nationals, whereas the embassy does business with the host country.

A British Consul can:

- Issue an emergency passport.
- Contact relatives and friends to ask them to help you with money or tickets.
- Tell you how to transfer money.
- Cash a sterling cheque worth up to £100 if supported by a valid banker's card.
- As a last resort give you a loan to return to the UK.
- Put you in touch with local lawyers or doctors.
- Arrange for next of kin to be told of an accident or death.
- Visit you in case of arrest or imprisonment and arrange for a message to be sent to relatives or friends.
- Give guidance on organisations that can help trace missing persons.

A British Consul can't:

- Intervene in court cases.
- Get you out of prison.
- Give legal advice or start court proceedings for you.
- Obtain better treatment in hospital or prison than is given to local nationals.
- Investigate a crime.
- Pay your hotel, legal, medical, or any other bills.
- Pay your travel costs, except in rare circumstances.
- Perform work usually done by travel agents, airlines, banks or motoring organisations.
- Find you somewhere to live or a job or work permit.
- Formally help you if you are a dual national in the country of your second nationality.

Stef and Ness were leading the workaholic lives typical of people in their 30s living in London, when Stefan was made redundant from his post as IT Management Consultant with one of the Big Four consultancies.

Since leaving university we had both worked full time. My daily routine as head of Customer Services was an hour-long commute either way, sandwiching what had become a standard 10-12 hour day in the office. Stefan's redundancy forced us to reconsider what our lives had become. The stresses and strains of the corporate machine were taking their toll and working away from home and high stress environments had become the norm. Work had become dominant for both of us and our relationship with each other was firmly in second place. Much later in our trip a radio interviewer on Canada's CBC 1 aptly described us as 'downshifters' - people in their late 30s who had had enough of the rat race and wanted to step down a gear or two to rebalance their life and capture the increasingly elusive work-life balance.

The opportunity to realise what for Stefan what was a lifelong dream was an exciting but also challenging prospect of leaving work behind and living out of a backpack for a year. Arriving at Heathrow was the culmination of a year's worth of preparation. We had both independently worked up our wish list of places we wanted to go to. Having initially planned a three-month extended holiday, we soon realised that we probably needed four years to do any sort of justice to our ultimate wish list and compromised with 12 months. There were no prescribed rules that shaped our decisions other than that we wanted to avoid what we saw as the typical backpacker destinations of Thailand, Australia and New Zealand. Some of our choices were based on what we knew about countries, others because we knew nothing at all and yet others were driven by an unquantifiable instinct that we would have a great time.

Of course we changed the plan as we went, spending more time in some places, less in others and sometimes avoiding planned countries entirely. In Vancouver, the decision to avoid Indonesia due to instability and unrest resulted in us heading through southern China, Laos, Vietnam and Cambodia instead. We will go back to the countries we missed at some stage.

Among the many highlights for us were Canada for its sheer expanse and variety, Paraguay for its quirkiness and the fact that not many people go there, the food of south-east Asia, (Malaysia in particular and the challenge of ordering meals in China with no common language to use) and Poland for its friendliness and welcoming approach to visitors. Seeing the Big 5 on the game reserves of Namibia and South Africa was stunning, as was Angkor Wat in Cambodia and walking on the volcanoes of Ecuador.

Connecting with the local people in a country and not just the tourist infrastructure was a definite bonus. Being watched, and laughed at, by the staff of a Chinese hotel restaurant while you battled (successfully) with crispy aromatic duck and chopsticks; buying a lamb at a market in Ecuador; hearing first hand the experiences of local people during the Pol Pot regime in Cambodia and the American war in Vietnam. Our experiences have given us a different perspective on world events and have reinforced that the perspective you see and hear at home is not necessarily a fully balanced view.

Re-connecting with each other was also a highlight. We became dependent on each other in a way we never had before. The only constant in each other's lives was waking up each morning and knowing that despite all the uncertainties that the day might bring, we knew we would end the day together. That provided much needed stability and allowed us to rediscover what we meant to each other.

We had the odd bad day but our only low spots were the inevitable cravings we got from time to time for home. Not the bricks and mortar but family, friends and creature comforts such as a night curled up on our own settee rather than propped up on a moderately comfortable bed in a hotel or B&B. There was an implicit pressure that our time away was so valuable that we had to use every day to see and experience new places, sights and sounds. We quickly learned that travelling is a tiring occupation and that as with any other, you need time to rest and recuperate. So a few days down time every month was soon factored into our agenda.

Next time we will keep a tighter reign on our finances. We would again take loads of photos and write our diaries but updating our website (www.aaltenvoogd.com) became a time-consuming and frustrating millstone because of the level of content we uploaded. Two years after our return, we are still adjusting to 'normality'. We've moved away from London to a beautiful part of Scotland and started new jobs. The memories have become part of our dictionary, we unconsciously compare experiences, sights, tastes, etc. to our wider frame of reference now. Our trip was an amazing journey to fulfil a lifelong fascination with different cultures and countries and a strong desire to experience them for ourselves.

PART 4

DOING SOMETHING WORTHWHILE

BECOMING A VOLUNTEER

The impulse to 'give something back' or 'do something worthwhile' can ring in the ears as empty clichés. But in the aftermath of recent devastating natural disasters such as the China earthquake, Burmese cyclone and before that the tsunami and increasing global awareness of the discrepancy between rich and poor created by the Make Poverty History campaign, there has been a noticeable shift among travellers with a social conscience. Many prefer to combine travel with trying to make a contribution to people less fortunate than themselves rather than pursuing hedonism and relaxation. They are signing on with companies that offer a chance to participate in some worthwhile way (if only briefly) rather than just gawp and lounge.

According to a National Survey of Volunteering, 11 million people would volunteer if only they were asked. In an age when the old jobs-for-life contract between employer and employee is breaking down, individuals are increasingly looking for rewarding experiences outside work that will add value to their life. They want to find activities that can bestow pride and a sense of achievement. Work may provide an outlet for some of these yearnings, but many individuals prefer to search elsewhere and the voluntary sector at home and abroad is a major beneficiary.

The first tentative step that working people might take in this direction is to volunteer locally. In the UK, many companies such as Marks & Spencer and HSBC have long run programmes to encourage their employees to take an active part in their communities. Major companies promoting social responsibility in this way such as Barclays, PricewaterhouseCoopers (PwC) and Nike encourage staff to become involved, for example in literacy and numeracy projects in schools. PwC has a Global Communities network whereby its staff share knowledge and skills with partner communities. Nike in the UK allows its employees to take six extra days off per year for volunteering. CSV works hard to encourage employee volunteering (www.csv.org.uk/services/employee+volunteering).

On this topic, the *Guardian* quoted an employee of a legal firm, '*There are so many benefits to volunteering; most of the time you get so caught up with work and working life that you forget what really matters.*' The British government strongly supports corporate initiatives to promote volunteering. Self-employed people working from home can benefit enormously from stepping outside their daily working grind intermittently or for an extended period to join a voluntary project.

Hardly anyone can be unmoved by news reports of disasters or by appeals from local and international charities on behalf of the struggling and the suffering — abandoned children, needlessly blind farmers, performing bears and so on. Usually a feeling of responsibility flickers past our consciences and is quickly suppressed. A career break allows you to believe that you can get usefully involved. But stepping in to right such wrongs is never straightforward and potential volunteers soon learn that a willingness to help is not sufficient. Aid work is a difficult field to break into, and agencies are increasingly cautious in the selection process for candidates to go overseas. You might think that being able-bodied and financially privileged might be sufficient but relevant experience and professional qualifications are almost always required.

The tsunami disaster of Boxing Day 2004 focused minds on helping in an emergency in an unprecedented way. The outpourings of financial help from around the world were reinforced by an upsurge in the number of people wanting to donate their time to help. As with all emergency relief work, skilled and experienced professionals are in demand while well-meaning amateurs potentially just get in the way. In the immediate aftermath, the United Nations Volunteers (www.unv.org) drew up an emergency roster of potential volunteers keen to help in the relief effort and reconstruction in south-east Asia. To be included on that, you had to have had experience in disaster response, be available at short notice, have worked in South Asia, be at least 25 years of age with a completed technical/university degree and fluent in English with some knowledge of local languages. Quite a tall order.

If all of this sounds discouraging, ordinary mortals should be aware that many organisations offer fee-paying volunteers the chance to experience life in the developing world by working alongside local people for a short period. The next chapter has details of programmes of dozens of charities and companies that can make it easy to go abroad as a volunteer, provided that you are willing to pay, usually in the range of £100–£300 a week. It is also possible to bypass the middleman, i.e. the agency or charity in your country, and go direct to small grassroots projects, some of which are experienced at incorporating paying volunteers from the developed world. It is for each individual to weigh up the pros and cons of paying a fee to a mediating agency, which is what **Polly Botsford**, a lawyer from London, did when arranging a project in Cambodia through *Outreach International* as part of her six-month gap year:

I went to a couple of extraordinarily off-putting open days full of anxious sixth formers and their less anxious parents. It may be that you do not need to go through an organisation. Many people I met had just turned up in a country and got a feel for what was going on. Organisations can be expensive and could be spoon-feeding. I do feel quite sorry for students who really do want to go and discover the world for themselves because sometimes it can be over-packaged, particularly perhaps for the 'maturer' traveller. On the other hand, the agency did provide useful contacts and structure and was particularly good in finding friendly language tutors, which was invaluable. There was no way I would have picked up Khmer as much as I did without that tuition.

If you decide that you do not need the safety net of a sending organisation in your own country, the Internet makes it possible to connect with local charities in a way that has never been possible before. **Geoffroy Groleau** is an economist and consultant from Montréal who decided to spend some months in India and wanted to dedicate part of his time to volunteering in the development field. He stumbled across the website of an Indian non-governmental organisation (NGO) and arranged to work for a month with Dakshinayan, which works with tribal peoples in the hills of Rajamhal and nearby plains.

ALTHOUGH GEOFFROY GROLEAU ENDED UP THINKING THAT HIS ENJOYMENT TOOK PRECEDENCE OVER HIS USEFULNESS, HE STILL ENJOYED HIS 'GAP' FROM PROFESSIONAL LIFE ENORMOUSLY:
The application process is simple and can be conducted fully over the Internet. The registration fee which must be provided before setting out for the project is the primary source of revenues for Dakshinayan. So there I was, stepping onto a train from New Delhi heading to Jharkhand.

The project provides an opportunity to acquire a better understanding of the myths and realities surrounding poverty in the developing world, and specifically about the realities of rural India. The tribal people of these villages do not need or want fancy houses or televisions, but simply an education for their children and basic healthcare in order to improve the life they have been leading in relative isolation for centuries. It was interesting for me to see that they lead a quiet and simple life based on the rhythm of harvests and seasons, in marked contrast to most Westerners. The primary role for volunteers is to teach English for a few hours every day to the kids attending the three Dakshinayan-run schools. I should also mention the numerous unforgettable football games with enthusiastic kids at the end of sunny afternoons. One should be aware that Dakshinayan is an Indian NGO fully run by local people, which in my view is another positive aspect. But it also means that volunteers will have to adapt to Indian ways.

Volunteers should expect to learn more from the people than they will ever be able to teach. Remember that the villagers know much more about their needs than we do, and they have learned long ago to use effectively the resources around them. On the other hand, the contacts with the outside world that the volunteers provide is a valuable way for the villagers to begin to understand the world that surrounds them. In my experience, the hardest things were to adapt to the rather slow rhythm of life and to the fact that as a volunteer you will not manage to change significantly the life of the villagers other than by putting your brick in a collective work that has been going on for many years.

Dakshinayan can be contacted c/o Mr Siddharth Sanyal, F-1169 Ground Floor, Chittarangan Park, New Delhi 110019 (☎ +91 9836596426; www.dakshinayan.org). Volunteers join grassroots development projects every month and contribute $300 for a month.

Committing to three, six or 12 months might be more than some people can manage in the first instance. If you want to test the waters, one solution is to book a holiday that incorporates an element of volunteering. The coinage 'voluntourism' has been used slightly sneeringly by some commentators; however these trips provide a snapshot of the needs of a specific locality and serve to introduce the paying visitor to the potential rewards of a more serious commitment of time and energy. The website www.voluntourism.org advocates the benefits for this kind of trip for both parties.

The following companies organise what might be called mini-gaps:

Different Travel – 3 Maritime Avenue, Marchwood, Hampshire SO40 4AN; ☎ 02380 669903; www.different-travel.com. Participants spend part of a two-week break working on development programmes in the host country: Sri Lanka, Thailand, Vietnam, India, Nepal, Malawi, Costa Rica or Ecuador.

Go Differently – 19 West Road, Saffron Walden, Essex CB11 3DS; ☎ 01799 521950; www.godifferently.com. Voluntourism trips to Southeast Asia.

Hands Up Holidays – ☎ 0800 783 3554; www.handsupholidays.com. Ethical tour operator working with local NGOs to arrange trips lasting 4–23 days worldwide.

Impact Travel – see entry.

Vivisto – 80 High Street, Winchester, Hampshire SO23 9AT; ☎ 0845 603 5719; www.vivisto.co.uk. Conservation and community experiences lasting four weeks in a range of countries.

REWARDS OF VOLUNTEERING OVERSEAS

By volunteering somewhere in the world on a humanitarian or environmental project, you can give your career break a structure and a goal, and integrate into a foreign society rather than just pass through on a holiday. Importantly, you will also acquire skills that are not available during the course of your normal professional life. A career break offers the chance to test and stretch yourself and make an enduring contribution if not to the world at least to your own development. If you want to use a career break to discover a country or culture, then volunteering is an attractive option.

Volunteers who return from stints abroad frequently rhapsodise about their experience and regard their time as a volunteer as an extraordinary episode in their lives. During a holiday in south-east Asia, **Dale Hurd** was enormously impressed by the friendliness and dignity of the people and the beauty of a culturally fascinating country, but at the same time appalled by the poverty and deprivation.

HAVING LONG BEFORE DECIDED TO DO SOME VOLUNTARY WORK OVERSEAS DALE HURD KNEW IMMEDIATELY THAT SHE HAD NO ALTERNATIVE BUT TO RETURN TO CAMBODIA TO DO SOMETHING MORE CONSTRUCTIVE THAN SIGHTSEEING. THROUGH OUTREACH INTERNATIONAL, SHE DEVOTED SIX MONTHS TO A PROJECT TRAINING KHMER TEACHERS AND WORKING WITH CHILDREN WHO WORK ON A RUBBISH DUMP IN PHNOM PENH, WHICH IN NORMAL CIRCUMSTANCES YOU WOULD NOT EXPECT TO PROMPT SOMEONE TO WRITE ABOUT THEIR EXPERIENCES UNDER THE TITLE 'THE TIME OF MY LIFE':

Sitting here, back in the freezing English spring, I look at my hundreds of photographs and dream I'm back in Cambodia in Phnom Penh, dripping in sweat, dodging motodops, blinded by the radiant smiles of the enchanting Khmer people. I had elected to train teachers at a French school called Pour un Sourire d'Enfant, which rescues children living near a vast rubbish dump, spending their days and most of their nights scavenging what bits of junk they can sell to finance their survival. They were in considerable danger from hypodermics, from pressurised tins that can blow up in their faces and from the huge machines that sometimes carelessly run them down. I visited the dump early one morning when the stench was suffocating, the sight of small filthy children dragging round the mounds of squalor unforgettable. I was warned to be careful when I filmed as the adults felt insulted and degraded; theirs was not a life they had made through choice but through desperation. Despite this situation where humanity seemed to have hit rock bottom, the children smiled and laughed, eager to communicate and make friends.

The vocational school, where I spent most of my time, comprised seven sectors: mechanics, gardening, secretarial, hairdressing and spa, maternity nursing, hotel work/housekeeping and restaurant. The beauty of this was that not only did they get a general education but also were able to graduate fully trained to go straight into a job. I'll never forget the graduation ceremony when I not only got a huge lump in my throat, but thought: one less prostitute, one less drug pusher, as I watched each immaculate, smiling student receive a certificate.

I could go on indefinitely about the experiences I had. I learnt an enormous amount about Cambodia and about myself. I found depths of tolerance within me that I never knew I had: when in England would I ever happily sit and wait for a bus for three hours, munching bananas and watching the world go by as I did at Snoul? When before had I got as much job satisfaction, or feel daily like a princess when the students said 'Oh, Dul, you are so beautiful today', when all I'd done was put on a clean shirt. I miss – terribly – the camaraderie and laughter of the teachers. I miss the heady fragrance of the jacaranda and the tantalising smells of cooking food in the streets; I miss Raidth running up from downstairs calling 'Mummee' with something delicious to eat; I miss Naieng the landlady playing badminton every night in the yard and nursing me so kindly when I was ill; I miss my students who greeted me so joyfully every day; I miss the landscape, slowly turning from blinding greens to dull golds and browns. Above all I miss the Cambodian smile. I miss everything. I had the time of my life and I can't wait to go back.

In addition to the energising break in routine, you may be able to improve or acquire a language skill and of course will learn something of the customs of the society in which you are volunteering. Not only will you gain practical experience in the fields of construction, conservation, archaeology or social welfare, you will acquire a more nuanced understanding of the complexities of delivering aid. But best of all you will probably experience some wonderful hospitality and friendship.

A number of organisations offer integrated programmes that might combine work, adventure and language learning. For example Trekforce (see *Directory* entry) has a five-month programme in Central America for candidates of all ages, consisting of a conservation work attachment in Belize, followed by an intensive Spanish language course in neighbouring Guatemala, and a period of teaching English in a Belize primary school. Meanwhile Frontier actively assists volunteers to pursue a career in conservation by offering a BTEC qualification in Tropical Habitat Conservation. Although these and similar organisations are popular among young people taking a gap year between school and university, they encourage older volunteers to participate as well.

CAREER BREAK OR CAREER DEVELOPMENT?

Does the term 'career break' do justice to the range of experiences obtained and new skills acquired by those who venture forth on a volunteering sabbatical? *'Almost certainly not,'* says Anthony Lunch, founder of MondoChallenge, 65% of whose volunteers fit this category. The need to get away is frequently a desire to challenge oneself in new directions, to move outside one's comfort zone, to experience different ways of life and to work in a new geographical location. There is usually also an element of wanting to put something back, of doing something useful for people less fortunate.

Undertaking a challenge of this kind often turns out to be more of a career *development* experience than just a break in one's normal routine. New skills are learned very quickly. Teaching in a small school in India, for example, when one has never taught before, provides daily practice in planning and rapidly hones communication skills. For women, the ability to work effectively in what is often a male-orientated society provides a sharp focus on negotiating skills and on the art of diplomacy.

Volunteers taking part in a small business programme face other challenges. *'They can forget the excel spreadsheets and three-year plans'*, say Anthony Lunch. *'It is today's actions and tomorrow's plan that really matter when trying to create livelihoods.'* A Proctor & Gamble marketing manager once likened his experience HIV business project in Tanzania to a *'six week MBA programme,'* which illustrates how a career break can be qualitatively different from a long holiday.

AGENCY FEES

As soon as you start to search for volunteering opportunities in books (like this) or on the Internet, you will quickly discover that volunteering can be expensive. Mediating agencies charge fees that are sometimes very high. Participants must either pay the fees themselves or raise funds. Most organisations provide detailed advice on how to obtain sponsorship and raise money.

Internet search engines are dominated by the high-profile international volunteer operations offering a packaged volunteer experience which may not suit everyone. Paying to volunteer is an issue with which adult gappers have to grapple. Attitudes to the fees charged by sending agencies (a typical monthly cost approaches £1,000) differ enormously from a feeling that they are good value to a conviction that they are a complete rip-off. For example it does not seem entirely reasonable for a company (as Sunrise International UK does) to market volunteering career breaks in China which cost the hapless participant £999 to spend just four weeks in Beijing teaching English.

Some companies are far more commercial than others and it is usually possible to tell from their style and literature. Essentially some are tantamount to specialist tour operators and charge accordingly for the infrastructure they provide. Occasionally suspicions are aired in the media and elsewhere that the service offered by the big agencies does not justify the fee. For example an advertising executive (whom the *Independent* has described as *'the brainiest man in adland'*), William Eccleshare, took advantage of a gap between high-level appointments to contribute his time to a worthwhile cause and later wrote about his experiences in the *Financial Times*:

Faced with a few months enforced garden leave earlier this year, I decided to use some of my sabbatical for a worthwhile cause. Volunteering for a tsunami relief project in Sri Lanka seemed ideal. Certainly my friends appeared to think so. It's interesting how keen others are to see a lifelong slave to capitalism do something with a vaguely altruistic air to it.

. . . We donned our pristine Homebase gardening gloves (the company had advised us to bring two pairs each) and started shifting rubble – whole bricks, clay, mortar – away from the wrecked houses and into a pile nearby. On the second day we were told to stop doing that and just separate the whole bricks for re-use into one pile; leave the rest of the rubble where it was, and put the clay into the foundations of what would become a new house. The next day the plan changed again: we were told the bricks we had spent the last two days saving were waterlogged and useless, and we should just put loose clay or cement in the foundations. It rapidly became apparent that what we were doing was pretty futile. By the end of the week, one of the group sighed and said that she wouldn't be surprised if we were simply moving back the same rubble that had been shifted by a previous team . . . I thought we could have achieved much more if the trip had been better planned. And I kept wondering about the money I'd spent (about £1,400 when you added airfares and other travel costs to the £800 fee).

In concluding, he accepts a charge of naïvety but feels that the marketing makes it difficult to see a commercial company for what it is when all the rhetoric is about helping others. It should be the company's responsibility to provide as clear and honest a briefing as possible about what the volunteer can should expect to achieve.

The sending agencies differ enormously in how serious they are about the sustainability and usefulness of the projects to which they send volunteers, and it is not always easy to distinguish among them. A source of guidelines on what to investigate when trying to choose among providers is the website www.ethicalvolunteering.org. The site's creator, Kate Simpson, did a PhD in gap year provision (see introduction to Part 5 Directory of Specialist Programmes).

Many of the companies in the Directory following this chapter are committed to supporting community development. Some sources of volunteer projects have a much lower profile on the Internet than others, but may suit your purposes better:

The 7 Interchange – www.the7interchange.com. 'Seven' stands for Social & Environmental Volunteer Exchange Network. This newly launched site lists free and low-cost volunteering opportunities worldwide and maintains a register of prospective volunteers. Volunteers are put in direct contact with host projects that need help.

The Ethical Project Company – Stowford Manor Farm, Wingfield, Trowbridge, Wiltshire BA14 9LH; ☎ 07703 725512; info@theethicalprojectcompany.com. Five-week projects in Tanzania and India for £1,100 plus flights; £100 goes directly to buy school supplies.

Globalteer – 54 Woodchester, Yate, Bristol BS37 8TX; ☎ 07771 502816; www.globalteer.org). A registered UK charity that promotes sustainable volunteering and recruits for development projects in many countries.

Original Volunteers – www.originalvolunteers.co.uk. See entry in *Directory*.

Ecoteer – (www.ecoteer.com) based in Plymouth. Collection of 157 projects worldwide that need volunteers and are willing to provide food and accommodation at no, or at little, cost. Ecoteer provides contact information to members (joining fee is £10) so they can organise their placement directly with the projects. Teaching English projects are among the most common. Membership is open to people of all ages, though most are students.

Most volunteers who have gone abroad through one of the sending agencies agree that they could (or would) not have had the experience without the backing of an organisation. Some of the most satisfying volunteer experiences have been with small specialised charities that may have a couple of committed representatives in the UK who know the project well. Madagascar seems to be a country where these are easy to fined (see Blue Ventures, Azafady and the Dodwell Trust). To take just a few examples: Village Africa is active in one village in Tanzania, Volunthai in northern Thailand and Ecologia in a community for orphans in western Russia (see entries).

With the benefit of hindsight, volunteers conclude that they did not need all the expensive services provided by a mainstream sending agency. You can simply search for 'Volunteer Ecuador' or 'Volunteer Zambia' on Google and find local projects which can be joined for next to nothing. Again, patient searching of the web will unearth opportunities for volunteering, perhaps through one of the mainstream databases (e.g.: www.idealist.org; www.traveltree.co.uk; www.wwv.org.uk). One specialist website is www.volunteersouthamerica.net, founded in 2005 by **Steve McElhinney**, after he had been looking himself for '*grassroots, zero-cost volunteer work*' in Argentina. Finding volunteering opportunities that did not involve paying a large amount of cash to a middle-man or third party was more difficult than he anticipated and he spent dozens of hours trying to track them down. He then posted his findings on the site and keeps it updated.

Older travellers with experience of the developing world may conclude that they do not need the safety net of a sending agency. **Till Bruckner** is a veteran world traveller who has developed a strong preference for fixing up teaching and voluntary placements independently after arrival rather than with the help of an agency. In fact he did go to Africa initially through a London-based organisation and later regretted that he hadn't put the £500 fee he had paid the agency into a donation box, since he feels that the money would have been much better spent by an international charity than on his placement as a teacher in a relatively privileged setting.

If you sign up as a volunteer with an organisation in your home country, it's hard to tell if you're needed at all. It might be run by a local businessman who wants to polish his ego and reputation by seeming charitable, or it might simply fail to address local needs. Some companies are offering nothing more than cultural adventure holidays with a politically correct twist and CV value. Nothing wrong with that, as long as people don't delude themselves that they're contributing to a better world by flying halfway around the planet (spraying the ozone layer with kerosene as they go).

My advice to anyone who wants to volunteer in Africa (or anywhere else) is to go first and volunteer second. That way you can travel until you've found a place you genuinely like and where you think you might be able to make a difference. You can also check out the work and accommodation for yourself before you settle down. If you're willing to work for free, you don't need a nanny to tell you where to go. Just go.

However for those who find this prospect daunting (and unless you are a mature and seasoned traveller you probably will), you will want to prearrange a more structured placement.

CAUTION

Potential volunteers should not get carried away imagining that they will be able to change the world. It is undoubtedly the case that some of the promotional literature, distributed by profit-making companies to enlist paying volunteers, shamelessly tries to exploit people's altruistic urges. The reality is that the experience of volunteering overseas is invariably of more benefit to the volunteer than to the community being helped. Some people argue that volunteer-tourism is the new colonialism, that poor suffering communities are being exploited as do-gooders' playgrounds. This negative interpretation should be resisted because all it does is quash the impulse to help others. It may be true that some volunteer schemes have been set up with the needs of the foreign volunteers taking priority over those of the local community. The local people may well enjoy the presence of the foreigners but in terms of contributing to ongoing change or building infrastructure, many of the programmes have little lasting impact. Older volunteers tend to have more awareness of the limitations of their contribution. For example retired teacher **Barbara Plane** from Newcastle looked back on her volunteer teaching with mixed feelings:

> *Despite all my travels, I was so naïve at the beginning. I will come away having learnt a lot from what I've seen and from the people I've met, and if I ever come again I would do it so differently. I wonder if Western-ers, full of good intentions, are really helping? Just because they speak English (and for some I would even question that!) doesn't mean they can teach it!!*

All the same, this is not colonial exploitation as some have argued. Nothing is removed from the foreign village except the experience for the Western participant, which can be transforming.

The insights gained by volunteers are often the most important long-term effect, resonating long after a gap year is over. Even those who have given the matter little thought when they are signing up for a £3,000 volunteering adventure in Africa or south east Asia often end up with their eyes being opened to the difficul-ties of delivering aid across cultural divides. A typical gap year volunteer might find him or herself working in a school in Ghana or Nepal or Costa Rica. Every day for three months he/she will stand in front of a class of 60 or 80 children trying to help them improve their spoken English by devising games for them to rearrange sentences in order, teaching them Beatles songs or nursery rhymes and having them compose haikus or put on a play. You could take a jaundiced view and say that in the scheme of things this contribution is negligible and mainly provides a chance for the local classroom teacher to put her feet up in the staff room. But our volunteer is sure to go home with a heightened sensitivity to cultural differences. Even if the development outcomes that follow on from a typical short volunteer placement are limited, foreign participants usually bring variety and laughter to the lives of children and adults they meet, forming bonds along the way. These issues are worth thinking through before committing yourself, so that you are more likely to choose with care your sending agency. A good agency will promote worthwhile programmes which grow out of local input while avoiding local rascals and rip-off merchants.

Some of the glossy marketing material distributed by the most commercial specialist operators shows only pristine beaches, jolly campfires and smiling black babies, with an upbeat text to match. It might be instructive to quote a more realistic version taken from the literature of an Icelandic exchange organisa-tion (EXIT):

> *As much as we would like Peru to live up to European standards, we have to warn you that institutions do not prepare for your arrival by organising a weekly work schedule or other special instructions. It's a big challenge to live and work in a poor Latin American country. It demands courage, some experience and the ability to adapt. It can be overwhelming, especially at first, to have to adjust to completely new conditions, communicate in a foreign language, etc. Things are not as you are used to, the climate, the food, the atmosphere – everything is different. During your work you will be faced daily with a harsh social reality and experience things very differently from the way a tourist would.*

Voluntary projects abroad often demand a large measure of flexibility. More mature volunteers with experience of the working world are often better placed than young students to cope in situations where the tasks are not pre-determined and where you may be left not knowing what you are supposed to do or be asked to carry out tasks for which you are ill-prepared. And they may also have more practical ideas for improving the experience of the next batch of volunteers, as **Barbara Plane** noted after her stint in Nepal:

> *We gave Bindu a list of small things we think would be beneficial upstairs in the lounge/eating area, e.g. plates, knives and forks, a washing up bowl – and they arrived the same day! I also suggested a Visitors Book that people could sign and make comments (not about the hotel – more about the sending agency, PoD), about places to eat, places to visit, tips and what to do and not to do – that sort of thing, I for one would have found that most helpful. We've started a 'Resource Pack' for future PoD volunteers.*

Privately run projects are particularly susceptible to causing disappointment if the individuals in charge fail to maintain high standards and continuity. For example volunteers have travelled to remote corners of the world to work on eco-projects only to find that the managers run them for profit. One eager volunteer turned up for an eight-week music project in Rio de Janeiro only to find that it was the summer holidays and the *Carnaval* and the college was deserted most of the time. Another was promised a garden design placement in Sri Lanka where the only task was weeding the headmistress's private garden because local males were not permitted to do this chore.

People who work in the developing world often experience just as much culture shock on their return home as they did when they first had to adapt to difficult conditions abroad (see Part 11, *Back to Normal or a Change for Life?*). Anyone who has spent time living among people for whom every day is a struggle to survive may find it very difficult to return to their privileged and comfortable life in the West. Many returned volunteers claim to feel sickened by the excesses of consumer culture and misplaced value systems. After returning from an HIV education programme in Zambia, **Carolinen Kippen** commented '*I really value what is important in life now, although that makes things difficult managing my expectations now I am back home – people just don't see things the same way I do now!*'

Volunteering is nothing like a conventional holiday and even volunteers for organisations with glossy seductive brochures often find the tasks they are assigned to be more physically and emotionally demanding than they anticipated. Teaching English to a group of smiling 8-year-olds in a west African village sounds fun and exotic when contemplated at home, but can land you in a very testing situation which might involve few creature comforts and demand a measure of stoicism. During a longer-term placement some volunteers are bound to face homesickness, loneliness or illness.

Raleigh stresses that for its volunteer expedition leaders, attitude of mind, not age, is the crucial factor in coping with the tough conditions of the Chilean Andes or the Mongolian steppes. If you have any concerns about physical endurance, it's best to consult your GP for a full medical. Explain the conditions you are likely to face and ask for advice.

Regional crises also flare up making volunteering potentially risky. For example most volunteer agencies have withdrawn from troubled Zimbabwe. To avoid nasty surprises you should do some research beforehand of political issues relating to democratic and religious freedoms, human rights and so on. Two starting points might be the Freedom House website (www.freedomhouse.org; despite the American bias) and the Paris-based Reporters Sans Frontières (Reporters Without Borders) website (www.rsf.org).

VOLUNTEERING ABROAD THROUGH A UK AGENCY

A growing number of British companies and organisations makes it possible for people of all backgrounds to take a career break of three, six or 12 months volunteering abroad. While some specialise in placements for gap year students between school and university, others cater to an older age group and many accept volunteers on a year out whatever their age.

Because the student gap year market has almost reached saturation, many mediating agencies for 18-year-olds have broadened the scope of their programmes to appeal more specifically to an older clientele. A number of the leading companies report that the real growth market has been among the over-30s with the over-50s close behind. Any upper limits may be flexible and should be challenged by a keen and energetic candidate. Madventurer, which started life as an organisation catering to university students, has noticed such a marked increase in the number of people joining as part of a career break that they now run projects just for adults (25+) taking a gap from their careers (see www.careerbreaker. com). MondoChallenge has always encouraged older volunteers to join its range of community-based projects on three continents. Its volunteer profile indicates that as many as 65% of volunteers are on a career break, 21% are post-university and 3% are retired, while the rest are students. Each agency has its own application procedures and it is best to telephone or look to their websites for detailed instructions. Many of these volunteer recruitment companies hold open days when you can meet the permanent staff and hear from former volunteers. If you have anxieties, try to establish precisely what safety net is in place in case of difficulties or emergencies.

OPPORTUNITIES FOR PROFESSIONALS

Mainstream voluntary bodies such as Voluntary Service Overseas (VSO), International Service, Skillshare Africa and Hands Around the World and many others act as matching agencies for overseas partners looking for specialist skills and expertise from the developed world.

VOLUNTARY SERVICE OVERSEAS

VSO is an international development charity which works on long-term partnerships with overseas organisations and is perhaps the most famous and longest established of volunteer sending agencies in the UK. Doing a stint as a volunteer with VSO (www.vso.org.uk) is a classic career break which thousands of Britons apply to do every year. Every year VSO recruits about 1,500 people from around the world with a steadily rising average age (now 41) and a maximum of about 75. Volunteers are recruited via its offices in the UK, Ireland, Europe, North America, India, the Philippines, Kenya and Uganda. In addition to its standard one- to two-year placements, short-term specialist assignments are now available for highly experienced professionals who can work at senior levels, as are business partnership placements for volunteers from the corporate world who can be seconded for periods of 6–12 months. VSO has a new international site (www.vsointernational.org), which gives an overview of the whole of VSO and a number of case studies. VSO recruits volunteers in the fields of education, Teaching English as a Foreign Language (TEFL), health, natural resources, technical trades and engineering, business and social work and many others. About half of all VSO projects worldwide are related to education, likewise there is a growing need for expertise in IT and small business advisers. During the 50 years since its creation in 1958, VSO has earned a reputation for the success of its programmes and its professional approach to recruiting volunteers. Recruitment is rigorous and intended to make sure that volunteer skills are matched most effectively with projects in the developing world. The advantage of volunteering with VSO is that its track record means that it is relatively well funded. Volunteers have their expenses covered and are also given a salary in line with local salaries plus various grants such as an equipment grant, national insurance, extensive training, reasonable accommodation with a private room and return travel. Most reassuringly, the health insurance package is described as the 'Rolls-Royce' of policies, providing comprehensive coverage. In addition, a payment is made on the return home to act as a cushion. On its 50th anniversary, the UK government announced a £13 million fund to support pensions for public sector professionals who volunteer with VSO.

This level of support requires a corresponding level of commitment and responsibility because most applicants will be asked to dedicate one or two years of their lives. VSO's Business Partnership Scheme encourages company bosses to allow volunteers to work overseas for shorter periods of between three and 12 months, partly to demonstrate their commitment to corporate responsibility. Companies such as Accenture, PricewaterhouseCoopers, Randstad and Shell have participated. The selection procedure takes place in several stages. Applications are assessed initially on paper to match volunteer skills to the requests made to VSO by its partners. If a certain skill does not meet a requirement then an application might be put on hold until opportunities arise. Then an assessment is made about each applicant's personal situation to see whether it affects their suitability. For example, does the applicant have children, a partner, financial stability, emotional stability? Often a couple will apply and only one of the couple will be able to find a suitable placement. References from current employers are checked at this stage and also a routine check takes place with the police to ensure that the applicant doesn't have a criminal record. Successful applicants then undergo intensive training in the UK and after arrival to prepare them for their assignments, including workshops on health and language immersion.

AN IT TRAINER IN HER LATE 40S, JAN LEE DECIDED THAT BEFORE SHE TURNED 50 SHE WAS FINALLY GOING TO FOLLOW THROUGH ON HER NEW YEAR'S RESOLUTION TO DO SOMETHING DIFFERENT:

After spending some time searching the Internet I discovered that VSO seemed to offer me all that I wanted – the opportunity to travel; the chance to live in and experience at first hand another culture; an appropriate job where I could fully utilise my skills and share my knowledge with local people in a developing country; and, perhaps most importantly for a 50-year-old single female embarking on her first real adventure, the protection and support of a large and well-respected organisation.

I soon began the process of filling in application forms; attending the selection day which weeds out those who are not fully committed, those with marked prejudices, those who are burning with a desire to change the world and other inappropriate candidates; and attending the various training offered by VSO to prepare you as much as possible for what you might meet overseas. My medical showed up a previously unknown condition which involved an operation and a six-month delay to my departure, but by November of that year I was ready to depart for Laos (which I learned is in Southeast Asia and not Africa) as an IT adviser to a government department dealing with Agriculture and Fisheries.

Any potential volunteer needs to know that the relationship with the host group will be delicate. Cross-cultural differences will be a challenge to accommodate and it is you who will have to do more adapting than the host project. Sometimes the advertised role will be different from the one you expected. Inevitably some local attitudes to volunteers are ambivalent. On the one hand, a placement from a charity such as VSO is prestigious and lends credibility to the indigenous programmes but on the other you might be perceived as something of a nuisance, a disruptive challenge to the established hierarchy. The trick is to earn the trust of your co-workers and to act as a catalyst for change rather than simply imagine you can act in an executive fashion. One past volunteer recommends not to sit around feeling frustrated and unhappy if the placement is not working out, but to try to negotiate improvements. If that doesn't work, consider asking VSO if it is possible to change jobs in-country.

OTHER AGENCIES RECRUITING PROFESSIONALS

A range of charitable organisations support 'operational' agencies such as Oxfam, UNICEF, UNHCR, etc., by recruiting for certain positions within their programmes. The types of assignment for which the client agencies need personnel almost always require previous field experience, typically at least six months with a known non-governmental organisation (NGO) in a developing country. The mediating agencies find people for specific jobs, not jobs for specific people. They receive many requests from those without previous field experience who wish to do short-term assignments but it is increasingly rare for such people to be placed, especially if they are first-timers who cost the agencies a lot of money in training and travel expenses. Competition for such placements is high, and international development work has become a competitive profession. Agencies are increasingly cautious in the selection process for candidates to go overseas because they have to ensure that the donor's money is being spent in the best possible way. Even with a relevant degree and further specialist qualifications, it can still be difficult to secure a position in the aid field.

Within most professions, an organisation refers specialists to appropriate volunteer vacancies overseas, including vets, dentists, pharmacists, pilots, even accountants. **Debbie Risborough** (see her case history on p. 64) got her job with Concern in Sudan through MANGO, Management Accountants for NGOs (www.mango.org.uk) – not to be confused with the fashion label. A current list of humanitarian vacancies for professionals is available on www.reliefweb.int. Skillshare International (www.skillshare. org) sends more than 60 qualified and skilled staff to work professionally in partnership with local people on development work throughout southern and east Africa and also India. Positions are varied and have included teachers for agricultural studies, business advisers, curators, fundraisers, catering tutors, ceramics/3D design lecturers, physiotherapists, engineers, bricklaying instructors and so on. Placements are for two years, and flights, national insurance payments, a modest living allowance/salary, rent-free accommodation, health insurance, small home savings allowance and equipment grants are provided. Applicants should be between the ages of roughly 25 and 65 and should have relevant qualifications and at least two years post-qualification work experience. If you are spending time in one place in the developing world you are bound to make the acquaintance of the aid community that will be plugged into the needs of local NGOs and international agencies. While **Till Bruckner** was staying in the Sudan he noticed that the overseas branches of Oxfam, Save the Children, etc., had huge volumes of reports to write, something that the local staff sometimes struggled to do in polished English. He discovered that his assistance was welcomed by some and so advises others to do likewise (see Part 11, *Back to Normal or a Change for Life?*, for further ideas from Till Bruckner on how to break into the world of professional development).

LISTING OF INTERNATIONAL VOLUNTARY ORGANISATIONS

British Red Cross – 44 Moorfields, London EC2Y 9AL; ☎ 0870 170 7000; www.redcross.org. uk. Their policy is not to send volunteers overseas. With branches in countries worldwide, only local volunteers are deployed.

Concern Worldwide – 52–55 Lower Camden Street, Dublin 2, Ireland; ☎ +353 1 417 7700; www.concern.net. See website for UK offices. Recruits mostly qualified professionals over 21 for development projects in Africa and Asia for one or two years.

Hands Around the World – PO Box 62, Lydney, Gloucestershire GL15 6WZ; ☎ 01594 560223; info@hatw.org.uk; www.hatw.org.uk. Run three-to six-month assignments primarily in Africa in a range of fields including for physiotherapists, radiographers/ultrasonographers, pharmacists, lab technicians, IT specialists and dairy farmers.

IESC Geekcorps – 1900 M St NW, Suite 500, Washington, DC 20036, USA; ☎ +1 202 326 0280; geekcorps@iesc.org; www.geekcorps.org. Geekcorps was set up by a group of IT professionals to help small businesses and institutions in the developing world. Although it is based in the USA, IT specialists do not need to be American citizens to apply. Most volunteers work for periods of three months in projects in Mali, etc.

International Service – Hunter House, 57 Goodramgate, York YO1 7FX; ☎ 01904 647799; www.internationalservice.org.uk. Founded as the United Nations Association, IS recruits professionals for two-year placements in Latin America, west Africa and the Middle East.

Médecins du Monde UK – 14 Herons Quay, London E14 4JB; ☎ 020 7515 7534; www.medecins-dumonde.org.uk. Must have a minimum of two years healthcare experience post qualification. Minimum placements are two to three months in emergency programmes, maximum one year.

Médecins Sans Frontières (UK) – 67–74 Saffron Hill, London EC1N 8QX; ☎ 020 7404 6600; office-ldn@london.msf.org; www.msf.org. MSF sends 2,000 medical volunteers to 60 countries providing medical support to victims of war and disaster, usually for 9–12 months. Most opportunities are for qualified medical professionals though there are also places for administrators and accountants. A knowledge of French is an asset.

Merlin – 12th Floor, 207 Old Street, London EC1V 9NR; ☎ 020 7014 1600; www.merlin.org.uk. Deploy medical volunteers at short notice to work in emergencies worldwide.

Oxfam – Volunteering Team, Oxfam House, John Smith Drive, Cowley, Oxford OX4 2JY; ☎ 0870 333 2444; www.oxfam.org.uk/what_you_can_do/volunteer/internship.htm. Oxfam recruits only full-time development professionals for overseas but relies on volunteers in the UK. Internships are available in several divisions and are mostly based in Oxford.

Progressio – Unit 3 Canonbury Yard, 190a New North Road, London N1 7BJ; ☎ 020 7354 0883; www.progressio.org.uk. Formerly the Catholic agency CIIR. Recruits development workers for one or two years.

RedR/IHE – ☎ 020 7233 3116; www.redr.org.uk. Disaster relief agency that trains and mobilises relief personnel for deployment to afflicted regions.

Skillshare International – 126 New Walk, Leicester, LE1 7JA (0116 254 1862; www.skillshare. org). Activities described above.

United Nations Volunteers – Postfach 260 111, D-53153 Bonn, Germany; ☎ +49 228 815 2000; www.unvolunteers.org. Keep a resource bank of skilled professionals and also send volunteers who have at least five years' professional experience to development projects for two years, although six- and 12-month assignments are becoming more common.

VSO – 317 Putney Bridge Road, London SW15 2PN; ☎ 020 8780 7500; enquiry@vso.org.uk; www.vso.org.uk. Offices in Ireland, Canada, the Netherlands and other countries.

SHORT-TERM VOLUNTEERING

WORK CAMPS

Voluntary work in developed countries often takes the form of work camps which accept unskilled people of all ages for short periods. The term 'work camp' is falling out of favour and is often replaced by 'project'. As part of an established international network of voluntary organisations they are not subject to the irregularities of some privately run projects. As well as providing volunteers with the means to live cheaply for two to four weeks in a foreign country, work camps enable volunteers to become involved in what is usually useful work for the community, to meet people from many different backgrounds (many of whom will be young) and to increase their awareness of other lifestyles, social problems and their responsibility to society.

Within Europe, and to a lesser extent further afield, there is a massive effort to coordinate work camp programmes. This means that the prospective volunteer should apply in the first instance to an organisation in his or her own country. The vast majority of camps take place in the summer months, and camp details are normally available online from March/April with most placements being made between April and June. If you want a printed copy of their international programme, you will have to pay £4–£6. For an overseas work camp is necessary to pay a registration fee (usually £100–£160), which includes board and lodging but not travel.

Many projects are environmental and involve the conversion/reconstruction of historic buildings and building community facilities, for example building adventure playgrounds for children, renovating an open-air museum in Latvia, organising youth concerts in Armenia, constructing boats for sea-cleaning in Japan, looking after a farm-school in Slovakia during the holidays, helping peasant farmers in central France to stay on their land, excavating a Roman villa in Germany, forest fire spotting in Italy, plus a whole range of schemes with the disabled and elderly, conservation work and the study of social and political issues. It is sometimes possible to move from project to project throughout the summer, particularly in countries such as France or Morocco where the work camp movement is highly developed.

Specialised work camps may appeal to mature volunteers with special interests and/or skills. **Jeffrey Lawson** from Florida ended up spending part of the autumn in Sweden, having traced a 'mixed age' work camp that suited him through the work camps organisation Volunteers for Peace (www.vfp.org). In contrast with many voluntary projects he checked, he found this one to be 'amazingly inexpensive' at $280 (and with no sleeping bag required):

In April, 2007, with mixed feelings of satisfaction and self-doubt I decided to volunteer for a three-week construction project in October in a small town in Sweden. As a premature retiree on the north side of 50, I was looking for an opportunity that combined moderate adventure (new places, faces and functions) with moderate self-sacrifice (without breaking my back or bank account) in appealing surroundings that would challenge my skills in a hands-on contribution to a local cause. I found all of that and enjoyably more in the town of Gamleby, a water-front settlement of about 4,000 souls situated 250km south of Stockholm. As indicated in the brief online description, the work camp was held at a small varv (boatyard) that had been established specifically to restore and preserve historic, Swedish wooden sailing vessels and traditional shipbuilding techniques.

Gamleby was my first overseas volunteer experience, and what attracted me was its connection to my Scandinavian heritage and my interest in wooden boats. What nearly deterred me was the scant information about the nature of the work (the advertised primary objective of the project was to complete a black-smith shop), the nature of the participants, and particularly my concern as how a 'senior citizen' would fit in among the multi-national 20-somethings I anticipated as workmates. I shared a room with Fabio (30), an affable, self-employed carpenter from the Italian part of Switzerland. Two other males ages 30 and 42 hailed from Holland and Germany. Our only female volunteer, just 22, was from Moscow.

I found the physical labour tiring, but the work did not trouble me. Apart from one or two days, the weather was beautiful, a late autumn for Sweden, with golden maple leaves fluttering to carpet the ground.

Our hosts were very pleased with our work. In fact, in the Friday edition of the regional newspaper of our second week, we were the featured front page story. The locals we met smilingly shook our hands and expressed appreciation for our efforts. Would I go back? Yes, indeed, and I hope one day to accept my hosts' open invitation to return and sail aboard the three-masted schooner VEGA.

Service Civil International is the largest work camp organisation with links to 40+ countries. The UK branch is International Voluntary Service (IVS).

Concordia Youth Service Volunteers Ltd – 19 North Street, Portslade, Brighton, Sussex BN41 1DH; ☎ 01273 422218; www.concordia-iye.org.uk. Registration costs £150.

International Voluntary Service (IVS Field Office) – IVS GB, Thorn House, 5 Rose Street, Edinburgh EH2 2PR; ☎ 0131 243 2745; scotland@ivs-gb.org.uk. Programme of camps published online in April. The cost of registration on work camps outside the UK is £190 which includes £35 membership in IVS.

UNA Exchange – United Nations Association, Temple of Peace, Cathays Park, Cardiff CF10 3AP; ☎ 029 2022 3088; www.unaexchange.org. Majority of camps cost £150–£175 plus £12 UNA membership.

Volunteer Action for Peace – 16 Overhill Road, East Dulwich, London SE22 0PH; ☎ 0844 20 90 927; www.yap-uk.org). UK branch of Youth Action for Peace/YAP, formerly the Christian Movement for Peace. Medium- and longer-term projects for older volunteers (sometimes with relevant skills) as well as short work camps mainly for young people. Joining fee is £150–£180.

ARCHAEOLOGY

Taking part in archaeological excavations is another popular form of voluntary work, but volunteers are usually expected to make a contribution towards their board and lodging. Also, you may be asked to bring your own trowel, work clothes, tent, etc. Archaeology Abroad (31–34 Gordon Square, London WC1H 0PY; ☎ 020 8537 0849; www.britarch.ac.uk/archabroad) is an excellent source of information, as it publishes annually on CD-ROM details of excavations needing volunteers; in 2007 between 700 and 1,000 definite places on sites were offered to subscribers. They do stress, however that applications from people with a definite interest in the subject are preferred. An annual subscription costs £20.

For those who are not students of archaeology, the chances of finding a place on an overseas dig will be greatly enhanced by having some digging experience nearer to home. Details of British excavations looking for volunteers are published in *British Archaeology*, a magazine from the Council for British Archaeology (St Mary's House, 66 Bootham, York YO30 7BZ; ☎ 01904 671417; www.britarch.ac.uk). The magazine is produced six times a year and lists archaeological digs to which volunteers can apply; an annual subscription costs £19. Digs are also listed on the website.

A huge number of digs take place throughout France in the summer months. Every May the Ministry of Culture (Direction de l'Architecture et du Patrimoine) publishes a national list of excavations requiring up to 5,000 volunteers which can be consulted on its website (www.culture.fr/fouilles). Most *départements* have *Services Archéologiques* which organise digs. Without relevant experience you will probably be given only menial jobs but many like to share in the satisfaction of seeing progress made.

Israel is another country particularly rich in archaeological opportunities, many of them organised through the universities. Information on volunteering at archaeological digs in Israel is also available on the website of the Israeli Antiquities Authority (www.antiquities.org.il) or on the Ministry of Foreign Affairs' website (www.israel-mfa.gov.il/MFA/History/Early+History+-+Archaeology). Digs provide an excellent means of seeing remote parts of the country, although Israeli digs tend to be more expensive than most, typically US$50 a day for two or more weeks.

CONSERVATION

Saving the planet is an issue that is quickly climbing up the international agenda as climate science proves how urgent the situation is. Scaling down one's consumption is often part of a gap year spent travelling or learning. But to make a more lasting contribution, it is worth slotting into a conservation project at home or abroad. Most fix up a placement in advance though this is not essential.

For a directory of opportunities in this specialised area, consult the book *Green Volunteers: The World Guide to Voluntary Work in Nature Conservation* (£12 from www.greenvolunteers.com) Many of the projects listed are ideally suited to people on a gap year. To take just one example, the Wakuluzu Trust in Kenya needs volunteers over the age of 22 who can stay for at least three months to work to save the Angolan Colobus monkey and preserve its coastal habitat. The cost of participating is modest: €425 per month plus about €20 a week for food. Details are available from the Colobus Trust (PO Box 5380, 80401, Diani Beach, Kenya; ☎ +254 40 320 3519; www.colobustrust.org) which was hit hard financially by the loss of tourism and cancellation of volunteer visits in the aftermath of the ethnic clashes of January 2008.

Animal lovers will find a wealth of opportunities. To take just one of the main conservation organisations, Global Vision International (see entry; www.gvi.co.uk) can arrange for people to work with vervet monkeys in South Africa, lemurs in Madagascar, turtles in Panama, Ghana, Zakynthos and Vanuatu, orangutans in Sumatra and various species in the Galapagos Islands. Elsewhere, the six-week expeditions in Borneo with the Orangutan Foundation are popular with career breakers, as are wildlife assignments in Africa with the main agencies listed in the *Directory of Specialist Programmes* in the chapter that follows. **Phil Bond's** lack of fitness in hot humid Borneo was instantly forgotten when an orangutan came over to him, put her hand in his lap and her baby played with the zip on his pocket.

Neil Munro was in his 60s (see his case history on p. 125) when he joined a lion-breeding project at a game park in Zimbabwe called Antelope Park (www.antelopepark.co.zw). He gravitated to two cubs who had had a traumatic start in life, perhaps because he had just emerged from a four-year family trauma in his own life. Neil knew nothing about lions before he went and had had limited contact with animals, but discovered to his pleasure that he was a natural. He was not overly frightened of the lions. Even on the occasion that two cubs did jump on him, he didn't lose his nerve, only hit them on the side of the face as the guides had instructed to show them who was in command. He was good at 'thinking like a lion' and worked patiently and devotedly to win the trust and affection of the two damaged cubs in his care for instance by crawling under prickly bushes with them (until one of them would sleep over his legs), adjusting their feeding routines and greeting them by rubbing heads, as lions do. He had lots of adventures in the bush – rode horses to inspect the perimeter fences and to check for poachers' snares, rode elephants to look at game, saw a deadly 2m long Egyptian cobra (which made a fellow volunteer scream and jump into his arms), a python (not so dodgy because not poisonous), watched impala, wildebeest, hartebeest, zebra, giraffes, etc. For the most part he got on very well with the other volunteers, who were of many nationalities and mostly young. Over time, his interaction with the lion cubs Casper and Cleo had a healing effect on them and unobtrusively on him too. The cubs gradually learned to play and not to be so dependent on each other. He thinks that because he (unlike most of the other volunteers) has children of his own, he was more understanding of their situation. He has been back since his original stay to visit 'his' cubs who clearly remembered him. He is now looking into the possibility of selling some land to fund further long-term stays in this beautiful corner of Africa.

Short-term conservation holidays are available through the BTCV (British Trust for Conservation Volunteers) which runs a programme of mainly two-week International Conservation Holidays in 17 countries including Iceland, France, Bulgaria, USA, Cameroon, Japan and Lesotho. Further details are available from the BTCV Conservation Centre in Doncaster (☎ 01302 572244/388888; international@btcv.org. uk; http://shop.btcv.org.uk). Accommodation, meals and insurance are provided from £350 to £770 a fortnight on international projects or £160 a week in the UK including training in conservation skills.

The Involvement Volunteers Association based in Australia (www.volunteering.org.au) arranges short-term individual, group and team voluntary placements in many countries including Australia, New Zealand, California, Hawaii, Fiji, Thailand, India, Lebanon and Finland. Many projects are concerned with conservation, while others assist disadvantaged people. Projects can be arranged back-to-back in different countries for a fee.

Well-known organisations such as Raleigh, Frontier, Trekforce and Coral Cay recruit expeditionary groups that operate as a project team for a period of two to three months. These agencies help and staff scientific expeditions by supplying fee-paying volunteers. These are, in effect, specialist tour operators, and it seems that there is a booming market for this sort of working holiday among the affluent who are looking for a holiday with a difference or a platform from which to launch a career break. Scientific expedition organisations and wildlife programmes that use self-financing volunteers include the following (most with entries in the 'Directory of Specialist Programmes').

African Conservation Experience – www.conservationafrica.net. Sends people to game and nature reserves in South Africa, Zimbabwe, Namibia and Botswana for between two weeks and three months where they have the chance to assist rangers and wardens and get some first-hand experience of animal and plant conservation. The participation fees are approximately £2,900 for one month, £4,900 for three months including airfares.

Biosphere Expeditions – www.biosphere-expeditions.org. Organises short wildlife conservation research expeditions to many unusual parts of the world such as the Altai Republic of Central Asia and the Caprivi Delta of Namibia and Botswana. Volunteers with no research experience assist scientific experts. Fees start at £1,000 for a fortnight.

Blue Ventures – www.blueventures.org. Conducts marine research and grassroots conservation projects in Madagascar.

Coral Cay Conservation – www.coralcay.org. Recruits paying volunteers to assist with tropical forest and coral reef conservation expeditions in Malaysia, Honduras, the Philippines and Fiji. A sample six-week project for a dive trainee is £2,230.

Earthwatch Europe – www.earthwatch.org/europe. International non-profit organisation that recruits over 4,000 volunteers a year for 120 expeditions to assist scientific field research around the world. Prices range from £175 for a short local project to £2,250 abroad.

Frontier – www.frontier.ac.uk. Operates a conservation programme to preserve coral reefs, savannas, forests and mangrove areas within a larger worldwide programme.

Global Vision International – www.gvi.co.uk. Offers research and conservation expeditions of varying lengths worldwide.

Greenforce – www.greenforce.org. Specialises in environmental expeditions. Wildlife conservation projects take place in Ecuador, Tanzania, South Africa and China; marine projects in Fiji and the Bahamas.

Operation Wallacea – www.opwall.com. Runs marine, rainforest or desert research projects in Sulawesi (Indonesia), Honduras, Egypt, Amazonian Peru, South Africa, Mozambique and Cuba.

Personal Overseas Development – www.thepodsite.co.uk. Runs Amazon jungle conservation programme in Peru as well as other opportunities in Belize and Thailand (see entry).

Trekforce Expeditions – www.trekforceworldwide.com. Operates in Central and South America, Morocco, Nepal, Borneo and Papua New Guinea to deliver remote conservation projects among others.

AS THE HEAD OF SCIENCE OF A SECONDARY SCHOOL IN CORNWALL, TOM INGER WAS INTERESTED IN ECOLOGY AND WANTED TO EXPLORE A REEF SYSTEM. THE OPERATION WALLACEA EXPEDITION TO INDONESIA ALLOWED HIM TO QUALIFY FOR AN OPEN WATER PADI QUALIFICATION AND THEN TO WORK ALONGSIDE A RESEARCH TEAM STUDYING THE HEALTH OF THE REEF.

Our task was to monitor numbers of species of bugs and lobsters, starfish and invertebrates. Bomb-fishing has irreparably damaged the coral and the damage needs to be quantified. OpWall shares the research results with the local communities in an attempt to change harmful practices.

There were 80 volunteers, mainly British and many of 'teacher age' including a family with two children aged five and six; the father is a diver and the mother a sociologist who was more interested in studying the local Bajo people. I had an absolutely brilliant time living in such a remote corner of the world, and also feel that the experience was professionally worthwhile too. Some of the Key Stage 3 and 4 lessons that I have given this year have been greatly improved by my first-hand experience.

ORGANIC FARMS

With an upsurge of interest in organic and local sourcing of foods, the organic farming movement is attracting a rapidly increasing following around the world, from Tunbridge Wells to Turkey with an ever-rising number of farms converting, at least partially, to organic methods of production. Organic farms are labour-intensive operations and everywhere they take on volunteers. Various coordinating bodies go under the name of WWOOF – World Wide Opportunities on Organic Farms. WWOOF has a global website (www.wwoofinternational.org) with links to the national offices in the countries that have a WWOOF coordinator. WWOOF organisations exist in the UK, Denmark, Finland, Sweden, Germany, Switzerland, Austria, Italy, Slovenia, Australia, New Zealand, Canada, Ghana, Ivory Coast, Togo, Japan, Korea and (most recently) Belize, Brazil, Chile, Kazakhstan, Romania and Taiwan. National WWOOF coordinators compile a list of member farmers willing to provide bed and board in a non-monetary exchange with volunteers who are genuinely interested in furthering the aims of the organic movement. These address lists are sent to members; membership in each country's organisation usually costs around €20/£15. Individual farm listings in other countries, i.e. those with no national organisation, are known as WWOOF Independents. It is necessary to join WWOOF before you can obtain addresses of these properties (£15 for Internet access to addresses, £20 for printed booklet).

WWOOF is an exchange: in return for your help on organic farms, gardens and homesteads, you receive meals, a place to sleep and a practical insight into organic growing. (If the topic arises at immigration, avoid the word 'working'; it is preferable to present yourself as a student of organic farming organising an educational farm visit or a cultural exchange.)

Before arranging an extended stay on an organic farm, consider whether you will find such an environment congenial. Many organic farmers are non-smoking vegetarians and living conditions may be primitive by some people's standards, so you might want to think carefully before organising a career break on an organic farm.

If you are starting in Britain, send a self-addressed envelope to the UK branch of WWOOF (PO Box 2675, Lewes, Sussex BN7 1RB; ☎ 01273 476286; hello@wwoof.org), which will send you a membership application form. The active Australian branch of WWOOF publishes its own *List of Independent Hosts* of farms and volunteer work opportunities in those countries with no national WWOOF group, which it sends to addresses overseas for A$32 (WWOOF Australia, 2166 Gelantipy Road, W Tree, Via Buchan, Victoria 3885; ☎ 03 5155 0218; www.wwoof.com.au).

A free Internet-based exchange of work-for-keep volunteers can be found at www.helpx.net where the majority of farms are located in Australia and New Zealand.

VOLUNTEERING WITHOUT MALARIA PILLS

Going abroad is not essential to becoming a volunteer. Thousands of opportunities within the UK do not require volunteers to pack a rucksack or learn survival skills. If the thought of leaving home for an extended period and living in a different place is unappealing, daunting or just unmanageable, volunteering closer to home may easily be incorporated into a gap year.

Some of the people most desperately in need of a career break (and uniquely placed to arrange one) are those people who work from home, freelance cartoonists, web designers, translators, crafts people, childminders, copy editors and so on. For many, feelings of isolation can be overwhelming, and they think back with fondness on the busy camaraderie of the office life left behind. Many feel that their social (not to say love) lives have gone into hibernation and they long for some new social outlets. One way of achieving this end is to join a congenial local project as a volunteer.

You might want to use a career break to find out about a different profession through volunteering. For anyone considering a career in youth and community work, counselling or social services, conservation or outdoor education and many others, it is standard practice to spend time initially as a volunteer. Anyone contemplating taking time out of the workplace this way can start gradually by volunteering locally while working full-time. This is becoming easier with the creation of schemes such as Business in the Community (www.bitc.org.uk) which has persuaded hundreds of companies to donate some of their employees' time to a local charity or community group. The best place to start familiarising yourself with volunteering opportunities at home is to consult your local Volunteer Centre which forms part of Volunteering England (www.volunteering.org.uk), linking volunteer centres all over the country. For example each London borough has its own. Each office is staffed by professional advisers who will develop a profile of your abilities and interests and then match you with a local organisation. They act as a high street recruitment agency for local charities, non-profit bodies and community groups and on average have databases containing between 1,000 and 3,000 opportunities. The last national survey discovered that half a million people had spent time volunteering after consulting their local volunteer recruitment office. Scotland's equivalent is called Volunteer Development Scotland (www.vds.org.uk).

Other sources of information include public noticeboards in libraries, the local hospital, etc. Local councils also work with volunteers and it's worth approaching the department that interests you, e.g. social services.

VOLUNTEERING ENGLAND, WHICH ADVISES VOLUNTARY BODIES, SUGGESTS YOU CONSIDER THESE ISSUES FIRST:

- *Before making contact with an organisation, think about what you want to know from them, and what they are likely to ask you.*
- *How much time can you give? At what time of day?*
- *What do you want to get from volunteering, e.g. meeting people or gaining new skills?*
- *What skills or experience can you offer?*
- *Will out-of-pocket expenses be paid? Does the organisation insure its volunteers?*
- *Will you need to obtain a police check from the Criminal Records Bureau?*

Volunteering in the UK can be a stepping stone to opportunities abroad or provide a taster of work in the field of development as it did for **Jen Dyer**. Although Jen had been enjoying her work in the office of a conservation expedition company, she decided to take a break to find out more about careers in the humanitarian and development sector. After much research, she discovered that an internship was the best option, since proper jobs required previous experience and qualifications she didn't have. She applied for all of the different internships Oxfam was advertising at the time and was interviewed by two departments, the Programme Resource Centre and the Media unit:

My internship was for three+ months for three days a week. I lived with a friend who was located conveniently close to Oxford which meant that I had lower rent and could finance my internship by continuing to work part-time for Operation Wallacea in Lincolnshire. Oxfam paid my expenses, which meant my living costs were very low and I just had to resist unnecessary items.

The best part of my internship may be yet to come. I have gained many contacts through Oxfam and am hoping that when I travel to Honduras with Opwall this summer I will be able to visit Oxfam's agricultural scale-up programme and see development work firsthand. I had one week where I was less excited about the work I was doing at Oxfam. I was helping with the migration of intranet pages to a new system which involved a lot of repetitive computer work without having much interaction with staff but I made up for that by attending the myriad of lunchtime talks available on Oxfam's work and pestering other staff members to have coffee and chats with me to hear their experiences and how their career in this sector came about...

The experience has helped me decide on my next course of action. I have now applied for a Masters degree at Manchester Uni in Environment and Development. Eventually I will look for employment in a sector which has now been revealed to me in more detail. I have enjoyed my internship entirely and it has been a wonderful experience where I have learnt an inordinate amount, not just about Oxfam's work but about working in a large NGO [non-governmental organisation], and in fact in a large company, as well as making some great friends.

PRACTICALITIES

The choices for volunteering in the UK are infinite and include both residential and non-residential work. Residential posts range from a week (say helping at a holiday centre for disabled children or rebuilding a dry stone wall) to a year (for instance at an outdoor centre for disadvantaged youths or at the Centre for Alternative Technology in Wales). By piecing together short stints as a volunteer in different places, it is possible to experience a range of activities and settings on a gap year within the UK.

Volunteer organisations that take on people to work with children or vulnerable adults have a statutory obligation to run a police check on new volunteers. Usually it is the responsibility of the organisation rather than the individual to apply to the Criminal Records Bureau (CRB). The standard fee charged for a CRB disclosure is £31 and an enhanced disclosure costs £36. Further details are available from www. crb.gov.uk or on the CRB Information Line (☎ 0870 90 90 811). Many organisations arrange accommodation, sometimes free as in the residential social care placements made by CSV (www.csv.org.uk/ volunteer/full-time; see entry), sometimes at a modest cost, as in the week-long conservation projects organised by the BTCV (British Trust for Conservation Volunteers). Most BTCV conservation holidays for paying volunteers are for short periods of a weekend or a week, but it is also possible to become a volunteer field officer for up to a year at one of BTCV's centres. Long-term volunteers are not restricted by age or qualification and are eligible for income support for the duration of their placement.

CSV places volunteers away from home around the UK for 4–12 month placements in a large variety of projects in the social care field. This includes working with the homeless, schools and hospitals, and mentoring young offenders and teenagers in care. Volunteers are given free board and accommodation and paid pocket money of £33 per week. CSV aims to recruit individuals up to the age of 35, though they also run a Retired & Senior Volunteers Programme for volunteers over 50. The CSV Employee Volunteering programme encourages companies to release employees on a part-time basis to volunteer locally in schools, etc.

Peter Luckham was at the upper end of the age range when he decided to give his managerial job in IT a rest and become a CSV volunteer, a scheme he remembered hearing about at university. For the first part of his six-month sabbatical he supported 63-year old Eddy who is partially blind and has learning difficulties. His next project was to work as a learning mentor at a special school in Hackney for boys with emotional and behavioural difficulties. It was while working there that he decided to resign from his job in London with a big investment bank and now works on a self-employed basis for a small IT consultancy that serves local small businesses in and around Bournemouth:

> *Originally I felt as though I was living in an isolated world, worrying about mortgages and pensions, but disconnected from the world around me. Now I'm in a continuous process of discovery. Volunteering has helped me have a wider experience of dealing with different people. It has helped me prove that I can do other things outside the IT world and that I don't need to be as dependent on the perceived security that a very commercially focused career provides. The experience of being a volunteer provided the space and a new structure to find out a little more about me, and what I really want. I wanted to give something back — maybe I have a little middle class guilt complex.*

VOLUNTEERING RESOURCES

If you are interested in short or long-term voluntary projects around the world, you might start by browsing www.do-it.org.uk, a national database of volunteering opportunities in the UK. If you want to sample volunteering abroad on a voluntourism trip, take a look at *Hands-on Holidays* (Crimson Publishing, 2007, £12.99) which describes hundreds of short volunteer travel opportunities. Try also www.voluntourism.org and the web portal www.responsibletravel.com, on which a search for 'Volunteer Travel' results in nearly 350 possibilities. Heavy Internet users should consider using www.everyclick.com as their search engine, since every click benefits your nominated charity.

The *World Service Enquiry* of the respected charity Christians Abroad (Bon Marché Centre, Suite 237, 241–251 Ferndale Road, London SW9 8BJ; ☎ 0870 770 3274; www.wse.org.uk) provides information and advice to people of any faith or none who are thinking of working overseas, whether short or long term, voluntary or paid. Their publication *The Guide to Volunteering for Development* was sold out at the time of writing but it is worth checking their publications page for updates. Challenges Worldwide (CWW) runs a free advisory service 'Ask an Expert' through a partner website (www.intervol.org.uk). Intervol is sponsored by CWW together with the government volunteering agency Timebank (www.timebank.org.uk). Free, impartial advice is provided to anyone wanting to volunteer internationally including information on reasons for using a volunteer sending agency, why it is necessary to pay to volunteer, training provision for volunteering overseas, the roles and responsibilities expected for and by volunteers, etc. The website also includes a number of case studies.

2Way Development – offers a different kind of service to people looking for international voluntary experiences. It provides independent, professional support to volunteers in the organisation of placements overseas, in all sectors of work. The one-off fee of £850 includes personal consultation, referral to ethical volunteering opportunities with NGOs, assistance with preparation and ongoing support.

Working Abroad – The Old School House, Pendomer, Yeovil, Somerset BA22 9PH; ☎ 01953 864458; www.workingabroad.com. As well as being a web-based resource of voluntary opportunities worldwide, Workingabroad.com will prepare a personalised report after you complete a detailed request form; the fee is £29/$52 by email, £36/$65 by post.

Christian Vocations – St James House, Trinity Road, Dudley, West Midlands DY1 1JB; ☎ 0870 745 4825; www.christianvocations.org. Publishes a searchable online directory of short-term opportunities with Christian agencies.

SOURCES OF INFORMATION

The revolution in information technology has made it easier for the individual to become acquainted with the amazing range of possibilities. One of the best website directories is www.traveltree.co.uk. It covers gap year ideas and volunteering opportunities worldwide as well as internships and educational travel. *Transitions Abroad* magazine maintains great on-line resources for volunteering (www.transitionsabroad.com). The best of the websites have a multitude of links to organisations big and small that can make use of volunteers. For example www.idealist.org (from Action Without Borders) is a US-based easily searchable website that will take you to the great monolithic charities such as the Peace Corps as well as to small grassroots organisations. It lists more than 13,000 non-profit and community organisations in 150 countries.

The website of Volunteering England (www.volunteering.org.uk) has a listing of UK agencies that send volunteers abroad, as well as disseminating a great deal of other information about volunteering generally. Worldwide Volunteering for Young People (7 North Street Workshops, Stoke sub Hamdon, Somerset TA14 6QR; ☎ 01935 825588; www.wwv.org.uk) maintains an authoritative search-and-match database of volunteering opportunities for 16–35-year-olds which is free. Although TimeBank is primarily intended to match British volunteers with UK projects, it has developed an online overseas directory in association with Intervol (www.intervol.org.uk). The Japan-based Go Make a Difference (www.go-mad.org) has links to unusual voluntary project. The search engine at www.do-it.org is very useful for finding suitable projects in the UK. Reach (☎ 020 7582 6543; www.reach-online.org.uk) brings together voluntary organisations in the UK and volunteers with career skills, mainly mature professionals and executives who are not in full-time work.

The first voluntary agency to spring to an American's mind is the Peace Corps (1111 20th St NW, Washington, DC 20526; ☎ +1 800 424 8580/+1 202 692 1800; www.peacecorps.gov) which sends volunteers, usually with appropriate skills and experience, on two-year assignments to 70 countries. It has undoubtedly done good work over the years though some volunteers come away with reservations about its focus.

KRISTIE MCCOMB WAS A PEACE CORPS VOLUNTEER IN BURKINA FASO AND GRADUALLY CONCLUDED THAT THE PROGRAMME PLACES LESS EMPHASIS ON DEVELOPMENT THAN ON CULTURAL EXCHANGE, I.E. SHARING AMERICAN CULTURE WITH THE HOST COUNTRY NATIONALS AND THEN SHARING THE CULTURE OF YOUR HOST COUNTRY WITH AMERICANS ON YOUR RETURN:

The cool thing for Americans is that you don't have to be qualified in anything to be accepted by the Peace Corps [PC]. There are many generalist programmes where you can learn what you need to know once you get there through the three-month pre-service training. I would encourage interested parties to be honest about what they can and cannot tolerate since not all volunteers are sent to live in mud huts. In a world changed by terrorism it is comforting to know how much of an active interest the US government takes in the safety and well-being of its citizens abroad. However some people might find this stifling and not adventurous enough. How well PC keeps tabs on volunteers in any given country depends on the local PC leadership but, regardless, you are still in a high-profile group of well-locatable people. Risk reduction is the buzz word in Washington these days.

Overall I am happy with my experience though I am often frustrated by the inertia, the corruption and bureaucracy that make me question whether anything will ever change. But you do gain a lot by (if nothing else) witnessing poverty on a regular basis. You quickly learn to recognise the difference between a problem and an inconvenience and to see how lucky we are as Americans to have some of the 'problems' we have.

MY GROWN UP GAP YEAR:
NEIL MUNRO

After 28 years as a lecturer in Scotland, Neil Munro was reeling from a family act of betrayal and ensuing legal frustrations that had resulted in a nervous breakdown and end to his marriage. An advertisement for 'Year Out Volunteer Placements' caught his eye in a geographic magazine in a doctor's waiting room, so he made contact with Travellers Worldwide and was soon signed up for a placement at Antelope Park in Zimbabwe. His four-month stay there turned out to be therapeutic as well as enjoyable:

A reasonably seasoned traveller, I set off happily enough. But illusions that I had overcome my traumas were soon shattered. Faced with X-ray apparatus and metal detectors at the airport, I froze, speechless and trembling violently. A kindly lady official soothed me with motherly support but my vulnerable condition was confirmed.

Antelope Park covers 3,000 acres of mixed vegetation, some woodland but mostly savannah grassland and spiky acacia bushes, where significant numbers of impala, zebra and wildebeest roam, along with eight giraffes and a family of warthogs. The lion breeding programme at Antelope Park is designed to achieve the release of lions into the wild and has approval from the WWF. Funding is by tourists who pay for activities such as 'Walking with Lions', cub viewing, game viewing, swimming with elephants, horse riding, etc.

To develop familiarity with the bush, the cubs (which have been bred in captivity to guarantee a strong gene pool) are walked free from about six weeks to 18 months old. During these walks they usually stay close to their human companions, viewing humans as senior members of their pride, while soaking up the feel of the bush. These encounters generate mutual interest, with the occasional stalk and chase by the larger cubs, which being well fed, are easily outrun but sometimes kicked by zebra. Learning can be hard!

I was to be working with two of these cubs, Caspar and Cleo. After a fascinating lesson on working with lion cubs, we were joined by some volunteers for my first lion walk, an incredible experience. I also learned that because Caspar and Cleo had had a sadly traumatic start to life, they were the only cubs not to have bonded with any humans, neither guides nor volunteers. This meant that they would not walk normally with the volunteers and my first walks with them were painful indeed. The cubs had to be harried and chased to walk any distance, and at every opportunity would scamper off in different directions, seeking the prickliest areas, then making plaintive calls to each other. Everyone involved became frustrated and before long the volunteers would give up, put down cushions and sit reading while Caspar and Cleo lay re-united under a shady bush.

(Continued)

Unlike the other volunteers, I have children and I think that is why I found the cubs' dependence on and devotion to each other so endearing. Seeing their insecurities as a challenge and wanting to help them, I began to lie with them, keeping my hand as near their noses as possible so they would get used to my smell. I also sat with them in the evenings when Caspar, realising that my legs were softer and warmer than the ground, began to sleep on top of them. Sitting in the dark under an African sky bright with stars with a lion cub on one's bare legs is a wonderful experience. Cleo would lie alongside me and let me stroke her but she was never as affectionate as Caspar.

Normal lion cubs just eat, sleep and play hunting games of ambushing, stalking, tripping and attacking. But Caspar and Cleo had never played so it was particularly rewarding when they began to do so. At last they had thrown off their insecurities to find walking and playing fun. Rehabilitation seemed complete and as the days went by, along with other volunteers, we explored extensively, finding some wonderful trees for the cubs to climb. I also helped the cubs overcome their fear of, and to drink from, the lake; a simple thing but their trust delighted me. Life was good for us all.

Soon bottle feeding Caspar and Cleo ended and it was time to move them to a main enclosure to continue their development. As we strolled across the lawns and footbridge for the last time I was reminded of my feelings when I walked my daughter up the aisle to be married, the same tearful pride filling my heart.

Some days later, having walked Caspar and Cleo, I was returning to camp with one of the volunteers who had become a friend, chatting about music. Spontaneously I found myself talking about my childhood and family, topics I had been unable to speak about for some three years due to my brother's betrayal. I realised that, just like Caspar and Cleo, I had recovered from my traumas - our mutual healing had initiated three new beginnings.

The parting, when it came, was emotional but subdued, my sadness mellowed by my recovery, a need to return home and by my sense of achievement in ridding Caspar and Cleo of their insecurities. Overall my placement was the most incredible experience of my life - a beautiful park, delightful people and wonderful animals. I will remember it all with gratitude and joy for the rest of my life. I have returned a restored individual, but not just restored, also mellowed, contented and optimistic.

PART 5

DIRECTORY OF
SPECIALIST PROGRAMMES

INTRODUCTION
CHOOSING AN AGENCY
DIRECTORY OF SPECIALIST PROGRAMMES
KEY US ORGANISATIONS

INTRODUCTION

Specialist agencies and organisations can arrange the logistics and save you a great deal of time and anxiety. They make placements, provide orientation and sometimes group travel and, crucially, provide back-up, usually in the form of an in-country representative who can sort out problems. Mediating agencies come in all shapes and sizes. Some are ethical non-profit charities that have links with local grassroots projects; some are bastions of the establishment with longstanding programmes in a range of countries. Still others are profit-making companies and are always seeking new projects in developing countries to which they can send paying volunteers. It is not always easy telling the difference between the various types of sending agency.

A plethora of organisations, both charitable and commercial, offers a wide range of packaged possibilities, from work experience placements in US businesses to teaching in Himalayan schools. Many of these organisations focus on the gap year market, targeting school-leavers taking a year off before university. The boom in year-out travel for 18 year-olds heading abroad after doing their A levels has resulted in an explosion of specialist companies. An increasing number of programmes from Siberia to Sulawesi are available to almost anyone able to pay.

Competition among the companies that once targeted school-leavers has become so acute that many of the agencies have been trying to broaden the appeal of their programmes to an older clientele. The directory that follows gives brief details of the programmes offered by companies, agencies and charities that place mature candidates in voluntary positions worldwide, sometimes integrated with language courses, expeditions, diving courses, etc.

With the marked growth in the number of adults undertaking such projects, the mediating agencies are beginning to design programmes for the older age range. There has been a recent tendency for projects of shorter duration, e.g. three to six weeks, to be introduced to cater for the well-heeled older person who does not want to take off more than a few weeks at once. Organisations that started out offering experiences to either adults or students realised that without changing anything except how they package and market their experiences, they can attract another population. It is possible that the majority of participants on a given scheme will be school-leavers which might potentially limit the social pleasures in store for someone wanting to take a career break. Anyone who is concerned about this possibility should simply enquire of the sending agency what the average age and full age range will be on the project that interests him or her. On her otherwise fantastic 14-month gap year, 38-year-old **Debbie Risborough** did not experience the buzz she expected to from a diving expedition she had booked in Fiji:

> *All the other people on the trip were in their gap year prior to uni so I was the odd one out, which I found very difficult. I would have preferred a wider age range in the group. One of the low points was knowing that I was stuck on an island with 15 18-year-olds for company for weeks and weeks and it really didn't matter how nice they all were.*

While 18 is usually quoted as the minimum age, an upper age limit is seldom specified. Even if an agency specifies 30 or 40, these upper limits tend to be flexible and an energetic candidate may have little trouble in being accepted. Most of these programmes are open to anyone with an adventurous spirit, good health, reasonable fitness, a willingness to rough it and enough money to pay for it. Many mature volunteers end up not minding working alongside 18-year-olds as much as they thought they would. **Nigel Hollington** knew that he wouldn't mind since he had always enjoyed the company of young people during his long teaching career. Over the 10 weeks of his wildlife project in Zambia with

Greenforce, differences of age and background seemed to melt away and he enjoyed the company of his 18-year-old roommate Mark. Stereotypes of carefree youth versus cautious middle age were overturned when they set off together to do a bungee jump. Nigel knew that Mark was absolutely terrified but felt that he could help him by remaining calm, so they achieved it together.

Another grown-up gapper, 43-year-old **Paul Edmunds**, worked on the outskirts of Accra in Ghana with mainly gap year students. He feels that the 18-year-olds who choose to do something worthwhile like this are a self-selecting group and tend to be more sensible and plucky than typical 18-year-olds. However because of his age, he did sometimes feel impatient with the emphasis placed by his agency (Travellers Worldwide) on safety and security. Occasionally he found living in a family, who assumed it was their role to act *in loco parentis*, rather claustrophobic and he sometimes regretted that he wasn't able to live independently, kind and welcoming as his host family was. For example he struggled with the Ghanaian diet and sometimes found the meals served by his host inedible, yet it was awkward going out to find a more palatable alternative.

CHOOSING AN AGENCY

Unless you have a reasonably specific plan for your gap year, you can become overwhelmed by the number of possibilities out there. Career gapper **Polly Botsford** has come to distrust the current mantra of extending choice and feels that there are too many destinations and options. '*You have this sense that you want to be original. My approach was to let the plans evolve. I let ideas sit a while and talked to lots of people over the course of about a year.*'

Of course there is no better starting point than this book for providing a survey of the options. The specialist website (www.thecareerbreaksite.com) carries lots of useful information, links and first-hand accounts. The longer established website www.gapyear.com has a special section for 'Career Gappers' (www.gapyear.com/25plus) with links to gap year providers (all listed in this Directory) and some case studies. Although the website, started and still run by Tom Griffiths, was originally aimed only at school-leavers, it has been expanding its provision although the majority of people using the message board are in their 20s. Gapyear.com's main rival on the web is FindaGap.com, although it remains loyal to its original constituency of young gappers.

The non-profit trade association, the Year Out Group (www.yearoutgroup.org) is working towards models of good practice and seeking to maintain high standards of quality among its member agencies. It promotes structured gap years for pre-university students, though many of its founding member companies also accept older participants. Their website contains useful guidelines and questions to ask when comparing providers, most of which are common sense, eg find out whether it is a charity or a profit-making company, look at safety procedures and in-placement support, ask for a breakdown of costs, and so on. The website www.gapadvice.org provides independent and unbiased information, research and advice on gap years for people of all ages, and devotes a section of its site to career breaks.

A growing number of UK organisations make it possible for people of all backgrounds to take a career break of three, six or 12 months volunteering abroad. Each organisation has its own application procedures and it is best to telephone or look to their websites for detailed instructions. Many of these volunteer bodies hold open days when you can meet the permanent staff and hear from former volunteers. People planning a career break might try to visit one of the annual specialised travel shows especially One Life Live held in March in London (www.onelifelive. co.uk) which has a Travel and Career Break zone. This exhibition gives you the chance to talk to companies offering career break travel and listen to specialist talks on the subject.

Lisa Bass describes the process of researching all the good causes that might be able to use her help as a volunteer 'harrowing' (see her case study on p. 6). **Hannah Stevens** wanted to leave her life in London and planned a one-year break which included a volunteering stint in Cambodia through Outreach International:

> *I spent a long time looking for an organisation that fitted my requirements, and when I found it, it just felt right. I passed the interview to see if we could handle living in a Third World country with flying colours, and then sought sponsorship from friends and family. Moving into a village for six months forces a whole new way of thinking, and I have loved adapting myself to those surroundings, and reassessing what is important in life. Whether our being there has done anything, I will never know, but I have giggled and laughed with people who'd never seen white skin, and it's those moments that I'll take with me.*

Practical considerations will revolve around the size of the fee and whether what is included justifies the expense. Usually accommodation will be arranged for you, insurance provided and logistics put in place, all of which is likely to cost several thousand pounds. The publicised fees charged by commercial agencies of £2,500–£3,500 do not generally include airfares from the UK to your destination.

People with a church affiliation and Christian faith have a broader choice of opportunities, since a number of mission societies and charities are looking for Christians. Whereas some religious organisations focus on practical work, such as working with street children, orphans, in schools, building libraries, etc., others are predominantly proselytising, which will only appeal to the very committed. Potential volunteers should be wary of joining a group that advocates a cultural or religious superiority or acts insensitively to local customs.

When trying to differentiate among gap year providers, the guidelines provided on www.gapyear-research.org/ethicalvolunteering.htm or www.ethicalvolunteering.org might prove helpful. The academic Kate Simpson, who is behind both websites, has compiled a searching list of questions under the heading 'How to be an ethical volunteer: picking the worthwhile from the worthless'. A good organisation should be able to tell an applicant exactly what work they will be doing and precise contact details for the overseas project. Assuming you care about such things (and even if you don't beforehand, you probably will after spending some time in a developing country), ask the company what financial contribution they make to the voluntary project. Some gap year companies wait until a paying customer has signed up before finding a placement abroad and these are often less satisfactory. Increasingly sending agencies are aware of the pitfalls and try to address them, primarily by being transparent about how the fees are spent. They aim to match volunteers' skills to community needs on sustainable projects on which volunteers work alongside, and not instead of, local people.

PERSONAL CONSULTATIONS

Trawling through books and websites may not be enough for some people who seek personal reassurance and expert advice. Several one-person businesses offer private consultations to anyone considering taking a grown-up gap year. **Tessa Mills** took her own adventurous gap year (see her case history on p. 25) which inspired her to set up the Gap Year Guru (www. theGapYearGuru.com) in 2007/8. Prospective clients can book a free 15-minute phone consultation and then proceed to more intensive coaching and advisory sessions, when client-specific recommendations and practical help will be given.

Similarly **Gillian Woodward** in her 60s did a solo round-the-world trip visiting 32 countries over three years and now works as a travel mentor, providing travel counselling to anyone who wishes to talk through a planned journey.

Career Break Coaching is a specialised service to assist people who want to take a sabbatical or gap year. **Kate Nelson** has been involved in coaching for many years and has also travelled the world and aims to support people in their quest for a fulfilling gap year.

The Gap Year Guru – Worlds End Studios, 132–134 Lots Road, Chelsea, London SW10 0RJ; ☎ 020 7193 8352; info@theGapYearGuru.com; www.theGapYearGuru.com. New business established in 2007/8. Hourly individual one-to-one consultations from £75 for the first hour.

TravelMentor – Gillian Woodward; ☎ 020 7221 4587/ mobile 07906 099535; Gillian.woodward@talk21.com; www.nottinghill counselling.co.uk. £55–£75 for a one-hour session.

Career Break Coach – Want More Coaching Limited, Hergest Ridge, Bishopstone, Wiltshire SN6 8PP; ☎ 07812 021438; katenelson@aol.com; www.careerbreakcoach.com. Usual consultation fee is £60.

CAREERS TEACHER TURNED VOLUNTEER

Because of the glut of year-out provision, it is possible to join interesting projects at short notice. Long-time teacher **Nigel Hollington** decided that the time had come for him to take a year out of teaching. After negotiating with his headteacher, who promised to keep a teaching job open for him in his Hertfordshire comprehensive where he was a valued member of staff, Nigel's first step was to rent out his house which would force him into action. Usually the expression 'burning your boats' means cutting yourself off, destroying your means of escape. But in the context of taking a major step such as deciding to rent out your house to finance some serious travels or volunteer projects, it can mean exactly the opposite. Paradoxically you might have to burn your boats (give up your job, move out of your house) to catch a boat to freedom and adventure.

Nigel had no fixed ideas of what he wanted to do or where he wanted to go, although he knew he wanted to fill the year with constructive things. By November, only a few weeks before he had to give up his house, he still had nothing fixed up and began to take a closer interest in the literature that passed through his hands in the careers' room at school. Greenforce's details caught his eye and he was impressed with their projects. He had an open mind about destinations and was soon signed up for the first expedition they had available, a 10-week conservation project in Zambia. Organisations whose literature contains dire warnings of the consequences of procrastination often have last-minute vacancies, so it is worth ringing around whenever you decide you want to go for it.

DIRECTORY OF SPECIALIST PROGRAMMES

The Directory *sets out the programmes of charities and companies that are equipped to arrange all or part of a gap year. Organisations that specialise in placing North American volunteers are listed at the end of this chapter, though some US organisations (like Travel Alive in Nicaragua) welcome all nationalities onto their programmes.*

2WAY DEVELOPMENT
2Way space, 1–4 Pope Street, London SE1 3PR, UK
- 020 7378 9600
- volunteer@2way.org.uk
- www.2way.org.uk

PROGRAMME DESCRIPTION: 2Way Development arranges skilled, long-term volunteer placements within local not-for-profit organisations in the developing world that work in pursuit of sustainable development and social justice. Skills and desires of volunteers are matched with areas of need within local development-related charities. Volunteers are looking to gain experience in international development, or expanding their skills by taking a career break.
DESTINATIONS: Africa, Asia, Latin America.
NUMBER OF PLACEMENTS PER YEAR: 100.
PREREQUISITES: Nationalities include British, American, Canadian, Australian and New Zealand. Average age 28. Educational and/or professional background in a skill (not specified) is needed.
DURATION AND TIME OF PLACEMENTS: 3–24 months (6 months average).
SELECTION PROCEDURES AND ORIENTATION: Interviews not essential, but informal interviews and event days are held every month in central London, where volunteers can meet staff to evaluate their decision.
OTHER SERVICES: Volunteers are supported while preparing for their placement before leaving home, e.g. you are provided with a training manual and given assistance with visa preparation. Other training courses can be recommended on request.
COST: £850.
CONTACT: Katherine Tubb, Director.

ADVENTURE ALTERNATIVE
PO Box 14, Portstewart, Northern Ireland BT55 7WS, UK
- /fax: +44 (0)2870 831258
- office@adventurealternative.com
- www.adventurealternative.com

Three-month programmes primarily for gap year students, career breakers, medical students or medical professionals in Kenya and Nepal.
PROGRAMME DESCRIPTION: Combine 8–12 weeks of teaching/community/charity or medical work, group activities (e.g. climbing, trekking, rafting, safaris) and independent travel. In Kenya participants teach and work in clinics and primary education in rural and slum schools or in an orphanage. In Nepal, participants help to build a village school or work in a Kathmandu primary school. Medical electives also available for doctors or student doctors.
DESTINATIONS: Rural Kenya and Himalayan Nepal.
NUMBER OF PLACEMENTS PER YEAR: 30 for Kenya, 30 for Nepal.
PREREQUISITES: Hard-working, committed, enthusiastic volunteers who are not fazed by the hardships of living in a developing country. All nationalities and ages welcome.
DURATION AND TIME OF PLACEMENTS: 8–12 weeks, but can be flexible.
COST: From £1,250 (includes food and accommodation) plus £300 in-country expenses (email, telephone, souvenirs) plus £600 for flights, insurance and other necessities.
CONTACT: Gavin Bate, Director; Chris Little/Andy MacDonald, Expedition Co-ordinators.

AFRICAN CONSERVATION EXPERIENCE
PO Box 206, Faversham, Kent ME13 8WZ, UK
- 0870 241 5816
- info@ConservationAfrica.net
- www.ConservationAfrica.net

PROGRAMME DESCRIPTION: Conservation work placements on game reserves in Southern Africa. Tasks may include darting a rhino for relocation, or an elephant for fitting tracking collars. Game capture, tagging, assisting with veterinary work, game counts and monitoring may be part of the work programme. Alien plant control and the re-introduction of indigenous plants are often involved.

DESTINATIONS: Southern Africa including South Africa, Botswana, Namibia and Zimbabwe.

PREREQUISITES: Reserves open to people of all ages who have reasonable physical fitness and ability to cope mentally. Enthusiasm for conservation is essential. Specific projects are run for 'grown-ups', which allow for better social interaction within the group.

DURATION AND TIME OF PLACEMENTS: 2–12 weeks throughout the year.

SELECTION PROCEDURES AND ORIENTATION: Candidates are matched to a suitable project on the information provided on their application form, but do have final say on their choice of project. Optional open days are held at various locations in the UK.

COST: Varies depending on specific reserve and time of year. Students can expect an average total cost of about £2,900 for 4 weeks, and up to £4,900 for 12 weeks, which includes international flights (from London), transfers, accommodation and all meals. Support and advice given on fundraising.

CONTACT: Alexia Massey, Logistics Manager.

AFRICA SABBATICAL
92 Kenilworth Avenue, Reading RG30 3DW, UK
- info@africasabbatical.com
- www.africasabbatical.com

PROGRAMME DESCRIPTION: Offers students and professionals volunteer activities in the fields of education, medicine, law or the media. Placements are found to match the requirements specified by prospective volunteers.

DESTINATIONS: Ghana, South Africa, Botswana, Malawi and Tanzania.

NUMBER OF PLACEMENTS PER YEAR: 100.

DURATION AND TIME OF PLACEMENTS: 4 months (on average).

PREREQUISITES: Average age of participants is 32. All nationalities accepted. Professional postings require suitable background (mostly medical). For other placements enthusiasm and commitment are needed.

SELECTION PROCEDURES AND ORIENTATION: Applications should be sent at least 3 months before departure. Candidates go through interviews, assessment, vetting and pre-departure processes. A full day pre-departure course addresses host country cultural values (dos and don'ts), security, politics, legislation, relationships, health issues, travelling and finances.

COST: About £2,500 including flights, accommodation, food, transfers and coordinator fees. Choice of accommodation

offered, from traditional housing to properties with modern facilities.

CONTACT: Harry Agyeman, Director.

AIDCAMPS INTERNATIONAL
483 Green Lanes, London N13 4BS, UK
- 0845 652 5412
- info@aidcamps.org
- www.aidcamps.org

PROGRAMME DESCRIPTION: Teams of volunteers of all ages work with partner non-governmental organisations (NGOs) on a range of projects, such as building rural primary schools and resource centres. Individual AidCamps placements are also available in conservation work, village water projects, teaching, etc.

DESTINATIONS: India, Nepal, Sri Lanka and Cameroon.

PREREQUISITES: Average age of volunteers is 40. If someone has particular skills/interests to offer, AidCamps will liaise with partner NGOs to arrange an appropriate individual placement.

DURATION AND TIME OF PLACEMENTS: Mainly short-term projects lasting 3 weeks. A longer term scheme called 'Individual AidCamps' is suitable for older gappers. Average duration of 5 weeks, but can be between 1 week and several months.

COST: Team participants pay £595 for 3 weeks, nearly three-quarters of which goes directly to the aid project. Homestay accommodation for individual AidCamps costs roughly £35–£50 per week.

CONTACT: Marios Cleovoulou, Founder and Managing Trustee.

ALL AFRICA VENTURES
Box 2031, Jeffreys Bay, 6331, South Africa
- +27 836 615 393; fax: +27 866 228 159
- allafricavolunteers@gmail.com
- www.allafricavolunteers.com

PROGRAMME DESCRIPTION: All Africa Volunteers assists the Animal Rehabilitation Centre between Port Elizabeth and Jeffreys Bay, with daily care and funding to feed and care for stranded and injured animals. There is a breeding programme for endangered species such as cheetah, blue duiker and servels, and a community project that operates in the surfing town of Jeffreys Bay.

DESTINATIONS: South Africa.

NUMBER OF PLACEMENTS PER YEAR: 50–100.

DURATION AND TIME OF PLACEMENTS: 1–3 months.

PREREQUISITES: Average age 18–35. All nationalities accepted. No specific qualifications needed, only life skills.

SELECTION PROCEDURES AND ORIENTATION: Applications due at least six weeks in advance of arrival.

COST: Varies with programme. Volunteer fee covers meals, lodging and programme sponsorship. Accommodation is provided in beach lodge (for community project) or log cabins in game area (for wildlife project).

CONTACT: Tyron van Tonder, Company Owner.

AMANZI TRAVEL

4 College Road, Westbury on Trym, Bristol BS9 3EJ, UK

℡ 0117 904 1924; fax: 0117 959 4678

✉ info@amanzitravel.co.uk

🖥 www.amanzitravel.co.uk

PROGRAMME DESCRIPTION: Worthwhile volunteer placements throughout Africa that provide opportunities to help conserve endangered wildlife, work on teaching and community development projects, and help at medical clinics and hospitals. Sample projects include working with big cats or at the first Lion Breeding/Release Project at Victoria Falls, helping at the Bushman Medical Clinic in Namibia, or looking after Aids orphans in Cape Town. Other projects include teaching disadvantaged children in schools in Zambia or Tanzania, coaching the local children's football team in Mozambique and helping with marine conservation along the Garden Route. Also offers a range of adventure activities and courses including learning to be a field guide or game ranger.

DESTINATIONS: Botswana, Kenya, Mozambique, Namibia, South Africa, Tanzania, Uganda, Zambia and Zimbabwe.

NUMBER OF PLACEMENTS PER YEAR: 200.

DURATION AND TIME OF PLACEMENTS: 2–12 weeks, with flexible start dates.

PREREQUISITES: All ages, including lots of people taking a career break, some mature volunteers and gap year students.

SELECTION PROCEDURES AND ORIENTATION: Comprehensive pre-departure pack and full orientation on arrival.

OTHER SERVICES: Help given with organising flights and travel insurance.

COST: From £400.

CONTACT: Gemma Whitehouse, Managing Director.

AVIF (ABLE VOLUNTEERS INTERNATIONAL FUND)

AVIF (UK) Fair Mount, Hartwith Avenue, Summerbridge, North Yorkshire HG3 4HT, UK

℡ 0777 171 2012

✉ volunteer@avif.org.uk

🖥 www.avif.org.uk

PROGRAMME DESCRIPTION: Assistance given to committed volunteers who want to work in rural Kenya. Summer placements are usually in or near primary or secondary schools that have requested volunteer participation.

DESTINATIONS: Kenya.

NUMBER OF PLACEMENTS PER YEAR: Up to 35 volunteers for 300+ children in 5 venues per summer.

PREREQUISITES: Enthusiasm, tolerance and dedication. Background in education would be helpful but even fully qualified teachers sometimes lack the necessary tolerance for work in Kenya.

DURATION AND TIME OF PLACEMENTS: 4-week placement in July/August following orientation.

SELECTION PROCEDURES AND ORIENTATION: Deadline for applications is June. Online interviews conducted via email and Skype.

OTHER SERVICES: At the end of each programme, AVIF organises an optional group safari from a base camp in Oropile, Maasai Mara, or a climb of Kilimanjaro with an experienced guide, Mary Kariuki.

COST: International airfares plus subsistence, e.g. £25 per fortnight.

CONTACT: Ms Alison Lowndes, Founder Trustee. Further information about AVIF can be found on Facebook, flickr and on the websites of associated hosts in Kenya.

AZAFADY

Studio 7, 1A Beethoven Street, London W10 4LG, UK

℡ 020 8960 6629; fax: 020 8962 0126

✉ info@azafady.org

🖥 www.madagascar.co.uk

PROGRAMME DESCRIPTION: Azafady is a UK-registered charity and Malagasy NGO providing opportunities to work with a grassroots organisation tackling conservation issues and extreme poverty in Madagascar. Working closely with local communities, volunteers on the Pioneer Programme take part in a range of practical construction work, conservation research and educational activities. The Lemur Venture scheme provides opportunities to study wild lemurs and their natural habitat. Programme particularly suited to adults interested in development and ecology (who may be looking for experience as an entry point into an ethical career, or who simply want to make a difference and have a meaningful career break experience).

DESTINATIONS: Southeast Madagascar.

NUMBER OF PLACEMENTS PER YEAR: 10–20 per group, 4 groups per year.

PREREQUISITES: Enthusiasm and cultural sensitivity. All ages welcome; average age range 18–70. Training given. Volunteers learn basic Malagasy so that they may work together with members of rural communities and gain a unique insight into the culture.

DURATION AND TIME OF PLACEMENTS: 4–10 weeks starting in January, April, July and October.

COST: Successful applicants pay for pre-project costs such as flight, insurance and visa, and are required to raise a minimum donation of £1,600–£2,200 dependent on project and duration. Applicants are provided with extensive fundraising resources and advice.

CONTACT: Claire Webber, Volunteer Coordinator.

BASE BACKPACKER HOSTELS

PO Box 5188, Wellesley Street, Auckland, New Zealand

+64 9 358 4877; fax: +64 9 358 4872

info@stayatbase.com

www.stayatbase.com

PROGRAMME DESCRIPTION: A network of superior, centrally located backpacker hostels in New Zealand, offering good value and quality local experiences. Beds are available for every budget and one-stop-shop services for travellers of all ages that include expert travel centres, New Zealand Job Search services, high speed wireless internet cafés and bars. New Zealand Job Search (www.nzjs.co.nz) is located in Base Auckland Central Backpackers (ACB) (Level 3, 229 Queen Street; 09 357 3996; info@nzjs.co.nz) and operates as a Job Agency for those on working holiday visas.

DESTINATIONS: Hostels throughout New Zealand including Auckland, Bay of Islands, Rotorua, Taupo, Wellington, Christchurch, Queenstown and Wanaka.

PREREQUISITES: Working holiday visa necessary to use New Zealand Job Search (unlimited number of visas valid for up to 23 months available for UK nationals aged 18–30).

COST: Starter pack includes 12 months' registration with Job Search, airport pick-up, two nights accommodation on arrival, etc for NZ$345.

BASE CAMP GROUP

30 Baseline Business Studios, Whitchurch Road, London W11 4AT, UK

/fax: 020 7243 6222

contact@basecampgroup.com

www.basecampgroup.com

Adventure training specialist company.

PROGRAMME DESCRIPTION: Instructor Courses and Performance Camps in snow, water and adrenaline sports including skiing, snowboarding, windsurfing, kitesurfing, surfing, diving, mountain biking, water-skiing and wakeboarding, paramotoring and skydiving.

DESTINATIONS: Diverse range of locations in the UK, Europe, North America and Australasia. For snow sports: Meribel and Val d'Isère (France), Whistler, Kicking Horse and Banff (Canada) and Queenstown (New Zealand). For water sports: Dahab (Egypt) and Cornwall (UK). For adrenaline sports: Whistler (Canada) and Figueres (Spain).

DURATION AND TIME OF PLACEMENTS: 2–11 weeks.

QUALIFICATIONS OFFERED. For snow sports: BASI in Europe, CSIA/CASI in North America and NZSIA in New Zealand. For water sports: Professional Association of Diving Instructors (PADI), BSA, BWS and IKO. For adrenaline sports: BMAA and PMBI.

NUMBER OF PLACEMENTS PER YEAR: 300.

PREREQUISITES: Course specific (see website).

COST: £300–£800 per week depending on length of programme and nature of sport. Usually includes all local requirements such as accommodation, food, coaching, exams, but not flights.

CONTACT: Alex Berman, Course Adviser.

BIOSEARCH EXPEDITIONS

Waytarer Lodge, Welbourn, Lincolnshire LN5 0QH, UK

01400 273323; fax: 01400 273003

expeditions@biosearch.org.uk

www.biosearch.org.uk

PROGRAMME DESCRIPTION: Expeditions to track and record game in the Nyika National Park of Malawi to build up a biodiversity index for the park, in cooperation with Malawi Department of National Parks & Wildlife and other institutions.

DESTINATIONS: Malawi. Preparatory weekend courses held at Hilltop Farm, Lincolnshire.

NUMBER OF PLACEMENTS PER YEAR: 25. Plus more attend weekend training camps in the UK.

PREREQUISITES: All nationalities accepted. Ages range from university students up to 70. Biosearch is actively encouraging more mature team members with established amateur and professional skills. Training weekends require no qualifications, just the desire to learn about adventure travel and bush living. Candidates for expeditions should have an inclination to natural history and conservation.

DURATION AND TIME OF PLACEMENTS: Standard 1-month expeditions in March and July. 2-day training weekends in the UK are open to all (whether or not they join a team in Malawi).
SELECTION PROCEDURES AND ORIENTATION: 48-hour training weekends held before expedition departures (see website for details).
OTHER SERVICES: Training continues on arrival in the bush. Accommodation in small tents on expedition, otherwise comfortable.
COST: £2,500 for African expedition.
CONTACT: Peter Overton, Project Director.

BIOSPHERE EXPEDITIONS
The Henderson Centre, Ivy Road, Norwich NR5 8BF, UK
℃ 0870 446 0801; fax: 0870 446 0809
✍ uk@biosphere-expeditions.org
⌨ www.biosphere-expeditions.org

PROGRAMME DESCRIPTION: Biosphere Expeditions is a non-profit-making organisation, offering hands-on wildlife conservation expeditions to all who seek adventure with a purpose. Volunteers with no research experience assist scientific experts.
Number of placements: 200–300.
DESTINATIONS: Worldwide, e.g. last year animal-monitoring projects included a climate change expedition to the Pyrenees, snow leopards in the Altai Republic of Central Asia, wolves and bears in Slovakia, cheetahs in Namibia, marine mammals in the Azores, coral reefs in Honduras, Arabian leopards in Oman, and pumas and jaguars in Brazil.
DURATION AND TIME OF PLACEMENTS: 11 days to 2 months, starting year round.
PREREQUISITES: No special skills or fitness required to join, and no age limit whatsoever.
COST: £990–£1,480 (excluding flights) for fortnight long expeditions. At least two-thirds of contributions benefit local project directly.

BLUE VENTURES
52 Avenue Road, London N6 5DR, UK
℃ 020 8341 9819
✍ enquiries@blueventures.org
⌨ www.blueventures.org

PROGRAMME DESCRIPTION: Volunteers needed for award-winning marine conservation project. Blue Ventures conducts marine research, coral reef conservation and grassroots conservation in south-west Madagascar. Volunteers participate in all research programmes and day-to-day management of field camps. Non-diving conservation work might involve cetacean surveys, accompanying local fishermen or beach clean-up operations. The Blue Ventures volunteer programme has been awarded a number of international responsible tourism awards and has pioneered successful conservation efforts in Madagascar.
DESTINATIONS: The village of Andavadoaka in south-west Madagascar has been the Blue Ventures expedition site since 2003. Blue Ventures has also coordinated marine projects in Tanzania, New Zealand, South Africa and the Comoros Islands.
PREREQUISITES: No diving or scientific background required as all necessary training is provided on site. The Blue Ventures international team of volunteers comprises all ages and walks of life.
DURATION AND TIME OF PLACEMENTS: Typical stay of 6 weeks, although shorter and longer stays are available.
COST: £2,100 for 6 weeks for volunteers requiring dive training; £1,900 for PADI Advanced divers or equivalent. Volunteers will be expected to provide personal diving kit (i.e. mask, snorkel, wet-suit, fins), torch, sleeping bag, malaria prophylactics, inoculations and flights. After the initial six weeks, the first three additional weeks are charged at a cost of £250 per week and £200 per week thereafter.
CONTACT: Richard Nimmo, Managing Director or Rajah Roy, Operations Manager.

THE BRITISH INSTITUTE OF FLORENCE
Piazza Strozzi 2, 50123 Florence, Italy
℃ +39 055 26 77 81
✍ info@britishinstitute.it
⌨ www.britishinstitute.it

Housed in two magnificent buildings on either side of the River Arno in the heart of the historic centre of Florence, and minutes from all the city's museums, galleries and churches, the British Institute of Florence has a long tradition of excellence in its teaching.
PROGRAMME DESCRIPTION: The Institute offers students the opportunity of experiencing the life and culture of Florence within the framework of a structured programme of study. Courses are offered in Italian language, history of art and life drawing, and some can be combined (excluding the short intensive History of Art courses). A regular programme of events including lectures, concerts and films, is held in the Institute's Harold Acton Library overlooking the River Arno.
Duration and time of courses: 1–12 weeks throughout the year.
COST: Fees vary according to the course chosen, e.g. a 4-week Italian language course costs €630, 4-week History of Art course costs €595 and 4-week combined Italian and History of Art course costs €1150.

ACCOMMODATION: Can be arranged in local homes, *pensioni* and hotels. Price for homestay accommodation starts at approximately €30 per night. There is a fee of €25 for arranging accommodation.

Founding member of the Year Out Group. BUNAC is a non-profit national student club offering worldwide work and travel programmes BUNAC also operates programmes for older participants.

PROGRAMME DESCRIPTION: Work New Zealand and Work Canada are open to 18–30 or 35 year-old UK passport holders. These flexible working visas exclusive to BUNAC, allow participants to work anywhere in that country and work does not have to be pre-arranged. Each cost-effective BUNAC programme provides full support before, on arrival and throughout the year; full visa processing and flexible flight options.

DESTINATIONS: Canada and New Zealand (plus other countries for younger travellers).

PREREQUISITES: Ages 18–30 /35 depending on visa. Work Exchange visa for New Zealand is open to people who have previously held a New Zealand working holiday visa.

DURATION AND TIME OF PLACEMENTS: 1–12 months.

COST: £5 BUNAC membership fee, plus programme fee of £429 for New Zealand (plus £50 or £80 for visa) and £175 registration fee for Canada.

Provider of language courses worldwide. In Latin America courses can be combined with volunteering placements. Cactus also acts as a business language and Teaching English as a Foreign Language (TEFL) training consultancy.

VOLUNTEER DESTINATIONS: Guatemala, Costa Rica, Peru, Ecuador, Bolivia, Brazil, Argentina, Chile and Mexico.

LANGUAGE COURSE DESTINATIONS: Language courses in Germany, France, Spain, Italy, Greece, Russia, China and more than 30 other countries.

PREREQUISITES: All ages and nationalities welcome.

DURATION AND TIME OF PLACEMENTS: Combination language and volunteer programme in Latin America: standard 4-week language course followed by 4 weeks volunteering but duration is flexible. Language courses from 1 week. TEFL courses are usually 4 weeks.

COST: From £999 for 12 weeks in Guatemala. Language course and TEFL training course costs searchable on Cactus website.

OTHER SERVICES: Admissions service and impartial advice given on recognised TEFL training courses such as the Cambridge CELTA and Trinity CertTESOL, as well as courses for experienced teachers, teachers of other languages and non-native teachers of English.

CALEDONIA LANGUAGES ABROAD

The Clockhouse, 72 Newhaven Road, Edinburgh EH6 5QG, Scotland

☎ 0131 621 7721/2; fax: 0131 555 6262

✉ courses@caledonialanguages.co.uk

🖥 www.caledonialanguages.com

Established in 1994, Caledonia's main focus is arranging language, culture and adventure travel abroad.

PROGRAMME DESCRIPTION: Caledonia offer short and long term language courses with accommodation (usually homestay, but other options are available) throughout Europe and Latin America. They also arrange volunteer work placements in Latin America, work experience programmes, language + activity courses (e.g. Spanish + dance in Spain, Cuba, Argentina and the Dominican Republic, Spanish + trekking in Cuba and Brazil, French + sailing in Nice) and language + learning courses (e.g. Italian + History of Art in San Giovanni, or French + cooking in Aix-en-Provence). Volunteer community projects in Latin America for language clients include: working with street children in Maceio, Brazil; conservation in the cloud forests of Costa Rica; a psychiatric hospital in Bolivia; kindergarten in Peru; or teaching English in Ecuador. Work experience programmes are also available working with partner language schools, companies and organisations, according to the client's skills and experience.

DESTINATIONS: Caledonia's partner language schools are in France, Spain, Portugal, Italy, Germany, Austria, Russia, Argentina,

Peru, Chile, Bolivia, Ecuador, Costa Rica, Brazil, Mexico, Dominican Republic and Guadeloupe. Cuba is one of Caledonia's main destinations; tailormade programmes can be made to suit individual requirements, with or without a language course.

PREREQUISITES: Complete beginner to advanced learners are catered for. A higher level of Spanish or Portuguese is needed to work on volunteer and work experience programmes.

DURATION OF COURSES: Minimum 1 week (or 3–4 weeks if combined with volunteer placement) up to 12 months. Classes start year round.

SELECTION PROCEDURES AND ORIENTATION: For volunteer and work experience programmes, a short language course is taken before work can begin, for cultural and linguistic familiarisation. Briefing meetings on the proposed work and occasionally pre-placement site visits are arranged. Full back-up support is given by the language school once in-country.

COST: Volunteers and work experience applicants must pay an arrangement fee of £250 plus VAT, fees for the pre-placement language course in the overseas country (e.g. £735 for four weeks in Peru or Ecuador with half-board accommodation), plus travel. Accommodation is with local families.

CAMP AMERICA

37a Queen's Gate, London SW7 5HR, UK

☎ 020 7581 7373

✉ enquiries@campamerica.co.uk

🖥 www.campamerica.co.uk

PROGRAMME DESCRIPTION: Camp America has been placing people from Europe, Asia, Africa, Australia and New Zealand on American summer camps for 44 years. Camp counsellors look after the children and/or teach sports activities, music, arts, drama and dance, etc.

DESTINATIONS: Throughout the USA.

NUMBER OF PLACEMENTS PER YEAR: 7,000+.

PREREQUISITES: Camp America is looking to recruit skilled adults for a variety of job choices. Experience in sport coaching, religious counselling, teaching, childcare, health care and lifeguarding is preferable.

DURATION AND TIME OF PLACEMENTS: Must be willing to depart between 1 May and 27 June for a minimum of 9 weeks. Up to 10 weeks of travel time available between camp and visa expiry at the end of October.

SELECTION PROCEDURES AND ORIENTATION: Face-to-face interview with locally appointed Camp America interviewer. Also Camp America host recruitment fairs allowing participants to meet and interview with Camp Directors from a variety of summer camps in London, Manchester, Edinburgh and Belfast in the late winter. Selectors aim to evaluate applicants' background, training and main skill areas to make suitable placements. Personal interview at US Embassy also required. Early application is advised.

COST: Medical insurance and application fees apply. All programmes offer free return flights from London and other selected international airports to New York, along with transfer to the camp, free accommodation and meals, up to 10 weeks of travel time after camp duties, Cultural Exchange US visa sponsorship, 24-hour support, medical insurance and pocket money which ranges from $525 to $1,375 (depending on age, experience and kind of counsellor).

PROGRAMME DESCRIPTION: The 'Life' programme incorporates a range of responsible travel experiences, consisting of community and conservation volunteer opportunities in east Africa. Placements include a healthy mixture of volunteer work with optional safaris and adventure challenges, including opportunities to climb Mount Kenya, Mount Meru or Mount Kilimanjaro and also take part in some diving on the coast.

DESTINATIONS: Kenya and Tanzania.

DURATION AND TIME OF PLACEMENTS: 1–4 weeks, year round.

COST: 4 weeks from £1,627.

CONTACT: Michelle Tutt, Expedition Coordinator.

COURSES OFFERED: Beginner, intermediate and advanced courses in French (Cannes, Nice, Montpellier, Tours, Bordeaux,

Paris, or for a more exotic option, Guadeloupe), Spanish (Seville, Nerja, Salamanca, Malaga or Madrid in Spain, plus Argentina, Chile, Mexico, Costa Rica or Ecuador), German (Berlin, Lindau, Munich, Cologne or Vienna in Austria), Italian (Florence, Rome, San Giovanni, Sorrento, Siena and Viareggio), Portuguese, Chinese, Russian, Greek and Arabic (in Morocco). Courses for mature students (50+) in Spain and France: Italian/Spanish/French + cookery; German or Spanish + skiing; Spanish + diving/surfing; French + surfing/sailing.

DURATION OF COURSES: 1–48 weeks with possibility of studying in more than one location during a year-out programme. At least one start date per month year round. Set dates apply to Language plus Activities or Mature Student programmes.

QUALIFICATIONS OFFERED: DELE preparation offered in Spain; DELF, Alliance Francaise and CCIP exams in France; TRKI exams in Russia. Full range of exams including the Z Daf exam offered in Germany and Austria.

COST: Languages for Life 16-week course in Seville or Madrid costs from £2,949 including shared apartment accommodation and 20 hours' tuition per week. A 12-week course with college residence accommodation and 20 lessons a week in Nice costs from £2,563.

ACCOMMODATION: Options include student apartments or residences, on-campus accommodation, host families, sole-occupancy apartments and hotels.

CHALLENGES WORLDWIDE
54 Manor Place, Edinburgh EH3 7EH, Scotland
℡ 0845 200 0342; fax: 0131 225 9549
✉ info@challengesworldwide.com
🖥 www.challengesworldwide.com

Challenges Worldwide (CWW), is expert in placing business professionals as volunteers in international development opportunities overseas. Volunteers skilled in core business areas are placed with local partner organisations to help strengthen their ways of working and focus on developing better education, health, livelihoods and environments.

PROGRAMME DESCRIPTION: Placements last 3 or 6 months and address issues such as management (project management, human resources, etc.), strategy, finance, research, monitoring and evaluation, social development, education and human rights issues. CWW matches your skills and experience to the needs of its partners to ensure your work is as sustainable as possible.

DESTINATIONS: Bangladesh, Belize, India, Sri Lanka, St Lucia, South Africa, Ghana.

NUMBER OF PLACEMENTS PER YEAR: 100.

PREREQUISITES: Average age is late 20s although volunteers can be aged 18–65. Volunteers need to have some level of relevant education or life/work experience (some placements require less experience than others).

DURATION AND TIME OF PLACEMENTS: 3 or 6 months. Recruitment takes place all year round.

SELECTION PROCEDURES AND ORIENTATION: Applicants are invited to attend a face-to-face interview in the UK and comprehensive pre-departure preparation and training session. Full mentor support provided by CWW UK operations manager as well as local placement leader in-country throughout placement.

COST: Placement fees are £2,500 for 3 months, £3,500 for 6 months. Placement fee covers accommodation, food, insurance, pre-departure training, recruitment costs, volunteer appraisal and support system while overseas, CV and debrief upon return.

CHANGING WORLDS
11 Doctors Lane, Chaldon, Surrey CR3 5AE, UK
℡ 01883 340960
✉ ask@changingworlds.co.uk
🖥 www.changingworlds.co.uk

Member of the Year Out Group. Small family-run company that aims to provide individual attention and full cultural immersion through challenging and worthwhile work placements with a safety net if required. Air Travel Organisers' Licensing (ATOL) Licence 6885.

PROGRAMME DESCRIPTION: Voluntary work placements in schools, journalism, hospitals, legal firms, orphanages, zoos, etc., and paid work placements in hotels and hospitality.

DESTINATIONS: Argentina, China, Dubai, Ghana, Honduras, India, Kenya, Latvia, Madagascar, New Zealand, Romania, Serbia and Thailand.

NUMBER OF PLACEMENTS PER YEAR: 120.

PREREQUISITES: Must have initiative, determination, adaptability and social skills, plus skills relevant to the job if possible. Open to all ages except paid work places in New Zealand, which are open to candidates under 30. Volunteers to Argentina and Honduras are expected to know or learn Spanish.

DURATION AND TIME OF PLACEMENTS: 3, 6 or 9 months. Placements begin throughout the year.

SELECTION PROCEDURES AND ORIENTATION: Interview days held in Surrey every 6–8 weeks. All participants attend a pre-

departure briefing; for those going to a developing country, this is a 2-day residential course. Participants are met on arrival in-country and attend orientation with the local representative before proceeding to placement. Local representatives act as support during placement. Changing Worlds is a member of Interhealth, which can provide health screening to all participants and act as travel health advisers.
COST: From £1,995 for 6 months in Dubai and £2,145 for 3 months in Latvia. Prices include return flights but exclude insurance (approximately £260 for 6 months) and in some cases food.
CONTACT: David Gill, Director.

CORAL CAY CONSERVATION
Elizabeth House, 39 York Road, London SE1 7NQ, UK
℗ 020 7620 1411; fax: 020 7921 0469
⊕ info@coralcay.org
💻 www.coralcay.org

Founding member of the Year Out Group. Hundreds of volunteers participate in Coral Cay expeditions every year to assist in conserving fragile tropical marine and terrestrial environments, building local capacity to protect these ecosystems in the long term.
PROGRAMME DESCRIPTION: The overall aim of Coral Cay Conservation is to train local communities and volunteers to understand the scientific, economic and social value of protecting rainforests and reefs, to maintain ecological biodiversity and promote long-term sustainability. The expeditions aim to help gather scientific data for the protection and sustainable use of tropical resources, and to provide alternative livelihood opportunities for local communities.
DESTINATIONS: Currently a small island in the Philippines called Leyte, on the Caribbean coast of Tobago and the tropical rainforest of Papua New Guinea.
NUMBER OF PLACEMENTS PER YEAR: 200–500.
PREREQUISITES: No previous experience is required. Volunteers come from a diverse range of backgrounds, ages and cultures. Scuba dive training is available up to PADI Dive Master level.
DURATION AND TIME OF PLACEMENTS: Expeditions depart monthly throughout the year. Volunteers stay for 1–16 weeks or longer.
COST: Sample prices £1,540 for 4 weeks as a dive trainee and £3,520 for 12 weeks if a qualified diver. Prices vary according to length of stay, type of project and level of training required. Prices exclude flights and insurance; fundraising advice is given.

COSMIC VOLUNTEERS
PO Box 11738, Philadelphia, Pennsylvania 19101, USA
℗ +1 610 279 2052
⊕ info@cosmicvolunteers.org
💻 www.cosmicvolunteers.org

Tax-exempt charity (33 0998120). Sending volunteers abroad since 2001.
PROGRAMME DESCRIPTION: Volunteering, internships and specialist travel programmes in developing countries. Volunteer programme includes teaching, medicine, orphanages, journalism, social work, HIV/Aids, environment, sports, organic farming and turtle conservation.
DESTINATIONS: China, Ecuador, Ghana, Guatemala, India, Kenya, Nepal, Peru, Philippines, South Africa, Thailand and Vietnam.
NUMBER OF PLACEMENTS PER YEAR: 400+.
PREREQUISITES: for all ages (16–60) with average about 24. Must have open mind and be fluent in English. Medical placements available only to health professionals and trainees.
DURATION AND TIME OF PLACEMENTS: 1 week to 6 months.
SELECTION PROCEDURES AND ORIENTATION: Applicants accepted year round. Must sign up at least 30 days before programme start date.
COSTS: Varies with programme, from $995 for 4 weeks volunteering in Nepal to $1,987 for 12 weeks in Ecuador. Spanish language classes are available in Ecuador, Guatemala and Peru.
CONTACT: Scott Burke, Founder and Director.

CROSS-CULTURAL SOLUTIONS
UK: Tower Point 44, North Road, Brighton BN1 1YR, UK
℗ 0845 458 2781/2782
US: 2 Clinton Place, New Rochelle, NY 10801
℗ +1 800 380 4777
⊕ infouk@crossculturalsolutions.org
💻 www.crossculturalsolutions.org

A non-profit international volunteer organisation founded in 1995 and registered charity in the UK (Number 1106741).
PROGRAMME DESCRIPTION: Opportunity for participants to work side-by-side with local people, on locally designed and driven projects. Volunteer programmes are designed to facilitate hands-on service and cultural exchange, with the aim of fostering cultural understanding.
DESTINATIONS: Brazil, China, Costa Rica, Ghana, Guatemala, India, Morocco, Peru, Russia, South Africa, Tanzania and Thailand.
NUMBER OF PLACEMENTS PER YEAR: 4,000+.

PREREQUISITES: All nationalities and ages welcome. Participants must be proficient in English.

DURATION AND TIME OF PLACEMENTS: 1–12 weeks. Frequent start dates run throughout the year.

COST: Programme fees start at £1,408 ($2,588) for a 2-week programme and cover costs such as staffing, volunteer placement, lodging, meals, ground transport and medical and emergency evacuation insurance. International airfares are not included.

CSV

National Full-Time Volunteering Team, 5th Floor, Scala House, 36 Holloway Circus, Queensway, Birmingham B1 1EQ, UK

℡ 0800 374991

✉ volunteer@csv.org.uk

🖥 www.csv.org.uk/volunteer/full-time

CSV is the largest voluntary placement organisation in the UK. Structured placements are available in a huge range of social care projects for those aged 16–35 who are able to commit to a minimum of 4 months volunteering.

NUMBER OF PLACEMENTS PER YEAR: approximately 800.

PROGRAMME DESCRIPTION: CSV volunteers help people throughout Britain in a wide range of social care projects, e.g.: working with adults and children with physical disabilities or learning difficulties; enabling people to access leisure and community facilities; supporting students with disabilities at university, homeless people, older people; assisting in schools; enabling adults with disabilities to live independently in their own homes; and mentoring and befriending young people at risk of offending or exclusion from education. CSV volunteers are full-time and live away from home anywhere within Britain.

PREREQUISITES: No previous qualifications or skills are required. You must have commitment and be flexible, as volunteers are placed where their help and skills are needed most. A full UK driving licence is useful but not required.

DURATION AND TIME OF PLACEMENTS: 4–12 months, beginning at any time of the year.

SELECTION PROCEDURES AND ORIENTATION: Interview days are held across the UK and start dates are available throughout the year. Volunteers receive regular supervision and back-up support from their local CSV office. A CSV certificate is given on completion of placement.

COST: No joining fee. CSV volunteers receive free accommodation and subsistence (which includes food and money to live on) and also travel expenses and relevant training. The current weekly allowance (2009) is £33 plus £39 food allowance if meals are not provided on the placement.

DEVELOPMENT IN ACTION

78 York Street, London W1H 1DP, UK

℡ 07813 395957

✉ info@developmentinaction.org

🖥 www.developmentinaction.org

Non-profit-making development education organisation (formerly Student Action India).

PROGRAMME DESCRIPTION: Voluntary internship type placements to partner Indian NGOs. Grassroots development projects ranging from teaching children in urban slums, administration and fundraising, to fieldwork and research. Volunteers are also required to produce a development education project, to be used as a resource in the UK.

DESTINATIONS: India, with projects in Pune, Udaipur, Indore, Bhopal, Pondicherry and Mumbai and surrounding areas.

PREREQUISITES: Motivation, an interest in global issues and commitment to the aims of Development in Action. No upper age limit or nationality restrictions.

DURATION AND TIME OF PLACEMENTS: 2-month summer placements or year out 5-month placements beginning in September.

SELECTION PROCEDURES AND ORIENTATION: University recruitment talks/careers fairs take place between January and March (see website for details). Application deadlines around the end of January and March; interviews held in February and April. Pre-departure training over one weekend, plus one week training on arrival.

COST: £660 for summer, £1,210 for 5 months (covers placement, training and accommodation). Flights, insurance, visa and subsistence costs are extra.

CONTACT: Ellen Roberts, UK Coordinator.

THE DODWELL TRUST

16 Lanark Mansions, Pennard Road, London W12 8DT, UK

℡ 020 8740 6302

✉ dodwell@madagascar.freeserve.co.uk

🖥 www.dodwell-trust.org

PROGRAMME DESCRIPTION: Hands-on experience in English teaching, working with children, French-language conversation tuition, conservation, research or zoology (depending on time of year).

DESTINATIONS: Madagascar.

NUMBER OF PLACEMENTS PER YEAR: 60–70.
DURATION AND TIME OF PLACEMENTS: 3 weeks to 8 months. Flexible timing.
PREREQUISITES: No skills required. All nationalities welcome provided English is spoken. Age range normally 20–55. Older volunteers welcome and families with children. Placements matched with volunteers' skills and interests where possible for example local radio and TV, French practice, IT computer literacy, tennis, choir, conservation and animal studies at zoo.
SELECTION PROCEDURES AND ORIENTATION: Interviews not essential, though frequent optional meetings and briefings are held in London. 2-day training and orientation course on arrival in Madagascar at placement. Volunteers usually placed in pairs.
COST: In-country placement costs from £590 for 3 weeks, £1,240 for 12 weeks. Self-contained accommodation with cooking facilities provided, in quaint small towns in highlands, rainforest, or seaside. Volunteers are responsible for obtaining visas and health insurance.
CONTACT: Christina Dodwell, Head of Projects.

DRAGONFLY
1719 Mookamontri Soi 13, A. Meuang Nakhon Ratchasima, 30000 Thailand
℡/fax: +66 4428 1073
dan@thai-dragonfly.com
www.thai-dragonfly.com

PROGRAMME DESCRIPTION: Volunteer projects include building, English teaching, wildlife conservation and orphanage care work.
DESTINATIONS: Thailand.
NUMBER OF PLACEMENTS PER YEAR: 150.
PREREQUISITES: Good working knowledge of English (or Thai!), flexibility and an open mind.
DURATION AND TIME OF PLACEMENTS: 1–52 weeks. On most projects, volunteers work full days on 5–6 days a week.
SELECTION PROCEDURES AND ORIENTATION: Preliminary contact online; application forms processed by email.
OTHER SERVICES: TEFL courses through local providers for teaching volunteers; choice of online option and courses based in beach towns in Thailand.
COST: Basic fees vary by project. Sample costs are £395 for first fortnight of orphanage work followed by £50 a week; £395 for 4 weeks of English teaching, £40 per week thereafter. Wildlife conservation costs £565 for 3 weeks, £65 per week after that.
CONTACT: Dan Lockwood, Project Manager.

EARTHWATCH INSTITUTE
Mayfield House, 256 Banbury Road, Oxford OX2 7DE, UK
01865 318838; fax: 01865 311383
info@earthwatch.org.uk
www.earthwatch.org/europe

Earthwatch is an international environmental charity which offers conservation volunteering opportunities on scientific research expeditions worldwide, not eco-tourist trips.

PROGRAMME DESCRIPTION: Earthwatch currently supports 120 expeditions in 55 countries. Research projects are divided into four primary research areas: climate change, oceans, sustainable resource management and sustainable cultures. As an environmental charity it uses volunteers to help gather data. Expeditions are designed at the request of scientists who are trying to find solutions to pressing environmental problems.
DESTINATIONS: Volunteer field assistants needed throughout Europe and worldwide. European projects include monitoring whales and dolphins in Scotland, Spain and Greece, or surveying Icelandic glaciers. International projects range from turtle conservation and coral reef research, to protecting wildlife in Kenya or the Peruvian Amazon.
NUMBER OF PLACEMENTS PER YEAR: approximately 4,000.
PREREQUISITES: Usual age limit is 18 with no maximum, though there are some family teams (minimum age 10). All nationalities accepted.
DURATION AND TIME OF PLACEMENTS: Projects last from 2 days to 3 weeks, throughout the year (see www.earthwatch.org/europe for calendar of dates).
SELECTION PROCEDURES AND ORIENTATION: No previous experience necessary. Volunteers fill out a questionnaire and health form before participating on the project; no interview is required.
OTHER SERVICES: All volunteers receive a briefing pack prior to going on the expedition, giving detailed information about the project, logistics and general information about the area. All volunteers receive training when they are at the expedition site before they start assisting the scientists. Accommodation provided, from huts in the Arctic to hammocks in the rainforest to safari lodges in Kenya.
COST: From £175 to £2,250, given as a charitable donation to support research. Cost covers training in the field, food, accommodation, medical emergency evacuation and the offsetting of greenhouse gases. It does not include travel to the rendezvous site.

ECOLOGIA YOUTH TRUST

The Park, Forres, Moray IV36 3TZ, Scotland

✆/fax: 01309 690995

✉ volunteer@ecologia.org.uk

🖥 www.ecologia.org.uk; www.kitezh.org

The Trust promotes creative change in Russia through youth, ecology and education, working closely with the Kitezh Community of foster families.

PROGRAMME DESCRIPTION: Volunteers, including gap year students and 2 or 3 adults, are placed at the Kitezh Children's Community for orphans in western Russia. Knowledge of Russian is not essential although students of Russian will quickly become fluent.

DESTINATIONS: Kaluga, Russia and Moscow.

PREREQUISITES: Reasonable knowledge of Russian language, TEFL or experience teaching English as a foreign language, experience working with children (sports, arts and crafts, music, drama), building, cooking and gardening. An interest in children and a willingness to participate fully in the life of the community are essential.

DURATION AND TIME OF PLACEMENTS: 1–3 months (additional months are at the discretion of the Kitezh Council). Moscow placement: 1 year.

SELECTION PROCEDURES AND ORIENTATION: Introductory questionnaire followed by telephone interview required. Police check in country of residence required. Extensive preparatory materials are sent including feedback from previous volunteers. Informal orientation given on arrival, weekly meeting with volunteer supervisor and ongoing support from Ecologia Youth Trust via email.

COST: 1 month costs £750, 2 months £900. Costs include invitation, visa + registration, transfer Moscow to Kitezh return and accommodation and food in Kitezh. Insurance and airfare not included; flights cost from £260 (depending on time of year). Cost of extended stay approximately £100 per month. Moscow placement: cover own travel costs. Accommodation and monthly stipend negotiable.

CONTACT: Liza Hollingshead, Director.

EDUCATORS ABROAD

5 Talfourd Way, Royal Earlswood Park, Redhill, Surrey RH1 6GD, UK

✆ 01737 785468; 01737 768254; fax: 01737 768254

✉ craig@educatorsabroad.org

🖥 www.educatorsabroad.org

Company that manages and operates the English Language Teaching Assistant Program (ELTAP) for universities in the USA and participants from other countries (www.eltap.org).

PROGRAMME DESCRIPTION: Volunteer/college-sponsored programme open to adults as a non-credit certificate option as well as to students. Participants assist teachers and students in ESL and EFL classes by bringing their native fluency in English to schools around the world.

DESTINATIONS: Over 25 countries on all continents.

DURATION AND TIME OF PLACEMENTS: 4 or 10 weeks throughout the year.

COST: $2,300–$4,200 depending on programme option, plus travel and in some cases room and board. Host schools assist with arrangements for accommodation and board.

CONTACT: Dr Craig Kissock, Director.

EXPERIENCE MEXECO

UK: 38 Award Road, Fleet, Hampshire, GU52 6HG, UK

✆/fax: 01252 629411

Mexico: #59 Valentín Gómez Farías, San Patricio Melaque, Jalisco

✆ +52 1 315 100 0818; +52 1 315 100 3730

✉ info@experiencemexeco.com

🖥 www.experiencemexeco.com or
   www.mex-ecotours.com

PROGRAMME DESCRIPTION: Sea turtle conservation, English teaching projects, community fundraising for special needs schools, physiotherapy placements and other community-based projects.

DESTINATIONS: Pacific coast of Mexico.

NUMBER OF PLACEMENTS PER YEAR: 30–35.

PREREQUISITES: All nationalities and ages (average 19–26). All backgrounds welcomed as any necessary training is provided. Spanish not a necessity as local staff speak English and Spanish.

DURATION AND TIME OF PLACEMENTS: 1–3 months.

SELECTION PROCEDURES AND ORIENTATION: Applications should be received no less than 1 month before desired start date, though earlier preferred. Interview not required.

COST: £799–£899 for 1 month, £1,899–£1,999 for 3 months; covers accommodation (homestay, private, or small tents on turtle project) and food throughout placement, plus insurance and 24-hour in-country support, but excludes flights.

CONTACT: Daniel Patman, Director.

FLYGAP – see Verbier Summits

Member of the Year Out Group. Flying Fish trains water and snow sports staff, and arranges employment for sailors, divers, surfers, windsurfers, skiers and snowboarders. Founded in 1993, Flying Fish provides travel, training, adventure and professional qualifications for those looking to enjoy some time out, take a gap year or start a career in water or snow sports.

PROGRAMME DESCRIPTION: A year out with Flying Fish starts with a course leading to a qualification as a surf or windsurf instructor, yacht skipper or sailing instructor, divemaster and dive instructor, or ski or snowboard instructor. For those not looking to work in the sports industry, this is a challenging recreational course, and training at professional level offers personal adventure and the ability to perform at a high level.

DESTINATIONS: Training courses are run at Cowes in the UK, at Sydney and the Whitsunday Islands in Australia, Bay of Islands in New Zealand, Dahab in Egypt, Vassiliki in Greece and Whistler in Canada. Jobs are worldwide, with main employers located in Australia, the South Pacific, the Caribbean and the Mediterranean.

NUMBER OF PLACEMENTS PER YEAR: 600, almost equal numbers of men and women.

PREREQUISITES: Ages 18–60+, from all around the world.

DURATION AND TIME OF PLACEMENTS: 2–19 weeks with start dates year round.

SELECTION PROCEDURES AND ORIENTATION: Applicants submit an application and, if looking for a career in the industry, may be asked to attend job interviews.

COST: Fees range from £1,100 to £11,000. Accommodation and airfares are provided, with normal wages during employment.

PROGRAMME DESCRIPTION. Frontier offers a huge range of volunteering opportunities in conservation and community work, and also internships such as journalism and medicine.

DESTINATIONS: Nearly 50 countries worldwide.

NUMBER OF PLACEMENTS PER YEAR: 500+.

PREREQUISITES: No specific qualifications required as training is provided. Marine expeditions include free scuba diving training. Possibility of studying in the field for a BTEC Advanced Diploma in Tropical Habitat Conservation or a BTEC Advanced Certificate in Expedition Management.

DURATION AND TIME OF PLACEMENTS: 4, 8, 10 or 20 weeks.

SELECTION PROCEDURES AND ORIENTATION: Open days are held twice monthly (Saturday mornings and Wednesday evenings, as listed on the website. After submitting an application and having a telephone briefing, applicants hear within a week whether they have been accepted. Prior to the expedition, a briefing weekend is held in the UK.

COST: Depending on location and duration, international volunteers raise from £1,200 for 4 weeks, £1,700 for 8 weeks, £2,000 for 10 weeks and £3,000 for 20 weeks. This covers all individual costs (including the UK weekend briefing), scientific and dive training, travel, visas, insurance, food and accommodation, but excludes flights.

FUNDACIÒN PRONIÑO ('FOR THE CHILDREN')

Barrio El Centro, Edificio Ecocentenario, El Progreso, Yoro, Honduras

℡/fax: (504) 647 3424

✆ proninohonduras@yahoo.com (for volunteer enquiries); streetkidshonduras@yahoo.com

🖳 www.streetkidshonduras.org; www.pronino.org

PROGRAMME DESCRIPTION: Proniño has three centres for street children based in El Progreso, Honduras. Las Flores provides for the initial needs of a child. La Esperanza is a transitional centre to help in the movement of the children from a closed centre to more freedom. Montaña is more of a home environment, where the children go to school and receive vocational training for their futures in society.

DESTINATIONS: El Progreso, Honduras.

PREREQUISITES: Ages 21–99. The most important quality needed is an ability to love, care and support the children. Any transferable skills that are appropriate to children are useful, e.g. for the education programmes (especially computer and English classes). People with a professional skill (such as psychologists or people with a building trade) are welcome to suggest a specific project they would like to set up.

DURATION AND TIME OF PLACEMENTS: Minimum 4 months, usually 6–12 months.

SELECTION PROCEDURES AND ORIENTATION: Applications accepted year round. Telephone interviews arranged after email application submitted. Participants receive a welcome pack with information about Proniño and the culture of Honduras. The first 2–3 weeks involve exposure to the centres and office, so the volunteer can decide where they can best help.

COST: Volunteer house is comfortable and classic Honduran, and costs approximately $120 per month; personal spending and living expenses about $50 per month.

CONTACT: Kevin Cestra, Volunteer Coordinator.

GAP AND CAREER BREAKS

PO Box 553,St Peter Port, Guernsey, Channel Islands

℡/fax: 01481 711206

✆ info@gapandcareerbreaks.com

🖳 www.gapandcareerbreaks.com

Small independent company offering a one-to-one personal service.

PROGRAMME DESCRIPTION: Range of programmes for volunteers to work in the social sector (communities, children, the elderly, healthcare, teaching), animals (e.g. private game reserves, animal sanctuaries, dolphins), environmental (beach cleanups, house/hut building) and so on.

DESTINATIONS: Bali, Bolivia, China, Ecuador, Ghana, Kenya, Mauritius, Paraguay, Peru, South Africa and Tobago, to date.

DURATION AND TIME OF PLACEMENTS: From 2 weeks to 2 years.

PREREQUISITES: Average age of clients so far is 39. Volunteers with skills in nursing, teaching, IT, building, electricians, plumbers or any other trade and profession can be placed, as well as volunteers with no particular skills.

SELECTION PROCEDURES AND ORIENTATION: Some programmes offer a choice of projects for the client to choose from on arrival.

COST: Sample prices for 4-week projects: £599 at an animal sanctuary on the Channel Islands, £685 beach-cleaning in Tobago, £775 for work with HIV/Aids patients in Mauritius and £895 for teaching in China. The longer the volunteer stays the cheaper per week the programme.

CONTACT: Carol Carlile, Director.

GAPS FOR GRUMPIES – see Madventurer

GAP YEAR IN ASIA – see WLS International

GLOBAL SPORTS XPERIENCE

UK: Thamesbourne Lodge, Station Road, Bourne End,
Buckinghamshire SL8 5QH, UK

0871 221 2929

Australia: 1300 664451

sports@globalxperience.com

www.globalsportsxperience.com

PROGRAMME DESCRIPTION: Specialist organisation that can
arrange for people wanting a career break to coach, play or
qualify in sports overseas. Also offers sporting and non-sporting
volunteer projects in Africa and Australia (teaching, building,
conservation). Sports include kite-surfing in the Caribbean, ski
instructor courses in Europe and Canada, scuba diving courses
in Thailand and Australia, kayak or mountain biking across
New Zealand and training programmes at international sports
academies.

DESTINATIONS: Asia, Africa, Australasia, Europe, North
America and Latin America.

NUMBER OF PLACEMENTS PER YEAR: 500–800.

PREREQUISITES: Most programmes require minimal or no
previous experience. Skilled professionals are also valued as
volunteer sports coaches, teachers, builders and medical staff.

DURATION AND TIME OF PLACEMENTS: 1 week to 1 year.
Volunteer projects have a minimum duration of 4 weeks.

SELECTION PROCEDURES AND ORIENTATION: Applications should be submitted at least 6–8 weeks before
departure to allow time to organise flights, jabs and visas.
References and background checks are required for
volunteer projects. Inductions and orientations are given on
arrival in destination country.

COST: Courses from £665 for 1 week. Volunteer projects from
£795 for 4 weeks.

GAP YEAR FOR GROWN-UPS

1st Floor, 1 Meadow Road, Tunbridge Wells TN1 2YG, UK

01892 701881; fax: 01892 523172

info@gapyearforgrownups.co.uk

www.gapyearforgrownups.co.uk; www.realgap.
co.uk

Part of the Real Travel Group including Real Gap Experience for the
18–30 market and Real Sport Experience (sport travel specialist).

PROGRAMME DESCRIPTION: Choice of volunteer and travel
options around the world, including a bespoke 'design-your-
own-gap-year' service. Range of travel and volunteer
programmes includes working with children and adults in
deprived communities, conservation volunteering, working with
wildlife, paid work, or learning a new skill such as a language,
PADI dive course or farm skills on an outback property.

DESTINATIONS: Australasia, Africa, Asia, Eastern Europe, Latin
America, North America and round the world.

PREREQUISITES: Programmes vary but most are open to all
ages and backgrounds.

COST: Varies with programme. Sample fees: £999 for an
adventure in Thailand, £899 for 2 weeks working on the Galapagos Islands protecting giant tortoises and £849 for
4 weeks in Tanzania working in an orphanage.

GLOBAL VISION INTERNATIONAL (GVI)

3 High Street, St Albans, Hertfordshire AL3 4ED, UK

01727 250250; fax: 01727 840666

info@gvi.co.uk

www.gvi.co.uk

PROGRAMME DESCRIPTION: 40+ conservation and community
expeditions, volunteer projects, courses and internships throughout Africa, Latin America, Europe, Asia and the USA. Courses for
prospective volunteers include intensive weekend TEFL courses
in the UK, Spanish lessons in Latin America, and outdoor survival
courses that include training to become a safari field guide in
South Africa and mountain skills schools in Patagonia. Training
options and support for career prospects are available on
selected projects. Some are also available to families.

DESTINATIONS: Mexico, Costa Rica, Guatemala, Honduras,
Nicaragua, Panama, Belize, Ecuador, Argentina, Brazil, Bolivia,
Chile, Peru, Nepal, India, Sri Lanka, Thailand, South Africa,
Kenya, Namibia, Ghana, Rwanda, Uganda, Seychelles, Tanzania,
Madagascar, Indonesia, Borneo, Vanuatu, USA and UK.

DURATION AND TIME OF PLACEMENTS: 1 week to 2 years.

SELECTION PROCEDURES AND ORIENTATION: Some projects
require a telephone interview; others require only a completed
application form online.

COST: From £325 for some short projects in Latin America,
to £2,995 for a year-long internship in South Africa. Price for
marine conservation expedition in Seychelles starts at £1,650
for 5 weeks, including scuba diving equipment, training and
accommodation.

GLOBAL VOLUNTEER NETWORK

PO Box 30–968, Lower Hutt, New Zealand

+64 4 569 9080; fax: +64 4 569 9081

info@volunteer.org.nz

www.volunteer.org.nz

PROGRAMME DESCRIPTION: Volunteers recruited for a variety of educational, community aid, health/medical, environmental/conservation, construction, wildlife programmes and cultural homestays in 22 countries. Fund-raising treks are also offered to Everest Base Camp, Mount Kilimanjaro, Machu Picchu and El Camino in Spain.

DESTINATIONS: Cambodia, China, Costa Rica, Ecuador, Ethiopia, Ghana, Honduras, India, Kenya, Mexico, Nepal, New Zealand, Peru, Philippines, Romania, South Africa, Thailand, Uganda, Vietnam and USA (Alaska and South Dakota).

DURATION AND TIME OF PLACEMENTS: 2 weeks to 12 months depending on the placement. Applications accepted year round.

NUMBER OF PLACEMENTS PER YEAR: approximately 2,000 (aiming for 2,500 in 2008/9).

PREREQUISITES: No special skills or qualifications needed in most programmes. All nationalities placed, although projects in China and Romania accept only Australians, Canadians, Europeans, Irish, British, American and New Zealanders.

COST: US$350 application fee to Global Volunteer Network covers personal staff support, programme guide, fundraising guide and software, access to your online journal and online video 'preparing for your trip'. Programme fees vary from US$697 per month in Ecuador to US$1,697 a month in Alaska, to cover training, accommodation and meals during training and placement, supervision and project transport (but not international airfares).

CONTACT: Colin Salisbury, Chief Executive Officer.

GREENFORCE

11–15 Betterton Street, Covent Garden, London WC2H 9BP, UK

✆ 020 7470 8888; fax: 020 7379 0801

✉ info@greenforce.org

🖥 www.greenforce.org

Member of the Year Out Group and a not-for-profit organisation. Previously a conservation volunteering organisation, but now offers in addition a full range of gap year activities including diving, teaching and internships. Recently merged with Trekforce but offers separate programme.

PROGRAMME DESCRIPTION: Participants work as fieldwork assistants on various marine and terrestrial projects, carrying out tasks such as tracking animal movements and studying coral reef species. Training is provided including diver training for the marine expeditions, and language training for the terrestrial expeditions. Internships, sport

volunteering, teaching, community work and many other projects also arranged worldwide.

DESTINATIONS: Fiji, the Bahamas, Tanzania, India, Nepal, Thailand, China, South Africa, Ecuador, Spain (interning in Valencia) and Australia (for working holiday makers).

NUMBER OF PLACEMENTS PER YEAR: 300.

PREREQUISITES: No previous experience is necessary and no qualifications are required, as training will be provided in the field.

DURATION AND TIME OF PLACEMENTS: 1–6 months in many countries; up to 12 months in China, Ecuador and Africa. Some short trips of 1–2 weeks as well.

SELECTION PROCEDURES AND ORIENTATION: Applicants may attend one of the regular, informal open evenings. A briefing pack is provided on application, giving information about fundraising and relevant medical advice, etc. Participants can attend a training day 6 weeks prior to joining the project (cost included in contribution). The first week of the expedition is spent undertaking further training and familiarisation with the project and host country.

COST: From £1,500 for 4 weeks and £2,300 for 10 weeks diving in the Bahamas, with similar prices for other countries. Fees cover training and instruction, food, accommodation and in-country transport, but not insurance and international flights. Diving equipment and training are provided for £300 in Fiji and the Bahamas, including PADI Open Water Advanced and Emergency First Response Qualifications. One member of each marine volunteer team is invited to stay on as an intern at no further cost; the position is aimed at those seeking to develop a career in conservation.

HELP (HIMALAYAN EDUCATION LIFELINE PROGRAMME)

30 Kingsdown Park, Whitstable, Kent CT5 2DF, UK

✆ 01227 263055

✉ help@help-education.org

🖥 www.help-education.org

HELP enables young people from poor communities in the Himalayas (Nepal and India) to improve their employment opportunities through education, by providing financial and volunteer resources to their schools.

PROGRAMME DESCRIPTION: Volunteer teachers and nurses work in needy schools targeted by HELP.

DESTINATIONS: Himalayan India (Sikkim, West Bengal, Uttarakhand, Ladakh and Himachal Pradesh) and Nepal (Kathmandu Valley, Pokhara and the mountains to the north of Pokhara).

NUMBER OF PLACEMENTS PER YEAR: 15 (approximately).

PREREQUISITES: Ages 19/20–60+. Teaching experience and/or TEFL qualifications are desirable but not essential. Nurses need to be qualified. Volunteers should be mature and resourceful people who can hit the ground running. Qualities needed include resilience and adaptability, an open mind, interest in other cultures, good mental and physical health, and tact and diplomacy. A love of and experience with children is vital.

DURATION AND TIME OF PLACEMENTS: 2 months usually. Volunteers can stay for a maximum of 6 months (for visa reasons).

SELECTION PROCEDURES AND ORIENTATION: Applications accepted year round. Telephone interview after receipt of online application form. Volunteers receive a briefing pack. Advice is given by email and/or over the phone.

COST. From £000 depending on volunteer's status and length of stay, including accommodation with host families or in school hostel.

CONTACT: Jim Coleman, Executive Director

HOPE AND HOME

Nepal Volunteer Program, Lazimpat, Kathmandu, (PO Box 119, Kathmandu) Nepal.

☏ +977 1 4415393; fax: +9771 4415176

✉ info@hopenhome.org; hopenhome@gmail.com

💻 www.hopenhome.org

Community-oriented opportunities for international volunteers in a quest to find sustainable solutions for education, health, conservation and development issues.

PROGRAMME DESCRIPTION: Volunteer opportunities are in the fields of teaching English, working in an orphanage, community health and environmental programme, school and community maintenance, and homestay/cultural exchange.

DESTINATIONS: Nepal (Kathmandu Valley, Pokhara, Chitwan and Nawalparasi).

NUMBER OF PLACEMENTS PER YEAR: 55–60.

PREREQUISITES: Ages 18–35. All that is needed is a genuine desire to help people.

DURATION AND TIME OF PLACEMENTS: 2 weeks to 3 months.

SELECTION PROCEDURES AND ORIENTATION: Online applications accepted year round.

OTHER SERVICES: Language class, cultural information and project information provided.

COST: Volunteer fees entirely fund programme and include homestay accommodation and food. From $250 for 2 weeks to $600 for 6 weeks to $800 for 3 months.

CONTACT: Rabyn Aryal, Director.

IALC (INTERNATIONAL ASSOCIATION OF LANGUAGE CENTRES)

Lombard House, 12/17 Upper Bridge Street, Canterbury, Kent CT1 2NF, UK

☏ 01227 769007; fax: 01227 769014

✉ info@ialc.org

💻 www.ialc.org

Language school association that accredits private language schools, with 92 members in 22 countries.

COURSES OFFERED: Diverse range of language programmes in nine languages worldwide, ranging from short-term general courses to specialised courses combining language with culture, cookery, dance, art, sport, etc. Some IALC schools offer work experience or volunteering.

APPLICATION PROCEDURES: Canterbury office is not a booking office. Contact details for member schools appear on the IALC website.

CONTACT: Jan Capper.

ICYE (INTER-CULTURAL YOUTH EXCHANGE)

Latin American House, Kingsgate Place, London NW6 4TA, UK.

☏ 020 7681 0983; fax: 020 7916 1246

✉ info@icye.co.uk

💻 www.icye.co.uk

ICYE is a registered charity (no. 1081907) and part of an international exchange organisation.

PROGRAMME DESCRIPTION: ICYE UK run long and short-term exchange programmes worldwide with an emphasis on inter-cultural understanding and integration into local communities. The majority of projects are social and community based, such as working with street children, working in orphanages, HIV awareness, working in disability support, mental health, conservation work, human rights work, construction and teaching. Volunteers live on projects or with host families.

DESTINATIONS: Long-term programme destinations include Bolivia, Brazil, Colombia, Costa Rica, Ecuador, Honduras, Mexico, Mozambique, Nigeria, Ghana, Kenya, South Korea, Taiwan, India, Nepal and Uganda. Short-Term Programme destinations are India, Nepal, China, Morocco, Ecuador and Costa Rica, Nigeria, Ghana, Kenya, Mozambique and Uganda.

NUMBER OF PLACEMENTS PER YEAR: The ICYE network arranges approximately 600 exchanges in 36 countries.

PREREQUISITES: Applicants must have a commitment to intercultural learning and the principles of ICYE. No formal qualification necessary, just enthusiasm and an open mind. ICYE's long-term programmes are open to 18–30-year-olds, although applicants can be considered on a case by case basis. Short-term programmes are open to volunteers aged 18+.

DURATION AND TIME OF PLACEMENTS: Long-term programme begins in August and January and lasts 6 or 12 months. The short-term programme runs all year with monthly departures.

COST: 12 months costs £3,900, 6 months costs £3,300. Long-term programme fees include the following: return flights and travel costs, insurance, visa support, accommodation, food, pocket money, pre-departure and on-arrival training, language course and administration. Prices for the short-term programme vary depending on length of stay and project choice. Volunteers are supported in their fundraising efforts and a discount of up to £300 is available for online fundraising.

CONTACT: Jenny Williams (Long-term Coordinator) and Cat Udal (Programme Coordinator).

IKANDO

Keta Close, Ring Road Central, Accra, Ghana

✆ +233 21 222726

✎ info@ikando.org

🖥 www.ikando.org

PROGRAMME DESCRIPTION: Volunteer and intern recruitment on behalf of organisations in Ghana. Placements in healthcare, medicine, psychology, journalism, law or teaching.

DESTINATIONS: Ghana.

NUMBER OF PLACEMENTS PER YEAR: 150–200 in 40 varying placements, some of them quirky.

DURATION AND TIME OF PLACEMENTS: 4–8 weeks. Flexible start dates year round.

PREREQUISITES: All nationalities. Range of ages (average 24). All skills can be placed such as architects, medics, teachers, lawyers, librarians and artists.

SELECTION PROCEDURES AND ORIENTATION: Online application and CV. Extensive written pre-travel information, welcome pack and in-country orientation provided.

COST: From £87 per week. Ikando house in the centre of Accra is fully furnished with security and housekeeping staff. It is set in a large garden with balconies overlooking the city.

CONTACT: Alexandra Daly, Volunteer Administrator.

IKO PORAN ASSOCIATION

Rua do Oriente 280/201, Santa Teresa, Rio de Janeiro (RJ), CEP: 20.240–130, Brazil

✆ +55 21 3852 2917; fax: +55 21 3852 2917

✎ rj@ikoporan.org

🖥 www.ikoporan.org

PROGRAMME DESCRIPTION: Volunteers are assigned to various autonomous development projects. Iko Poran is always forging new links with Brazilian NGOs that can use the services of volunteers.

DESTINATIONS: Brazil (Rio, Salvador, Amazonia).

NUMBER OF PLACEMENTS PER YEAR: 300–400.

PREREQUISITES: Average age range 20–30 but accept volunteers up to 70. All nationalities welcome.

DURATION AND TIME OF PLACEMENTS: 3–24 weeks, according to volunteer's availability. Maximum of 24 weeks for visa reasons.

SELECTION PROCEDURES AND ORIENTATION: Applications accepted up to one week before departure. Volunteers fill out an extensive application form detailing their interests, abilities and reasons for joining an international volunteer programme. Police certificate needed by volunteers who want to work with children.

OTHER SERVICES: Upon arrival volunteers are picked up from airport and given an orientation that includes a welcome pack, information about neighbourhood facilities, public transport, maps and guides, safety tips and so on. Portuguese language lessons can be arranged.

COST: Programme fee is R$1,500 (US$925/£470) which covers lodging in one of Iko Poran's comfortable volunteer houses for the first 4 weeks and a donation of R$400 to the project. Additional weeks cost R$180 including accommodation.

CONTACT: Luis Felipe Murray, General Coordinator.

IMPACT TRAVEL

71 Inver Road, Blackpool, FY2 0RQ, UK

✆ 01253 315975

✎ info@impacttravel.co.uk

🖥 www.impacttravel.co.uk

Impact Travel believes in socially responsible travel, that communities visited should be supported.

PROGRAMME DESCRIPTION: Selected few gap year style volunteer projects in India and Nepal, such as working in needy schools and orphanages. Also offer short escorted trips including participation for a week in a community volunteer project.

DESTINATIONS: India and Nepal.

NUMBER OF PLACEMENTS PER YEAR: 30.

DURATION AND TIME OF PLACEMENTS: 1 week – 1 year for volunteering, but most are no more than 1 month.

PREREQUISITES: No age or nationality restrictions.

SELECTION PROCEDURES AND ORIENTATION: Interviews essential and can be arranged to suit the volunteers. Cultural awareness training and specific advice on teaching preparation is available so that volunteer teachers are ready to face their classrooms.

COST: From £200 for one week (project only) to £800 for one month placements with accommodation. Escorted flagship tours costing £2,000 include extensive travel itinerary, quality accommodation (with homestay options), transport and an insight into the communities visited.

CONTACT: Jeremy Mannino, Company Partner.

THE INTERNATIONAL ACADEMY

King's Place, 12–42 Wood Street, Kingston-upon-Thames, Surrey KT1 1JY, UK

0871 971 0376; fax: 029 2066 0204

info@theinternationalacademy.com

www.theinternationalacademy.com

Part of the Student Travel and Adventure Group (STAG) of TUI Travel, the leading international leisure travel group.

PROGRAMME DESCRIPTION: Ski and snowboard instructor training courses run in partnership with the resident ski and snowboard schools in various resorts. Courses lead to recognised CSIA, CASI and NZSIA qualifications. Professional programmes are aimed at personal development and the improvement of technical/teaching skills.

DESTINATIONS: Courses are run in Whistler/Blackcomb and Banff/Lake Louise in Canada, and Cardrona Alpine Resort in New Zealand.

DURATION OF COURSES: 5–12 weeks with various start dates throughout the year.

COST: Courses include flights, airport/resort transfers, lift pass, accommodation, breakfast and evening meals, instructor training/tuition, exam fee and certification. Prices of 5-week ski or snowboard courses in the Canadian Rockies range from £4,050, and 12-week courses range from £6,550.

IST PLUS LTD

Rosedale House, Rosedale Road, Richmond, Surrey TW9 2SZ, UK

020 8939 9057

info@istplus.com

www.istplus.com

Work, teaching and study abroad programmes for UK students, graduates and professionals.

PROGRAMME DESCRIPTION: Programmes that are open to grown-up gappers include Professional Career Training (PCT) in the USA (for ages 20–40), Work & Travel Australia (maximum age 30), Work & Travel New Zealand (maximum age 30), Teach in China (maximum age 65) and Teach in Thailand (maximum age 65). IST Plus also offers a Volunteer Programme, helping disadvantaged children in Thailand (recommended maximum age 30).

DESTINATIONS: China, Thailand, USA, Australia, New Zealand.

NUMBER OF PLACEMENTS PER YEAR: Unlimited.

COST: Australia £275; New Zealand £195; Asian teaching programmes £725–£825; PCT in the USA starts at £525, excluding travel. Volunteer Thailand programme from £325.

---

i-to-i MEANINGFUL TRAVEL

Woodside House, 261 Low Lane, Horsforth, Leeds LS18 5NY, UK

0871 220 2215; fax: 0113 205 4619

info@i-to-i.com

www.i-to-i.com

---

i-to-i Meaningful Travel works in partnership with hundreds of locally run projects around the world to offer the chance to make a difference on a trip in a safe, supported, and sustainable manner; they can help arrange a life-changing travel experience whether for two weeks or two months.

PROGRAMME DESCRIPTION: Volunteer abroad projects include conservation, community work, building, sports, work experience placements and humanitarian tours. i-to-i also organises a variety of TEFL training courses, including a 20-hour weekend course offered across the UK, Ireland, Australia and the USA, a 40-hour online course and various combinations. i-to-i also offer a free job placement service to assign course graduates paid TEFL work in a selection of countries.

DESTINATIONS: for volunteers are Argentina, Australia, Brazil, Cambodia, China, Costa Rica, Ecuador, Ghana,Honduras, India, Indonesia,Kenya, Malaysia, Mozambique, Nepal, Peru, Philippines, South Africa, Sri Lanka, Swaziland, Taiwan, Tanzania, Thailand, Uganda, Vietnam and Zambia. Paid teaching China, South Korea, Thailand,Indonesia, Japan, Taiwan, Czech Republic, Greece, Hungary, Slovakia, Spain, United Kingdom, Ecuador and Honduras.

NUMBER OF PLACEMENTS PER YEAR: 15,000 (including course participants).

PREREQUISITES: Most volunteer projects require no experience or qualifications, although some skills development placements (e.g. media) require a CV. Paid teaching graduates must go through interview process.

DURATION AND TIME OF PLACEMENTS: Volunteer projects from one week to six months, starting year round. Paid teaching placements range from three months to twelve months (depending on location).

SELECTION PROCEDURES AND ORIENTATION: Venture placements include full pre-departure support but there is no formal selection process. i-to-i provide full project information packs and in-country orientation plus accommodation and meals. All teaching placements include a free i-to-i Online TEFL course.

COST: Volunteer abroad from £295 (excluding airfares). TEFL training from £195 (www.onlinetefl.com).

I-VOLUNTEER
D-134, East Kailash, New Delhi 110065, India
📞 +911 65672160; fax: +911 26217460
✉ jamal@ivolunteer.org.in
💻 www.ivolunteer.in

A not-for-profit Indian charity working to promote volunteering in India including international volunteers.

PROGRAMME DESCRIPTION: i-Volunteer provides hands-on volunteering opportunities with communities to help volunteers acquire an understanding of the development challenges facing India. Volunteer work in partnership with more than 300 host organisations in areas such as livelihoods, childcare, HIV/Aids, education, health, environment and micro-finance.

DESTINATIONS: India. i-Volunteer has centres in New Delhi, Mumbai, Bangalore and Chennai with links to urban and rural NGOs all over India.

NUMBER OF PLACEMENTS PER YEAR: 4,000+ (of whom 50+ are international volunteers).

PREREQUISITES: All ages. No particular skills needed. Only requirements are a passion for volunteering and an interest in exploring.

DURATION AND TIME OF PLACEMENTS: 2 months–2 years (shorter attachments from 1 week also possible).

SELECTION PROCEDURES AND ORIENTATION: Applications are accepted round the year. Volunteers receive preparatory materials before departure and in-country orientation, plus mid-term review and final assessment.

COST: Deposit of $100 needed to secure place. Fee for 1-month placement is $1,000 which covers board and lodging plus travel within India.

CONTACT: Mohammad Jamal, Manager.

JAPAN EXCHANGE & TEACHING (JET) PROGRAMME UK
JET Desk, Embassy of Japan, 101–104 Piccadilly, London W1J 7JT, UK
📞 020 7465 6668
✉ info@jet-uk.org
💻 www.jet-uk.org

The JET Programme is a well-established initiative in the field of cultural exchange and provides opportunities for those contemplating a career break or change of career.

PROGRAMME DESCRIPTION: Government-run JET Programme allows graduates to spend one or more years teaching or working with local government in Japan.

DESTINATIONS: Throughout Japan.

NUMBER OF PLACEMENTS PER YEAR: 200+ from UK going to educational institutions all over Japan.

PREREQUISITES: Must have a bachelor's degree, UK passport and be under 39 years of age by the time of departure. TEFL training or experience preferred but not essential.

DURATION AND TIME OF PLACEMENTS: 12-month renewable contracts starting in late July or August. Normal working hours are 35 hours per week, although teaching hours are between 15 and 20.

SELECTION PROCEDURES AND ORIENTATION: Application period begins in late September with a deadline on the last Friday in November. Interviews take place in London and Edinburgh in January and February with decisions given in April.

OTHER SERVICES: JET finds placement, organises visa and insurance, hosts 2-day pre-departure orientation day in London or Edinburgh, beginners' TEFL training and basic Japanese language course, 2-day orientation in Tokyo, language books and return flights provided.

COST: None. Minimum salary of 3,600,000 yen paid (currently just less than £17,000). Participants pay for rent (30,000–70,000 yen) plus 40,000 yen per month compulsory contributions. Return airfares provided to those who complete contract.

LANGUAGE COURSES ABROAD LTD
67 Ashby Road, Loughborough, Leicestershire LE11 3AA, UK
📞 01509 211612; fax: 01509 260037
✉ info@languagesabroad.co.uk
💻 www.languagesabroad.co.uk

Spanish Study Holidays, the parent company of Language Courses Abroad, was founded in 1991 by a team of language teachers, as an advisory service for students wishing to study Spanish in Spain.

PROGRAMME DESCRIPTION: In-country full immersion language courses offered at more than 100 schools, in Spanish, French, German, Italian, Portuguese, Russian, Chinese, Japanese and Greek.

PREREQUISITES: All ages, including clients in their 30s, 40s and older. Club 50+ language courses are offered in a number of destinations for people in their 50s and older (details on www.languagesabroad.co.uk/third_age.html).

DURATION AND TIME OF PLACEMENTS: 1–36 weeks

ACCOMMODATION: Shared self-catering student apartments, private studio apartments, host families, student residences or hotels.

CONTACT: Scott Cather, Language Travel Adviser.

LAUNCHPAD AUSTRALIA

PO Box 2525, Fitzroy, Victoria 3065, Australia

☎/fax: +61 3 9445 9375

✉ workingholiday@launchpadaustralia.com

🖥 www.launchpadaustralia.com

PROGRAMME DESCRIPTION: Offers a variety of international work, study, cultural and volunteer opportunities.

DESTINATIONS: Europe, Asia, South America, Africa.

NUMBER OF PLACEMENTS PER YEAR: Unlimited.

PREREQUISITES: None. Some volunteer programmes require related experience.

COST: Varies hugely depending on programme.

CONTACT: Danielle Salman, Managing Director.

THE LEAP OVERSEAS LTD

121 High Street, Marlborough,

Wiltshire SN8 1LZ, UK

☎ 0870 240 4187; 01672 519922; fax: 01672 519944

✉ info@theleap.co.uk

🖥 www.theleap.co.uk

PROGRAMME DESCRIPTION: Voluntary placements in Africa, South America, Asia and Australia, that incorporate a variety of experiences and locations. Projects are involved with eco-tourism, conservation and community projects. For example in Kenya volunteers can escort guests on safari, track elephants in the bush and teach football or English to local kids.

DESTINATIONS: Placements are based in game parks, jungle and coastal locations in Africa (Kenya, South Africa, Mozambique,

Tanzania and Zambia), South America (Guyana, Costa Rica, Argentina and Ecuador), Asia (Cambodia and India) and Australia.

NUMBER OF PLACEMENTS PER YEAR: Approximately 300. The majority of participants are school leavers aged 18–20, though career breakers are specially catered for and sent together with others of a similar age.

PREREQUISITES: Ages 18 and up. Must be committed, enthusiastic and motivated, able to work well in a team and prepared to get stuck in.

DURATION AND TIME OF PLACEMENTS: Departures in January, April, July and September for 6 or 10 weeks.

COST: From £1,700 for 6 weeks; solo placements lasting up to 3 months cost £2,400 including accommodation, food, transport and back-up. Excludes travel, visas and insurance

CONTACT: Guy Whitehead, Director.

MADVENTURER

1 Pink Lane, Newcastle upon Tyne

NE1 5DW, UK

☎ 0845 121 1996; 0191 260 3491

fax: 0191 280 2860

✉ team@madventurer.com

🖥 www.madventurer.com; www.careerbreaker.com; www.gapsforgrumpies.com

Madventurer combines development projects and adventurous overland travel for all ages.

PROGRAMME DESCRIPTION: Expeditions that give career breakers, gap year individuals and students the opportunity to undertake a range of voluntary work for a grassroots community or environmental project (building, teaching, sports instruction, healthcare and conservation), with the option then to travel on an overland adventure (trekking, rafting, touring). Placements can sometimes be arranged to complement area of academic study. The specially designed career break projects are for individuals aged 24 or over who are looking for a unique experience during their time out from work.

DESTINATIONS: Peru, Ghana, Tanzania, Kenya, Fiji, India, Thailand, Vietnam, Uganda, and South Africa.

PREREQUISITES: Career Break projects for all ages.

DURATION AND TIME OF PLACEMENTS: 2, 4 or 6 weeks.

SELECTION PROCEDURES AND ORIENTATION: Full-time crew support venturers both before departure and overseas on project sites. Thorough pre-departure information, advice, support and fundraising pack provided.

COST: Sample prices for 6 week trips: £1,195 in Asia, £1,295 in Africa; £1,395 in Peru and Fiji (not including flights).

CONTACT: Elaine Lawler (elainel@madventurer.com).

MONDOCHALLENGE

Malsor House, Gayton Road, Milton Malsor, Northampton NN7 3AB, UK

📞 01604 858225; fax: 01604 859323

📧 info@mondochallenge.org

💻 www.mondochallenge.org

PROGRAMME DESCRIPTION: MondoChallenge is a not-for-profit organisation which sends volunteers (post-university, career break, early retired, etc.) to help with teaching and business development programmes in Africa, Asia, South America and Eastern Europe. Programmes are community based, providing volunteers with an insight into local cultures and a chance to experience a different way of life first-hand.

DESTINATIONS: Nepal, India, Sri Lanka, Tanzania, Kenya, The Gambia, Senegal, Ecuador, Chile and Romania.

NUMBER OF PLACEMENTS PER YEAR: 200 approximately.

PREREQUISITES: All ages – average is 35. All nationalities accepted; about half are non-UK based with a large number of volunteers from North America, Europe and Australia. For teaching projects, minimum qualification is A level or equivalent in subjects to be taught. For business development, a minimum of 3 years business experience is required. Must be able to cope with remote posting and to relate to people of other cultures. Enthusiasm, flexibility and good communication skills are essential.

DURATION AND TIME OF PLACEMENTS: Usual stay is 2–4 months and start dates are flexible.

COST: £1,300 for 3 months. Board and lodging in local family homes costs an extra £15 (approximately) per week.

CONTACT: Anthony Lunch, Director.

NEPAL KINGDOM FOUNDATION & MUIR'S TOURS

Nepal House, 97A Swansea Road, Reading RG1 8HA, UK

📞 0118 950 2281

📧 mo@nkf-mt.org.uk

💻 www.nkf-mt.org.uk

Fair trade and eco-adventure travel company that organises volunteer placements.

PROGRAMME DESCRIPTION: Options include English teaching, care for street children (Kolkata), handicraft projects with Tibetans in exile, research on wild horses in Mongolia and looking after huskies in Norwegian Lapland.

DESTINATIONS: Nepal, India, Mongolia, Peru and Norway.

NUMBER OF PLACEMENTS PER YEAR: 75.

DURATION AND TIME OF PLACEMENTS: 3–8 weeks.

PREREQUISITES: Average age of volunteers is 48. All nationalities provided they speak fluent English. Specialist skills not needed for many positions. Candidates must be enthusiastic, articulate, organised and flexible enough to deliver volunteer programmes.

SELECTION PROCEDURES AND ORIENTATION: Applications preferred 2 months prior to departure. Notes of what to expect and how to carry out main role are provided, plus meet and greet service.

COST: From £200/$390 registration, plus daily charge to cover homestay, food and other expenses (usually $20–$90). In some cases higher registration fees are charged for people without relevant experience.

CONTACT: Maurice Adshead, Manager.

Unit 3B, The Plough Brewery, 516 Wandsworth Road, London SW8 3JX, UK

℡ 0845 365 1525

✉ info@nonstopadventure.com

🖥 www.nonstopadventure.com; nonstopski.com; nonstopsnowboard.com

Nonstop Sail business was sold in 2008.

PROGRAMME DESCRIPTION: Ski and snowboard instructor and improvement courses in the Canadian Rockies.

NUMBER OF PLACEMENTS PER YEAR: 500 (30% are aged 30+).

DESTINATION: Canada (Fernie, Whistler, Banff and Red Mountain).

PREREQUISITES: Participants should have at least 1 week's previous snow experience. Couples welcome.

DURATION: Ski & snowboard courses are between 2 and 11 weeks.

QUALIFICATIONS OFFERED: Internationally recognised CSIA (Canadian Ski Instructor Alliance) and CASI (Canadian Association of Snowboard Instructors). Also CAA (Canadian Avalanche Association) Recreational Avalanche 1 certificate and St John's Ambulance Basic first aid certificate. Freestyle and race coach qualifications can also be obtained.

OTHER SERVICES: Work experience may be arranged with local ski school and contacts with other ski schools for instructing jobs provided. Ski accommodation in twin rooms (some quad, triple and single rooms available) in houses/lodge equipped with kitchens and living rooms with stereo and cable TV.

COST: £2,300–£7,150 which includes flights, transfers, accommodation, weekday meals, lift pass, resort transport, professional coaching, weekend trips and (depending on course booked) CSIA/CASI examination, first aid course and avalanche course.

CONTACT: Georgie Bush, Sales Manager.

OPERATION WALLACEA

Wallace House, Old Bolingbroke, Nr Spilsby, Lincolnshire PE23 4EX, UK

℡ 01790 763194; fax: 01790 763825

✉ info@opwall.com

🖥 www.opwall.com

PROGRAMME DESCRIPTION: Marine and rainforest scientific research projects in Indonesia (south-east Sulawesi) and Honduras; desert and marine projects in Egypt; sailing expeditions down the Amazon in Peru; bush and marine projects in South Africa; and turtle monitoring and marine projects in Cuba. Projects aim to carry out good scientific conservation work to enable local people to protect their own environment from destructive practices. Volunteers from all walks of life and ages assist with surveys of marine, desert, bush and rainforest habitats.

DESTINATIONS: Indonesia, Honduras, Egypt, South Africa, Mozambique, Cuba and Peru.

PREREQUISITES: Minimum age 16. Enthusiasm needed.

DURATION AND TIME OF PLACEMENTS: 2, 4, 6 or 8 weeks between June and September.

SELECTION PROCEDURES AND ORIENTATION: No deadlines. Dive training to PADI, OW or BSAC and full training given onsite (reef ecology, jungle training, bushcraft, etc.), included in cost of expedition.

COST: £950 for 2 weeks, £1,750 for 4 weeks, £2,400 for 6 weeks and £2,800 for 8 weeks, excluding flights.

CONTACT: Pippa Disney.

ORANGUTAN FOUNDATION

7 Kent Terrace, London, NW1 4RP, UK

℡ 020 7724 2912; fax: 020 7706 2613

✉ info@orangutan.org.uk

🖥 www.orangutan.org.uk

PROGRAMME DESCRIPTION: Volunteers are based in the Lamandau Reserve near Tanjung Puting National Park in Kalimantan, Indonesian Borneo, the Foundation's current release site for ex-captive and rehabilitated orangutans. Volunteers will get to spend time at Camp Leakey, the historical research site of Dr Biruté Galdikas and may also work in other areas of the Park. Previous projects have included general infrastructure repairs, trail cutting, constructing guard posts, and orangutan release sites. Volunteers should note that there is no direct work or contact with orangutans.

NUMBER OF PLACEMENTS PER YEAR: 36.

DURATION AND TIME OF PLACEMENTS: 6 weeks, 4 teams of no more than 12, departing May, June and August.

PREREQUISITES: Participants must be members of the Orangutan Foundation (£20 per year). They must work well in a team, be fit and healthy and adaptable to difficult and demanding conditions. There is no upper age limit.

SELECTION PROCEDURES AND ORIENTATION: All potential UK volunteers are expected to attend an interview at the Foundation office in London. Phone interviews can be conducted for non-UK applicants. Successful UK applicants are expected to attend a pre-departure briefing day.

COST: Approximately £700, includes all accommodation, food, equipment, materials and transport for the duration of the programme, but does not include international and internal travel to the project site. Prices are confirmed before places are offered and will depend on inflation and exchange rates.
CONTACT: Elly Sanderson, Development and Volunteer Coordinator (elly@orangutan.org.uk).

ORIGINAL VOLUNTEERS
Riverside House, 5 Lovelotaithe, Norwich NR1 1LW, UK
📞 0800 345 7582; 01603 627007
📧 contact@originalvolunteers.info
🖥 www.originalvolunteers.co.uk

PROGRAMME DESCRIPTION: Social care and conservation placements throughout the world.
DESTINATIONS: Mexico, Guatemala, Costa Rica, Honduras, Ecuador, Peru, Argentina, Brazil, Ghana, Kenya, South Africa, Tanzania, India, Nepal, Thailand.
NUMBER OF PLACEMENTS PER YEAR: 300.
DURATION AND TIME OF PLACEMENTS: 2–4 weeks with possibility of combining 2 or more placements.
PREREQUISITES: All ages and backgrounds accepted.
SELECTION PROCEDURES AND ORIENTATION: Informal training given on arrival by local staff or long stay volunteers.
COST: One-off registration fee of £295 plus £20–£40 per week to cover room and board on-site. Accommodation is usually self-catering in shared houses or apartments, with 2/3 volunteers to a room. Sample prices from £100 for 4 weeks in Honduras to £160 in Kenya. Possibility of free placements in Thailand.
CONTACT: Caroline Revell, Senior Projects Advisor.

OUTREACH INTERNATIONAL
Bartletts Farm, Hayes Road, Compton Dundon, Somerton, Somerset TA11 6PF, UK
✆/fax: 01458 274957
📧 info@outreachinternational.co.uk
🖥 www.outreachinternational.co.uk

Member of the Year Out Group. Outreach International is a specialist organisation that places committed volunteers in carefully selected meaningful projects.
PROGRAMME DESCRIPTION: Volunteers can make a valuable contribution to their project while experiencing the pleasures of living and working with local people and immersing themselves in a foreign culture. The projects are small, worthwhile, varied and handpicked. They include humanitarian and aid work, community development, helping in orphanages, teaching English/sports/computer skills to street children, horse riding therapy, teaching in schools on the Pacific coast of Mexico, helping at medical centres, working at centres for disabled children, dance, art and craft projects, conservation work with giant sea turtles and environmental work in the Amazon rainforest. Projects are visited regularly by the Outreach director and other team members. In order to minimise the cultural impact of projects, volunteers are usually placed in pairs and never in a large group. Some placements are ideal for gap year volunteers while others provide a good opportunity for individuals wishing to pursue a career in International development.
DESTINATIONS: Mexico, Costa Rica, Ecuador and the Galapagos Islands, Sri Lanka and Cambodia.
PREREQUISITES: Ideal for confident people with a desire to travel, learn a language and offer their help to a humble

community. Some of the projects need volunteers with skills in physiotherapy, law, report writing, accountancy, computers (IT) and in management. The majority, however, do not need specific skills. Energy, enthusiasm and commitment are more important than official qualifications.

DURATION AND TIME OF PLACEMENTS: Short- and long-term placements lasting a month or more. Flexible departure dates thoughout the summer and also in January, April, and September.

SELECTION PROCEDURES AND ORIENTATION: Outreach International aims to meet all applicants within 3 weeks of applying and let them know what the chosen placement will involve. Each placement has its own project manager, and volunteers have 24-hour in-country support from a full-time coordinator.

COST: £2,700 for 3 months. Includes full insurance (public liability, health and baggage), language course, in-country support, food, accommodation, local travel, all project costs, fundraising, teacher training and pre-departure briefing days in the UK. Extended stays cost approximately £475 per month.

CONTACT: James Chapman, UK Director.

OVERSEAS WORKING HOLIDAYS (OWH)

Level 1, 157 Ann Street, Brisbane, Queensland 4000, Australia

℡ +61 1300 651 639; +61 7 3011 7460; fax: +61 7 3011 7854

1/150 Queen Street, Melbourne, Vic 3000, Australia

℡ +61 3 9248 5500; fax: +61 3 9248 5515

✉ info@owh.au

🖥 www.owh.com.au

Youth travel agency mainly for Australians who want to work and volunteer abroad. Part of the Australian-owned Flight Centre.

PROGRAMME DESCRIPTION: Working holiday programmes in USA, Canada, UK and New Zealand (the latter is open to all nationalities eligible for a working holiday visa). Volunteer placements in India, Kenya, Thailand, Cambodia and Philippines among others.

NUMBER OF PLACEMENTS PER YEAR: 1,500.

DESTINATIONS: Worldwide.

PREREQUISITES: Nationality and age restrictions differ with programme.

DURATION AND TIME OF PLACEMENTS: Variable. Duration of working holiday visa, i.e. winter or summer seasons in Canada (Nov to May or Mar to Oct).

PEAK LEADERS

Mansfield, Strathmiglo, Fife KY14 7QE, Scotland

℡ 01337 860755; fax: 01337 868176

✉ info@peakleaders.com

🖥 www.peakleaders.com

Time out and gap year ski and snowboard instructor courses and performance camps, with possible job offers to high quality candidates on completion.

PROGRAMME DESCRIPTION: Ski and snowboard instructor courses including choice of modules (powder, moguls, free skiing, free riding, park and pipe, ski tuning), along with the services of an experienced leader throughout. Peak Leaders' Ski and Snowboard Instructor courses can also include avalanche awareness, mountain first aid, team leading, back country, freestyle, ski school shadowing and off-piste skiing.

DESTINATIONS: Courses are in Switzerland (Saas Fee, Zermatt and Verbier), Canada (Whistler and Banff), Argentina (Bariloche in Patagonia), New Zealand (Queenstown) and Indian Kashmir (2-week powder experience in Gulmarg).

DURATION OF COURSES: 4–12 weeks. Instructor training in Argentina and New Zealand finishes in September/October, the Saas Fee course finishes in November and high quality, well-organised candidates can get jobs in Europe or Canada by Christmas.

COST: From £3,250 for short courses, up to £7,250. Includes instruction, flights (in some cases), hotel with half board, lift tickets and certification.

OTHER SERVICES: Optional extras are offered like skidoo driving, backcountry training, Spanish and French language and stopover in Buenos Aires. Job advice available.

PEOPLE AND PLACES

1 Naboths Nursery, Canterbury Road, Faversham, Kent ME13 8AX, UK

℡ 08700 460479; fax: +44 203 002 5608

✉ info@travel-peopleandplaces.co.uk

🖥 www.travel-peopleandplaces.co.uk

Volunteer recruitment organisation which was Highly Commended in the Virgin Responsible Tourism Awards 2007. Places volunteers of all ages (mainly 25+) with skills and experience to share. Also works in partnership with Saga Holidays on their volunteer programme (www.saga.co.uk/volunteer) for people aged 50+.

PROGRAMME DESCRIPTION: Various volunteer placements as requested by local communities, liaising with host country partners' project management teams. Examples include: community development work in Bali, training programmes for the unemployed in southern Africa, education development in Nepal, and marine research and child care support.

DESTINATIONS: South Africa, The Gambia, Mozambique, Swaziland, Madagascar, Nepal, India, Pakistan and Indonesia.

NUMBER OF PLACEMENTS PER YEAR: 300+.

PREREQUISITES: Most volunteers are aged 35–45 with a maximum of about 75, though there is no maximum age if volunteers are healthy and can do the work. All nationalities accepted. Volunteers' skills and abilities are more important than age and are matched with needs of individual projects, e.g. child counselling, education/healthcare training or experience, IT skills, practical and trade skills.

DURATION AND TIME OF PLACEMENTS: Most are 4–8 weeks though some are shorter and others last up to 12 weeks.

SELECTION PROCEDURES AND ORIENTATION: Flexible start dates; usually 1 month is needed for screening and placement preparation. Telephone or face-to-face interview required plus Criminal Records screening or equivalent.

OTHER SERVICES: Each volunteer receives comprehensive pre-departure information, including a briefing on responsible volunteering and the communities in which they will be working.

COST: £1,025 for 4 weeks including orientation, half-board accommodation (normally homestay), airport transfers and support throughout. All volunteer fees are paid direct to the host country, and at least 80% of it stays there. Each project description includes details of how and where the volunteer's money will be spent. Volunteers are clearly told in advance how the donation element will be spent for the specific project on which they are working.

CONTACT: Kate Stefanko (Placement Director), Sallie Grayson (Programme Director).

PERSONAL OVERSEAS DEVELOPMENT (PoD)
Linden Cottage, The Burgage, Prestbury, Cheltenham, Gloucestershire GL52 3DJ, UK
✆ 01242 250901
✉ info@thepodsite.co.uk
🖥 www.thepodsite.co.uk

PoD is a small non-profit organisation that arranges placements and courses for volunteers to develop their skills.

PROGRAMME DESCRIPTION: Flexible programmes are designed to provide the essentials for a fulfilling break, which can also be incorporated into existing travel plans. Packages include training, support and accommodation if required. Opportunities include: caring for elephants and wild animals; joining an Amazon jungle conservation project; scuba diving and marine conservation; community building projects; volun-

teering at orphanages and care homes; and teaching English and running summer English camps.

DESTINATIONS: Belize, Cambodia, Malawi, Nepal, Peru, Tanzania and Thailand.

PREREQUISITES: No specific requirements for most placements, just a positive attitude.

DURATION AND TIME OF PLACEMENTS: From 1 week to 1 year, with flexible start dates throughout the year.

SELECTION PROCEDURES AND ORIENTATION: All applicants submit an online application and depending on the project, receive a telephone interview and submit references. A Criminal Records Bureau Check may also be conducted. A detailed information pack is sent to volunteers pre-departure, and local training and introductions are undertaken on arrival in-country.

COST: Short programmes start at £250. Sample prices include 2 months dog and cat care in Thailand for £495/3 months village teaching in Tanzania for £1,195.

CONTACT: Mike Beecham and Alex Tarrant.

PROJECTS ABROAD
Aldsworth Parade, Goring, Sussex BN12 4TX, UK
✆ 01903 708300; fax: 01903 501026
✉ info@projects-abroad.co.uk
🖥 www.projects-abroad.co.uk

Founding member of the Year Out Group. Company arranges voluntary teaching posts as well as placements in care, conservation, animal care, medicine, journalism and other fields around the world.

DESTINATIONS: Argentina, Bolivia, Brazil, Cambodia, China, Costa Rica, Ethiopia, Ghana, India, Jamaica, Mexico, Moldova, Mongolia, Morocco, Nepal, Pakistan, Peru, Romania, Senegal, South Africa, Sri Lanka, Thailand and Togo. Destinations and placements can be combined in a 'Grand Gap'.

NUMBER OF PLACEMENTS PER YEAR: 3,000–4,000.

PREREQUISITES: Volunteers range from 16 to 70.

DURATION AND TIME OF PLACEMENTS: Very flexible, with departures year round. Placements last from 2 weeks to 12 months.

SELECTION PROCEDURES AND ORIENTATION: Paid staff (250 in total) in all destinations who arrange and vet placements, accommodation and work supervisors. They meet volunteers on arrival and provide a final briefing before the placements.

COST: Placements are self-funded and the fee charged includes insurance, food, accommodation, airport pick-up and drop-off and overseas support. 3-month placements cost between £1,395 and £3,000+, depending on placement and destination, excluding travel costs.

QUEST SABBATICALS

The North West Stables, Borde Hill Estate, Balcombe
Road, Haywards Heath, West Sussex RH16 1XP, UK

✆ 01444 474744; fax: 01444 474799

✉ emailus@questoverseas.com;
info@questsabbaticals.com

🖥 www.questsabbaticals.com;
www.questoverseas.com

Part of Quest Overseas, a founding member of the Year
Out Group. Quest Overseas specialises in combining worth-
while voluntary work projects and challenging expeditions to
Africa and Latin America for volunteers of all ages.

PROGRAMME DESCRIPTION: Expedition specialists with
projects and adventure travel in South America and Africa.
Phases include language tuition, volunteer projects such as
working with children or animals, diving surveys and working in
rainforests; 6-week expedition with adventure activities such as
surfing, diving and hang gliding.

DESTINATIONS: Ecuador, Peru, Chile, Bolivia, Brazil, Swaziland,
Tanzania, Mozambique, South Africa, Botswana and Zambia.

NUMBER OF PLACEMENTS PER YEAR: 200+.

PREREQUISITES: An estimated 20% of clients are on career
sabbaticals. No qualifications needed, just enthusiasm.

DURATION AND TIME OF PLACEMENTS: Range of departures
from 3 weeks to 3 months.

SELECTION PROCEDURES AND ORIENTATION: Application deadline 2 weeks before departure. Interviews can be in
person or by phone.

OTHER SERVICES: All participants receive a joining pack
and access to help and advice. They are also invited to a
2-day training event, which covers all topics in preparation for
overseas travel and project work.

RALEIGH

Third Floor, 207 Waterloo Road, London SE1 8XD, UK

✆ 020 7183 1270/1

✉ volunteermanagers@raleigh.org.uk

🖥 www.raleigh.org.uk

Raleigh is a leading youth charity with 24 years experience
of organising transformational and challenging expeditions
around the world. The charity works with young people from all
backgrounds and nationalities to enable them to make a positive contribution to society, and to help facilitate their personal
and social development.

PROGRAMME DESCRIPTION: Volunteer managers (aged
25–75) use their professional and personal skills to support young
people in undertaking sustainable community, environmental
and adventure projects overseas. These projects are designed
in partnership with government ministries, local communities
and NGOs to ensure that they are worthwhile and sustainable.
Volunteer managers will either be based at Raleigh headquarters
in the expedition country or on project sites. The experience is well
suited to anyone interested in education development, looking for a
constructive and challenging way to spend a career break or as a
motivational tool for a possible change of career.

DESTINATIONS: Costa Rica, Nicaragua, India, Malaysia, Borneo.

NUMBER OF PLACEMENTS PER YEAR: 300–350 staff (9–10
programmes per year).

PREREQUISITES: Applicants must be aged over 25 and have
relevant skills and experience in at least one of the following: administration, building and carpentry, communications and creativity, driving, finance, logistics, medic/nursing/paramedic (qualified),
photography, project management, Spanish interpretation, trekking
and outdoor instruction, or working with young people. A 'can-do'
attitude and the energy and desire to benefit communities and
young people from around the world are also necessary.

DURATION AND TIME OF PLACEMENTS: Up to 13 weeks (including 2 weeks' in-country training before the programme begins and a week after the expedition ends).

SELECTION PROCEDURES AND ORIENTATION: Successful applicants are invited to an assessment weekend which simulates potential team challenges through physical exercises and problem solving.

COST: Volunteer managers are asked to contribute £1,500 to cover their training costs and living expenses (around £860 using Gift Aid). Bursaries are available for some positions (e.g. doctors, nurses and qualified outdoor professionals).

CONTACT: Eileen Fisher, Volunteer Manager Recruitment Coordinator.

RIGHT TO PLAY

65 Queen Street West, Thomson Building, Suite 1900, Box 64, Toronto, Ontario M5H 2M5, Canada

- 416 498 1922; fax: 416 498 1942
- recruitment@righttoplay.com
- www.righttoplay.com

International NGO committed to improving the lives of children in the most disadvantaged areas of the world, by using the power of sport and play for development, health and peace.

PROGRAMME DESCRIPTION: International volunteers help implement sport and play programmes by training local community members and community leaders in Right to Play resources.

DESTINATIONS: Developing countries depending on project needs.

PREREQUISITES: Appreciation for sport and play as a tool for community development; experience in: workshop facilitation, adult education, coaching, project administration, leadership development and training of trainers. Volunteers who have previous experience of implementing projects in an international development context.

DURATION AND TIME OF PLACEMENTS: 1-year placements.

REMUNERATION: RTP pays for training expenses, in-field accommodation and transport, health insurance and vaccination costs up to Can$500. Also pays an honorarium of US$8,000 for 1 year.

CONTACT: Kerry Emmonds, International Volunteer Services Manager.

ROBBOOKER VOLUNTARY ORGANIZATION (RVO)

Box RY 655 Railways, Kumasi, Ghana

- +233 51 47956; mobile: +233 24 4591378; fax: +233 51 34493
- info@robborg.org; volunteer@robborg.org
- www.robborg.org

RVO was registered in Kumasi, Ghana in 2000, and is dedicated to service projects across Ghana.

PROGRAMME DESCRIPTION: Volunteer projects in Ghana include orphanage work, HIV/Aids eduction, healthcare and community work. Internships and teaching placements are also available.

DESTINATIONS: Throughout Ghana.

NUMBER OF PLACEMENTS PER YEAR: 50.

PREREQUISITES: Ages 17–45. All nationalities. No special qualifications needed.

DURATION AND TIME OF PLACEMENTS: 2–12 weeks.

SELECTION PROCEDURES AND ORIENTATION: Written applications accepted on an ongoing basis. Pre-departure profile on Ghana is sent to volunteers before departure. In-country orientations about project and host families are given to volunteers on arrival.

OTHER SERVICES: Language (Twi) and cultural studies can be arranged.

COST: From $600 for 2 weeks to $1,200 for 12 weeks plus extra $75 per week thereafter. Programme fee includes homestay accommodation and all meals, airport transfers, access to free Internet, donation to project, etc.

CONTACT: Richmond Amoakoh, Director.

RURAL CENTRE FOR HUMAN INTERESTS (RUCHI)

Bandh, Bhaguri 173233, District Solan, Himachal Pradesh, India

- +91 1792 207002 ; +91 1792 207003
- info@ruchin.org
- www.ruchin.org

The TOTEM programme enables people to work in one of 200 villages for spells of 2 weeks (or longer) as volunteers in India.

PROGRAMME DESCRIPTION: Volunteers can choose between the Environmental Management Programme, the Social Development Programme and the Health and Sanitation Development Programme.

DESTINATIONS: Himachal Pradesh, India.

NUMBER OF PLACEMENTS PER YEAR: 10.

PREREQUISITES: For ages 20–60. All candidates are welcome to apply. The key acceptance criterion is whether the candidate has enough international travel experience to handle the basic conditions in a grassroots organisation.

DURATION AND TIME OF PLACEMENTS: 3-week placements for working professionals, starting on fifth day of every month (though start dates are flexible). Extensions can be negotiated for up to 6 months.

COST: $1,000 for 3 weeks; cost for longer placements negotiable. Fee includes transport from Kalka or Chandigarh railway station, use of private car with driver when at RUCHI, accommodation and all vegetarian meals.

SAGA VOLUNTEER TRAVEL

The Saga Building, Enbrook Park, Folkestone, Kent CT20 3SE, UK

✆ volunteer@saga.co.uk

🖳 www.saga.co.uk/volunteer

Division of Saga launched 2006 linked with the Saga Charitable Trust.

PROGRAMME DESCRIPTION: Volunteer placements, some offered in conjunction with People and Places (see entry).

DESTINATIONS: South Africa, Nepal, Sri Lanka (2009) and St Lucia (2009).

COST: From £2,599 for 4 weeks (including flights and hotels as part of a complete package).

SCHOOLHOUSE VOLUNTEERING

Schoolhouse, Anderson Road, Ballater, Aberdeenshire AB35 5QW, Scotland

✆ 01339 756333

✆ info@schoolhousevolunteering.com

🖳 www.schoolhousevolunteering.com

New volunteering programme that has grown out of Schoolhouse English, a family-run language school in Scotland, plus a long-standing connection of the owners with Sri Lanka and India.

PROGRAMME DESCRIPTION: Volunteer English teachers and teaching assistants are placed in government schools through the Ministry of Education in Colombo and a partner organisation in Tamil Nadu.

DESTINATIONS: Sri Lanka and India.

NUMBER OF PLACEMENTS PER YEAR: New company so numbers not known.

DURATION AND TIME OF PLACEMENTS: Minimum one term, starting in October or January (when directors will be on hand to oversee settling-in period).

PREREQUISITES: Directors are keen to work with older volunteers.

SELECTION PROCEDURES AND ORIENTATION: Personal service given to volunteers in the form of pre-placement training and cultural orientation. Assistance given with obtaining visas. Volunteers will stay with host families or in a serviced house with a group of other volunteers. Support given throughout placement.

COST: For Sri Lanka; first month £1,065, plus £465 for each additional month. For India; first month £1,025, plus £425 per month. Price includes 6-day residential school house certified training and preparation course, 3-day orientation course, accomodation, most meals and local transport.

CONTACT: Alan and Cathy Low, Directors.

SPW (STUDENTS PARTNERSHIP WORLDWIDE)

2nd Floor, Faith House, 7 Tufton Street, London SW1P 3QB, UK

☏ 020 7490 0100

✆ info@spw.org

🖳 www.spw.org

European, American and Australian volunteers aged 18–28 are recruited to work in partnership with counterpart volunteers from Africa and Asia. In pairs or groups they live and work in rural communities for 5–12 months. Their input builds awareness, and begins to change attitudes and behaviour to important health, social and environmental issues among young people and communities. All volunteers take part in training which covers health, hygiene, sanitation, nutrition and the environment, with a particular emphasis on HIV/Aids prevention and care. SPW is a non-profit making charity.

PROGRAMME DESCRIPTION: SPW runs health education and environment programmes. These programmes tackle youth problems from different perspectives. All placements are in rural areas.

DESTINATIONS: India, Nepal, South Africa, Tanzania, Uganda and Zambia.

NUMBER OF PLACEMENTS PER YEAR: 200 places for European, American and Australian volunteers.

PREREQUISITES: A level or equivalent qualifications. Volunteers need to be physically and mentally healthy, hard working, open-minded, enthusiastic and have good communication skills.

DURATION AND TIME OF PLACEMENTS: 4–8 months with starting dates throughout the year.

SELECTION PROCEDURES AND ORIENTATION: Every applicant is required to attend an information and selection day in London. This also gives them the opportunity to meet staff and ex-volunteers. Following selection, volunteers are accepted on a first come first served basis, so early application is recommended.

COST: Minimum donation of £3,600 to the charity. All costs are then covered by SPW, including open return flight, accommodation, basic living allowance, insurance, in-country work permit, UK briefings and general administrative support, and extensive overseas training and support.

STARFISH VENTURES

PO Box 9061, Epping, CM16 7WU, UK

✆/fax: 0800 197 4817

✉ enquiries@starfishventures.co.uk

🖥 www.starfishventures.co.uk

Starfish Ventures is a British company founded in 2003 which specialises in supporting development projects in Thailand. Volunteers work closely with Starfish's Thai partner organisations (such as the Education Administration of Surin Province and Thailand's Marine and Coastal Protection Organisation). In addition to placing volunteers, Starfish delivers financial aid and provides expertise and project management.

PROGRAMME DESCRIPTION: Volunteer programmes in teaching, development, animal welfare, conservation, construction and medicine.

DESTINATIONS: Throughout Thailand including Surin, Maehongson, Phuket and Rayong.

PREREQUISITES: Ages 18–70 (older volunteers may be accepted but will need to discuss insurance cover and any medical conditions). All nationalities accepted. Criminal Records Bureau (CRB) certificate essential for UK applicants, non-UK residents must provide evidence of no criminal record.

DURATION AND TIME OF PLACEMENTS: 2–12 weeks, longer placements can be arranged.

SELECTION PROCEDURES AND ORIENTATION: Applicants must apply at least 6 weeks prior to the volunteer's chosen departure date. Suitable projects are suggested on basis of applicant's CV. Volunteers joining a Teaching Venture attend a TEFL training weekend. Comprehensive briefing kit given. Thai coordinators help candidates orientate themselves in their new surroundings, make regular checks throughout placement and provide a 24-hour support service.

COST: £700 (2 weeks) to £1,400 (12 weeks). Includes preparatory TEFL training weekend (only for teaching placements), airport pickup and transfer to placement destination, insurance, in-country coordinator and 24-hour support, travel within Thailand, plus accommodation in private room in privately rented house or guesthouse.

CONTACT: Dan Moore (Founder) or Steve Williams (Director).

SUDAN VOLUNTEER PROGRAMME

34 Estelle Road, London NW3 2JY, UK

✆ 020 7485 8619

✉ davidsvp@blueyonder.co.uk

🖥 www.svp-uk.com

PROGRAMME DESCRIPTION: Sudan Volunteer Programme works with undergraduates and graduates who are native English speakers and who wish to teach English in Sudan. Teaching tends to be informal in style, with 4–5 hours of contact a day. Volunteers can plan their own teaching schemes, such as arranging games, dramas, competitions and tests for assessing skills learned by the students. Accommodation is in flats shared with other volunteers.

DESTINATIONS: Sudan, mostly in and around Khartoum area and especially Omdurman.

PREREQUISITES: TEFL certificate, experience of travelling in developing countries and some knowledge of Arabic are helpful but not obligatory. Volunteers must be in good health and be native English speakers, and have experience of living away from home. Older candidates with teaching experience are welcome to participate.

DURATION AND TIME OF PLACEMENTS: Preferred minimum 8 months. Shorter summer placements are possible.

SELECTION PROCEDURES AND ORIENTATION: Applications accepted year round. Two referees are required. Prior to departure, medical check-up required plus selection interviews, orientation and briefings. Volunteers are required to write a report of their experiences and to advise new volunteers.

COST: Volunteers must raise the cost of the airfare to Sudan (currently £485) plus £60 (cost of the first 3 months insurance). SVP pays subsistence, accommodation and insurance beyond the initial 3 months.

CONTACT: David Wolton (at email above).

TASK BRASIL TRUST

PO Box 4901, London SE16 3PP, UK

✆ 020 7735 5545; fax: 020 7735 5675

✉ info@taskbrasil.org.uk

🖥 www.taskbrasil.org.uk

TASK stands for Trust for Abandoned Street Kids.

PROGRAMME DESCRIPTION: Volunteer projects in Rio de Janeiro working with children and teenagers from troubled backgrounds. Volunteers are involved in the day-to-day care of the children and in offering activities such as art, English lessons, sports, music and swimming, or in outreach work on the streets of Rio. Other volunteer work takes part at the projects themselves, and volunteers assist Task Brasil staff in their work (e.g. on the streets, or in Casa Jimmy caring for teenage mums and their babies).

DESTINATIONS: Rio de Janeiro, Brazil.

NUMBER OF PLACEMENTS PER YEAR: 100.

PREREQUISITES: Average age 26. Experience working with children/adolescents. Ability to teach English (TEFL) and/or organise activities such as arts, sports, music or swimming is also useful.

DURATION AND TIME OF PLACEMENTS: 1–12 months. Volunteers accepted year round. Should apply at least 2 months before start date.

SELECTION PROCEDURES AND ORIENTATION: Interviews in UK are essential and candidates must attend induction meetings.

OTHER SERVICES: Volunteers attend preparatory sessions including at least one meeting with ex-volunteers to discuss what volunteering consists of and to pose any questions they have.

COST: Self-catering shared accommodation and food are provided. Placements cost £1,000 for up to three months, £1,500 for up to six months and £2,500 for up to a year. Volunteers over 21 work on the streets of Rio. Placements cost £1,200–£2,500.

CONTACT: Sany Ittoo, Admin Assistant.

TRAVELLERS WORLDWIDE
2A Caravelle House, 17/19 Goring Road, Worthing, West Sussex BN12 4AP, UK
℅ 01903 502595; fax: 01903 708179
✏ info@travellersworldwide.com
🖥 www.travellersworldwide.com

Founder member of the Year Out Group. Volunteer programme for people taking a career break, gap year or want to do something constructive in retirement.

PROGRAMME DESCRIPTION: Voluntary work overseas on different types of project, open to all individuals and groups. Projects include teaching conversational English (and other subjects such as sports, music, drama, art, maths, geography, IT), care and orphanage placements, conservation programmes including rehabilitation of endangered species, marine projects, African wildlife courses, structured work experience in sectors such as law, journalism, media and medicine; language courses (e.g. Spanish, Mandarin, Brazilian Portuguese, Swahili, Tamil) and cultural courses (meditation, photography, tango, music, martial arts).

DESTINATIONS: Argentina, Australia, Bolivia, Brazil, Brunei, China, Ghana, Guatemala, India, Kenya, Malawi, Malaysia, New Zealand, Peru, South Africa, Sri Lanka, Tanzania, Thailand, Zambia and Zimbabwe.

NUMBER OF PLACEMENTS PER YEAR: 1,000+.

PREREQUISITES: Open to ages 17–90. Approximately 30%–40% of Travellers' volunteers are between late 20s and retirees. No formal qualifications required. Travellers runs a weekend TEFL course in the UK (check details at www.tefltime.com).

DURATION AND TIME OF PLACEMENTS: 2 weeks to 1 year with flexible start dates all year round.

COST: Sample charges from £675 for 2 weeks to £1,425 for 12 weeks with additional weeks at £80 each. Prices include food and accommodation, plus transport, airport pick-up, local support and back-up. Travellers staff overseas, but do not include international travel, visas or insurance. (Travellers can arrange the latter but many volunteers prefer the flexibility of organising their own.)

TREKFORCE EXPEDITIONS
Garden Studios, Betterton Street, London WC2H 9BP, UK
℅ 020 7866 8110
✏ info@trekforce.org.uk
🖥 www.trekforce.org.uk

Trekforce is on the executive committee of the Year Out Group and is carbon neutral in association with the World Land Trust.

PROGRAMME DESCRIPTION: Expedition programmes ideal for career gappers as well as young gappers, focusing on rainforest conservation, community and scientific projects. Programmes can incorporate a combination of expedition project work, a Spanish language course, teaching in rural communities, trekking, adventure and dive phases. Expedition leader course also available.

DESTINATIONS: Central America, South America, Morocco, Nepal, Borneo, Papua New Guinea and Australia.

PREREQUISITES: All ages. Must be generally fit and healthy.

DURATION AND TIME OF PLACEMENTS: Programmes last 1–5 months, all year round.

SELECTION PROCEDURES AND ORIENTATION: Interested participants may attend a one-to-one in the office. Regular open days are also held. Briefing day in the UK and in-country training are provided for expedition members.

COST: From £1,200 for 2-week project to £4,100 for a 5-month Ultimate Gap Year and £910 for a work abroad programme including a guaranteed job in Australia. Fundraising advice is given to all volunteers.

PROGRAMME DESCRIPTION: Range of volunteer programmes in developing countries. Project types include community development, conservation, medicine and teaching. Also paid and unpaid work experience programmes, mostly in Europe (including government funded vocational training programmes).

DESTINATIONS: Volunteer programmes in Asia, Africa, North and South America and Australasia. Work experience in Europe, Australia and New Zealand.

NUMBER OF PLACEMENTS PER YEAR: 400+.

PREREQUISITES: Average age of participants 25, with plans to develop the older market. All nationalities accepted, subject to visa requirements. Generally there are no specific skills required, just enthusiasm, an open mind and a willingness to get involved.

DURATION AND TIME OF PLACEMENTS: From 1 week to 2 years.

SELECTION PROCEDURES AND ORIENTATION: Some programmes require 3 months notice, others need much less processing time. All programmes have some form of orientation/induction/training in the host country, and some include a UK-based induction programme. There are no interviews.

OTHER SERVICES: Accommodation varies. Some programmes offer comfortable fully furnished rooms with en-suite facilities; in other cases, participants will be camping in the wilderness for short periods with limited facilities.

COST: Varying programme costs.

CONTACT: Barry Johnson.

Career break experiences in Latin America, Africa and Asia consisting of 3 distinct phases: 1. Learn the language 2. Volunteer with the community 3. Explore and enjoy. Development projects are funded by the VentureCo Trust, a UK registered charity. ATOL license 5306.

PROGRAMME DESCRIPTION: A combination of language courses, community development projects and expeditions, allows career gap travellers to explore off the beaten track, learn about the host country and give something back to the communities where they stay.

DESTINATIONS: VentureCo has 13 itineraries operating in 19 countries across Latin America, Africa and Asia.

NUMBER OF PLACEMENTS PER YEAR: 175.

PREREQUISITES: Career gap ventures for those 21 and over Gap year ventures for ages 17–20. No upper age limit. Must have enthusiasm and an open mind.

DURATION AND TIME OF PLACEMENTS: Ventures range from 2 to 15 weeks. Departures year round.

SELECTION PROCEDURES AND ORIENTATION. Attendance at an open evening, held in London on the first Tuesday of every month, can be booked by phone or online. Pre-departure travel course held in the UK lasting 1 or 3 days depending on venture. Planning, leading and organisational roles throughout the venture are shared among the team.

COST: Venture costs range from £600 for a 2-week volunteer project, to £1,895 for a 6-week summer venture and from

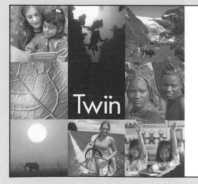

£3,705 for a full 12-week career gap venture. Cost includes a 3-day travel safety course, accommodation, in-country transport, language tuition, project funding and food and expedition activities. Flights, airport taxes, insurance and visas are not included.

CONTACTS: Jenny Hill and Seth Harris, Venture Co-ordinators.

VERBIER-SUMMITS PARAGLIDING

Chalet Anguillita, Chemin de la cote 15, 1934 Verbier, Switzerland

☏ +41 (0)79 313 5677; fax: +41 (0)27 776 1134

✉ stu@verbier-summits.com

🖥 www.verbier-summits.com; www.flygap.com

PROGRAMME DESCRIPTION: Paragliding holidays in the Alps specially suited to people taking career breaks.

DESTINATIONS: Switzerland.

NUMBER OF PLACEMENTS PER YEAR: 200.

DURATION AND TIME OF PLACEMENTS: 1-week beginner's course to 8-week instructor's course.

PREREQUISITES: All nationalities. Average age 30–45. Participants receive thorough training, both theory and practical. Participants with no flying experience can gain a pilot's licence.

COST: From £1,000 for a week to £5,000 for 8 weeks. Includes luxury accommodation and 5-star cuisine.

CONTACT: Stuart Belbas, Director.

VESL (VOLUNTEERS FOR EDUCATIONAL SUPPORT & LEARNING)

19 Bryson Road, Polworth, Edinburgh EH11 1ED, Scotland

☏ 0845 094 3727

✉ info@vesl.org

🖥 www.vesl.org

Formerly Volunteers for English in Sri Lanka, VESL is a charity registered in the UK and an NGO in Sri Lanka, and sends volunteers to work on projects in Asia.

PROGRAMME DESCRIPTION: Volunteers and qualified teachers are sent to run English language summer schools and for long er periods in remote communities in the southern, central and north-eastern provinces of Sri Lanka. Work is being done in response to the tsunami.

DESTINATIONS: Sri Lanka mainly, also India and Thailand, with possibility of expanding to other countries.

NUMBER OF PLACEMENTS PER YEAR: Up to 40.

PREREQUISITES: Minimum age 18, though most volunteers are older. Volunteers should be enthusiastic, motivated and up for a challenge. TEFL experience and some experience overseas are helpful but not a requirement.

DURATION AND TIME OF PLACEMENTS: 3–6 month projects throughout the year and also 4/5 week summer programmes in July and August.

SELECTION PROCEDURES AND ORIENTATION: Applications accepted throughout the year. All candidates are invited to information and selection days that take place throughout the UK.

COST: From £400 to £850-£950. Includes induction and training day, in-country travel, insurance, visas, food, accommodation and comprehensive back-up and support.

CONTACT: Tom Harrison, Programme Director.

VOLUNTEER AFRICA

PO Box 24, Bakewell, Derbyshire DE45 1YP, UK

✉ support@volunteerafrica.org

🖥 www.volunteerafrica.org

PROGRAMME DESCRIPTION: UK charity recruits volunteers to work on community projects in Tanzania, e.g. in rural development or working with children.

DESTINATIONS: Singida and Tabora regions of Tanzania.

PREREQUISITES: All ages above 18.

DURATION AND TIME OF PLACEMENTS: 4, 7, 10, 11 or 12 weeks.

OTHER SERVICES: Other vacancies in Africa with various charities and aid agencies are also posted on this website.

COST: Fees are £1,050 (4 weeks), £1,380 (7 weeks), £1,710 (10 weeks), £1,950 (11–12 weeks), a proportion of which are a donation to the host programme.

CONTACT: Moya Cutts, Volunteer Coordinator.

VOLUNTEER PETEN

Parque Ecologico Nueva Juventud, San Andres, Peten, Guatemala

✆ (502) 5711 0040

✉ volunteerpeten@hotmail.com

🖥 www.volunteerpeten.com

Not-for-profit organisation which recruits volunteers to help protect and manage a 150-acre reserve in San Andres, provide environmental education to all the schools in the area, aid and assist small community organisations, schools, and families, and to provide quality volunteer opportunities for travellers and students.

PROGRAMME DESCRIPTION: Volunteer projects are concerned with ecological management or education. Ecological management includes maintaining a 150-acre reserve, trail management, gardening, tree nursery management, medicinal plants, reforestation projects, and ecological restoration projects. Education includes environmental education, general education in local schools, library management and activities, extracurricular activities, and adult education. Volunteers also work on various construction projects throughout the year.

DESTINATIONS: San Andres, Peten, Northern Guatemala.

NUMBER OF PLACEMENTS PER YEAR: 180.

PREREQUISITES: Average age 25. Volunteers should be open-minded and hard working.

DURATION AND TIME OF PLACEMENTS: 4–12 weeks.

SELECTION PROCEDURES AND ORIENTATION: Rolling acceptance of volunteers. Orientation, tour of facilities and projects, use of equipment and tools, and daily supervision by staff.

COST: $350 for 4 weeks, $650 for 8 weeks and $900 for 12 weeks, which includes room and board with local family, training, all activities, and use of resources on a project.

CONTACT: Matthew R. Peters, Director.

VOLUNTEER ZAMBIA

216 Mosi Oa Tunya Road, Livingstone, Zambia

✆ +260 213 323432; fax: +260 213 323433

✉ info@volunteerzambia.com

🖥 www.volunteerzambia.com

PROGRAMME DESCRIPTION: Community volunteer opportunities in education, sports coaching, health, vocational college based training and wildlife management.

DESTINATIONS: Zambia.

DURATION AND TIME OF PLACEMENTS: Minimum 1 month.

PREREQUISITES: Average age of participants is 25–40. Volunteers should have any adaptable vocational qualification, maturity, a realistic and flexible attitude and an independent nature.

SELECTION PROCEDURES AND ORIENTATION: Start dates year round. Interview preferred, can be arranged via Skype. Participants are met at Livingstone International Airport, and introduced to their project.

OTHER SERVICES: Independent tourism advice, activities, safaris and onward travel centre via African Horizons (www.adventure-africa.com).

COST: From $250 per week, including shared or private self-catering accommodation with security, TV and swimming pool. Wildlife volunteers may stay in permanent tented accommodation at the project site.

CONTACT: Becx Whitefield (In-house Manager) or Richard Sheppard (Owner).

VOLUNTHAI (VOLUNTEERS FOR THAILAND)

86/24 Soi Kanprapa, Prachachoun Road, Bahng Sue, Bangkok 10800, Thailand,

✆ +1 202 403 1540

✉ info@volunthai.com

🖥 www.volunthai.com

PROGRAMME DESCRIPTION: Volunteer teaching in 20 target schools with homestay. Volunteers teach conversational English in the classroom for 3–4 hours a day.

DESTINATIONS: Rural areas in remote provinces of Thailand.

NUMBER OF PLACEMENTS PER YEAR: 100.

DURATION AND TIME OF PLACEMENTS: 1 month minimum.

PREREQUISITES: Ages 21–60. College degree required. Must be speaker of English, native or non-native. Must be willing to live with and learn from the locals.

SELECTION PROCEDURES AND ORIENTATION: Rolling admissions. Online interviews. Volunteers are met in Bangkok for an introduction, and then go to the headquarters in rural Chaiyaphum for a 2-day training in Thai culture and language. A Thai teacher is available at the homestay to help with teaching and to answer any questions.

COST: Modest monthly fee ($375 for two months) to cover comfortable homestay and three fine Thai meals a day. Volunteers pay for their own travel costs.

CONTACT: Michael Anderson, Founder and Leader.

VSO (VOLUNTARY SERVICE OVERSEAS)

317 Putney Bridge Road, London SW15 2PN, UK

✆ 020 8780 7500; fax: 020 8780 7300

✉ enquiry@vso.org.uk

🖥 www.vso.org.uk; www.vsointernational.org

International development charity which works on long-term partnerships with overseas organisations worldwide. Offices also in Dublin, Ottawa, Nairobi, New Delhi, Quezon City and Utrecht. More detailed information about VSO may be found in Part 4, *Doing Something Worthwhile.*

PROGRAMME DESCRIPTION: Volunteers are assigned to suitable projects abroad, primarily in the fields of education, health, natural resources, technical trades and engineering, IT, business, management and social work.

DESTINATIONS: Worldwide.

NUMBER OF PLACEMENTS PER YEAR: 750+.

PREREQUISITES: Must have professional skills or experience that can be matched with an overseas need. Average age of volunteers is 41; maximum age about 75. High level of commitment required.

DURATION AND TIME OF PLACEMENTS: 1–2 years. Short-term specialist assignments now available for highly experienced professionals who can work at senior levels. Business partnership placements for volunteers from the corporate world who can be seconded for periods of 6–12 months.

SELECTION PROCEDURES AND ORIENTATION: Rigorous selection procedures and extensive training provided.

COST: None. Volunteer receives living expenses and wages in line with local workers, plus accommodation, flights, insurance and training.

WARREN SMITH SKI ACADEMY

Switzerland: Chalet Zapreskie, 1936 Verbier, Switzerland

✆ +41 79 359 6566

UK: ✆ 01525 374757

✉ warrensmith@snowsportsynergy.com

🖥 www.warrensmith-skiacademy.com

gap-year-ski-instructor-course.htm

PROGRAMME DESCRIPTION: Gap year ski instructor courses and ski performance improvement courses.

DESTINATION: Verbier, Switzerland.

NUMBER OF PLACEMENTS PER YEAR: 30 BASI trainees per year.

DURATION AND TIME: 9 weeks (10 Jan to 14 Mar 2009).

PREREQUISITES: Minimum age 16; average age 35.

QUALIFICATIONS OFFERED: BASI Level 1 + Level 2 qualifications. In 2008, academy achieved 100% pass rate.

COST: £6,499 with accommodation, £4,299 without accommodation.

ACCOMMODATION: Half board, excellent food, en suite, in centre of Verbier.

CONTACT: Warren Smith, Director of Coaching.

WLS INTERNATIONAL LTD

29 Harley Street, London W1G 9QR, UK

✆ 0870 479 5145; fax: 0870 479 7631

✉ info@GapYearInAsia.com

🖥 www.GapYearInAsia.com

PROGRAMME DESCRIPTION: Affordable volunteering programmes in Asia.

DESTINATIONS: China, Cambodia, India, Nepal, the Philippines, Thailand and Vietnam.

NUMBER OF PLACEMENTS PER YEAR: 350.

DURATION AND TIME OF PLACEMENTS: 1–12 weeks.

PREREQUISITES: All nationalities welcome. Most participants are aged 20–35 but no limit. Volunteers must have enthusiasm, flexibility and a willingness to help. Candidates should be willing to prepare ideas for English lessons in advance of their trip.

SELECTION PROCEDURES AND ORIENTATION: Most candidates book a month in advance but last-minute placements are available.

COST: Sample prices £505 for 4 weeks in Nepal (plus £50 for each extra week), and £585 for 4 weeks in the

Philippines plus £55 per extra week. Accommodation in guesthouse or as homestay.

CONTACT: Kurt De Corte, Programme Manager.

WORLDWIDE EXPERIENCE

Guardian House, Borough Road, Godalming, Surrey GU7 2AE, UK

01483 860560; fax: 01483 860391

info@worldwideexperience.com

www.worldwideexperience.com

PROGRAMME DESCRIPTION: Global conservation and community development combined programmes. Worldwide Experience specialises in conservation projects in South Africa working on some of the world's leading game reserves, rehabilitation centres and ocean research projects.

DESTINATIONS: South Africa, Kenya, Namibia, Malawi and Sri Lanka.

NUMBER OF PLACEMENTS PER YEAR: 100–150.

PREREQUISITES: Minimum age 17, no maximum. No particular skills needed but should be passionate about conservation. All nationalities accepted.

DURATION AND TIME OF PLACEMENTS: 2, 4, 8 or 12 weeks. Summer holiday, gap year and sabbaticals.

SELECTION PROCEDURES AND ORIENTATION: Applications accepted year round. Open days are arranged, e.g. in London, to meet potential volunteers and to discuss details of placements. Full medical and personal checklist is supplied during preparation. Company is a member of IATA so can issue air tickets on request.

COST: From £1,199 for a 4-week placement to £3,599 for a 12-week placement. Inclusive of meals, accommodation, transfers and placement activities.

YHA (YOUTH HOSTEL ASSOCIATION)

Recruitment Department, Trevelyan House, Matlock, Derbyshire DE4 3YH, UK

01629 592656

jobs@yha.org.uk

www.yha.org.uk

Seasonal youth hostel assistants are required to help run the YHA's 208 youth hostels in England and Wales.

EMPLOYMENT AVAILABLE: Assistants undertake various duties including catering, reception work and assisting the manager with all aspects of the day-to-day running of a hostel.

NUMBER OF PLACEMENTS PER YEAR: 300.

PREREQUISITES: Experience in one or more of the relevant duties is desirable, but lots of enthusiasm and excellent customer service is essential.

DURATION OF EMPLOYMENT: One week Between February and October.

WAGES: Competitive salary and benefits package. Employee accommodation available at most locations, for which there is a nominal charge.

SELECTION PROCEDURES AND ORIENTATION: Recruitment mainly in December and around Easter, with some recruitment and selection events during winter.

YOMPS

10 Woodland Way, Brighton, East Sussex BN1 8BA, UK

0045 000 1100; fax 020 7149 9933

info@yomps.co.uk

www.yomps.co.uk

PROGRAMME DESCRIPTION: Multi-country trips suitable for career breaks combining adventure, training courses, exploration, volunteering and cultural experiences.

DESTINATIONS: South Africa, Namibia, Malawi, Kenya, Botswana, Zambia, Zimbabwe, Mozambique, Mexico, Ecuador, Venezuela, Chile, Peru, Thailand, Fiji and Switzerland.

NUMBER OF PLACEMENTS PER YEAR: 200+.

DURATION AND TIME OF PLACEMENTS: 2 weeks to 1 year; average adventure lasts 8–12 weeks.

PREREQUISITES: All nationalities. Most participants are aged 19–25 but older candidates welcome. Sometimes specific skills are required.

SELECTION PROCEDURES AND ORIENTATION:
Applications accepted year round. Interviews sometimes required (by telephone). Field manual provided pre-departure and project orientation on arrival.

COST: Prices from £649 for short trips. Sample cost of 3/6-month Venezuela explorer trips is £1,995/£3,499. Prices include accommodation which varies according to trip, e.g. a chalet (Switzerland), a tented camp (South Africa), a seafront volunteer base (South Africa/Mexico), a coastal volunteer base on the southern shores of Lake Malawi, a specifically designed overlanding vehicle (Southern Africa), under the stars (Namibia), a rural guest house (South Africa), an Amazonian rainforest research base (Ecuador) and camping out in the Patagonian wilderness (Chile).

YOUTHREACH

11 Community Centre, Ground Floor, Saket,
New Delhi 110017, India

☏ +91 11 41649067; +91 11 41664084/5;
fax: +91 11 26533520/25/30

✉ yrd@youthreachindia.org

🖥 www.youthreachindia.org

PROGRAMME DESCRIPTION: Youthreach matches volunteers with NGOs working to assist disadvantaged children, women, the environment, animals, disability and HIV/Aids. Tasks for volunteers range from teaching academic subjects/art and craft, to skilled professionals contributing their time by building the capacities of the staff/grassroots workers of NGO partners.

DESTINATIONS: India (Delhi and environs, Bangalore and Hyderabad).

NUMBER OF PLACEMENTS PER YEAR: Approximately 30.

PREREQUISITES: Age range 25–40+. All nationalities are welcome. Many skills can be put to use from graphic design to occupational therapy.

DURATION AND TIME OF PLACEMENTS: Very flexible: 4–52 weeks.

SELECTION PROCEDURES AND ORIENTATION: Ongoing acceptance. Various projects are described on the volunteer portal of the website and prospective volunteers identify which would suit their skills and preferences before submitting CV and cover letter. Youthreach then tries to match volunteer with NGO and stays in touch every fortnight or month of their stay, so that a structured volunteering programme can be worked out.

OTHER SERVICES: No accommodation provided. Most foreign volunteers live in guest houses/hotels.

COST: Nil.

CONTACT: Priyanjana Ghosh, Senior Coordinator, Mass Volunteerism Programme.

KEY US ORGANISATIONS

Of the thousands of organisations large and small offering programmes of possible interest (primarily to North American grown-ups planning a gap year but often to people of any nationality), here is a selection of important ones for prospective volunteers, travellers or learners.

Adelante LLC – 601 Taper Drive, Seal Beach, CA 90740; ☎+1 562 799 9133; info@adelanteabroad.com; www.adelanteabroad.com. Internships, volunteer placements, teaching abroad, language classes and semester placements from 1 to 12 months in Spain (Barcelona, Madrid, Seville and Marbella), Costa Rica, Mexico, Uruguay and Chile. Prices from $1,995 for 1 month in Chile or Mexico, to $5,895 for a semester in Seville.

AFS International Youth Development – ☎ +1 800 AFS INFO; vol.reg@afs.org; www.usa.afs.org. Full intercultural programme lasting 4/6–12 months in 54 countries for volunteers aged 18–29. Most programmes include language training prior to volunteer placement, homestay accommodation and participation in local voluntary projects.

Agriventure – International Agricultural Exchange Association, Calgary, Canada; ☎ 403 255 7799; www.agriventure.com. For details of the international farm exchange see Part 6 Working and Living Abroad.

Association for International Practical Training (AIPT) – ☎ +1 410 997 3069; www.aipt.org. Short/long-term placements in more than 80 countries through the International Association for the Exchange of Students for Technical Experience (IAESTE) available to students in science, engineering, math, agriculture or architecture. Other work exchange schemes with selected countries.

Alliances Abroad Group – ☎ +1 512 457 8062; +1 888 6 ABROAD; www.allianceabroad.com. Variety of overseas placements including work placements in the UK, France and Australia; teaching in Spain, China and Argentina; and volunteer placements in Ecuador, Costa Rica, Brazil and Peru. Participants pay fees to cover placement, accommodation and emergency insurance.

AmeriSpan –Philadelphia, PA; ☎ +1 800 879 6640; info@amerispan.com; www.amerispan.com. Language training organisation which arranges internships and volunteer placements lasting 2 weeks to 6 months in many Spanish-speaking countries.

ArchaeoSpain – Conneticut ☎ +1 866 932 0003; www.archaeospain.com. Summer archaeological programmes for anyone over 18 in Spain and Italy. Sample cost $2,000+ for a month working on a Roman excavation in Spain.

BUNAC USA – ☎ +1 203 264 0901; www.bunac.org. Administer a number of work exchange programmes (some open only to students).

Camp Counselors (CCUSA) – www.ccusa.com. Work Experience programmes in Australia/ New Zealand (18–30) and summer camp counsellors in Russia (no upper age limit).

CDS International Inc – 871 United Nations Plaza, 15th floor, New York, NY 10017–1814; ☎ +1 212 497 3500; info@cdsintl.org. Executive level internships for young American professionals aged 23–34 in Germany. Programmes also in Russia (ages 25–35), Argentina, Spain and Switzerland.

Cross-Cultural Solutions – New Rochelle, NY; ☎+1 800 380 4777; www.crossculturalsolutions.org. See entry above with UK address.

Earthwatch Institute – ☎ +1 800 776 0188; www.earthwatch.org. International environmental charity which engages people worldwide in scientific field research and education to promote the understanding and action necessary for a sustainable environment. Earthwatch recruits over 4,000 volunteers a year to assist scientific field research projects around the world. Prices range from $670 to $2,600, excluding travel to the location.

English Language Teaching Assistant Program (ELTAP) – sponsored by the University of Minnesota, Duluth, MN; craig@educatorsabroad.org; www.eltap.org. Participants can be students or adults on a non-credit certificate option. They bring their native fluency in English to schools in over 25 countries on all continents. Placements last 4 or 10 weeks throughout the year. Programme fee of $2,300–$4,200 depending on programme, plus travel and in some cases room and board. Total cost from $3,000 for 4 weeks. Host schools assist with arrangements for accommodation and board. $300 placement fee, plus course fee and travel (total usually $3,000–$4,000). Accommodation and board provided by host schools. Available to students (non-credit certificate option for adults).

Experiential Learning International – Denver, CO; ☎ +1 303 321 8278; www.eliabroad. com. Volunteering programmes in Argentina, Bolivia, China, Costa Rica, Ecuador, Ghana, Guatemala, India, Kenya, Uganda, Tanzania, Nepal, Philippines, Vietnam and Poland; plus intern placements in some countries. Cost for 12 weeks varies from $695 for China to $2,300 for Tanzania.

Explorations in Travel Inc – Guildford, VT; explore@volunteertravel.com; www.volunteer-travel.com. International volunteers for rainforest conservation, wildlife projects, etc., in Ecuador, Costa Rica, Belize, Guatemala, Puerto Rico, Mexico, Nepal, Australia and New Zealand.

Foundation for Sustainable Development – San Francisco, CA; ☎ +1 415 288 4873; www.fsdinternational.org. Short summer and longer-term internships for anyone over 18, in the field of development in certain Latin American and African countries plus India. Usually volunteers in Latin America will be expected to converse in Spanish. Prices from $3,000 for 9 weeks.

Global Citizens Network – St Paul, MN; ☎ +1 800 644 9292; www.globalcitizens.org. Volunteer vacations in Kenya, Nepal, Mexico, Guatemala, Peru, Tanzania, Arizona and New Mexico.

Global Crossroad – Irving, TX; ☎ +1 800 413 2008; www.globalcrossroad.com. Volunteer teaching and internships in 26 countries. Paid teaching in China (1–12 months). Placement fees from $799 for China to $2,125 in Togo.

Global Service Corps – San Francisco, CA; www.globalservicecorps.org. Cooperates with grass-roots organisations in Thailand and Tanzania and sends volunteers and interns for 2 weeks to 3+ months. Sample fee $3,305 for 6 weeks in Tanzania.

Global Vision International – Boston, MA; ☎ +1 888 653 6028; www.gviusa.com. US office of British company of same name (see entry above).

Global Volunteers – ☎ +1 800 487 1074; www.globalvolunteers.org. Volunteer vacations in many countries.

Institute for Cultural Ecology – Hilo, Hawaii; ☎ +1 808 640 2333; www.cultural-ecology.com. Academic internships in Fiji, Thailand and Hawaii working on marine biology projects, environmental advocacy or custom designed projects in student's major. 4, 6, 8 or 12 weeks. Sample fees: $1,895 for 4 weeks, $3,850 for 12 weeks, eg reef mapping on the Fiji coast.

International Cultural Adventures – ☎ +1 888 339 0460; www.ICAdventures.com. Cultural, educational and volunteer service experiences in Peru and Sikkim (India). Fees for 6-week summer programmes from $3,150, and from $4,150 for 12-week extended programmes beginning in Feb/March and September.

Kibbutz Program Center – New York; ☎ +1 212 462 2764; mail@kibbutzprogramcenter.org. Volunteer placement service for people aged 18–35 for Israeli kibbutzim; $100 registration fee, $250 programme fee.

Living Routes – Amherst; ☎ 888 515 7333; www.livingroutes.org. Semester, summer and year-abroad programmes based in eco-villages around the world that help people of all ages gain the knowledge, skills and inspiration to build a sustainable lifestyle. Current programmes in India, Scotland, Senegal, USA, Mexico and Peru.

Operation Crossroads Africa – New York, NY; ☎ +1 212 289 1949; http://operationcrossroadsafrica.org. 7-week summer projects in Africa and Brazil. $3,500 including airfares.

Peace Corps – 1111 20th Street NW, Washington, DC 20526; ☎ +1 800 424 8580; www.peacecorps.gov. Sends US citizens on two-year volunteer assignments to 70 countries; the average age of volunteers is 27 with no upper limit.

Projects Abroad – New York, NY; ☎ +1 888 839 3535; www.projects-abroad.org. US office of British company (see entry above).

ProWorld Service Corps – Bellingham, WA; ☎ +1 877 733 7378; www.myproworld.org. Offers a range of internships lasting 2–26 weeks with aid agencies in Peru, Belize and Mexico. Fees start at $2,485, which include Spanish tuition followed by placement with an NGO and lodgings for the first four weeks.

Radical Sabbatical – Annapolis, MD; ☎ +1 410 990 1171; www.radicalsabbatical.net. Short exploratory journeys worldwide for small groups of like-minded people (aged 45–60) who are dedicated to withdrawing from routine.

Schools Without Borders – Toronto ☎ +1 416 534 6342; www.schoolswithoutborders.com. Registered Canadian charity dedicated to fostering leadership through 3/12-month volunteer placements in Brazil, Nepal, Kenya, India and Thailand. Minimum age 21.

Travel Alive Inc – Oak Park, IL; ☎ toll-free 866 380 3042; info@travelalive.com; www.travelalive.com. Provides Spanish language study, family stay and volunteer opportunities in Nicaragua and Ecuador. Sample prices $1,730 for 4 weeks, $3,170 for 10 weeks.

Volunteer Abroad – ☎ +1 888 649 3788; www.volunteerabroad.ca. Worldwide volunteer placements lasting 8–24 weeks run by Travel Cuts, the national student travel agency of Canada. Open to professionals taking a career break and retirees as well.

Wildlands Studies – ☎ +1 707 621 5665; www.wildlandsstudies.com. Conservation projects lasting 6 weeks in the US (including Alaska and Hawaii), Belize, Thailand, Nepal, etc.

World Endeavors – Minneapolis, MN; ☎ +1 612 729 3400; www.worldendeavours.com. Volunteer, internship and study programmes lasting 2 weeks to 2 months in Brazil, Costa Rica, Ecuador, Philippines, China, Nepal, India, Thailand, Ghana and Jamaica.

WorldTeach Inc. – Cambridge, MA; ☎ +1 617 495 5527; www.worldteach.org. Non-profit organisation that places several hundred paying volunteers as teachers of English as a Foreign Language (EFL) or English as a Second Language (ESL) in countries which request assistance. Currently, WorldTeach provides college graduates for 6–12 months to Costa Rica, Ecuador, Chile, Guyana, China, Poland, Namibia, Pohnpei (Micronesia) and the Marshall Islands. Fee is $3,990–$5,990, though some programmes are fully or partially funded by the host country.

MY GROWN UP GAP YEAR:
NIGEL PEGELER

Nigel wanted to ensure that his contribution to a development project in South Africa would be sustainable, and he has clearly succeeded. He became involved in a cycle project in the rural village of Mapoch, about 40km north-west of Pretoria, after being matched with this project by the British agency People and Places (see entry).

I was initially interested in volunteering in Madagascar as it is somewhere I would love to visit. But Kate at People and Places [P&P] emailed me about Mapoch and she suggested that my skills could be very well used on this project. I read the diary of a former volunteer who said that the residents of the village spend nearly a day walking to the doctor and back. At this point I had a bright idea and mentioned to P&P's local partners in South Africa that it would be a great idea to get some bicycles in the village. I am passionate about cycling and know quite a bit about cycle charity projects, so we worked together designing a cycle repair maintenance and sales project for the village.

The idea of the project was to introduce bicycles into a poor African community and give the people cheap transport. During the month I was there we turned a grocery shop run by Pastor Peter into a cycle shop, built some bicycles from spares and renovated some donated bicycles which we put in the shop for sale. The difference a bicycle can make to a poor South African is amazing. I was told about a district nurse who visited her patients on foot and saw eight patients a day but after being given a bicycle she can visit 18 patients, as she is paid per visit her income has doubled and more people get treatment. By setting up a cycle shop we have ensured the bicycles will be maintained and we have created employment for the villagers and they will have cheap transport which for some of the children will mean they do not have to spend hours each day walking to school.

As I have a holiday entitlement of 27 days a year I was entitled to take a month off work, although taking this amount of time during the summer holidays is not normal for a school caretaker as we often have a lot of building and repair work carried out when the school is closed. I asked the head teacher for the time off and she fully supported me in what I wanted to do. In total £660 was donated to the project by work colleagues, friends and even people who I have never met. The money was spent on buying tools, cycle parts and spares, two new bicycles for the villagers, an awning outside the shop for shade and finally buying parts to build a cycle trailer as a prototype and leaving enough parts to build another one. The amount of money that some people donated stunned me.

Returning to home routines has been bloody impossible to be honest. Life back in England seemed so pointless even after only a month away. In South Africa I could really help people who needed it, people who have so little but are still happy. The rewards have been immense. I feel empowered to do much more voluntary work, and have a belief in myself and what I can achieve. I have learnt a lot about the culture and customs of South Africans and have been amazed by their resilience and resourcefulness in the face of adversity.

MondoChallenge volunteers often got involved with extra-curricular activities at schools

1 ● ● ●

Volunteers supervise small grant schemes in Tanzania, enabling families affected by HIV/AIDS to sustain livelihoods

2 ● ● ●

Rise and shine in the Himalaya!

3 ● ● ●

4 MondoChallenge volunteer assisting at a Maasai women's market

5 Teaching in Buddhist temples

Volunteers run arts & crafts activities in Ecuador 6 ● ●

MondoChallenge volunteer vs. Monk's XI 7 ● ●

8 A rural agricultural MondoChallenge project in Darjeeling, India

9 Small grant recipient (and MondoChallenge volunteer) run a street stall

10 IT training in a Tanzanian village

MY GROWN UP GAP YEAR:
RAHEEL KHAN

Challenges Worldwide has sent a number of legal volunteers to key volunteer posts. Raheel Khan went to Belize to raise awareness of domestic violence.

I decided on voluntary work after many years of increasing disillusionment as a corporate lawyer where the only impact I made through successful cases was on the balance sheet of my client bank or company. I had a desire to make a positive difference and use the skills that I had for what I perceived to be the greater good. I was even considering leaving the profession altogether. It was at this juncture in my life that I came across Challenges Worldwide, which offered me an opportunity not only to expand my existing skill set, but also to discover new skills and gain experience working in a completely different setting and with a completely different agenda whilst still working as a lawyer.

Being a somewhat bolshy city lawyer I specifically asked for a demanding placement which was commensurate to my years of post qualification experience. My principal objectives whilst working as a volunteer lawyer with the Women's Department in Belize was on the implementation of the new law concerning domestic violence. This was at a time when the Domestic Violence Bill 2007 was about to come into force, the first substantive legalisation in this area in 13 years. I had no prior experience of working on gender issues or law and undertook my placement with a certain amount of trepidation. Nevertheless I set my mind to seeing all the challenges as part of the adventure.

I was also asked to write and publish a men's handbook on domestic violence as a counterpart to the existing Women's Handbook. I publicised this work through interviews on national television and radio. One of my most rewarding experiences was hearing my summary of the new legislation being read out on national television by the Attorney General as part of one of his speeches. I wonder what the chances are for this ever happening in the UK? I would never have dreamt that being a lawyer could make such a positive difference to the lives of so many people. By the end of my placement I wished I had committed myself for a longer spell. I had genuinely fallen in love with the people and the country.

My time in Belize has been rewarding in so many ways, but I really think I got the most out of it by living as a Belizean so far as I could. My host family was wonderful and supportive and not only provided me with a stable home life but also knew how to have a good time! My weekends alternated between spending time with them and exploring Belize and its beautiful Cayes with my fellow Challenges volunteers.

In terms of my career I had come to Belize unsure about what I wanted to do after over six years as an insolvency solicitor. I now know that international development law is the way forward for me.

PART 6

WORKING AND LIVING ABROAD

INTRODUCTION

Who has not dreamed of living in a place far from home, perhaps a favourite holiday destination or a place that lives in your imagination? Perhaps you want to try living elsewhere as an experiment to gauge how you might cope with moving abroad indefinitely. But how can you translate this yearning into the reality of spending an extended period of time somewhere else, of transforming yourself from a tourist into a temporary resident? The choices at your disposal are simply to set up home and stay there, which is expensive without an income (unless you are living in a country with a very low cost of living), to find paid work or to undertake some formal studies. (Volunteering is covered in a separate chapter.)

The reasons why people choose to settle temporarily in a foreign place are multitudinous. Climate is the reason most often cited. Often it's something as straightforward as wanting to be near a partner who comes from that place or has been posted there. Living abroad is by far the best way to master a foreign language. Sometimes the urge to spend time abroad is motivated by a simple craving for novelty and curiosity about a place and culture which has caught your attention. Two-week holidays can be unsatisfactory from many points of view and may have engendered a desire to experience a foreign culture from the inside rather than as an onlooker.

Using a gap year to dip your toe into foreign societies and cultures needs to be distinguished from becoming an expatriate, which by definition means that you have taken up residence in another country. On a personal level, it all depends on what you classify as home and how you regard your time abroad. Calling your time abroad a 'career break' implies that you are suspending your normal professional routine temporarily and intend to return to 'real life'. Inevitably these definitions can become blurred over time. It is very common for people who are lucky enough to own a holiday home abroad to increase the percentage of time they spend there.

WORKING ABROAD

If seeing the world is your motivation for a career break, finding an opportunity to live and work in a foreign country might give you the most rewarding experience. Travelling on its own may not answer your need to get under the skin of a different culture. By setting up a temporary home abroad you'll have the chance to make new friends, learn another language and experience, not just observe, how people in different parts of the world actually live. It will be a challenging experience as you'll need to learn fast and find ways of landing on your feet in a place where customs and laws will be different from those back home.

For those who aren't going to be able to save enough beforehand to fund a long holiday from work or can't rely on an income by renting out their house, money may have to be earned. Taking up paid work on the road may bridge any looming financial crises. This may involve the most menial jobs such as picking fruit to more skilled work such as translating technical and academic papers. The latter kind is not always preferable, as **Chris Miksovsky** concluded. He found well paid computer work in both Sydney and Melbourne offices with ease. However, after a few months he realised that the reason he had left home was to get away from spending his days in an office, so he headed north to work on a sheep or cattle station and was thrilled with the contrast.

For others, finding work abroad acts as an admission ticket to an unfamiliar society. Above all, if you're hoping to learn a foreign language, it's arguably the best way of creating your own crash course. It will give your gap year structure, particularly if you are spending a lengthy period of time in one place, and it will be a chance to meet other people in their own habitat and make new friends.

Another great advantage of working abroad is that it will look good on your CV, which is important if you're concerned that a career break might be viewed as an indulgence or wasted time by a prospective employer on returning home. Of course the acquisition of a language will be a plus. An intimate knowledge of another country can also be used to your advantage in many areas of commerce and the media.

Paul Jones, now in his 30s, had already given up a full-time position in the IT industry in his native Australia in order to go freelance so had 'gotten over' any anxieties about having a secure job. So when he took the decision to go overseas for a while, he was lucky enough to have the freedom to choose when:

> *Having been working for a number of years and having transferable skills in IT, it made sense to find work in Europe in my field to finance my trip. Prior to leaving, I found a job by using the Internet and having interviews over the phone. I still like the fact that I got my first job by having an interview on my mobile phone that was the clearest while standing on a city street that provided a nice drowning out kind of noise. Not the best conditions for an interview but it worked. The job happened to be in the Netherlands where I hadn't particularly wanted to go but that was the job that I was accepted for first, so I took it as a stepping stone. After a number of months in a job I didn't like in a country that I never found an affinity for, I found a job in Bristol which has been my base since.*

For some fortunate individuals, their employer will arrange for them to live and work abroad. In this case help is automatically provided to navigate the problems of legal status, housing and adapting to a strange culture. However, the nature of your profession or the absence of international postings within a company may prevent you from effortlessly going to work in New York, Rome or Hong Kong. Many individuals will need to find alternative ways of immersing themselves in a foreign culture without the help of an employer.

Volunteering is popular (see Part 4, *Doing Something Worthwhile*) because much of the logistical support is set up, either by a charity for whom you'll be working or by a mediating agency that recruits fee-paying volunteers on behalf of local projects. Joining a voluntary project simplifies the process of finding a radically different niche from your usual one. Trying to find some kind of paid work will be more difficult but not impossible.

Working abroad is one of the means by which people can immerse themselves in a foreign culture, to meet foreign people on their own terms and to gain a better perspective on their own culture and habits. The kind of job you find will determine the stratum of society in which you will mix and therefore the content of the experience. The professional who is engaged in a job swap with someone in their profession or who is attached to an overseas office of their old employer will have a less radical break than the adult on a gap year who decides to do something entirely different such as teaching English in the Far East or scuba diving in the Red Sea.

Sweeping generalisations about the valuable cultural insights afforded by working in a foreign land should be tempered with a careful consideration of the reality of doing a job abroad. True 'working holidays' are rare, though they do exist. For example people have exchanged their labour for a free trip with an outback Australian camping tour operator or a free stay in a Spanish hill resort merely by promising to speak English (mentioned later in this chapter). This is easier if you have certain skills such as mechanical or culinary ones. But jobs are jobs wherever you do them, and there is little scope for visiting art galleries and historic sights or even developing a social life if you are stranded in an obscure industrial town teaching English six days a week or manning the reception in a damp caravan for a camping holiday operator.

VISAS AND PERMISSION TO WORK

The great hurdle to overcome in gaining work abroad, particularly in popular destinations like the USA and Australia, is obtaining the legal right to work. The situation is much more favourable in the European Union (EU) where citizens of any member country can work, live and study in any of the other member states with a minimum of bureaucracy. This is perhaps one of the greatest benefits of the single market, making a working stint in Denmark, Greece, Hungary, Malta, etc., wholly feasible.

The EU consists of the original 15 member states (Austria, Belgium, Denmark, Finland, France, Germany, Greece, Ireland, Italy, Luxembourg, the Netherlands, Portugal, Spain, Sweden and the UK) plus the 10 that joined in May 2004 (Cyprus, Czech Republic, Estonia, Hungary, Latvia, Lithuania, Malta, Poland, Slovakia and Slovenia) and Romania and Bulgaria since 2007. Reciprocal transitional controls may be in place in some of the accession states; the consular representatives will be able to advise.

The standard situation among all EU countries is that EU nationals have the right to look for work in any member state for up to three months. Most countries are in the process of abolishing the requirement at the end of three months to obtain a residence permit from the police or the local authority, but always make local enquiries. Work permits/work visas outside the EU are not readily available. It is easy to understand why most countries in the world have immigration policies that are principally job protection schemes for their own nationals. Nevertheless it can be frustrating to encounter bureaucratic hassles if you are merely taking a break from your employment at home and want to earn a little money by picking up a job here and there on your travels.

The standard procedure for acquiring a work permit or work visa is to find an employer willing to apply to the immigration authorities on your behalf months in advance of the job's starting date, while you are in your home country. This is usually a next-to-impossible feat unless you are a high ranking nuclear physicist or a foreign correspondent, or are participating in an organised exchange programme where the red tape is taken care of by your sponsoring organisation. In some countries, an exception is made for special employment categories such as teachers of English and live-in child-carers.

Official visa information should be requested from the Embassy or Consulate of the country you intend to visit; the *London Diplomatic List* contains up-to-date contact details for all diplomatic representations in London and is published in print and online by the Foreign & Commonwealth Office (☎ 0870 600 5522 to order it from The Stationery Office; www.fco.gov.uk). Being caught working illegally in any country potentially jeopardises any chance to work there in the future or even to visit as a tourist, and may even result in the ignominy of deportation.

For specific information on the red tape governing work in the USA and Australia, see relevant sections below.

PLANNING IN ADVANCE

At the risk of oversimplifying the range of choices, anyone who aspires to work temporarily abroad must either fix up a definite job before leaving home or take a gamble on finding something on the spot. Some jobs can be pre-arranged either through private contacts or by enlisting the help of a mediating organisation or agency but, as in any job hunt, it is much easier to land a job if you can present yourself face to face to a prospective employer, which is worth more than any number of speculative applications from home. If nothing else your presence in the flesh reassures the employer that you are serious about working and available to start as soon as a vacancy crops up.

'Easy' ways to fix up a job abroad do exist, for example to teach English in Taiwan, work on an organic farm or look after children for a European family. The price you pay for having this security is that you commit yourself to a new life, however temporary, sight unseen. Wages in these cases are negligible so that these are tantamount to volunteer jobs even if they do require eight hours of work a day.

It is a truism to state that the more unusual and interesting the job, the more competition it will attract. For example it is to be assumed that only a small percentage of applicants for advertised jobs actually get the chance to work as history coordinators for a European tour company, assistants at a museum bookshop in Paris or underwater photographic models in the Caribbean, whereas other less glamorous options can absorb an almost unlimited number of people, for example working as a counsellor or sports instructor on an American children's summer camp.

Secretarial and employment agencies from Brussels to Brisbane can be especially useful to those with the right qualifications. For example Manpower has several thousand branch offices in 72 countries; most addresses are linked from their UK or US sites (www.manpower.co.uk; www.manpower.com) or try other multinationals such as Drake (www.drakeintl.com) and Adecco (www.adecco.com) with about 7,000 branches in 60+ countries. No matter how briefly you have worked for an agency, request a letter of reference or introduction which may allow you to bypass the typing and other tests.

Reputable international recruitment agencies in Britain, the USA and elsewhere may be looking for personnel qualified in your area of expertise for short-term contracts in fields such as accountancy and IT. For example Robert Walters, with 23 offices in 13 countries (www.robertwalters.com), specialises in recruiting contract staff for jobs worldwide in the fields of accountancy and finance, banking, legal, information technology, sales and marketing, human resources, support and administration. Interviews can be pre-arranged for candidates at their city of arrival and in the case of high-calibre candidates, tele-conference links are set up.

IMPROVING YOUR CHANCES

A number of specific steps will improve your chances either of being accepted on an organised work scheme or of convincing an employer in person of your superiority to the competition. For example, before leaving home you might take a course in a foreign language or acquire a portable skill such as teaching English as a foreign language, cooking, or scuba diving – all skills which have been put to good use by people on a gap year working abroad.

Even if you are not lucky enough to have friends and family scattered strategically throughout the world, it is always worth broadcasting your intentions to third cousins, pen friends to whom you haven't written since you were 12 and visiting professors, in case they divulge the addresses of some useful contacts. The more widely publicised your work and travel plans are, the better your chance of being given a lead. Any locals or expatriates you meet after arrival are a potential source of help. Any skill or hobby from jazz to running (e.g. seek out the Hash House Harriers popular with expatriates worldwide) can become the basis for pursuing contacts.

JOB HUNTING ON ARRIVAL

One of the most useful sites is the free community noticeboard Craigslist which started in San Francisco in 1995 but has spread to 450 cities from Auckland to Buenos Aires, Moscow to Cairo. With notification of about half a million new jobs a month, it is probably the biggest job board in the world, as well as carrying accommodation listings and everything else. It also lists many unpaid jobs and internships.

However, not all jobs are found on the Internet or by word of mouth. Local English language newspapers such as Mexico City's *The News*, the *Bangkok Post* or the *Athens News* may carry job advertisements appropriate to your situation, or may be a good publication in which to place an advertisement offering your services. If (for example) you want a job translating documents in a company office or teaching English in a school but there appear to be no openings, volunteer to do some unpaid translation or assist with a class one day a week for no pay; if you prove yourself competent, you will have an excellent chance of filling any vacancy which does occur.

The ease with which you can find work may depend partly on your knowledge of the language, although neither this nor a circle of ready-made friends is essential. The independent and confident traveller quickly accumulates names of contacts and advice from travellers, expats and residents in preparation for setting up a home from home abroad. With the advent of the Internet it's possible to carry out an enormous amount of research and make online contact with relevant companies and organisations before leaving home.

SEASONAL WORK

For a complete break from the stresses of a professional life, perhaps casual or seasonal work is the answer. Two categories of employment appeal most to seasonal workers because they appeal least to a stable working population: agriculture and tourism. Farmers from Norway to Tasmania (with the notable exception of developing countries) are not able to bring in their harvests without assistance from outside their local communities, though piece-work apple-picking in Tasmania or strawberry-picking in Denmark is unlikely to appeal to many career breakers. The tourist industry in many areas could not survive without a short-term injection of seasonal labour. Big cities create a wealth of employment opportunities for people not driven to compete in a professional capacity.

While opening up an enormous range of possibilities, the Internet can be a bewildering place to look for a job. One of the best specialist recruitment websites is www.seasonworkers.com, a website that has been designed to help people conduct a tailored search for a summer job, outdoor sports job, ski resort job, gap year placement or course quickly and easily. A couple of years ago it won in the 'Best Recruitment' category in the Travel and Tourism web awards. Its search system differentiates between courses, gap year placements and paid jobs in many categories, and its forum can helps users get a first hand view of the activity they are considering.

The website www.eurosummerjobs.com links to the EURES search engines. EURES, the government-run Europe-wide employment service operates as a network of EuroAdvisers, who have specialist expertise on living and working in other member states. The searchable database of general vacancies can be found at http://europa.eu.int/eures/index.jsp.

One of the biggest summer employers is PGL Travel Ltd (Alton Court, Penyard Lane, Ross-on-Wye, Herefordshire HR9 5GL; ☎ 0870 401 4411; www.pgl.co.uk/recruitment) which run outdoor activity holidays for children in locations around the UK, France and Spain. It employs over 2,500 seasonal staff a year for a huge range of jobs from sailing instructors to drivers, catering staff to French-speaking tour guides; staff are needed for the whole summer season April–September, rather than list for June–August.

TEACHING ENGLISH

Although the English language is still the language which literally millions of people around the world want to learn, finding work as an English teacher has become more difficult in recent years, as an increasing number of people of all ages are acquiring specialised training. The number of public and private institutes turning out certified Teaching English as a Foreign Language (TEFL) teachers in the UK, North America and the Antipodes has greatly increased, creating a glut of teachers chasing the good jobs, especially in the major cities of Europe such as Paris and Prague.

Having sounded that warning note, there are still areas of the world where the boom in English language learning seems to know no bounds, from Ecuador to China, Slovakia to Vietnam. A university degree is sufficient to find a respectable job in Thailand, Japan, China, Taiwan and a few others. In small private schools and back street agencies, being a native speaker and dressing neatly are sometimes sufficient qualifications to get a job. But for more stable teaching jobs in recognised language schools, you will have to sign a contract (usually a year to qualify for a visa). **John Routledge** describes how English teaching can fill a gap year and beyond on the website www.onestopenglish.com:

> *I had been working in south London as a software developer and had had enough of the whole 9 to 5 job culture (it was more like 8 to 6 every day). So I went to Chiang Mai, Thailand's second city. I had only planned to stay for a few months at the most and hadn't considered teaching English. My sister was a teacher in England and from what she told me, it really didn't seem like my kind of thing – lots of lesson planning, low pay and not much respect from the students. Four years and five months later, I'm still here and fully immersed in TEFL teaching. I went for an interview at the university and to my surprise they weren't at all interested in my CELTA or my three years' experience at the private language school. They were most interested with my honours degree. I'm still teaching there now and really enjoying it and never wake up dreading going to work.*

The Brighton-based company Cactus TEFL has established itself as the place to go to get all kinds of information on Teaching English Abroad (www.cactustefl.com). Their jobs website is at www.cactustefl. com/jobs/index.php and they publish the free *Little Book of TEFL Jobs*, which is packed with advice for the teacher searching for a job in TEFL, and advertisements from schools which regularly employ teachers (request a copy on info@cactustefl.com). Cactus TEFL also works with a large number of TEFL training course providers worldwide and has an efficient search engine to find a suitable course.

TEFL TRAINING

The only way to outrival the competition and make the job hunt (not to mention the job itself) easier is to do a training course in Teaching English as a Foreign Language (known as TEFL, pronounced 'teffle'). Intensive certificate courses are typically delivered over four weeks and cost between £800 and £1000. In the UK the two standard recognised certificate qualifications that will improve your range of job options are the Cambridge Certificate in English Language Teaching to Adults (CELTA) administered and awarded by the University of Cambridge Local ESOL Exam Unit (address in *Resources* listing below) and the Certificate in TESOL (Teaching English to Speakers of Other Languages) offered by Trinity College London. Both courses involve at least 100 hours of rigorous training with a practical emphasis (full-time for four weeks or part-time over several months which might suit grown-ups who are not ready to give up their jobs but want to equip themselves for a future break). Although there are no fixed prerequisites apart from a suitable level of language awareness, not everyone who applies is accepted.

A listing of the 280 centres offering the CELTA course is available from the University of Cambridge in exchange for a large self-addressed envelope or can be searched on their website (www.cambridg-eesol.org/teaching). Here is a small selection:

Basil Paterson Edinburgh Language Foundation – 66 Queen Street, Edinburgh EH2 4NA; ☎ 0131 225 3802; celta@basilpaterson.co.uk. 10 courses per year; £950.

Ealing, Hammersmith & West London College – Gliddon Road, London W14 9BL; ☎ 0800 980 2185; www.wlc.ac.uk. £800 or £895 non-EU.

Embassy CES – International Teacher Training Institute, Gensing Manor, Dane Road, St Leonards on Sea, Sussex TN38 0QJ; ☎ 01424 464820; training@studygroup.com. Full-time CELTA courses offered monthly in Hastings and Cambridge.

International House – 16 Stukeley Street, Covent Garden, London WC2B 5LQ; ☎ 020 7611 2414; www.ihlondon.com. Certificate course runs at least monthly; £1,240. Also offers courses at IH Newcastle.

Language Link – 181 Earls Court Road, Earls Court, London SW5 9RB; ☎ 020 7370 4755; www.languagelink.co.uk. £795 full-time, £890 part-time over 12 weeks. Places Certificate holders in its network of affiliated schools in Russia, Vietnam, China and Uzbekistan.

Stanton Teacher Training – Stanton House, 167 Queensway, London W2 4SB; ☎ 020 7221 7259; www.stanton-school.co.uk. £785 including Cambridge registration fee of £96.

St Giles College Highgate – 51 Shepherd's Hill, London N6 5QP; ☎ 020 8340 0828; www.tefl-stgiles.com. £925. Also offered at St Giles in Brighton.

Centres offering the Trinity College Certificate include:

EF English First Teacher Training – 26 Wilbraham Road, Fallowfield, Manchester M14 6JX; ☎ 0161 234 0797; www.englishfirst.com. EF aims to recruit successful trainees to work for EF schools worldwide, mainly in China, Russia and Indonesia. Subsided training provided to candidates willing to sign contracts for those three countries.

Golders Green Teacher Training Centre – 11 Golders Green Road, London NW11 8DY; ☎ 020 8731 0963; www.englishlanguagecollege.co.uk. 5-week course, £799 plus exam fee.

Inlingua Teacher Training & Recruitment – Rodney Lodge, Rodney Road, Cheltenham, Gloucestershire GL50 1HX; ☎ 01242 250493; training@inlingua-cheltenham.co.uk. £1,045 plus moderation fee. Can help place successful candidates in posts in inlingua schools in Ecuador, Italy, Germany, Russia, etc.

The Language Project – 27 Oakfield Road, Clifton, Bristol BS8 2AT; ☎ 0117 909 0911; www.languageproject.co.uk. £1,295 including moderation fee. Also offer Introduction to TEFL/TESL (£245 for two-day course).

Cambridge CELTA courses are offered at more than 150 overseas centres from the Middle East to Queensland, including seven in the USA, including St Giles in San Francisco (www.stgiles-usa.com), International House San Diego (www.ih-sandiego.com) and Teaching House in New York (www.teachinghouse.com). Other centres for American readers to consider are Transworld Schools (701 Sutter Street, 6th Floor, San Francisco, CA 94109; ☎ +1 888 588 8335; 415 928 2835; www.transworldschools.com), San Diego State University/American Language Institute (50 Campanile Drive, San Diego, CA 92115–1914; ☎ +1 619 594 8740; www.americanlanguage.com/home.html) and the Boston Language Institute (648 Beacon Street, Boston, MA 02215; www.teflcertificate.com) which offer highly regarded *sui generis* certificates with extensive job placement assistance.

Many advantages can be gained by signing up for a TEFL course in the place where you want to work, from Barcelona to Bangkok. Most TEFL training centres have excellent contacts with language schools and can assist with the job hunt. Scores of independent providers provide TEFL training courses of varying lengths, though note that qualifications may not be recognised outside their own organisations. Examples of proprietary courses include:

The Boland School in the Czech Republic (Brno, ☎ +420 541 241 674; www.boland-czech.com) and in China (Suzhou, ☎ +86 512 6741 3422; www.boland-china.com) offers intensive 140-hour teacher training diploma programmes The cost is €1,300 in the Czech Republic (plus accommodation) and €1,250 in China (plus about €300 for single-room accommodation).

Bridge-Linguatec Language Services – 915 S. Colorado Blvd, Denver, CO 80246, USA; tefl-celta@bridgelinguatec.com; www.bridgetefl.com. Language training company which offers TEFL teacher certification and job placement programmes in Asia, Europe and Latin America. Also offers online TEFL course.

TEFL International – www.teflinternational.com offers its course in dozens of locations worldwide from Seoul to Seville.

World TEFL School – www.worldteflschool.com. 4-week course offered around the world.

TEFL RESOURCES

Teaching English Abroad (Susan Griffith, Vacation-Work, £14.99). The 2009 edition is the definitive guide to short- and long-term opportunities for trained and untrained teachers.

British Council – Information Centre, Bridgewater House, 58 Whitworth Street, Manchester M1 6BB; ☎ 0161 957 7755; www.britishcouncil.org. Distributes information on getting started in TEFL.

University of Cambridge ESOL Examinations – 1 Hills Road, Cambridge CB1 2EU; ☎ 01223 553355; esol@ucles.org.uk; www.cambridgeesol.org/teaching. Administers CELTA and other specialised qualifications in English Language teaching.

Trinity College London – 89 Albert Embankment, London SE1 7TP; ☎ 020 7820 6100; www.trinitycollege.co.uk. Administers the Certificate in TESOL. Course locations provided on website.

WHAT ENGLISH TEACHING INVOLVES

It is difficult to generalise about what work you will actually be required to do once hired. At one extreme you have the world traveller who is hired by a businessman to correct English pronunciation on a one-to-one basis and at the other you get teachers contracted to teach a gruelling 30-hour week split between early morning and evening classes requiring extensive preparation.

Native speaker teachers are nearly always employed to stimulate conversation rather than to teach grammar. Yet a basic knowledge of English grammar is a great asset when pupils come to ask awkward questions. The book *English Grammar in Use* (Raymond Murphy) is recommended for its clear explanations and accompanying student exercises. Other useful books for unsupported English teaching placements include *Getting Beginners to Talk* (Jim Wingate, Prentice Hall) and *Lessons from Nothing* (Bruce Marsland, Cambridge).

Each level and age group brings its own rewards and difficulties. Beginners of all ages usually delight in their progress which will be much more rapid than it is later on. Not everyone, however, enjoys teaching young children (a booming area of TEFL from Portugal to Taiwan) which usually involves sing-songs, puzzles and games. Intermediate learners (especially if they are adolescents) can be difficult, since they will have reached a plateau and may be discouraged. Adults are usually well-motivated though may be inhibited about speaking. Teaching professionals and business people is almost always well paid. Discipline is seldom a problem, at least outside western Europe. In fact you may find your pupils disconcertingly docile and possibly also overly exam-oriented.

Most schools practise the direct method (total immersion in English) so not knowing the language shouldn't prevent you from getting a job. Some employers may provide nothing more than a scratched blackboard and will expect you to dive in using the 'chalk and talk' method. If you are very alarmed at this prospect you could ask a sympathetic colleague if you could sit in on a few classes to give you some ideas. Brochures picked up from tourist offices or airlines can be a useful peg on which to hang a lesson. If you're stranded without any ideas, write the lyrics of a pop song on the board and discuss.

The wages paid to English teachers are usually reasonable, and in developing countries are quite often well in excess of the average local wage. In return you will be asked to teach some fairly unsociable hours since most private English classes take place after working hours, and so schedules split between early morning and evening are not at all uncommon. It is also possible to arrange an informal exchange of English conversation for discounted accommodation or lessons in the destination language. Vaughan Town or Pueblo Ingles (www.vaughantown.com) is a unique programme whereby a holiday village in Spain (between Madrid and Barcelona) is 'stocked' with native English speakers and Spanish clients who want to improve their English. The English native-speaking volunteers participate alongside the Spanish adults in an intensive week of activities, sports, games and group dynamics and, in exchange for making English conversation, receive free room and board. All they have to do is cover the travel expenses to Madrid and then agree to speak in English mainly to Spanish business executives while engaging in a well-orchestrated schedule of activities.

Of course many people on an extended break teach English on a voluntary basis. **Peter and Debra Hardy** from Devon, aged 46 and 51, decided to take time out to do some voluntary teaching in Thailand through Starfish Ventures. Pete had to negotiate unpaid leave from his job as a veterinary practice manager, which was the major limiting factor on their time:

> *We can both honestly say that it was one of the great experiences of our lives, and if anybody is debating whether to embark on a Starfish project, then do it. I have never taught before, but the intensive weekend TEFL course set me up well for the job. I was a bit apprehensive on my first day teaching, but I needn't have been. The Thai kids are wonderful – very keen to learn, very respectful, and a total joy! After a busy but hugely enjoyable English Camp at one school, we even taught the kids to play rounders and cricket! My only regret was that we were only there for one month – I could happily have stayed for many more. The Starfish organisers in Surin were a fountain of knowledge and helped us arrange trips on our days off to Kho Samet, Cambodia and Kho Chang (don't miss that one!)... We are now trying to persuade all our friends to get off their backsides and be volunteers.*

ENGLISH FOR SPECIFIC PURPOSES

English for Specific Purposes (ESP) refers to the practice of teaching groups of employees the specific vocabulary they will need in their jobs, preferably by a native speaker of English with experience of that job. This means that anyone with a professional background such as business, banking, tourism, medicine, science and technology can try to be matched to an appropriate group of language learners from airline staff to exporters. Employees want lessons in which they can pretend to be telephoning a client or chasing a missing order. People on a gap year are often far more suited to this kind of teaching than a freshly qualified TEFL teacher would be.

When applying to an organisation which serves this business market, try to demonstrate your commercial flair with a polished presentation including a business-like CV. **Andrew Sykes** felt that he owed the success of his job hunt in Tours to his experience of accountancy rather than to his TEFL Certificate:

> *I wrote to lots of schools in France and elsewhere that didn't stipulate 'experience required' and was fairly disheartened by the few, none-too-encouraging replies along the lines of 'if you're in town, give us a call.' Sitting in a very cheap hotel bedroom halfway down Italy in early November feeling sorry for myself and knowing that I was getting closer and closer to my overdraft limit and an office job back in the UK, I rang the schools that had replied. 'Drop in,' the voice said, 'and we will give you an interview.' So I jumped on the next train, met the director on Monday and was offered a job on the Tuesday morning, initially on an hour-by-hour basis and then in December on a contract of 15 hours which was later increased to 20 hours a week.*
>
> *What got me the job was not my TEFL Certificate nor my good French. It was the fact that I was an ex-accountant. I had been one of the thousands enticed by the financial benefits of joining an accountancy firm after graduation. But I hated the job and failed my first professional exams. Ironically the experience gained during those years of hell was invaluable because in France most employers are looking for business experience (whereas in Italy they want teaching experience).*

You will in the end be teaching people not objects, and any experience you can bring to the job (and especially the job interview) will help. However ashamed you may be of telling everyone in the pub back home that you were once a rat catcher, it may be invaluable if the school's main client is Rentokil.

THE JOB HUNT

Here is a list of some of the key English Language Teaching recruitment sites:

- www.esicafe.com
- http://education.guardian.co.uk/tefl – the *Guardian's* TEFL pages
- www.englishjobmaze.com
- www.eslworldwide.com
- www.jobs.edufind.com
- http://jobs.guardian.co.uk/jobs/education/tefl – job vacancy listings on the Guardian Unlimited website
- www.TEFL.com

- www.tefl.net
- www.tefljobs.co.uk
- www.tefllogue.com

The best time of year is between Easter and July. Very occasionally a carefully crafted CV and enthusiastic personality are as important as EFL training and experience.

Other websites that are country specific, e.g. www.ohayosensei.com (jobs in Japan) and www.ajarn.com (teaching in Thailand) are listed in the relevant country chapters. Recruitment agencies that at one time matched teachers' CVs with international vacancies have been almost entirely supplanted by online recruitment. The major language school chains hire substantial numbers of teachers, many of whom will have graduated from in-house training courses. Among the major employers of EFL teachers are:

Bénédict Schools – www.benedict-schools.com
Berlitz – www.berlitz.com
EF English First – www.englishfirst.com; see p.170 for more information
International House – www.ihworld.com
Language Link in London – www.languagelink.co.uk
Linguarama – www.linguarama.com
Saxoncourt – www.saxoncourt.com
Wall Street Institute International – www.wallstreetinstitute.com

For schools, a web advertisement offers an easy and instantaneous means of publicising a vacancy to an international audience. CVs can be emailed quickly and cheaply to advertising schools, which can then use email themselves to chase up references. Arguably it has become a little too easy to advertise and answer job advertisements online. At the press of a button, your CV can be clogging up hundreds of computers. After sweating his way through a CELTA course one summer, **Fergus Cooney** (an aspiring musician from Scotland) turned to the Internet to find a job:

> *After installing myself in the cheapest net café in Edinburgh I began reading and posting emails here, there and everywhere. I also posted a message on Dave's eslcafé.com, a message stating 'Qualified teacher seeking job'. Within two days I was inundated with many dozens of replies requesting my CV and, more surprising, with job offers everywhere from Andorra to Zonguldak, through Italy, Poland, Turkey, Russia and too many to count from Korea, Taiwan and China. Jackpot, I thought. (I have since realised that many schools/agents must have an automatic reply system that emails those who advertise in the way I did.) I quickly began sifting through the replies but not as quickly as they kept arriving in my inbox. Before a few days had passed, I had become utterly confused and had forgotten which school was which, which Mr Lee-Soo was which, etc. So I deleted them all, got a new email address and posted a second more specific message on Dave's: 'Teacher with degree + CELTA seeks job in Italy/Spain.' This had the desired effect. A couple of days later my inbox began to fill though not overflow with replies. I still had to delete many from China, etc., but could work with the rest and chose a school in Calabria...*

... A choice he later came to regret (but that is another story).

A wealth of opportunities exists for untrained but eager volunteers willing to pay an agency to place them in a language teaching situation abroad. For example IST Plus runs the Teach in Thailand and

Teach in China programmes for graduates up to the age of 65. Many such as the Sudan Volunteer Programme have entries in the *Directory*.

Other people on a career break simply wait until they arrive at their destination to look around for money-making teaching opportunities.

American **Bradwell Jackson's** holiday travels throughout his 20s and 30s persuaded him to reinvent himself as a long-term world traveller and as of 2008 he is finding his travels by teaching English:

> After reading the book **Work Your Way Around the World**, *I made the decision to quit my job, leave my home, give most of my belongings to charity and sell my car, so that I could wander the earth freely. I wondered if it was really possible to get a job teaching English so easily. Well I found out that it is. I was sitting at a metro stop in Mexico City, looked up and saw an English school right across the street. Providence, I thought. I was right. I sauntered on upstairs, cheerfully asked if they needed an English teacher, and about an hour and a half later, I was told when to start my training. It really was that easy.*

Later he depended on luck again when he ended up teaching in a most unlikely corner of the world: Nouakchott in Mauritania, West Africa:

> *I was wandering around Nouakchott on what I was intending to be my last day there. I saw a fellow Westerner walking on the other side of the street and decided I would talk to her. It just so happened that she knew where the local, well nigh the only, English school was. We stopped by this school and they told us to come back in a couple of days, and I decided to change my plans and stay long enough to check out the school. My luck was in because the director showed up and we seemed to get on well. She asked me to give a tryout lesson in front of the other teachers. This I did, with great confidence, and was told to start straightaway.*

With all this English teaching experience under his belt, Bradwell decided to apply in the conventional way for the next destination, which was to be China in the run-up to the Olympics. His application to Aston English Schools (www.astonrecruiting.com) was successful and on arrival in Tangshan he was immediately captivated by China in general and by his school and colleagues in particular. Looking back at his months in west Africa, he thinks the only way he survived those hot Mauritanian summers, all that sand, and the fact that there was nothing to do was because of the warmth and generosity of so many African people.

FREELANCING

An alternative to working for a language school is to set yourself up as a freelance private tutor. While undercutting the fees charged by the big schools, you can still earn more than as a contract teacher. Usually you will have to be fairly well established in a place before you can attempt to support yourself by private teaching, preferably with some decent premises in which to give lessons (either private or group) and with a telephone.

It is always difficult to start teaching without contacts and a good working knowledge of the language. When you do get started, it may be difficult to earn a stable income because of the frequency with which pupils cancel. It is unrealistic for a newly arrived freelancer to expect to earn enough to live on in the first six months or so.

Getting clients for private lessons is a marketing exercise, and all the avenues that seem appropriate to your circumstances have to be explored. Here are some ways you can market yourself:

- Put a notice up in schools and universities, supermarkets or corner shops, and run an advertisement in the local paper if you have the use of a telephone.
- Send neat notices to local public schools, announcing your willingness to ensure the children's linguistic future.
- Compile a list of addresses of professionals (lawyers, architects, etc.) who may need English for their work and have the resources to pay for it. Then contact them.
- Call on export businesses, distribution companies, perhaps even travel agencies.

These methods should put you in touch with a few hopeful language learners. If you are good at what you do, word will spread and more paying pupils will come your way, though the process can be slow.

If you are more interested in integrating with the local culture than making money, exchanging conversation for board and lodging may be an appealing possibility. This can be arranged by answering (or placing) small advertisements in appropriate places. The American Church in Paris notice board is famous for this.

WORKING IN TOURISM

The travel and tourism industry employs a staggering 72 million people. A season of working as a tour guide, holiday rep or sports instructor might exactly suit someone taking a gap year although, on the whole, the work is hard and the pay low.

Everywhere you look on the Internet, potentially useful links can be found. A surprising number of tour operators and other travel company home pages feature a Recruitment or Human Resources icon which you can click to find out about jobs with that operator. Dozens of sites may prove useful such as www.seasonal-jobs.com (part of www.voovs.com) and www.resortjobs.co.uk (part of www.natives. co.uk). Two US-based websites – www.coolworks.com and www.jobmonkey.com – are recommended for seasonal jobs in the tourist industry. Check out the Independent travellers magazine *Wanderlust* (cover price £3.80 in selected newsagents; £22.80 subscription for eight issues a year; www.wanderlust.co.uk). You might find a few relevant advertisements in its Jobshop column (www.wanderlust.co.uk/job-shop) for example vacancies with adventure travel companies for 25–35-year-old Spanish speaking tour leaders in the eastern Mediterranean or in Latin America. Opportunities for cycle holiday leaders or hill-walking guides are also notified in specialist outdoor magazines. Often a first aid certificate and driving licence are required and in some cases a specialist certificate such as the MLTE (Mountain Leader Training).

Many tourist destinations are in remote places where there is no local pool of labour. Itinerant job-seekers have ended up working in hotels in some of the most beautiful corners of the world from the South Island of New Zealand to Lapland. People with some training in catering will probably find themselves in demand. In addition to hotel and restaurant kitchens, cooks and chefs can put their talents to good use in a range of venues from luxury yachts to holiday ranches, safari camps to ski chalets.

RESORTS

It is not at all unusual for people who have been working in business or industry for a few years to want to work in the sun for a while. Mediterranean resorts in places such as the Canaries, Ibiza and Corfu are bursting at the seams with tourist establishments that need to be staffed – mostly by young party animals.

But if you target the right resorts and the right companies, you can find something suitable for a grown-up gap year. More mature candidates may be appreciated by companies catering to that market, a hope expressed by a woman from Yorkshire who posted a request for relevant information on the 'Living and Working Abroad' branch of Lonely Planet's Thorntree website:

> *I've done the career thing: 17 years in banking, finishing up as a relatively senior manager. But I'm opting out of the rat race now with a handy redundancy payment in my pocket. I passionately want to live on an unspoilt Greek island. I don't mind being paid peanuts, a pit for accommodation is fine, and a bicycle is an improvement on the transport I'll have in the UK (my feet). I haven't applied to just an ordinary holiday company but rather to a specialist in unspoilt Greek islands. Their prices are a little higher and their clientele a little older. I should know since I've holidayed with them four times. Each time the rep was over 30 and once he was over 50 so I don't worry about being too old.*

HOSTELS

At the age of 29, it hadn't occurred to **Steph Fuccio** to strap on a backpack until she spent time working in a travellers' hostel in San Francisco and met a series of creative travellers. They inspired her to save like mad and make a trip to the part of Italy from which her family originates. By making use of the international hostel site www.hostels.com, Steph had little difficulty pre-arranging a hostel job:

> *I was working at a really cute, small hostel in Rome called Hostel Casanova and was working 7 days a week (I was a bit scared about running out of money since this was the first leg of the trip). As well as getting to stay there for free, they paid me 20 euros per day in cash which was really nice. Rome was so cheap (from a San Francisco point of view) and with great weather, it was easy to save. I came to Italy with $700 cash and a plane ticket, I left with about $600 and a plane ticket to England and Ireland. I was there about 5 weeks total.*

TOUR OPERATORS

A list of special interest and activity tour operators (to whom people with specialist skills can apply) is available from AITO, the Association of Independent Tour Operators (33A St Margaret's Road, Twickenham TW1 1RG; www.aito.co.uk). In the USA, search the website of the *Specialty Travel Index* (www.specialtytravel.com).

WHEN ROGER TURSKI CAME TO A CRISIS IN HIS CAREER AND WANTED A GAP YEAR, HE KNEW IMMEDIATELY THAT HE WANTED TO GO TO AFRICA TO WORK AT A SAFARI LODGE, AND WAS ABLE TO ARRANGE THIS WITH THE HELP OF AN AGENCY THAT SPECIALISES IN MAKING PLACEMENTS IN ECO-TOURISM IN AFRICA AND ASIA:

I decided I needed a career sabbatical and wanted to combine this with my passion for the African Bush. At 39 years of age my desire was to spend time through voluntary work at a Game Lodge in Southern Africa. Within a few clicks of the Internet I came across The Leap, and after a call to the director, I knew I had found the kind of thing I was looking for. I was thrilled at the type of experiences on offer which were much closer to the career sabbatical I was after than some normal gap year projects.

My time in Botswana was nothing short of magical. The safari company has four lodges as part of their operation (three in Botswana and one in Zambia) and I spent time in all of them learning and experiencing a life that few imagine possible. Realising that I was there to work, I was quite happy to be given tasks that utilised some of my city-born skills. Initially I helped the company resolve some logistical issues they were having with maintaining correct levels of food and general supplies within each lodge. In doing this I picked up some new skills along the way and have come away with a rudimentary but solid knowledge of how to run a safari operation. Eventually I moved on to helping with relief management of the camps whilst the permanent managers were on leave. This was quite a responsibility as the guests pay a premium price for a luxury safari holiday and demand the service that goes with it. I did of course have many, many opportunities to see the wildlife. Some events will stay with me for the rest of my life. Coming across your first pride of lions, alone in a completely open vehicle, is quite an experience.

SPECIAL EVENTS

Great bursts of tourist activity take place around major events which require armies of people to work. For example up to 70,000 volunteers will be needed to help at the London 2012 Olympic and Paralympic Games. As is commonplace at high profile international sporting events, people who work on-site are usually doing so merely for the thrill of being part of the action. Volunteers who are neither paid nor provided with accommodation are invited to work eight-hour shifts for a minimum of 10 days. Sports lovers planning a career break in 2010 might like to keep their eye on the press for opportunities in Vancouver where the Winter Olympics are due to take place.

OVERLAND TOUR LEADERS

Leaders are needed to escort groups on tours within Europe by a range of companies. Drivers need to have a Passenger Carrying Vehicle (PCV) or a Heavy Goods Vehicle (HGV) licence, which costs several hundred pounds to obtain. Working in Africa, Asia and Latin America as an adventure tour leader is usually only for people in their late 20s and 30s willing to train for one of the specialist licences and with some knowledge of mechanics. Competent and well-travelled expedition staff are in demand by the many overland companies and youth travel specialists which advertise their tours and occasionally their vacancies appear in magazines such as the London giveaway *TNT* (www.tntmagazine.com) and *Wanderlust*.

Here is an annotated list of overland operators; others are listed on the Overland Expedition website www.go-overland.com.

RESOURCES

The Adventure Company – jobs@adventurecompany.co.uk; www.adventurecompany.co.uk/work-for-us.aspx. Tour leaders 25+ with first aid qualification and knowledge of languages (preferably) to lead tours worldwide.

Dragoman – ☎ 01728 861133; www.dragoman.co.uk. Has a good reputation and looks for leader drivers over 25 willing to train for the PCV licence in its workshops (if they don't already have one). Minimum commitment of two years for expeditions to Africa, Asia, South and Central America.

Exodus – www.exodus.co.uk. Suitable candidates (aged 25+) for leader positions in Africa, Asia and the Americas can acquire the appropriate licence during the months of training. Knowledge of Italian, Spanish, French or Japanese highly valued.

Explore Worldwide Ltd – www.exploreworldwide.co.uk/worldwide/tourleaders.jsp. Europe's largest adventure tour operator employing more than 100 tour leaders for Europe, Africa, Asia and the Americas. Must have first aid certificate and preferably a second language. Must be UK resident and over 25. Training given (refundable bond of £250).

Imaginative Traveller – tljobs@imtrav.net; www.imaginative-traveller.com/jobs. Tour leaders for at least 12 months for Middle East, China, Thailand, Vietnam, etc. £250 good will deposit required.

Intrepid Travel – www.intrepidtravel.com/quicklink/employment. Group Leaders come from all walks of life and join a New Leader Training course at their own expense

Kumuka Expeditions – humanresources@kumuka.com; www.kumuka.co.uk. Qualified diesel mechanics with a PCV or HGV licence needed to be drivers. Tour leaders (minimum age 23) chosen according to experience and personality.

Oasis Overland – www.oasisoverland.co.uk/work.html. Africa, Middle East, Egypt and Latin America. Minimum age 22.

The job of expedition tour leader may sound glamorous but it can be daunting unless you know well the countries and places through which you will be expected to chaperone your group. The journalist **Rosemary Behan** who took a gap year gave an account in the *Daily Telegraph* of a small group tour she joined in south-west China:

> *Our group numbered seven plus our Australian guide. We were concerned to learn that she had never been to China before, but we hoped for the best. It soon became clear that our guide was seriously out of her depth, barely managing to shepherd us on to local buses and trains, let alone give us the expert insight into the country we had all hoped for. On the other hand, simply having someone to take responsibility for our daily transport and accommodation needs did allow us more time for reflection.*

SKI RESORTS

Ski resorts generate many vacancies in the tourist industry. Staff are needed to operate the ski tows and lifts, to be in charge of chalets, to patrol the slopes, to dispense and maintain hired skis and of course to instruct would-be skiers. Either you can try to fix up a job with a British-based ski tour company before you leave (which has more security but lower wages and tends to isolate you in an English-speaking ghetto), or you can look for work on the spot where there will be a lot of competition from the young and footloose.

Specialist online ski recruitment agencies that match job-seekers with alpine vacancies will be of interest: Free Radicals (www.freeradicals.co.uk), Natives (www.natives.co.uk), www.findaskiresortjob.com and the smaller Ski Staff (www.skistaff.co.uk). Free Radicals, for example, calls itself a one-stop shop for ski season jobs for Europe and America, while Natives declares itself simply to be the 'Season Workers' website', where many ski jobs as well as summer jobs are posted before the season. Gravity Recruitment (www.gravityrecruitment.co.uk) and Alprecruit (www.alprecruit.co.uk) are more recently launched services which aim to help job-seekers find seasonal jobs winter or summer, especially those with a catering qualification.

For ski instructing courses see entries for Basecamp Group, Flying Fish, Global Sports Xperience, The International Academy, Nonstop Adventure, Peak Leaders and the Warren Smith Ski Academy. Some chalet companies hire older applicants; for instance Snowline (140–142 Wandsworth High Street, London SW18 4JJ; ☎ 0844 557 1323; www.snowline.co.uk) welcomes applications from 'couples and mature applicants' to do a winter season in Val d'Isère, Méribel, La Tania, la Plagne or Morzine. Le Ski (www.leski.com/alpinejobs) is another company that will consider older applicants to manage chalets in France. In fact a few seasons ago they hired **Susan and Eric Beney** in their autumn years:

> *We took potluck with the resort and on reflection should have done a bit more homework on resorts. La Tania was very limited; La Plagne would have been one hundred percent better. We worked long hours, six days a week, and were probably a bit too conscientious due to our age (we have just become grandparents). It's still a good way to experience a season in the Alps, but just be prepared to be overworked and underpaid. Listen to the young folk who have got the work down to a fine art and really know how to cut corners since they are there to ski and socialise.*

INTERNATIONAL JOB EXCHANGES

Even though a job swap means that you will be performing the same job as you do at home, it will involve a significant change in your life and therefore qualifies as a gap year for grown-ups. You'll have the chance to relocate abroad, meet new colleagues and put yourself in a new, challenging environment. If you're keen to live abroad without giving up your job and its income then this could be an ideal way of taking a break from the usual routines at home and work.

Employees of multinational companies are sometimes lucky enough to be offered a posting abroad so that their career break is laid on for them. A growing trend is for companies to send personnel abroad on temporary secondments rather than full blown expats. The term 'flex pats' has been coined for this.

More and more people, especially Americans, seem to be working remotely from abroad. They manage to carry on an online business from anywhere in the world, as advocated on websites such as www. laptophobo.com and www.NuNomad.com.

TEACHER EXCHANGES

The UK government supports the idea of teacher sabbaticals and local education authorities (LEAs) may even make funding available. Qualified teachers can join a post-to-post exchange through the government-sponsored League for the Exchange of Commonwealth Teachers (LECT; 60 Queens Road, Reading RG1 4BS; ☎ 0118 902 1171; www.lect.org.uk) which places British teachers with at least five years' experience in one-year or shorter posts, in schools in Australia, Canada and New Zealand. LECT manages a number of other professional development programmes for teachers.

The British Council administers the Fulbright UK/US Teacher Exchange from its Northern Ireland office (Norwich Union House, 7 Fountain Street, Belfast BT1 5EG; ☎ 028 9024 8220; fulbright@britishcouncil.org) which funds British teachers at any level to spend a term or a year in the USA. Alternatively investigate the Visiting International Faculty (VIF) Program based in North Carolina (☎ +1 919 967 5144; www.vifprogram.com) which places about 1,700 teachers from many countries in 1,000 schools throughout the USA. **Jo Elgar**, a reception teacher from Derby, thoroughly recommends career breaks. She was lucky because her school kept her job for her while she took a year out to teach in a Tanzanian village (through Personal Overseas Development (PoD) and Village Africa) and to travel:

> *I was itching to get out of Derby and see the world. They say 'the grass is not always greener,' but in my case it was, although by the end of my year out I was itching to get back to my old pastures. I found with teaching that it was nice to have a change of scenery – I came back feeling very refreshed and enthusiastic and eager to share my experiences with the children. Plus, while in Tanzania I was able to use my teaching skills and develop new ones. It was just the challenge I needed. The bonus was that I had a whole year out, so after six months in Tanzania, I continued to travel down East Africa, on an overland tour, visiting six countries. Then from Jo'burg I resumed my round-the-world ticket: next stop Australia, then New Zealand, Southeast Asia, ending in Bangkok. I was away 10 months in total with the last two months to chill and earn some cash before work.*

Teacher exchanges can also be arranged independently. **Anne Hogan** was teaching at a college of further education when it occurred to her that she would love to spend a term in the USA. She wrote to about 10 English departments which were strong in her field of interest (children's literature) and received several replies. The most promising was from a college in North Carolina. Further investigation revealed that it looked a good place to spend the winter months. She negotiated directly with her counterpart who was satisfied to exchange a big house for a small one, and wasn't unduly concerned that Anne didn't own a car.

Organisations involved in teacher recruitment including the British Council and Voluntary Service Overseas (VSO) usually welcome applications only from trained and experienced teachers. Similarly, the long established CfBT (address below) recruits teachers on behalf of foreign Ministries of Education, mainly for Brunei, Malaysia and Oman.

Certified American and international teachers seeking appointments abroad in international schools should contact International Schools Services which offers a recruitment/placement service year round and sponsors three large international recruitment fairs each year. Similarly Search Associates tries to match qualified teachers with vacancies in international schools worldwide via its website and also teacher/recruiter job fairs held in Kuala Lumpur, Sydney, Dubai, London, Toronto and others between January and July.

If you are a qualified teacher and think you might want to look for a job after arriving in an English-speaking country, you should take along your diploma and any letters of reference you have. It is a good idea to correspond ahead of time with the education authority in the district which interests you, to find out what their policy is on hiring teachers with foreign qualifications. Some countries with teacher shortages (such as New Zealand and Hong Kong) advertise their vacancies abroad and even sometimes offer incentives such as a NZ$4,000 re-location grant and automatic two-year visas (www.teachnz.govt.nz/overseas_index.html). Private recruitment agencies can also help teachers find temporary jobs in other English-speaking countries (though most of the traffic is from overseas to the UK especially London).

CfBT The Teaching Agency – 60 Queens Road, Reading RG1 4BS; ☎ 0118 902 1000; enquiries@cfbt.com; www.cfbt.com.

Christians Abroad – Bon Marché Centre, Suite 233, 241–251 Ferndale Road, London SW9 8BJ ; ☎ 0870 770 7990; www.cabroad.org.uk. Some paid but mainly volunteer teaching posts in China, Hong Kong, Japan, Tanzania and Nigeria; voluntary opportunities for minimum three months in Kenya, Zambia, Tanzania, Tonga, Uganda and Kenya.

International Schools Services – 15 Roszel Road, PO Box 5910, Princeton, New Jersey 08543, USA; ☎ 609 452 0990; www.iss.edu.

Search Associates – www.search-associates.com.

Voluntary Service Overseas (VSO) – 317 Putney Bridge Road, London SW15 2PN; www.vso.org.uk.

INTERNATIONAL TRAINING

Some professional organisations for law, agriculture, business, social work, etc., sponsor work exchanges for career development around the world, particularly in the USA, Canada, Australia, New Zealand and South Africa.

Doctors have a well-established network of contacts for finding temporary secondments to hospitals abroad. In response to the many enquiries it receives from medics looking for a stint abroad the

British Medical Association (BMA; www.bma.org.uk) carries information on planning a temporary career abroad. The *BMJ* carries classified adverts for long and short-term postings abroad (www.bmjcareers. com). Similarly, nurses and physiotherapists are a highly mobile population, especially with the morale so low in the National Health Service. The Royal College of Nursing (20 Cavendish Square, London W1M 0AB; www.rcn.org.uk) provides information for its members who want to work abroad. Of course many medical charities recruit volunteers (see Part 4, *Doing Something Worthwhile*).

In some of the capital cities of the world, specialist agencies and human resources companies can set up internships for ambitious young professionals in the field of their choice.

INTERNATIONAL VOCATIONAL EXCHANGES

Agriventure is the name of the International Agricultural Exchange Association's (IAEA) exchange programme which operates in Australia, New Zealand, Canada, the USA and Japan. Agriventure (IAEA, Speedwell Farm Bungalow, Nettle Bank, Wisbech, Cambridgeshire PE14 0SA; ☎ 01945 450999; www.agriventure.net) has many years' experience arranging for young agriculturalists up to the age of 30 to live and work with approved host families. Many types of agricultural/horticultural placement are available for between six and 12 months. Participants pay between £2,000 and £4,200 which includes airline tickets, visas, insurance, orientation seminar and board and lodging throughout with a host family. Trainees are then paid a realistic wage.

The International Exchange Programme (IEP UK, Lamont House, 18 Leicester Road, Uppingham, Rutland LE15 9SD; ☎ 0845 347 0105; ☎ 01572 823934, www.iepuk.com) places trainees under 35 and with at least a year's hands-on practical experience in horse racing and equine work, agriculture, horticulture or oenology (wine-making) in the USA, Australia, New Zealand, South Africa and Europe including Ireland. IEP can assist candidates in getting a J-1 visa for up to 18 months of working in the USA and a 416 working holiday visa for Australia; the placement fee is about £2,000 including airfares.

WORKING IN THE USA

Visas are a perennial bugbear for anyone who is interested in doing paid work in the USA. The exchange visitor visa J-1 is available only through approved exchange organisations responsible for work and travel programmes, mostly for students, and only to candidates who pass an interview at the US Embassy. Joining a Summer Camp Counsellor programme such as Camp America (www.campamerica.co.uk) or BUNAC (www.bunac.org.uk) is the most straightforward way to spend time working in the USA with a J-1.

For a brief list of approved exchanges and internship programmes in the USA, including some for specific groups (from qualified lawyers to unemployed Northern Irish nationals) contact the Educational Advisory Service of the Fulbright Commission or check the website (www.fulbright.co.uk/eas/workexchange//index.html).

Apart from the J-1 visa available to people on approved exchange visitor programmes, the other possible visas must be applied for by the employer on the applicant's behalf which will take at least three months. The H category covers non-immigrant work visas in special circumstances. The H2-B is for temporary or seasonal vacancies which employers have trouble filling with US citizens. For example, the chronic shortage of workers on the ski fields of Colorado means that many employers can obtain the necessary Labor Certification confirming that there are no qualified American workers available to do the jobs. A petition is then submitted by the employer to the Immigration and Naturalisation Service (INS). The maximum duration of the H2-B visa is 10 months though most come in for about six months to work at amusement parks, as lifeguards, in retail and fast food. They must work only for the employer that has petitioned for their visa.

The H-1B 'Specialty Occupation' visa for professionals with a degree is available for 'prearranged professional or highly skilled jobs' for which there are no suitably qualified Americans. The allocation of H-1B visas rose sharply a few years ago, partly to alleviate the shortage of IT specialists, but has been declining again (so that the 2007 allocation was 61,000). A university degree is a prerequisite and all the paperwork must be carried out by the American employer who must pay a training fee.

The H-1C is available only to nurses. The H-3 'Trainee' visa is the other possibility. Applicants must indicate in detail the breakdown between classroom and on-the-job time, and why equivalent training is not available in their own country.

INTERNSHIPS AND WORK EXPERIENCE

Internship is the American term for traineeship, providing a chance to get some experience in your career interest as part of your academic course. These are typically available to undergraduates, recent graduates and young professionals.

Several organisations in the UK arrange for students and young professionals to undertake internships and work experience in the USA.

The Association for International Practical Training (AIPT) – Maryland; info@aipt.org, administers the UK/US Career Development Programme. This programme is for people under 35 with relevant qualifications and/or at least two years of work experience in their career field. A separate section of the programme is for full-time students in Hospitality & Tourism or Equine Studies.

CDS International – 871 United Nations Plaza, 15th Floor, New York, NY 10017–1814; ☎ +1 212 497 3500; www.cdsintl.org, offers Professional Development Program in the USA lasting two to 18 months in a variety of fields including business, engineering and technology. The opportunities for internships are open to young professionals, aged less than 35. Participation fee for stays of up to six months is $850, longer stays $1,200.

IST Plus – Rosedale House, Rosedale Road, Richmond, Surrey TW9 2SZ; ☎ 020 8939 9057; www.istplus.com, runs Professional Career Training programmes for candidates aged 20–40 as well as helping full-time students to arrange course-related placements in the USA lasting three to 18 months. IST Plus supplies practical advice on applying for work and a searchable database of internships/work placements. Those who qualify get a J-1 visa. The programme fees start at £500.

Internship programmes are also available through **InterExchange** (161 Sixth Avenue, New York, NY 10013) and **Alliances Abroad Group** (1221 South Mopac Expressway, Suite 250, Austin, Texas 78746; ☎ +1 512 457 8062; ☎ +1 888 6 ABROAD; www.allianceabroad.com) which authorise J-1 visas and arrange internships in Denver, San Francisco and Washington DC.

WORKING IN AUSTRALIA AND NEW ZEALAND

Australia has reciprocal working holiday arrangements with Britain, Ireland, Canada, the Netherlands and a number of other countries. Applicants must be between the ages of 18 and 30 and without children. The visa is for people intending to use any money they earn in Australia to supplement their holiday funds. Working full-time for more than six months for the same employer is not permitted (increased from three months in 2006) and full-time study or training can now last up to four months.

The working holiday visa is valid for 12 months after entry, which must be within 12 months of issue. People who have done at least three months of seasonal work in regional Australia or worked in specified primary industries are eligible to apply for a second working holiday visa. Application can be made via the Australian Immigration Service website (www.immi.gov.au) or using a specialist agent such as Visas Australia (☎ 01270 626626; www.visas-australia.com) where you will pay a premium.

Most people apply for a Working Holiday Maker (WHM) visa online, in which case there is no need to provide proof of savings of £2,000, nor do you send in your passport. Applying online via the Australian Department of Immigration website (www.immi.gov.au) is usually straightforward and hassle-free and should result in an email confirmation within two days, which is sufficient to get you into the country. Your passport isn't physically inspected until you arrive in Australia when you must take it along to an office of the Department of Immigration and Citizenship (DIAC) to obtain the visa label. The official non-refundable visa fee is currently A$190 (£90).

A number of agencies such as BUNAC, CCUSA and Real Gap (www.realgap.co.uk) offer working holiday packages for both Australia and New Zealand to anyone eligible for the working holiday visa (under 31), from basic DIY packages including the first couple of nights accommodation (from £200) to more deluxe versions that include visa, insurance, job offer guarantee and other benefits.

The dense network of 'backpackers' (i.e. private hostels) is a goldmine of information. Foreign job-seekers often find employment in the hostels themselves too. Working in the cities may not provide much of a contrast with your home situation, so consider spending time in the bush or the outback. Many gap year dreams revolve around campfires by moonlight and close contact with wildlife and nature. One way of experiencing the authentic Aussie outdoors is to sign up for a one-week course as a station/farm assistant (jackaroo or jillaroo).

Horsecraft, cattle mustering, ute driving and trail biking are tasks that may occupy your days. The course organisers often provide a referral service to other stations in case you want to stay on working as a farm hand (provided you have a working holiday visa in your passport). Courses in Queensland are available from Rocky Creek Station in Biggenden (☎ +61 7 4127 1377; www.isisol.com.au/rockycrk-farmstay). Intensive four or five-day farm training courses will cost roughly A$125 a day. A course at the Leconfield School of Jackarooing in New South Wales (www.leconfieldjackaroo.com) is longer and therefore costs more (A$895–A$995 for 11 days).

The New Zealand government no longer imposes a quota on the number of working holiday visas available to Britons aged up to 30 who can work for up to 23 months. Base Backpackers with its headquarters in Auckland offers a Work & Travel Starter Package for NZ$345 which includes 12 months registration with New Zealand Job Search (including a job offer guarantee), orientation sessions, the first few nights' accommodation and many other perks (www.stayatbase.com/work).

NESTING ABROAD

Finding a temporary home in Marrakesh or Memphis, San José or Salamanca is an idyllic dream for many, giving them the chance to enjoy a rejuvenating interlude in their lives. A stint spent living abroad is bound to be exciting and memorable as you navigate your way round a different society, interact with the locals in the bar or corner shop, adapt to a different language and sense of humour and come to understand how different societies develop according to history, geography and climate. On a more basic level, simply mastering the bus or postal systems or signing up for an evening class will impart a feeling of achievement. Perhaps you'll have the chance to rent your own place, even if is just a bedsit or a garret. Once you have a base in a foreign country, you will begin to feel as though you are really living there, however briefly.

An American journalist Alice Steinbach did just this by leaving behind all that was familiar – not only home, job, family and friends, but her own concept of self – to spend long periods living in Paris, London, Oxford and Italy. Her book *Without Reservations* is a warm and thoughtful account of this gap year, and could well inspire other women whose children have left home to do likewise.

Sometimes your travels will lead you into an unexpected episode of living abroad. On the road you may fall in love with a person or place and find a way to extend your stay for months. Travelling without any intention of working, **Rachel Pooley** and **Charlie Stanley-Evans** were driving through Africa when they were offered the lease on a backpacking hostel in Malawi for £1,000 which they ran for six months, living contentedly by the shores of Lake Malawi. To give themselves their own project they built a house of brick and straw and made a garden. They even considered buying the hostel outright and settling down indefinitely, but they decided that the expatriate life was not for them in the long term. But they describe this period spent managing the lodge as the most worthwhile experience of the whole trip and enabled them for a time to live in a 'heavenly place'.

After a period of volunteering in the Himalayas through HELP and working for the Orangutan Foundation in Borneo, **Natasha Allden** went on to spend three months in New Zealand partly as a working visitor on a farm through Farm Helpers in Palmerston North, New Zealand (www.fhinz. co.nz) where she led horse treks in Kawakawa, Northland. She was smitten, and not just with the country, because at last report she was applying for permanent residency in order to marry her partner, a Maori.

After leaving his legal practice to take a round-the-world trip, **John Taylor** and his wife **Lavinia** would never have anticipated that they would find themselves working in the West Australian wheat belt. Instead of continuing their travels to see the world, John and Lavinia stayed on, spending five years in Australia altogether. But they faced a problem common to many couples. John enjoyed the self-sufficiency of life in Western Australia and could quite happily have stayed for good. With its vast landscapes and ample agricultural work he could envisage a rewarding working life there. Lavinia, however, missed England, especially its social mores. There were some aspects of life in Australia to which she simply couldn't reconcile herself so in the end they both returned to their roots.

Having been tempted by an alternative way of life on the other side of the world, they faced a decision that is more difficult for a couple than a single person, and even more so for a family. Nevertheless a conscious decision to emigrate is a momentous one and marks the most conclusive kind of life change prompted by a gap year. For some individuals putting their work on hold is a catalyst for much needed larger changes in their life.

JOINING THE EXPAT COMMUNITY

In every major city of the world you'll find an international community of expat teachers, medics, aid workers, journalists, diplomats, anthropologists, business people, missionaries and not a few eccentrics suspended between two cultures. So it is difficult to feel completely stranded abroad. You may particularly value the support and assistance of the expat community if you don't speak much of the local language or if you need their help to find work.

Dan Boothby had read Arabic as an undergraduate and had lived in Syria as a student. Later he decided to leave his job as an awards coordinator with the British Academy of Film and Television Arts (BAFTA) to move to Cairo where a good friend lived, whom he hoped would introduce him to the local social scene. He was already in possession of a TEFL Certificate and planned to use teaching to support himself while he worked on a novel. He found it almost alarmingly easy to find one-to-one teaching work which he did not enjoy all that much but it paid the bills.

In retrospect he wishes that he had tried to break into local journalism as there were plenty of opportunities in local English language magazines. Yet the time away from London allowed Dan to read incessantly and pursue his own literary endeavours.

It was a very easy life but I felt penned in by a cultural divide. I had little contact with Egyptians and it's very difficult for European men to meet Egyptian women. It was rather frustrating for a single man.

Still, the constant round of ex-pat parties meant that Dan wasn't short of company and he travelled extensively in his spare time. Dan took some savings with him but wishes that he had had more (who doesn't?). He lived very cheaply on a houseboat divided into flats. Turning 30 in Egypt was a disturbing experience for Dan and he began to wonder whether he had exhausted the pleasures of drinking beer on a boat. He felt he had to return to London to take up some professional challenges:

It was a very easy life in Cairo and it gave me time to think. I decided that I quite like the rat race and I returned to London more mellow and confident. But I am a serial 'sabbaticalist' until I find out what I want to do long term... After London, the chaos of Cairo was initially appealing but I finally decided that living there resembled an open prison because of the cultural divide.

Of course you may try to function outside the expat scene and concentrate your energies on meeting and befriending the locals, as **Glen Williams** did in Madrid:

Madrid is a crazy place. During the gaps in my teaching timetable (10–2 and 4–7) I pretend to study Spanish (I'm no natural) and just wander the back streets. I suppose I should try to be more cultural and learn to play an instrument, write poetry or look at paintings, but I never get myself in gear. I think most people teach English here as a means to live in Spain and learn the Spanish language and culture. But there is a real problem that you end up living in an English enclave, teaching English all day and socialising with English teachers. You have to make a big effort to get out of this rut. I am lucky to live with Spanish people (who do not want to practise their English!).

STAYING ON

Making the decision to take a career break abroad can be the prelude to an adventure that might take you in unexpected directions and last far longer than intended. Some people simply don't come home. The longer you stay away, the more difficult it will be to reintegrate (see the chapter *Reverse Culture Shock* in Part 11).

Every individual will have to weigh up the gains and losses of staying or returning. The majority will have too many attachments and obligations back home to contemplate a permanent move. Sometimes the intention of eventually moving home disappears almost imperceptibly as it very gradually transpires that a career and the future are being built abroad. There's an irresistible attraction about living in a place you come to as an adult. You have more freedom to invent yourself and shed inhibitions. Away from family, school friends, college peers and work colleagues, individuals can start afresh without the burdens of old baggage.

LIVING IN THE SOUTHERN US, KATHY HINES COOPER SUDDENLY FELT AN IMPERATIVE TO UNFURL A DREAM. WITH A 'NOW OR NEVER' ATTITUDE TO THE RISKS, SHE MADE THE DECISION PRACTICALLY OVERNIGHT TO HEAD ACROSS THE ATLANTIC. AFTER DISCOVERING HOW HARD IT IS FOR AMERICANS TO GET A VISA TO WORK IN HER FIRST CHOICE COUNTRIES OF FRANCE AND ITALY, SHE TURNED HER ATTENTION TO POLAND. SINCE HER GREAT-GRANDFATHER WAS BORN IN PRUSSIA IN 1847 (LATER RETURNED TO POLAND), SHE SOON TRANSFERRED HER ENTHUSIASM, AND WITHIN A WEEK OF DOING A TEFL TRAINING COURSE IN THE UK HAD BEEN OFFERED A JOB:

Some years ago, I (a middle-aged American woman) got a wild hair to do my thing. What I really wanted to do was to live in Europe. When I got bored one evening, I went to the bookstore and bought one of your first books on a whim. I was hooked and am now here in Poland, experiencing this fabulous country, living in the small city of Raciborz, teaching in international businesses.

'Poland? You're kidding?' Such remarks from most, not all, family and friends only pushed me through this wild and crazy time of completely changing my life. A new country, culture, language, food, profession, no friends and all faced alone, acquainted with nary a person, except for the typed signature of emails from the Director of Studies of the hiring language school in Opole.

And that was seven years ago. I never expected to stay this long. I was sure it was a path towards getting back west, to France or Italy. I never tried. My heart is here; my life is here nine months a year. In the summers I return to America to my family.

Currently, my pay has quadrupled from when I arrived, mostly due to the EU entry and having built a name for myself in the local school. I no longer have roommates, but a flat of my own. Living conditions run from comfortable (always warm in winter) to fabulous, as in my tastefully Tuscan marble decorated flat that is freshly decorated, however in a Stalinist 'cubist' building.

How gratifying it is to be so well respected as a teacher. Offer your expertise, background, and life. They will take it and accept you for who you are, as long as you are accepting of their cultures and lifestyle. Expect to be offered home cooked dinner, theatre and opera outings, family holidays (don't eat for two days prior please), weekend trips to the country or seaside. Would you like to experience castle hunting, Krakow, Warsaw, the surrounding mountains, snow skiing at its best, winter kulig (sleigh) pulled by horses and enjoying fresh kielbasa braised on a stick over an open fire pit in the depths of the snow? To me this is heaven on earth, and my destiny.

Some post-gap year changes of direction can be dramatic in the extreme. **Philippa Vernon-Powell** had been a very high-profile businesswoman and consultant in London earning up to £200,000 a year. In her late 30s, she decided to do an eight-month volunteer stint in Mexico with Outreach International at a shelter for street children in the resort of Puerta Vallarta, which turned her life around. She returned to London and within a short time had raised £17,000 to buy beds, a washing machine, books and sports equipment for the struggling shelter. She has now set up her own street children rehabilitation project in Puerta Vallarta, New Life Mexico, and is staying on to run it (www.newlifemexico.com).

Alienation from the materialistic values of the West often afflicts career gappers who have spent time in a developing country. Some find it impossible to slot easily back into what they have come to view as pleasure-seeking ways. **Kate Ledward** knew that accountancy was not her dream ticket to a happy life even before she went to Africa. Having become aware that her previous trips to Tanzania and Kenya had not satisfied her curiosity about Africa, she decided she needed to return. She stumbled across the charity SPW and was impressed with their methodology in partnering each overseas volunteer with a local volunteer and then sending the mixed nationality group into rural villages. Not only were the Ugandans perhaps the most hospitable, happy and friendly people Kate had ever met, the country was also breathtakingly beautiful.

When I returned to the UK, I was not able to settle. Having spent a further 18 long months back in the Financial Services sector, and indeed studying for Financial Planning exams, I kept my passion for the work I did in Uganda alive by volunteering on an organic farm at weekends and taking a short community course in organic growing. Now clear of the gloomy debts from university, I am free to return to one of my dreams come true, and am flying back to my beloved Africa to explore a path that I am now more certain than ever is the one I wish to follow.

PART 7

TRAVEL AND ADVENTURE

INTRODUCTION

Traditionally, the gap year between school and higher education is associated with a period of travel, time spent working abroad or a combination of the two. Many new graduates also head off travelling immediately after finishing their courses and before settling into a career. But why can't you have the same adventures at the age of 35 or 55?

Possibly travelling and/or working abroad held no appeal when you were younger. Perhaps a shortage of funds, a lack of confidence or a reluctance to interrupt vocational training and career progression were factors. As a more mature traveller you might have a clearer idea about which countries and cultures you want to visit. Arguably, travel is wasted on the young. There is a tendency these days for very young students to travel rather indiscriminately to far-flung corners of the globe, to places they are not really interested in just to meet up with other travellers, to eat, drink and socialise in exactly the way they would at home but without as many inhibitions. At just 18, travellers are more likely to follow the crowd (and the party) than those who are 28, 38 or beyond.

Whatever age you are, nothing can compare with the joy of the open road. The sense of possibility, adventure and even danger can bring feelings of exhilaration unavailable in the workplace. When travelling in developing countries, you can shed – at least temporarily – the clutter and accoutrements of modern life in the Western world, for a time to live more simply.

Another of the less trumpeted pleasures of independent travel is the feeling of being free and unfettered. Anyone who has been working in a big organisation or even operating within a family where the other members tend to dictate the rules (e.g. on holidays the man usually takes charge of the map) may have forgotten the unalloyed pleasure of exercising choice of activities and destinations from an infinite number of possibilities.

Almost anyone who has had some experience of independent travel catches the bug and longs to see more and spend a longer time abroad. It might stem from a personal passion such as learning languages or saving the rainforest or a fascination left over from childhood with an exotic destination, e.g. Madagascar or Patagonia. Cheap air travel has opened up parts of the globe once reserved for the affluent. Today there's little surprise (but usually some envy) when you tell your colleagues that you are planning to go trekking in the hinterland of Rio de Janeiro or diving in the Philippines. Inside many an office worker lurks a secret Indiana Jones longing for a challenge.

Some people take time out from work to embark on a particular journey they have long set their hearts on following. These journeys range from straightforward backpacking to expeditions using specially acquired equipment to an organised adventure trip in which you pay a specialist to help you, which might range from mountain trekking to long distance motorbiking. Options include white water rafting, hot air ballooning, mountain climbing, off-road driving, scuba diving and sailing, perhaps even around the world.

Older travellers taking a gap year may be in a position to travel in greater comfort than would have been possible in their student days, while others may choose to revert to their youth and go backpacking and hostelling. **David Moncur** had always felt a bit sniffy about backpackers hostels but since he wanted his redundancy money to last as long as possible, he used hostels in Australia and found that he absolutely loved them. He discovered it was very energising to be in the company of so many young people, though he also found some people closer to his own age to chat to as well. Backpackers' hostels are far more convivial than hotels.

Maddie Kilgour from Scotland, who negotiated six months off from her administrative job, thoroughly enjoyed the non-volunteering phase of her trip, booked with VentureCo, when she travelled on her own:

> I went off on my own on a journey of discovery. Most of this was in Peru – and I absolutely loved it. I travelled in buses, on boats, in cars, on foot. I clambered up mountains, walked through deserts, flew over the Nazca lines, followed Inca trails via graveyards and pyramids. It was the most fabulous journey of my life. Had I known that on my return I would be so quickly made redundant, I would have extended my time in Peru.

For many, travel represents escape and discovery. By immersing yourself in the unknown it is temporarily possible to disorient yourself and undergo a process of detachment from banal and tedious routines and responsibilities that hem in the lives of all adults. At a more practical level, an extended break gives an almost unique period (post-education) to explore in depth other regions and cultures of the world. In the 19th century, many individuals never travelled more than 10 miles to the next town.

HAVING AWARDED HIMSELF SEVERAL CAREER BREAKS OVER THE YEARS, MIKE BLEAZARD WAS LUCKY ENOUGH TO BECOME PAIR-BONDED IN HIS MID-30S WITH JANE O'BEIRNE WHO SHARED HIS COMMITMENT TO STEPPING OUT OF THE RAT RACE:

When Jane got together with Mike, she was discontented with the solicitor's office where she worked. After one particularly frustrating day at work, she blurted out 'Shall we take off round the world?' Mike nodded his assent and seven months later they did. They were both in the fortunate position of being able to save money quite handily in that period of planning – Jane by moving into the flat that Mike owned so that she saved everything she would have spent on rent and Mike by getting a staggeringly well-paid contract (£50 an hour) turning techie-speak into human language. They were each able to budget £7,000 for the six-month trip on top of round-the-world airfares plus they had the rent of £800 a month coming in from Mike's flat. They did not want to rough it for six months but intended to intersperse periods of spartan travel with short bursts of luxury. They looked into doing some voluntary work but the (very expensive) schemes that they came across didn't grab them.

Their initial destination was southern Africa to see the solar eclipse that took place in early December 2002. They headed to Cape Town for Christmas to meet up with friends from Cambridge who turned out to be planning to get married secretly so Mike and Jane were invited to act as best man and maid of honour. They then flew to the Seychelles from Nairobi (losing one of their cameras to a corrupt airport official). Most of the African leg of their trip had been pre-arranged whereas once they moved on to Australia they could improvise a bit more. Yet they realised that much of the time they spent driving the Great Ocean Road (for example) was spent planning the next leg of their journey to New Zealand and they decided to try to concentrate more on the present moment. Their most treasured possession that they never let out of their sight was a gadget capable of storing 12,000 digital pictures (a collection that they delighted in promising to show to families and friends in its entirety).

In retrospect they were glad that they had done the trip in the order that they did: starting with the strangeness of Africa, relaxing into the familiarity of Anglo culture in Australia and New Zealand and finally entering the most challenging phase, travelling around South America with minimal Spanish. They noticed that the average age of travellers met in Chile, Argentina and Brazil was higher than it had been earlier in their trip and they came to the conclusion that adults on gap years are better equipped and more committed to leaving the beaten track than gap year students and other young backpackers who congregate in Cape Town, Kathmandu and Sydney.

Patagonia was firmly on their itinerary but because they were a little apprehensive about venturing into the tail end of the continent at the tail end of the season, they reckoned that they had better pre-arrange their trip. They tried to do this through a well-meaning agent in Santiago, though none of the arrangements they made with him came off. For instance they arrived at a 10,000-strong penguin colony near Punta Arenas to find just four lonely penguins, since five days before the colony had decided to swim off.

With hindsight, they would have done better making arrangements after arrival in Patagonia for visiting national parks, going trekking and finding accommodation. It wasn't until near the end of their trip that they shared a Zen moment in a bus station in southern Chile: they realised that they had absolutely no idea where they would end up that day. They opened their guidebook, liked the sound of a volcano in the vicinity and proceeded to find out if any bus was going that way, but not until after they had retired for a coffee. They felt more free than they had perhaps in their whole lives. As the months had passed, so had their anxiety about mapping out what was to come.

From the plane between Santiago and Punta Arenas they had seen an astonishingly beautiful mountain. A Chilean passenger informed them that this was Mount Fitzroy and they resolved to return by land. After many hours on a bus over unmade roads and crossing the border into Argentina, Mike and Jane were exhilarated to have the chance to hike to the base of Mount Fitzroy and look up its sheer vertical rock walls on which they had looked down from the aeroplane.

COMBINING TRAVEL AND WORK

If on an adult gap year, you wish to work or volunteer abroad (topics that are covered in other chapters), you will have more skills and maturity to bring to a foreign employer or project. Some older travellers consider it self-indulgent or shallow simply to travel. For London lawyer **Polly Botsford**, for example, it was important to work and not only travel. Because she thinks that '*you can get jaded very quickly and then end up a mechanical tourist*,' she decided to divide her six-month gap equally between travelling and working. Through Outreach International Polly arranged to work for a non-governmental organisation (NGO) in Cambodia that campaigns against the illegal trafficking of children and young girls.

Likewise **Daniel Smith** aspired to more than just travel in his four-month break from his job in publishing. He had long wanted to go to India but didn't just want to go backpacking or hang around in Goa. After looking at lots of different volunteer opportunities he ended up spending time in the publishing arm of an enterprising arts charity in Calcutta.

Interestingly, quite a few career gappers who have combined volunteering and travel end up enjoying the volunteering more. **Jackie Smith** and her husband Peter took a six-month sabbatical in India and Southeast Asia after many years of working, part volunteering through MondoChallenge and part travelling:

> Since our return we both agree that staying in a small rural village and living with the principal of a local school for two and a half months was the highlight of our six months away. It was fantastic being part of the community if only for a short time. People got to know us and included us in local festivals such as Diwali, which included an impressively run bingo competition on the field opposite our school as well as lots of food, drink and blessings. I do think that if we travelled again we might do a longer volunteer placement and perhaps even less time being a 'tourist' – maybe even something like VSO. While the world is a huge place and there is always something new to see, we felt that you really can't beat meeting local people, getting to know them and their way of life and sharing stories. It is the only real way to get anywhere near understanding a place and making some sort of connection.

TRAVEL CHOICES

People travelling on a gap year later in life will be looking for a unique travel experience, one that is different from their annual holidays in Wales or Provence. Open-ended travel is considered to be distinct from tourism which can be roughly defined as a trip abroad in which itinerary and accommodation are booked in advance. Yet the growing number of tour operators is now blurring the difference by providing challenging adventure holidays on foot or by vehicle over difficult terrain, or by catering to people who want to donate their time and labour to a specific cause like conservation or teaching (see Part 5, *Directory of Specialist Programmes*). These packages attempt to introduce travellers to a more authentic experience of countries such as Peru or Thailand. Trips might include a variety of experiences, for example jungle trekking, cookery lessons, and free-time sightseeing.

ORGANISED TRAVEL

Heading into the wild blue yonder is a daunting prospect for most adults taking a break unless they are hardened independent travellers from away back. In many cases it will make sense for a solo traveller to consider joining some kind of structured programme, whether an organised trek in the Himalayas, an overland expedition through East Africa or an adventure trip through South America possibly combined with Spanish lessons and/or a volunteer placement. Environmentally and culturally sensitive tour operators design trips to introduce Westerners to a region, country or culture by employing expert guides who can share their insights and knowledge. These trips address a growing market of people who want a trip that's organised for them without losing the experience of adventure and discovery that comes from independent travel. As this book tries to demonstrate, the choice of worthy small and large companies organising short and long trips is quite staggering. For someone in the early stages of thinking about a gap year, the range of possibilities can be overwhelming.

A possible starting place is one of the annual winter travel shows, for example the *Daily Telegraph* Adventure Travel Show (www.adventureshow.co.uk) held every March at Olympia, or Destinations (www.destinationsshow.com) at Earl's Court in London and the National Exhibition Centre in Birmingham, or perhaps most relevant of all – One Life Live (www.onelifelive.co.uk), which features a travel and career break zone in association with the travel magazine *Wanderlust*. Many relevant companies exhibit at these shows and it is a good chance to compare what is on offer. When **Paul Carroll** reached his late 20s, he came to the conclusion that there was something seriously wrong with the work–life balance in his pressurised IT job. So he took himself off to the Destinations show in Earl's Court:

> *There I saw lots of companies, but few offering specialist programmes for trekking, backpacking and generally challenging itineraries. VentureCo was one, and White Peak Expeditions another. I took a VentureCo brochure that happened to be labelled 'Career Gap'. Later I sifted through all the brochures I had collected from the show and from the Internet and eventually chose VentureCo. I was very impressed as they are very careful with their selection of individuals through a series of interviews.*

Paul went on to book a four-month expedition to Patagonia with VentureCo (see Directory entry). Afterwards he travelled independently for several more months in South America and experienced nature like he had never imagined: '*glaciers, volcanoes, mountain ranges, condors, wild cats, rainforest, jungle, pampas, salt lakes, geysers, etc...*' This proved a useful half-way house between going it alone and having a trip pre-arranged.

Another way of achieving this balance is to create an itinerary with the help of a specialist travel agent. An intriguing new concept in travel is being pioneered by the online travel organisation Rickshaw Travel (☎ 01273 718034; www.rickshawtravel.co.uk) which launched in 2008. The concept is based on short travel programmes or 'modules' which last a few days each. Customers can go à la carte and pick and mix from a wide selection of these. Once they have selected the modules, the agency can join the dots by booking sleeper trains, ferries and accommodation, which is all locally owned, authentic and cosy. This kind of travel booking is for people who do not want to do a group tour, flop in a resort or stay in bland international hotels, but they do want the security of booking in the UK with a bonded tour operator. So far the countries covered are Thailand, Vietnam, India, Nepal and South Africa, with Mexico in the pipeline.

For more conventional travel bookings, well-established agents such as Trailfinders, STA Travel and Flight Centre should be familiar with options suited to the longer-term traveller. You might want to consider hop-on hop-off transport aimed primarily at backpackers in which, typically, you travel in a group of up to 20 on an adapted bus which travels on more off-the-beaten-track routes than conventional bus tours. Passengers are free to get off at any stop, stay as long as they like and resume their journey when they're ready and the next one passes through within a time limit, usually of between two and six months.

If solo travel does not appeal, as it often does not for novice travellers or women travelling alone, organised group travel offers many advantages. It can become an excellent way of meeting new people and sharing experiences rather than facing the potential loneliness and anxiety of solitary, independent travel. Many appealing alternatives to the conventional coach tour for OAPs exist around the world; for example in the USA consider the escorted trips aimed at people 18–38 offered by Trekamerica (☎ 0845 330 6095; www.trekamerica.co.uk) or by Green Tortoise in San Francisco (☎ +1 800 867 8647 within North America or +1 415 956 7500; www.greentortoise.com) which uses vehicles converted to sleep up to 36 people that make interesting detours and stopovers. On Green Tortoise trips, which place more emphasis on outdoor activities such as hiking and canoeing than sightseeing, about a third of clients are aged 25–35 and 6% are older.

Overlanding by motorbike appeals to some, possibly more to mid-life men than other groups. Specialist companies such as Globebusters (www.globebusters.com) and Kudu Expeditions (www.kuduexpeditions.com) offer up to four-month motorcycle journeys through Africa and America, which are accessible to anyone who can afford them.

INDEPENDENT TRAVEL

The clear alternative is to travel completely independently in as basic or as luxurious a style as you choose. Students do not have the monopoly on backpacking. There is no reason why at an older age you shouldn't aim for something more than relaxation and predictability. If you decide to take the independent route, it's a good idea to map out a plan or itinerary in advance because you will probably want to make at least some flight bookings, while retaining the pleasure of following your nose. Many round-the-world tickets cost less than £1,000 (before tax) and allow you to hop through different countries and continents at your own pace.

So give yourself enough flexibility to act on impulse. You may meet locals who take you off the beaten track to visit their homes or recommend a beach or waterfall overlooked by the guidebooks.

Inspiration can come from someone met in the pub, from the travel section of your local bookshop, television documentaries or from the travel pages of papers such as the *Independent* or travel magazines such as *Wanderlust*. The worthy organisation Tourism Concern published a book in 2006 called

The Ethical Travel Guide, which describes 300 places in 60 countries guaranteed not to be tourist traps.

Americans might consult the classic *Vagabonding: An Uncommon Guide to the Art of Long-Term World Travel* by veteran shoestring expeditioner Rolf Potts. The author defines 'vagabonding' like the adult gap year of this book, i.e. taking time off from your normal life to discover and experience the world on your own terms. He also maintains a link-laden website (www.vagablogging.net). The author argues persuasively that time is a more precious commodity for travellers than money, and liberates you from having to over-organise your itinerary in advance. Another title of interest is *The Practical Nomad: How to Travel Around the World* whose author, Edward Hasbrouck, is at the time of writing engaged in a round-the-world trip which has taken in 27 countries so far (Avalon Travel, $22). The book is a '*how-to handbook of advice and tips for independent, on-your-own travel*'.

Many people are anxious about the language barrier when contemplating travel within or beyond Europe. With a phrase book and a lack of inhibition about playing charades, this perceived hindrance usually melts away.

The best source of information on what to see and how to get there is other travellers, met on the road or in Internet forums such as the invaluable Lonely Planet Thorntree (www.lonelyplanet.com/thorntree). Here members can post any query under the sun about border crossings, departure taxes or tourist site rip-offs, and expect a prompt and illuminating answer.

PLANES, TRAINS AND AUTOMOBILES

There follow some general guidelines for finding bargains in train, coach, car, ship and air travel. More detailed information on specific destinations can be found in travel guides from Lonely Planet, Rough Guides and others. The amount of travel information on the Internet is staggering and this chapter cannot hope to tap its resources. There are websites on everything from sleeping in airports (the fabulous www.sleepinginairports.net) to sharing lifts across the USA and Canada (www.erideshare.com). Many sites have pages of intriguing links: to name just one, try www.budgettravel.com.

BOOKING FLIGHTS

For long-haul flights, especially to Asia, Australasia and most recently Latin America, discounted tickets are available in plenty and there should never be any need to pay the official full fare on a scheduled flight. Unfortunately no one is exempt from surcharges so you should be aware that printed prices can very quickly go out of date in this economic climate. Since 2004, fuel surcharges have gone up over a dozen times and now weigh in at up to £111.50 per flight (depending on the length of the flight). With most people predicting that the price of oil is set to rise further, everyone has to be braced for further increases.

The lowest fares are still found by doing some careful shopping around on the telephone and Internet. Even if you choose not to book online and want the reassurance of dealing with a human being, the web can still be a great starting point for information about prices and options.

Discount agents advertise in London weeklies such as *TNT* and *Time Out*, as well as in the travel pages of newspapers such as the Saturday *Independent*. Phone a few outfits and pick the best price or check relevant websites (www.cheapflights.co.uk; www.expedia.com; www. opodo.com). Viewers can log onto their destination and then see a list of prices offered by a variety of airlines and agents. The cheapest flights are sometimes available from lesser known airlines such as Aeroflot or Bimanair, the airline of Bangladesh, which are considered dubious by cautious types. East European carriers (e.g. Tarom) and Asian carriers (e.g. Eva Airways) are often worth investigating for low fares. Try to overcome your reluctance, since flying with them is guaranteed to be more interesting than flying on Air Canada or British Airways. When **Sarah Spiller** fell in love with Sri Lanka after joining a turtle conservation project and persuaded her husband that they should buy a holiday house there, she made several trips on Sri Lanka Airlines and feels that she is already on holiday the minute she steps aboard.

ROUND-THE-WORLD FLIGHTS

The most common round-the-world itineraries are ones that have been specially marketed by groups of airlines that cooperate and have formed various 'alliances'. A good travel agent will quickly tell you which alliance of airlines (if any) is best suited to your needs. Fare levels change according to how many stops and what distances you want to cover, so you will need to make some careful calculations about your route, and whether you want to travel 26,000 miles or up to 39,000 miles (which might mean a £700 difference in price). Note that if you don't particularly want to include North America on your itinerary, you may not really need a round-the-world ticket.

Round-the-world fares currently start at £780 for a six-stop ticket departing in low season (between mid-April and mid-June). By far the most popular departure season is between 16 January and 15 April, followed by 15 August to 30 November, when the same ticket would cost around £900. The sting in the tail is that nowadays, taxes and fuel charges rarely add on less than £500 to these costs. On this ticket you could do for example: London–Bangkok – overland to Singapore – Cairns – Sydney – Christchurch – overland to Auckland – Fiji – San Francisco – London. From time to time, bargain basement round-the-world fares still pop up for around £1,000 including add-ons, but with very limited stop options, e.g. London – Hong Kong – New Zealand – San Francisco – London. Travel Nation (www.travelnation.co.uk) are specialists in more complicated multiple stop and round-the-world flights. One of the points that Travel Nation's managing director Haydn Wrath often makes when advising how much to spend and how many stops to take in, is that unlike most other products, you get proportionately more for your money if you spend more on a round-the-world ticket. For example a £2,000 round-the-world ticket gives a much better cost to stop ratio than a £1,000 ticket will.

Generally speaking round-the-world itineraries must continue in one direction with no backtracking and invariably must be completed within 12 months with no possibility of extending. Fares that differ between low, shoulder and peak season depend on your date of departure from home. If possible, try to start your round-the-world trip between September and November or April and June. The cheapest fares involve one or more gaps which you must cover overland, though be aware that the land mileage still counts towards the maximum.

Check www.roundtheworldflights.com (☎ 0844 844 2540), sister website to www.globalvillage travel.com, www.travelmood.com/round-the-world-flights.asp or any of the agents recommended below. The cheapest pre-tax fares at the time of writing were Air New Zealand's route via Hong Kong or Los Angeles starting at £535 and Virgin's four-stop £570 ticket. More typical round-the-world fares start at £850 plus tax. The cheapest fares involve one or more gaps which you must cover overland. Taxes and surcharges continue to escalate and for a round-the-world fare will add an eye-watering £350–£550.

The standard round-the-world stopovers are Singapore/Bangkok, Sydney/Auckland and Los Angeles/New York with a free stopover in the Pacific such as Fiji or the Cook Islands thrown in.

The main airline alliances offering round-the-world fares are:

The Great Escapade – www.thegreatescapade.com. Can be booked using Virgin Atlantic, Singapore Airlines, Silkair and Air New Zealand. It is possible to stay inside the 29,000 mile limit and still visit eight or more countries, for a fare starting at £869.

One World – www.oneworld.com. Member airlines includes British Airways, Qantas, Cathay Pacific, American, Finnair, Iberia, Japan (JAL), Lan Chile, Malev and Royal Jordanian. The One-World Explorer round-the-world fares are calculated according to season of travel and number of continents included. A three-continent itinerary starting in the low season costs £1,239 plus tax and a five-continent trip in a high season is well over £2,000.

Skyteam – www.skyteam.com. Member airlines are Aeroflot, AeroMexico, Air France, Alitalia, Continental, Czech Airlines, Delta, KLM, Korean and Northwest. Choices range from the basic 26,000 mile maximum with up to five stops for £1,250 (excluding tax) to 39,000 miles with 15 stops for £2,000 + tax.

Star Alliance – www.staralliance.com. World coverage is provided by 17 airlines including Air New Zealand, Singapore Airlines, Air Canada, Lufthansa, United, Lot (Polish), TAP Portugal, SAS and South African Airways. Its special round-the-world fare allows five stops and up to 26,000 miles for £1,289 plus tax and surcharge. The website allows you to download a round-the-world mileage calculator tool.

Other options to consider include the World Discovery Plus available from BA, Qantas and Cathay Pacific. The restriction here is 29,000 miles and seven stopovers including three in Australia. Departures in the low season (mid-April to mid-June) are very good value at £845 plus tax, rising to £1,169 in the peak summer or Christmas season. The excellent travel agent Western Air in Devon (www.westernair.co.uk/roundtheworld.html) provides some sample mileages on its website: London – Santiago (Chile) – Sydney – Perth – Tokyo – London comes in at 28,033 miles.

Before contacting agents, spend some time poring over an atlas and deciding where you are sure you want to go and on what approximate dates. A specialist agent will quickly be able to tell you whether one of the alliance promotions is better than a DIY itinerary. It is possible to include almost anywhere on a round-the-world itinerary – at a price. For example it is usually disproportionately expensive to zigzag between hemispheres, so flying London – Johannesburg – Mumbai – Sydney – Tokyo – Santiago could end up being astronomically expensive. Be prepared to compromise on your wish list of destinations.

LONG- AND SHORT-HAUL FLIGHTS

Some of the principal agencies specialising in long-haul travel are listed here. All of these offer a wide choice of fares including round-the-world fares. Telephone bookings are possible, though these agencies are often so busy that it can be difficult to get through.

Flight Centre – ☎ 0870 499 0040; www.flightcentre.co.uk. Branches around the UK.

Journey Latin America – 12–13 Heathfield Terrace, Chiswick, London W4 4JE; ☎ 020 8747 3108; www.journeylatinamerica.co.uk. A fully-bonded agency which specialises in travel to and around all of Latin America. Consistently offers low fares and the most expertise. One of the best flight deals at the time of writing was on Iberia to Rio or on Air France to Caracas for about £500.

Marco Polo Travel – 24A Park Street, Bristol BS1 5JA; ☎ 0117 929 4123; www.marcopolotravel.co.uk. Discounted airfares worldwide.

North South Travel – Moulsham Mill Centre, Parkway, Chelmsford, Essex CM2 7PX; ☎ 01245 608291; www.northsouthtravel.co.uk. Discount travel agency that donates all its profits to projects in the developing world.

South American Experience Ltd – Welby House, 96 Wilton Road, Victoria, London SW1V 1DW; 0845 277 3366; www.southamericanexperience.co.uk. Latin American specialist with good customer service.

STA Travel – ☎ 08701 630026; www.statravel.co.uk. Has about 65 branches in the UK and more than 450 worldwide. Although it specialises in deals for students and under-26s, it can also assist older travellers planning a gap year.

Trailfinders Ltd – 194 Kensington High Street, London W8 7RG; ☎ 0845 058 5858 worldwide; ☎ 0845 050 5940 Europe; www.trailfinders.com. Also more than a dozen branches in UK cities plus Dublin and five in Australia.

Travelbag – 3–5 High Street, Alton, Hampshire GU34 1TL; ☎ 0870 814 4440; www.travelbag.co.uk. Originally Australia and New Zealand specialist, owned by ebookers.

Travelmood – 214 Edgware Road, London W2 1DH; ☎ 08700 664566; www.travelmood.com. Branches in Islington, Guildford, Bristol, Solihull, Leeds, Liverpool and Dundee.

Travel Nation – Hove, Sussex; ☎ 0845 344 4225; www.travel-nation.co.uk. Expert advice including for complex itineraries. The website allows you to search round-the-world routes on www.travelnation.co.uk/roundtheworld/route_chooser.php and by budget on www.travelnation.co.uk/roundtheworld/budget (with all taxes and fuel surcharges shown).

When purchasing a discounted fare, you should be aware of whether or not the ticket is refundable and whether the date can be changed and if so at what cost. **Roger Blake** was pleased with the round-the-world ticket he bought from STA that took in Johannesburg, Australia and South America. But once he embarked he wanted to stay in Africa longer than he had anticipated and wanted to alter the onward flight dates:

> *That is the biggest problem of having an air ticket. I had planned for six months in Africa but I've already spent five months in only three countries. I have been into the British Airways office here in Kampala to try my verbal skills but have been told the 12-month period of validity is non-negotiable. A lesson for me and a warning to future world travellers, to check before they buy whether or not the ticket is refundable/extendable.*

Jen Moon is another adult gapper who found it difficult to predict how long she and her two young daughters would want to stay in any one place on their four-month adventure:

> *Dividing the time was the hardest bit as I didn't know what to expect. In fact dates changed three times before I finally paid and three dates changed during the trip. Thank God for Trailfinders and unfixed dates.*

Similarly, 28-year-old **Tara Leaver** splashed out on an ambitious round-the-world route with the One World Alliance (British Airways, Air New Zealand, etc.) for about £1,300 including Central America, South America, Easter Island, Tahiti, New Zealand, Australia and South East Asia. Apart from her first month which she pre-arranged in Costa Rica, she didn't want to over-plan for the rest of her year off.

In the USA, check the discount flight listings in the back of the travel sections of the *New York Times* and *Los Angeles Times*. Discounted tickets are available online from Air Treks in San Francisco (☎ +1 877 247 8735; www.AirTreks.com) which specialises in multi-stop and round-the-world fares. By far the cheapest airfares from the USA are available to people who are flexible about departure dates and destinations, and are prepared to travel on a standby basis. The passenger chooses a block of possible dates (up to a four-day 'window') and preferred destinations. The company that tries to match these requirements with empty airline seats being released at knock-down prices is Air-Tech in New York (☎ +1 212 219 7000; www.airtech.com). The transatlantic fares being advertised at the time of writing were US$269 one way from the east coast, excluding tax, a registration fee of US$29, a FedEx delivery charge of US$18+ and a possible fuel surcharge when departing from Europe. Discounted fares of US$325 return between the USA and Mexico or the Caribbean are also available.

From the UK to Europe it is generally cheaper to fly on an off-peak no-frills flight out of Stansted, Luton or regional airports than it is by rail or bus, although off-peak fares on Eurostar can be competitive. Cheap airlines include:

Ryanair – www.ryanair.com
Easyjet – www.easyjet.com
BMI baby – www.bmibaby.com
Flybe – www.flybe.com
Jet2 – www.jet2.com (Leeds-based)
Thomsonfly – www.thomsonfly.com (Coventry-based)

This style of flying has spread to the continent and discount airlines have proliferated including:

Clickair – www.clickair.com (Spanish)
Air Berlin – www.airberlin.com (German)
German Wings – www.germanwings.com (German)
Transavia – www.transavia.com (Dutch)
Wizz Air – www.wizzair.com (Polish)
Smart Wings – www.smartwings.com (Czech)
SkyEurope – www.SkyEurope.com (Central European)
Blue1 – www.blue1.com (Finnish)
Norwegian – www.norwegian.no (Norwegian)

Central sources of information include www.flycheapo.com and www.whichbudget.com. Scheduled airlines such as BA have had to drop fares to compete and are always worth comparing.

After saying all this, the environmental impact of flying should not be overlooked. Anyone who has seen Al Gore's film *An Inconvenient Truth* will want to give some thought to minimising their carbon footprint. The following companies provide the means for you to offset your emissions with a donation to fund tree-planting or other mechanisms to reduce the impact of air travel on the environment: CarbonNeutral Company (www.carbonneutral.com), Climate Care (www.climatecare.org) or the Reduce my Footprint initiative overseen by the Association of British Travel Agents (☎ 020 7637 2444; www.reducemyfootprint.travel).

RAIL AND COACH

One of the classic gap year experiences is to InterRail around Europe (www.interrail.net), an experience which is readily available to people over 26, albeit at a higher price than it is to young travellers. It may sound a little tame compared with round-the-world flights or Himalayan treks, but it can provide an amazing taste of the delights of Europe. In the past, tickets were divided into zones, but this system has been simplified. Now one Global pass covers the whole of Europe for one calendar month from £475 for those 26 and over. A shorter duration of 22 days is also available for £370. If you plan to make a few long journeys in a certain number of days, investigate Flexipasses – they permit five days of travel within 10 days, or 10 days of travel within 22 days. Also you can buy one-country passes that will cover three, four, six or eight days of travel within one month. A number of specialised agencies sell InterRail products and add slightly different mark-ups. Passes can be bought online (in which case you will probably have to pay an extra £5 or so for Special Delivery) or in person at branches of STA Travel and similar outlets. Websites to check include www.trainseurope.co.uk (usually the cheapest), www.raileurope.co.uk, www.railchoice.co.uk, www.railpassshop.com or the marvellous website for train travellers everywhere (www.seat61.com). Within Europe, consult the *Thomas Cook European Rail Timetable* whereas the bible for rail travellers outside Europe is the *Thomas Cook Overseas Timetable* (£15.99 each). The *Overseas Timetable*, published each May, is valuable for coach as well as train travellers since there are many areas of the world from Nepal to Papua New Guinea where public road transport is the only way to get around, short of flying. Except where smooth air-conditioned buses provide an alternative to third class rail travel, coach travel is generally less expensive than trains.

Eurolines is the group name for 32 independent coach operators serving 500 destinations in all European countries from Ireland to Romania. Promotional prices start at £30 return for London – Amsterdam if booked seven days in advance. Bookings can be made online at www.nationalexpress.com/eurolines or by calling 08705 808 080. So called 'funfares' mean that some off-season fares booked ahead from the UK are even lower, eg £6 to Brussels or Paris. Private coach operators still serve eastern Europe such as Poltours (www.poltours.co.uk) which links London with various Polish cities and Prague for £50 one way, £75/£85 return. However cheap airlines such as Wizz Air sell return tickets to Polish cities for less than half that (£30 return to Cracow was available at the time of writing).

GREAT RAILWAY JOURNEYS

Undertaking one of the great rail journeys of the world is something that might easily appeal to people taking a gap year at any age. Anyone who has read any of the abundant literature of rail travel such as Paul Theroux's *Great Railway Bazaar* and Eric Newby's *The Big Red Train Ride* about the Trans-Siberian may have had their appetite whetted and want to take a longer-than-usual holiday to travel by train between Moscow and Beijing or on the Trans-Canada from Toronto to Vancouver. Some lesser known routes might also appeal such as the Blue Train of South Africa, the Eastern & Oriental Express of Malaysia or the Sierra Madre Express of Mexico.

You can plan a rail journey independently or via a specialist agency such as *Great Rail Journeys* In York (☎ 01904 521936; www.greatrail.com). Specialist travel agents can arrange the Trans-Siberian trip for you, for instance the excellent travel company Regent Holidays (☎ 01983 863013; www.regent-holidays.co.uk) which pioneered tourism in Cuba, Eastern Europe and Central Asia. For lesser known routes such as the Silk Route Railway through Kazakhstan and China, you will have to put it together yourself, possibly with the help of the very useful website www.seat61.com, which has links to specialist booking agencies. If you are already in China, you can simply organise the ticket and visas yourself as **Barry O'Leary** did:

> I had discovered that if you book the Trans-Siberian on your own and don't pay for an agency to rip you off and organise everything yourself it's actually really cheap. Sure you have some hassle getting visas for China, Mongolia and Russia but isn't that all part of the fun? The total cost to get from Beijing to Moscow with three visas was only about £250, not bad for six days on a train and some tasty meat and celery stuff.

Alternatively you can use a Chinese agency such as Monkey Business located in Beijing's Red House Hotel (www.monkeyshrine.com). For detailed advice, see the *Trans-Siberian Handbook* (Bryn Thomas, Trailblazer, £13.99) or *The Trans-Siberian Railway* (Lonely Planet, £14.99).

CARS

If you are considering taking your own vehicle, contact your local AA or RAC office for information about international driving permits (IDPs), motor insurance, green cards (international motor insurance card for outside Europe), etc. Members of motoring organisations should ask for free information on driving and services provided by affiliated organisations in other countries. Although plenty of sources (especially the motoring organisations that sell them) recommend obtaining an IDP for £5.50, your national licence is sufficient for short stays in most countries. The relevant RAC webpage (www.rac.co.uk) also provides a list of countries (such as Albania and Japan) in which an IDP is required.

In some countries such as Australia and the USA you might decide to buy a cheap car or camper van after arrival and hope that it lasts long enough for you to see the country. Buy a standard model for ease of finding spares. Some travellers have even managed to sell a vehicle at the end of their trip.

An underrated alternative to hitch-hiking is to use a lift-sharing agency of which there are dozens of outlets across Europe, especially in Germany, where there are Citynetz offices in most of the major cities. For a varying fee (usually about £10–£20 plus a share of the petrol) they will try to find a driver going to your chosen destination. The Backpackers Ultimate Guide runs Bugride, an online lift-sharing exchange in Europe. The websites www.hitchhikers.org and http://europe.bugride.com list long-distance rides within Europe, for example a random check revealed seats in a car going from Munich to Amsterdam (for a share of the expenses of €35); occasionally lifts are offered free of charge. There are dozens of lift-sharing outlets across Europe, especially in Germany, where there are Citynetz offices in Berlin, Dusseldorf, Freiburg, Hamburg, Munich, etc. Most require you to register which is free in some cases or costs €10–€20 in others. Try Allostop in France (www.allostop.net), Taxistop/Eurostop in Belgium (www.taxistop.be) and Citynetz-Mitfahrzentrale in Germany (www.citynetz-mitfahrzentrale.de). Matches can seldom be made straightaway, so this system is of interest to those who can plan ahead.

DRIVING EXPEDITIONS

Anyone planning to take a vehicle off the beaten track will need to be pragmatic and able to rise to various challenges. Diesel is more easily obtained than petrol and, in general, a diesel engine is more reliable and requires less maintenance. Taking your own vehicle is an expensive way to travel but the freedom it offers is worthwhile if you have the resources. In some parts of the world, it is unwise to leave your car or van unattended, in which case you will usually receive local advice about how to hire a watchman. For example, in Egypt '*boabs*' or apartment building concierges/doormen often double as guards and charge a dollar or two a night.

Crossing borders with your own vehicle is often fraught with difficulties and expense. For example, **Rachel Pooley** and **Charlie Stanley-Evans**, whose experiences of driving a Land Rover through Africa are recounted in the next section, found themselves being charged extra 'costs' by border officials. This was particularly bad in Romania, Bulgaria, Turkey, Syria and Egypt (but not Jordan). Crossing into Egypt by ferry from Jordan, they were asked to pay a staggering £200 because the Land Rover had an engine over 2000cc. Exercising some ingenuity, they claimed to constitute a 'group' because, as Rachel claimed, she was pregnant with twins; but this ploy did not succeed and their budget took a mighty hit. In your projected budget, allow for these unforeseen levies. Red tape in Egypt was also onerous and they spent two weeks in Cairo organising the paperwork to ship the vehicle to Kenya.

Other problems include poor roads, difficulty interpreting road signs in an alien script and suicidal driving styles. Entering Cairo, a huge sprawling city choked with traffic, Rachel and Charlie were stumped by an inability to read the Arabic road signs or ask for directions. Sometimes it may also be difficult to buy fuel. It is crucial to carry plenty of spare supplies. Syria and Jordan are countries with almost no campsites, and they were once forced to pitch their tent on a roundabout in Aleppo, after asking permission from the local police. The discomfort of staying in the middle of a Syrian Piccadilly Circus was aggravated by the absence of public toilets for women.

DESERT DRIVING

Motorists must be sure to be suitably equipped for journeys across inhospitable terrain – modern folklore is laced with stories of skeletons being discovered a few miles from broken-down cars in desert regions. The first essential when planning a journey off the beaten track is to ensure your vehicle is fit for the task. It should be mechanically sound, and suitable for the roads you intend to use. Always seek local advice, preferably from a motoring organisation or the police, on whether your vehicle is fit for the journey you plan to make. You should notify a responsible person of your intended route and ensure that you let them know when you arrive safely at your destination.

At least two spare wheels are advisable; the heat on desert roads can melt the bitumen which then sticks to tyres. Punctures are commonplace on unsealed roads so make sure you know how to change a tyre (and that the wheel nuts are not jammed) before you leave civilisation. Petrol stations are thin on the ground and potentially low on fuel supplies so substantial supplies of fuel and water should be carried, not least in case you need to help out a less well-prepared motorist. The standard calculation of the amount of water needed is 10 litres per person per day. A selection of spare parts such as a fan belt and electrical fittings is also advisable, as well as shovel, axe and tow rope. In an emergency, crawl under the vehicle for shade and drink the radiator water, provided it has no chemical additives. If possible, do not exert unnecessarily, reduce your salt intake, increase your sugar intake and keep a fire going so that the smoke might be spotted. Never leave your vehicle in the event of a breakdown since you have a much better chance of being rescued.

One of the hazards on unsealed (or newly surfaced) roads is of flying stones hitting the windscreen. Some drivers take the precaution of placing their fingers on the windscreen whenever they meet an oncoming vehicle, which absorbs the shock of the impact and reduces the risk of shattering. If the windscreen breaks, however, use gloves or a cloth to punch out a hole to see through. It is a good idea to carry a plastic windscreen for emergency use.

USEFUL CONTACTS FOR LAND ROVER DRIVERS

Scores of off-road driving centres can be found throughout the UK. Many are members of the British Off-Road Driving Association (www.borda.org.uk/members.html).

Brownchurch Ltd – Bickley Road, Leyton, London E10 7AQ; ☎ 020 8556 0011; www.brownchurch.co.uk. Markets overland equipment and heavy-duty roof racks for Land Rovers. Full list of items with prices available on their website as well as information on expedition planning.

Keith Gott Land Rover Specialists – Greenwood Farm, Old Odiham Road, Alton, Hampshire GU34 4BW; ☎ 01420 544330; www.keithgott.co.uk. Specialist dealer that services and customises Land Rovers for range of clients including the Foreign Office and the National Trust. The company can equip a vehicle for any journey, for example by extending water and fuel tanks, and by providing roof racks, tents and showers.

Land Rover – www.landrover.com/gb. The company website is an online catalogue with extensive information about the current models, used vehicles and how to find dealers around the UK and globally, which might be useful if you needed to find spare parts on a journey. Click on the Adventures – Land Rover Experience link to find nine centres where you can do half or full-day off-road training courses (normal price £175-£275+).

DESIGNING YOUR OWN ADVENTURE

Hitting the road can take many forms. At the most basic you can walk. Walking one of the world's best or lesser known long distance footpaths, whether the spine of Corsica or the Southern Alps of New Zealand, would be a worthy ambition for a gap year and a means of getting to grips with the landscapes and people of one region. Closer to home many grown-ups take up the challenge of a long-distance path such as the Pennine Way and are amazed, despite the fact that it is a household name, that they have it virtually to themselves. Unless you plan to take a 'gap decade' you are unlikely to want to emulate the project of Briton **Karl Bushby** who is attempting to walk 36,000 miles around the world, which he has dubbed the Goliath Expedition (http://goliath.mail2web.com). He has been having endless headaches with renewing his visa in Russia but is determined to prevail.

One 28-year-old Dutch woman is at the moment journeying to the South Pole in a tractor (www.tractortractor.org). The drawback is that you become dependent on a piece of machinery that might prove difficult to protect and maintain in remote areas of the world. However, a vehicle offers autonomy and allows you to chart your own course.

Each of the tales from the road profiled in this chapter illustrates some of the choices available if you are contemplating a gap year to travel the world. These individuals chose different means of travel through different regions. Each has a unique story to recount and each represents just one of the thousands of journeys that travellers take every year in which they hope to experience adventure and a measure of self-discovery too. Beyond the picket fence and the privet hedge lie the excitement and challenges of travel.

INTO THE HEART OF AFRICA

Rachel Pooley, aged 24, and **Charlie Stanley-Evans**, aged 28, both decided to leave their jobs in London and drive to Cape Town. Rachel had been working for a mental health charity and Charlie had been employed in the wine trade. Together they felt an urge to travel and so planned a long-distance trip by road. Initially, Rachel's father felt she should be thinking about settling into a career, but neither had commitments and they wanted to see Africa. They were bored with London and wanted change. Charlie made a good profit from the sale of his flat, so he had capital to put into the expedition.

For £18,500, Rachel and Charlie bought an old MOD Defender TDI/long wheel chassis from a specialist dealer, Keith Gott (address above), who then built a new body and new engine to allow them to sleep in the vehicle and on the roof. Brownchurch supplied a roof rack with tent, which could be put up in half a minute on wooden boards and could be stored at the front of the rack. Other important supplies included jerry cans for water, which could be warmed in the sun during the day to supply water for a shower. Looking back on their hugely ambitious journey, one practical mistake they identified was not taking a fridge for food and drinks. But they do not regret their decision to take neither a phone nor a camcorder because it forced them to take a closer look at what they were seeing.

They spent three months planning what to take and trying to anticipate all their requirements for day-to-day life in the tropics and also for emergencies. To prepare themselves they took an off-road driving course and learnt motor maintenance, all about air and oil filters and how to change tyres. They took 500lb of spare parts including special air snorkel attachments to keep out dust and water.

Leaving in April, their trip took them through Europe and to Turkey on the threshold of Asia and its more alien cultures. They travelled on through Syria and Jordan to Egypt where they shipped the Land Rover to Kenya with P&O, which they had booked in advance because it was impossible (as it is now) to travel through Sudan. Picking up the jeep in Kenya they then took it through safari game parks and into neighbouring Tanzania.

Without the vehicle, their experience of Africa would have been wholly different. It enabled them to escape the well-worn routes covered by crowds of other tourists and to take their own safari into fascinating places such as the Tsavo West National Park. They slept either in the Land Rover or on the roof. At other times they could use campsites with loos and showers.

In Malawi they accidentally fell into buying a six-month lease on a backpacker's hotel, the Mwaya Beach Lodge on the edge of Lake Malawi. This was the highlight of their journey through Africa but wholly unplanned. Despite the difficulties of supplying the lodge with food, dealing with difficult guests, and managing the staff of nine people, it taught them skills they could use back home in Britain. They built a house for themselves with brick and thatch for £200 together with a garden. '*We were tempted to stay long-term and buy the lodge, which had potential. It was a heavenly place and we enjoyed the work but the life of ex-pats in Africa is a little strange. We met too many who were stoned or drunk,*' says Rachel.

From Malawi they headed south through Zimbabwe and into the Kruger National Park in South Africa, Namibia and onto Cape Town. In general their African adventure was hugely rewarding:

> *We learnt a lot about each other and other people. It makes us appreciate life more now. We are less concerned about work and fussier about the work we choose to do. The mentality in Africa is very different because there's no concept of planning ahead. Each day is a new challenge.*

In retrospect they see the Land Rover as crucial to their experience of Africa. They still own it and use it as a rather sturdy car in the English countryside and are now thinking of making a similar trip in Europe or the Americas.

Of course other means of transport can be equally exciting in Africa, even public transport. **Mark Tanner** is a New Zealander in his late 20s who thinks that '*It's a shame more people don't take time out from the job*'. He aims to take off about every year in three from office life where he works as a product marketing manager. Most recently, he took six months off to teach English in Khartoum through the Sudan Volunteer Programme (see entry) followed by a very ambitious paddling expedition. Along with a Canadian friend, Mark became the first man to paddle from the source of the Blue Nile to the Mediterranean Sea, a journey that took just short of five months and covered 5,000km. An account of their epic journey complete with descriptions of terrifying rapids, crocodile attacks and hostile locals can be found at www.niletrip.com. For Mark, volunteering in Sudan was a useful precursor to the rafting adventure:

> *I guess you could say the time in Sudan was a gap year for grown-ups. Teaching was a breeze compared to the paddle, but it prepared me for many of the cultural challenges during the paddle. Also having taught at the University of Khartoum helped give me creditability with officials during the paddle.*

TRAVELLING BY BICYCLE

One of the most rewarding and accessible ways of travelling is by bicycle. You remain in control of your own route and can veer off the beaten track to take the back roads while still maintaining a healthy mileage each day. Cycle touring represents freedom. It is a cheap and clean form of transport. For improving physical fitness, you can't improve on a bike journey. A bicycle allows the rider to stop to appreciate the views or sights along the route. Due to their speed and relative quietness, cyclists have a much better chance than other road users of seeing animals and birds. It can often provide a peg for interacting with the local population both in areas where cyclists abound and in areas where cyclists are a rarity and have novelty value. Enormous pleasure can be derived from the knowledge that you are crossing a landscape under your own steam. Walking achieves the same end but cycling allows you to travel much further in the same time.

Provided you take the right equipment it's possible to be very versatile, either taking roads or mere tracks. You can also skip regions that hold no interest for you by putting your bike on a train or bus. It is not unknown for trucks to stop and offer a lift to a cyclist, especially one labouring up a mountain. Bear in mind that you don't need to be an experienced cyclist to use a bicycle for a long-distance journey. Everyone can obtain a bike and find a pace that is comfortable. An average target in relatively benign terrain might be 50 miles a day, which might seem daunting to a novice, but is manageable for most reasonably fit people. By comparison experienced and super-fit cyclists can cover twice that.

Let us imagine that in your youth you were a keen (not necessarily avid) cyclist. You remember with great fondness your cycling holidays in the Cotswolds, round the Ring of Kerry or along the Loire Valley. Perhaps your dedication to cycling survived into your working life and you have used your trusty machine on and off for commuting to work. The arrival of children has inevitably cramped your cycling style and if you're lucky you have got your money's worth out of the bicycle rack you bought at Halfords in a fit of enthusiasm. Come to think of it you haven't been on a decent long ride for a decade and certainly not taken your bicycle abroad. It is an astonishing statistic that the British own 21 million bicycles (more than they do cars), the majority of which are gently rusting in garages and sheds.

A gap year might provide a chance to resurrect an interest in this most wholesome of pastimes. The National Cycle Network in the UK (www.sustrans.org.uk) covers more than 12,000 miles of designated cycle routes, many of them along disused railway lines and canal towpaths. But you needn't confine your aspirations to the UK. With a large scale map and a comfortable bicycle with a good gear range, you can enjoy cycling almost anywhere.

AMBROSE MARSH IS A CANADIAN PHYSICIAN WHO ENJOYED A COUPLE OF EXTENDED CYCLING TRIPS AROUND EUROPE IN THE 1970S. AS HIS 50TH BIRTHDAY APPROACHED, HIS WIFE LEAH ASKED HIM WHAT HE WOULD MOST LIKE TO DO.

He thought about it for a while and decided that he would like to do some travelling on his own followed by an adult cycling trip in an interesting part of the world. She cheerfully agreed to look after their two young children while he cycled from Madrid to Bilbao and explored the Basque country. He sent a round robin email to his address book, inviting friends to join him on his 'birthday-boy-designed perfect celebration'.

After the spirit-sapping climb north from Madrid airport, the small group had a marvellous time following the network of minor roads. They were helped in their route finding by the book Cycle Touring in Spain *by Harry Dowdell (Cicerone Press, £14) but still managed to get into various scrapes and have adventures. One of his companions had a shiny new bicycle with such high-tech pedals that she sometimes couldn't loosen them before falling over and on one occasion cut her leg quite seriously. The moral is, always get to know your machine thoroughly before setting off on a long cycle ride.*

Tom Moreton, aged 28, and his friend **Paul Beaton**, aged 30, departed from Newcastle to cycle to Istanbul. Tom had set up a web design business precisely so that he could be self-employed and take time out to travel for extended periods. Whereas his mother was very encouraging about this trip, some of his contemporaries remained unconvinced that it was a good idea to leave his home and business for four months. Neither Tom nor Paul had much experience of cycling over distances or steep terrain but they decided that their bicycles provided the best way of seeing Europe. They took 119 days to travel via Norway, Sweden, Germany, Poland, the Czech Republic, Slovakia, Austria, Slovenia, Croatia, Hungary, Romania and Bulgaria to Turkey.

With the help of country-specific maps on which camping grounds were marked, they could plan their route each day, choosing minor roads whenever possible. Occasionally it was not possible to reach a campsite or hostel by nightfall, though this was of minimal concern in Norway and Sweden where you are legally allowed to pitch a tent as long as it is not within 100m of a house. Occasionally they were forced into a hotel and at the other extreme to camp illegally in a lay-by. The technical problems they encountered were remarkably few: a spoke, a buckled wheel and a broken gear changer. In Prague it was difficult to find repairs for some damaged ball bearings. On one occasion in Bulgaria they accidentally found that they had filtered onto a motorway which was not very pleasant, especially when they received a hostile reception from a group of prostitutes. Roads in Turkey were very narrow without hard shoulders. But at no point on their journey did they feel endangered by the conditions.

Their equipment did not require a huge investment. They chose hybrid mountain bike frames made by Trek (current price from £260). These bikes are made for touring rather than for travelling on rough terrain. After researching tents, they plumped for one produced by Mountain Brand, which cost £80 and is used by the World Health Organization. For storage Tom and Paul used a Canadian-made pannier system known as PanPack, which sits on the back of the bike and converts into a backpack. They found that this item of luggage had too many straps to remove with ease, so they tended to leave them on the bikes and felt that they were not sufficiently waterproof. In retrospect they wish they had taken a pair of rubberised panniers produced by Ortlieb of Germany. They took a small tool kit, spare inner tubes, puncture repair kits and spare brake cables.

An even more ambitious cycling journey in the opposite direction was undertaken by teacher **Sally Haiselden** between finishing her contract at an international school in the Sudan before Christmas and returning to Cambridge in the summer. Almost from her arrival in Africa more than two years before, Sally had been harbouring thoughts of cycling home. Her friends and acquaintances had provided her with lots of reasons not to do it: 'But there are snakes and scorpions!', 'What about water?', 'It is a long way!', 'You will be tired', 'But you are a woman. You are alone'. She says, '*It's not as though I had not thought about the risks but such talk made me more stubborn and determined.*'

In 200 days, she cycled a truly impressive 8,855.27km through Sudan, Egypt, Jordan, Syria, Turkey, Bulgaria and along the Danube to Germany, Holland and home. At times she became addicted to the self-indulgent lifestyle of being without stress, responsibility, schedule or appointments. Some news from home made her realise how lucky she was to have the time, money and particularly the health to be able to do what she wanted. A year or so on, she had once again embraced stress, responsibility and strict timetables since she was teaching a lively Year Five class at a Cambridge primary school. Her cycling diary can be read at www.salcycleshome.org.

Keen cyclists can benefit from joining the Cyclists' Touring Club, Parklands, Railton Road, Guildford, Surrey GU2 9JX; ☎ 0844 736 8450; www.ctc.org.uk, which provides free technical, legal and touring information to members; membership costs £35.

BACKPACKING – TRAVELLING BY YOUR WITS

The purest form of travelling is by hitching rides or on public transport, cheek by jowl with the local people. Many dream of indulging their wanderlust, following their noses, crossing a country by any means possible. By creating your own route and using your wits to find your way, you'll find yourself obliged to interact with local people rather than being cocooned in a foreign-run tour.

Yet you will seldom be entirely isolated. Almost everywhere in the world from Baluchistan to Patagonia, you'll encounter other travellers and expats. Often you will find yourself inside an informal community of travellers who stay in the same hostels, travel on the same ferries and swap travellers' tales. This camaraderie of the road often provides a welcome grapevine and support system far from home. But sometimes it is a depressing reminder of how small the world has become for privileged Westerners.

You are more likely to learn where the locals shop, eat and socialise if you have the courage to keep your nose out of a guidebook. Of course guidebooks can be very useful and reassuring for novice travellers. But they are sometimes bestowed with more authority than they deserve. Often, two or three years might have elapsed between your arrival and when the guide was researched. Urban life is especially fluid and city listings quickly go out of date.

When engaging with local people, always follow the golden rule of trusting your instincts. It may be stating the obvious, but you should never accept an invitation to go somewhere or participate in an activity that makes you feel uncomfortable or threatened. Even if you run the risk of offending a 'host', you need to keep your internal compass functioning. Bear in mind that foreigners may be viewed as easy targets for some form of exploitation, principally financial. If you feel that an offer sounds too good to be true then it is likely to be just that.

Don't lose sight of why you're travelling. Often, it will be hard work and occasionally gruelling. Travelling in reasonable comfort is exhausting enough. Sightseeing is often a pleasure but it is taxing too, so give yourself plenty of time out for relaxation, whether reading in cafés, writing entertaining emails to friends and family, strolling in foothills or lounging on a sunny beach. Occasionally, it's a good idea to splash out on a comfortable hotel, particularly if you are feeling under the weather. Clean sheets, air-conditioning and a laundry service are reviving treats after several weeks on the road and are usually worth the extra expense.

While juggling bus or train timetables and the need to find suitable accommodation, try not to rush. The slow pace of life as a traveller, especially in the developing world, is something to be savoured, not bemoaned. Dawdling allows you to appreciate different experiences and sensations in places to which you may never have the chance to return. Dashing hither and yon should be left to the very young who, in the words of the veteran traveller and writer Dervla Murphy, '*seem to cover too much ground too quickly, sampling everywhere and becoming familiar with nowhere… it would be good if the young became more discriminating, allowing themselves time to travel seriously in a limited area that they had chosen because of its particular appeal to them, as individuals.*' This is something that more mature travellers on a gap year can aim to achieve. Remember that your sabbatical is designed precisely to give you the time you normally lack on a conventional holiday from work.

Once you have been carrying your pack for a couple of weeks, caught the right buses, met a few other travellers, you will probably laugh at your pre-travelling misconceptions of danger and risk. The economy end of independent travel is a burgeoning market worldwide, especially in Australasia, Latin America and Africa and you will soon find a bewildering choice of destinations with suitable facilities. If you are trying to capture the essence of travel and want to make a distinctive break from your annual holiday then open-ended backpacking guarantees a chance to find your own adventure.

At the same time that it offers the romance of travel, backpacking is undeniably arduous and uncertain. Sleeping on crowded trains or hiking through mosquito-infested jungles may hold little appeal. For some, pitching a tent on Dartmoor in a drizzling mist and bedding down in a soggy sleeping bag require plenty of courage and daring. People past their thirties may decide that they don't want to rough it any more or to replicate student life, and will travel accordingly. They may have little interest in experiencing foreign cultures at a grassroots level and may prefer to concentrate on some other aspect, such as making a study of the art and architecture, history or language of a foreign culture. (See Part 9, *New Skills and New Projects*.)

PRE-NUPTIAL TRAVELS IN AFRICA

After his engagement, **Nick McNulty** decided at the age of 28 to be brave and leave his job as a manager in a West London Health Authority to travel through Africa, because it represented what he thought of as his last opportunity to follow a whimsical dream. African wildlife and its intrinsic mystery had always appealed to him. It made sense to head off before he became settled with a new family. Nick backpacked across the length of Africa the old-fashioned way by hitching rides with new friends or on local transport, like a 19th-century explorer now aided by maps, banking, modern transport and the occasional support of the British Council's various libraries across the African continent.

Nick McNulty attributes many of his best experiences to his own '*bumbling naïveté*', without which he believes he wouldn't have seen so much. By under-planning his trip and moving with a greater degree of spontaneity, Nick enjoyed being able to avoid the mass of tourists. On his journey he made friends with Ahmed with whom he travelled from Algeria to Benin. Nick stayed first with Ahmed's family and then with a brother in a Ghanaian slum, unusual experiences which he attributes to his backpacking style of travel. Nick also found rides with a couple of German wheeler-dealers driving a Mercedes across Africa to sell in Nigeria. '*I found myself on what was less the hippy-trail and more the route of would-be entrepreneurs. Many Africans I met were also pursuing money-making schemes.*'

In Kenya he met up with his fiancée, **Anna**, who took a shorter break from the BBC to meet him. Together they continued the journey into Tanzania and Madagascar. Eventually a glimpse of the lights of Cape Town clustering round the massive form of Table Mountain felt like a homecoming to Nick. The trip did not seriously change the dynamic of his career as he returned to the National Health Service in a similar role, but the experience has had a lasting impression: '*The trip was great. It has been one of the best things I've done in my life with the exception of marrying my wife and becoming a parent.*' Anna believes the trip was a wonderful time for them to spend together before their marriage. For her part the travels inspired Anna to produce a series on post-colonial Africa for the BBC's World Service.

Like any trip, theirs was not trouble-free. On the border crossing between Algeria and Niger, Nick sat on the border with his two German travelling companions for six days because the border had been closed. Waiting for the guards to resolve the problem, they had to cope with a shortage of food and with boredom, which was eased by playing repeated games of chess amid the Sahara's unending dust and rubble. On another occasion Nick had some money stolen and an accidentally unpaid credit card bill at home forced him to survive on $100 for two weeks. In Benin, a policeman confiscated his passport leaving him feeling very vulnerable to the possibility of corruption.

Nick's gap year illustrates that it's possible to travel in a leisurely way across a vast continent in a spontaneous and loosely planned fashion. Because relying on your wits and travelling solo requires courage and self-confidence, it's arguable that this option delivers the greatest rewards.

ADVENTURE TRAVEL

A gap year is an ideal time to indulge a taste for adventure. Some will consider one of the classic overland journeys across continents or will want to pit themselves against the elements on the high seas (see section on *Sailing* below). But staying put and going native can provide the backdrop for any number of adventures.

While staying in the town of Kratie in Cambodia for six months of her gap year, **Hannah Stevens** was more willing than most to experiment with new experiences:

> *I took a few days off work to travel with three friends up to Ratanakiri in the North East of Cambodia. We went trekking through the rubber plantations on an elephant to a hidden waterfall that was directly out of* The Jungle Book. *In fact I'm pretty sure I heard Baloo singing in the distance! The whole thing was absolutely phenomenal, and I had to keep reminding myself that this is where I live! It certainly made me smile! Sometimes, I can't quite work out how I've ended up here in such a glorious place, with wonderful people and a rich culture.*
>
> *On one journey, I found myself volunteering to sample the local cuisine, fried tarantulas! The head was absolutely hideous and popped in my mouth, drowning my taste buds in brain fluid; but the legs and body were fairly acceptable, somewhat crunchy, but certainly edible. I spent the following four hours of the journey picking leg hair out of my teeth, and doing fairly repulsive burps! I think I'll pass next time! With the rainy season come crickets! Swarms of noisy, ugly, flying cockroaches. But, unlike six months ago, I don't squeal and flap, but catch and eat them! Chop off their legs, rip out their guts, stick a peanut up their bum, and deep fry them. Genuinely delicious, and it keeps us occupied. Coming soon to a dinner party near you!*

Like tarantulas and crickets, the thrill of risk-taking may be an acquired taste but it is one which can bring enormous satisfaction. When long-time Religious Education teacher, **Nigel Hollington**, set off to join a Greenforce conservation project in Zambia, he knew that he would be expected to handle rodents, and decided to confront his phobia head on. He packed an extra-strong pair of gardening gloves for the purpose and did not shirk when the moment came. His year off included a succession of minor triumphs such as this, which he found extraordinarily satisfying.

Pushing yourself to the edge of danger can hold a special appeal. More conventional challenges like bungee-jumping, white water rafting, parasailing and various other adrenaline sports are tempting to many independent travellers (but make sure your insurance policy will cover them).

OVERLAND JOURNEYS

Venturing across vast continents, dark or otherwise, can be a daunting prospect for an independent traveller. An alternative is to make the journey with one of the numerous established overland tour operators, most of which charge between £100 and £150 a week plus a food kitty of about £50 a week. The longer the trip the lower the weekly cost, for example Oasis Overland trips (www.oasisoverland.co.uk) start at £85 per week plus £35 a week local payment (for food and camping fees) on a 40-week trans-Africa trip and go up to around £150 a week plus kitty for shorter South American trips. Adventure tour operators follow a huge number of routes through all the continents of the world. Whereas some overland routes are fraught with difficulty, others are comfortable and almost routine.

The old hippy overland route to India and Nepal has been problematical for many years though not impossible if travelling from Iran to Pakistan, by-passing Afghanistan, which is completely off-limits. The situation in Sudan means that it is not feasible to travel overland from Egypt to Kenya, though various routes penetrate the rest of the continent. Zimbabwe is also off-limits to most trips at present.

Even more than on ordinary group trips, personal dynamics are crucial to your enjoyment on an overland journey. **Carol Peden**, a doctor in her 40s who took six months off, joined two separate trips with Intrepid Travel and describes how they differed:

> *I did some travelling with an Australian based company called Intrepid. Their southern India trip was fantastic, great food, wonderful Indian experiences and fun travelling companions – a group of 12 and 10 of us were singles and we all got on really well. On another Intrepid trip, we travelled through China for three weeks by train, but this was not as successful as the first. This time my 11 travelling companions consisted of a family of four including two disgusted teenagers who did not speak for the whole trip, a trio of bird-watchers and two loved up couples, which was very lonely for me. With hindsight I would have checked out small group travel more carefully, e.g. would I be the only single in the group?*

There is surely an element of luck in the composition of any group. Another woman career breaker in her middle years had been travelling for months on her own in Canada, New Zealand and south-east Asia. She felt a bit daunted at the prospect of travelling in India, so she signed up with a Dragoman trip from Chennai to Mumbai. It so happened that one of her fellow travellers seemed to take against her, and she found that a small group purposely excluded her, which made her feel more lonely than if she had been on her own. Out of her nine-month trip, this proved to be the low point, though she still does not regret joining the trip and saw much to enjoy in India.

Petrol-heads might be tempted by the poor man's/woman's variation on the Paris-Dakar Rally. Teams that enter the Plymouth-Banjul Challenge (www.plymouth-banjul.co.uk) must travel to the capital of The Gambia in an old banger, and then auction their vehicle on arrival for good causes. In 2007 Tony Wheeler, founder of Lonely Planet Publications, and his wife Maureen joined the race in a 1989 Mitsubishi they bought in Devon for £350 (although rules stipulate that the vehicle should cost no more than £100). In 2008, two new rally destinations were added: Baku and Timbuktu.

OVERLAND TOUR OPERATORS

A selection of overland companies is listed here. Others may be found on the Overland Expedition Resources website (www.go-overland.com). Many overland companies advertise in the adventure travel magazine *Wanderlust*, available in large newsagents (www.wanderlust.co.uk).

Absolute Africa – ☎ 020 8742 0226; www.absoluteafrica.com. Adventure camping safaris in Africa.

Acacia Adventure Holidays – ☎ 020 7706 4700; www.acacia-africa.com. Africa specialist with over 200 tours lasting from three to 70 days. A free 112-page colour brochure provides detailed tour information.

Bukima Adventure Travel – www.bukima.com. Has introduced specialist tours to Africa, Egypt and South America for the over-40s as well as a programme of other tours open to ages 18–55.

Dragoman Overland Expeditions – ☎ 01728 861133; www.dragoman.com. Expeditions to Africa, Asia, South and Central America. Travellers are carried in a specially adapted vehicle which is a cross between a jeep, minibus and army truck.

Exodus – ☎ 0845 863 9600; www.exodus.co.uk. One of the leading adventure travel companies in the UK, organising adrenaline-fuelled activities graded according to difficulty to give you guidance about physical endurance. In addition to overland expeditions, Exodus offer trekking holidays, cycling holidays, multi-activity holidays and trips in Europe lasting from one to 24 weeks. 500 tours in 90 countries, mostly for an older, civilised clientele.

Explore Worldwide Ltd – ☎ 0845 013 1537; www.explore.co.uk. Small group adventure and special interest tour operator worldwide, with similar range of destinations, clientele and prices as Exodus.

Imaginative Traveller – 1 Betts Avenue, Martlesham Heath, Suffolk IP5 7RH; ☎ 0800 316 2717; www.imaginative-traveller.com. Runs small group adventures around the globe, some of which are based on voluntary work. Ring them to request a brochure on your chosen continent or region. Trips last up to a month.

Intrepid Guerba – ☎ 0203 147 7777; 01373 826 611; www.intrepidtravel.com. Small group adventure tour operator

Journey Latin America – ☎ 020 8747 8315; www.JourneyLatinAmerica.co.uk. A fully-bonded agency which specialises in travel to and around all of Latin America. Runs dozens of escorted tours throughout the continent using private or public transport, and also offers some activity adventure trips such as cycling in Costa Rica and rafting in Peru.

Ke Adventure Travel – ☎ 017687 73966; www.keadventure.com. Organises adventure trips on bike or by foot around the world from the Himalayas to Brazil. Most trips last two to four weeks. Was recently voted the best trekking outfitter in the world by *National Geographic*.

Kumuka Expeditions – ☎ 020 7937 8855; 0800 068 8855; www.kumuka.com. Itineraries through Africa and Latin America including the 'Andean Adventure' which takes groups from Quito, Ecuador to Santiago, Chile over 56 days (£1,350 plus $1,535 local payment).

Oasis Overland Ltd – ☎ 01963 363400; www.oasisoverland.co.uk. Africa, the Middle East and South America.

Tucan Travel – ☎ 020 8896 1600; brochure request ☎ 0800 804 8415; UKsales@tucantravel.com; www.tucantravel.com. Offices in London, Sydney and Cusco. Open age group adventure tours and independent travel worldwide including Antarctica. Budget Expeditions is its brand for the 18–35 age range. Sample Budget price is £1,000 for 49 days travelling between Rio and Santiago via Patagonia plus local fund of $550.

Wagon Trails – ☎ 01772 741600; www.wagontrails.co.uk. Short tours of southern Africa and a 43-week London to Capetown trip (costing £3,500 plus £1,475 kitty).

World Expeditions – ☎ 020 8545 9030; www.worldexpeditions.co.uk. Long established adventure travel company with large choice of journeys on all continents including the Arctic and Antarctic. Trips lasting up to 30 days for all ages and fitness levels.

Collectively these companies employ large numbers of competent expedition staff including leaders and cooks, though most companies require a longer commitment than would be available on a career break. See 'Overland Tour Leaders' in earlier section *Working in Tourism*.

CHARITY CHALLENGES

Some UK charities offer adventurous group travel to individuals who are prepared to undertake some serious fundraising on their behalf. Typically the fundraising target that must be met by participants is in the range of £1,500–£3,000. These are energetically marketed so are often advertised in the travel advertisements of the *Independent* and other broadsheets. Household names such as the National Deaf Children's Society the Youth Hostels Association, LEPRA and the Big Issue Foundation organise their own sponsored trips, as do many more obscure good causes. Charity trips seldom last longer than a fortnight so are perhaps not of central interest to people on a career break. But the chance to participate in a group activity which at the same time funds a good cause is welcomed by some, especially those who don't relish the prospect of taking an adventurous trip on their own. Cycling, trekking, canoeing, rafting, mountaineering, all are on offer in most corners of the world. These trips have proved particularly popular among women in middle life who lack the confidence to undertake an adventurous trip on their own and who often find it easier to justify a trip abroad if it is for a good cause as well as for their own pleasure.

Specialist companies organise 'open challenges' which allow you to nominate the charity you want to support. Companies that organise a range of overseas charity challenge events include:

Across the Divide – ☎ 01460; www.acrossthedivide.co.uk
Charity Challenge – ☎ 020 8557 0000; www.charitychallenge.com
Classic Tours – ☎ 020 7619 0066; www.classictours.co.uk
Different Travel – ☎ 02380 669903; www.different-travel.com
Discover Adventure – ☎ 01722 718444; www.discoveradventure.com
Kuoni Challenge for Charity – ☎ 01306 744477; www.challengeforcharity.co.uk
Tall Stories Challenge Events – ☎ 020 8939 8739; www.tallstories.co.uk

Note that experienced tour leaders and medics may be needed for these trips and offered subsidised or free places.

While these events have proved a popular way of raising money for a favourite charity, some critics have argued that it is an inefficient way of raising money for worthy causes. In fact, Cancer Research UK, which at one time ran regular fundraising treks to Patagonia, China and Kilimanjaro, recently decided to reduce its International Challenge programme in the interests of cost effectiveness. As much as half of the money raised by each sponsored traveller goes towards paying for their holiday (flight, accommodation, etc.), something which family, friends and colleagues who support the fundraising might come to resent. One solution is to simply pay that portion out of your pocket and raise funds for the rest. Charity challenges do appear to achieve the dual goals of raising money and raising awareness of the charity's purpose and achievements by engendering a sense of occasion. Of course anyone undertaking a challenging trip independently can use it to raise money for a good cause.

Whereas many challenges involve gentle exertion that healthy people of any age can enjoy, others are for more committed sportsmen and women.

SIMON BALL, A 37 YEAR OLD DESIGNER, TOOK PART IN THE SPANISH THREE PEAKS CHALLENGE TO RAISE MONEY FOR CARE INTERNATIONAL:

I had taken part in charity events in the past, including the UK Three Peaks Challenge and various road races, but the Three Peaks Challenge in Spain attracted me because not only did it look extremely challenging, it was also being held in an area that I might otherwise not get to visit. Trekking and mountain biking three peaks in three days also appealed to my sporting sensibilities.

I first heard about the challenge from a colleague who was also planning to take part. We set to work straightaway appealing for sponsorship from suppliers and sub-contractors that work for our company. We suggested a recommended amount for people to donate as this helps to maximise potential for fundraising. I would normally do plenty of cycling, but to prepare for this challenge I had to increase my training volume several months beforehand.

The challenge itself was a fantastic experience. Being in a beautiful natural environment, with a group of diverse, but in many ways like-minded, people and setting yourself a unique personal challenge is an experience you will never forget. During the challenge we stayed in a mountain refuge that was clean and functional, although I didn't enjoy the cold showers. But the accommodation and its remote location were a key part of the atmosphere of the challenge and the group.

The physical and mental exertion of the challenge is something you really have to try to prepare yourself for. But when you get there, you have to just give it 100%. It is important to remember that it is a challenge not a trial, and you should always try to enjoy yourself and feel good about what you are doing. Two moments from the experience really stand out in my mind. Firstly standing on top of the Alcazaba and taking in the view – I had tears in my eyes (it must have been the altitude) and, secondly, racing off-road down from the top of Veleta. A truly unforgettable experience.

EXPEDITIONS

One romantic idea for people planning a break from the daily grind is to join an expedition venturing into the more remote and unspoiled parts of the world from Tierra del Fuego to Irian Jaya. Previously, you could be invited to join a party of latter-day explorers in exchange for some menial duty such as portering or cooking. However, expedition organisers and leaders nowadays demand that participants have some specialist skills or expertise to contribute beyond mere eagerness. For example, an advertisement for people needed on an Arctic expedition included among its volunteer requirements a post-doctoral archaeologist, an electronics officer for proton magneto-meter maintenance and an antenna theorist. One suspects that they weren't inundated with applications.

The *Royal Geographical Society* (1 Kensington Gore, London SW7 2AR; ☎ 020 7591 3030) encourages and assists many British expeditions. The Expedition Advisory Centre at the RGS published a booklet *Joining an Expedition* in 2001 listing about 60 organisations that regularly arrange expeditions; this can now be read free online (www.rgs.org). The EAC also hosts a weekend 'Explore' seminar every November on Expedition and Fieldwork Planning, which covers fundraising and budgeting for expeditions as well as issues of safety and logistics. If you want personal advice on mounting an expedition, you can make an appointment to visit the EAC (eac@rgs.org). The Society's historic map room is open to the public daily from 11am to 5pm. The Expedition Advisory Centre has generously put online most of the grant-giving organisations listed in its publication *The Expedition Handbook*. Although many grants are ring-fenced (eg must live within 8 miles of Exmouth Town Hall) it is worth checking and applying as widely as possible. Raleigh (www.raleigh.org.uk) is the longest established and most experienced expedition organisation, having run hundreds of expeditions overseas. Their aim is to provide challenging experiences that develop skills and transform lives through its five and 10-week expeditions consisting of community, environmental and adventure projects. While young people aged 17–24 can sign up as participants, those 25–75 can volunteer as managers. Building schools or collecting scientific data are examples of projects undertaken in Raleigh's four expedition countries, Costa Rica, Nicaragua, India and Malaysian Borneo.

Raleigh employs older volunteers to organise expedition logistics for groups of young Raleigh volunteers. Their website has a special section on Career Breaks/Retirement because they need self-funding volunteers from diverse working backgrounds to take on roles such as project manager, accountant, doctor, nurse, engineer, photographer, builder, trek leader and communications expert. Not all of the 40 roles on an expedition require specialist knowledge. The main requirement is an affinity with youth development, a positive attitude and a willingness to raise funds of approximately £1,350 for five weeks and £1,950 for 10 weeks to cover all expenses except flights. Selection takes place through written applications and an assessment weekend that simulates potential team challenges through physical exercises and problem solving (cost £40). Volunteers must know how to swim and speak English. Former expedition staff acknowledge that the expeditions are hard work but the experience is unique, rewarding and contributes to career development. This is something that is officially acknowledged by some employers (such as the Ministry of Defence) that occasionally sponsor their employees to participate on Raleigh expeditions.

Going on an expedition is a great way to test yourself, which is something **Jane Belfourd** would probably agree with since she almost stepped on a giant boa constrictor when she was on a Raleigh expedition in Costa Rica. And stockbroker **Alex Henney** took time off work to join the Polar Race to the North Pole (www.polarrace.com). **Alasdair Taylor** (age 26) traded the comfort of his city life as a management consultant in London for three months in the wilds of Patagonia and the chance to get his hands really dirty. As part of a 40-strong volunteer staff team on a Raleigh expedition in southern Chile, Alasdair led groups of eleven 17–25-year-olds from around the world on a mission to build footpaths in Queulat National Park and then took them on to Colonia to collect moraine samples to be used to calculate what drives the world's climate:

I am covered in mud, it's raining and I am looking up at an amazing hanging glacier with three waterfalls pounding down from it into the laguna below. Around me is my team of wet, mud-splattered people, all still smiling. This is a far cry from my work in the UK! And I mustn't complain about the weather – we were unexpectedly blessed with endless sunshine for the first month or more. I came to Chile for the extremes that it offers, weather certainly being one of them. I actually expected life on expedition to be more uncomfortable than it is. There have been far fewer crises than one would anticipate on an expedition this large (we are 170 people in total) and doing such a range of activities. One of the self-improvements I will cherish is my newly found ability to sleep on any floor, the fact that I can now be almost pleasant in the morning and an appreciation of the finer things in life!

World Challenge Expeditions (☎ 08704 873173; leaderinfo@world-challenge.co.uk) takes on several hundred expedition leaders to supervise school expeditions to developing countries. Trips take place in the summer and the minimum commitment is four weeks. Applicants must be at least 24, have an MLTB (Mountain Leader Training) and some experience of working with young people and preferably of travelling in developing countries. Expenses are covered and a stipend may be negotiated. Leadership training courses take place in Derbyshire

Every two or three years XCL Ltd (Reaseheath, Nantwich, Cheshire CW5 6DF; ☎ 01270 625825; www.xcl.info) runs three-week expeditions for approximately 30 adults from diverse backgrounds. Previous expedition destinations have included seldom-visited Guyana in South America, Ethiopia and Uganda in Africa, and Sikkim in India. Community projects include teaching in indigenous communities, running business workshops, conservation work, sports development and basic construction work. The next destination in 2010 is Guyana; the cost will be approximately £2,500.

Those with a specialised project might discover that targeted funds are available from trusts and charities. However many, such as the Mount Everest Foundation (www.met.org.uk/mefguide.htm), are earmarked for high-level expeditions undertaking first ascents, new routes and scientific research on mountains, which are beyond the capabilities of all but the most serious climbers.

Wilderness Medical Training (The Coach House, Thorny Bank, Garth Row Kendal, Cumbria UK LA8 9AW; ☎ 01539 823183; www.wildernessmedicaltraining.co.uk) puts on courses in expedition medicine for lay people as well as doctors. Its foundation course is called 'Far From Help' and teaches the use of prescription medicines. Courses last from two days (from £240) to seven days for their annual Expedition Skills course (£795).

SAILING

Sailing is a versatile sport that can form the basis of an adventurous gap year. Learning to sail the oceans is a perfect way to fill a gap in your career. It is possible for experienced sailors to charter a boat with or without crew, or act as crew for someone else with a boat, for short or long crossings. The pleasures of open-ended island hopping in the Aegean, Caribbean or South Pacific are easily imagined though difficult to realise. Sailing represents the ultimate freedom to chart your own course and, for some, a chance to stretch mental and physical limits by sailing around the world in a yacht race.

On a sailing adventure you are bound to see dolphins, whales, flying fish and rare birds. You get in touch with nature by seeing and feeling the rhythms of the sea. You learn about sailing, meteorology, navigation. But there are also drawbacks. You will probably have seasickness at the beginning. You will have to deal with a panoply of adverse weather conditions and probably experience terror at least once, especially when you move into the path of a supertanker. You have to get up in the middle of the night to take the watch. Every little task is made more difficult by the constant movement of the boat. It may be that there will be no wind for days at a stretch. But if you are prepared to cope with all this, a sailing trip can be exhilarating in the extreme.

In the context of a career break, sailing is a truly escapist activity. Out at sea you have no choice but to stop thinking about work and home because the daily tasks will require all your concentration. Long-distance sailing allows you to suspend your life while simultaneously demanding an intense and unique form of communal living.

HAVING FINISHED HER ACCOUNTANCY EXAMS, JENNIE SANDERS WASN'T SURE WHAT SHE WAS AIMING FOR NEXT AND SUDDENLY FELT AS THOUGH ALL SHE HAD AHEAD WAS A LIFETIME OF WORK:

I had often seen adverts for sailing courses in the back pages of sailing magazines and thought how much I would like to do one. I knew that my employer PricewaterhouseCoopers invest a great deal in training up new graduates and are understandably eager to hang on to them once they are qualified. The company is also keen to promote flexible working policies, and career breaks are one option they offer to staff who have worked for them for at least four years. So I followed up one of the ads and booked on a 3[half]-month course with Flying Fish in order to indulge my passion for sailing (I had been sailing with my family since the age of 10) and qualify as a professional skipper.

The first month in north Wales was fairly windy and wet, but with Australia to look forward to, no one seemed to mind too much. We spent most of the first month learning (or refreshing) the basics and doing classroom work including chart work. No sailing experience was required; in fact one participant hadn't even been on a ferry before. Whereas some of the grown-up trainees found it strange going back to a classroom, living in shared accommodation (on the boats at very close quarters) and being told when to be where, I found it relaxing not to have to think about what to do next.

Soon we were all off to Sydney where we were installed in an apartment right on the beachfront in Manly – amazing. Sailing consisted of day sailing on Sydney harbour and some longer passages including night sailing up and down the east coast of Australia, as well as some racing. We took it in turns to be skipper, in order to get in the necessary practice to pass the Yachtmaster exams.

The course was expensive [the current price is £9,650], but by using my savings, working for a couple of months whilst I was away, and making the most of a six-month interest-free loan when I returned, I managed to do virtually everything I wanted to whilst I was away. Following the course I got a sailing job in a marina in Sydney (a far cry from sitting in front of a computer in an office in London!). Originally I had applied to my employer for a six-month unpaid break but decided to extend it to nine months since I was having such a good time. This allowed me to travel up the East Coast of Australia on to Fiji for a couple of weeks and then return to the UK to do some more sailing, including to the Scilly Isles and Ireland, as well as taking my final Yachtmaster exam.

After passing the exam, I decided that I couldn't put off the return to work any longer. Pricewaterhouse-Coopers had agreed to keep my job open (although they didn't guarantee it would be in exactly the same department) but it was felt that my technical knowledge at work might get too out of date if I stayed away for a year or more. When I was quizzed by one of my bosses as to what I had got out of the course, I was able to stress that the forward planning, organisation and people managing involved in being a skipper would be of potential benefit at work. In fact a few months after my return, I was promoted to manager. The return to work was more difficult than I had anticipated, for instance finding people who had previously been junior to me promoted ahead of me and also working to tight deadlines didn't come easily again.

I never worried that my career break would harm my career. I am now a corporate tax manager with six people working under me. As well as having improved my work skills, I now race in a very competitive sports boat class, which I do every Sunday nine months of the year. It gives me something to look forward to all week, and keeps me active and refreshed so that I am able to do my job better. I hope to take another career break when I can, but next time I'll use it to sail round the world.

To judge whether sailing might be an idea to pursue for your own career break, dip into the

wealth of sailing literature, including a classic such as Joshua Slocum's *Sailing Alone* or a light-hearted account of sailing with small children in *One Summer's Grace* by Libby Purves about sailing around the British Isles with her husband Paul Hoincy and their two children aged 3 and 5. If you are committed enough to go after an advanced qualification such as the Yachtmaster which might lead to a career change, see the chapter Sail and Dive Training in Part 9 New Skills and New Projects.

CREWING ON YACHTS

In every marina and harbour, people are planning and preparing for long trips. There may be requests for crew posted on harbour notice boards, in yacht clubs or chandlery shops from Marina Bay in Gibraltar to Rushcutter's Bay in Sydney. The most straightforward (and usually the most successful) method is to head for the nearest yacht marina and ask captains directly. The harbour water supply or dinghy dock is usually a good place to meet yachties.

People who display a reasonable level of common sense, vigour and amiability, and take the trouble to observe yachting etiquette should find it possible to persuade a yachts person that they will be an asset to his or her crew. As one skipper comments, '*A beginner ceases to be a passenger if he or she can tie half a dozen knots and hitches, knows how to read the lights of various kinds of ships and boats at night, and isn't permanently seasick.*' Obviously, it is much easier to become a crew member if you have some experience. But there are opportunities for people who lack experience at sea, and it is unwise to exaggerate your skills. Once you have worked on one yacht it will be much easier to get on the next one. The yachting world is a small one. It is a good idea to buy a log book in which you can enter all relevant experience and voyages, and be sure to ask the captains of boats you have been on for a letter of reference.

Inexperienced crew are never paid and most skippers will expect a contribution towards expenses; at least US$25 a day is standard for food, drink, fuel, harbour fees, etc. but not airfares to join the yacht or visa fees. The more experience you have, the more favourable arrangements you will be able to negotiate. Also, your chances are better of having a financial contribution reduced or even waived if you are prepared to crew on unpopular routes, for example crossing the Atlantic west to east is much tougher than vice versa. If you demonstrate to a skipper that you take safety seriously enough to have learned a little about the procedures and if you are clean and sober, sensible and polite, you are probably well on your way to filling a crewing vacancy. Offshore sailing is a risky business and you should be sure that the skipper to whom you have entrusted your life is a veteran sailor. A well-used but well-kept boat is a good sign. A good starting place for novice crew might be to get to grips with a good yachting book such as *RYA Competent Crew* which contains invaluable information on technical sea terms and the basics of navigation.

Even better would be to sign up for a sailing course. The first level, Competent Crew, can be reached in a five-day course at any Royal Yachting Association recognised centre for £400–£500. If you are planning your trip a long way in advance, scour the classified columns of *Yachting Monthly, Yachting World* or *Practical Boat Owner*, though advertisers are likely to require a substantial payment or contribution towards expenses on your part. Increasingly skippers use the Internet to find paying crew. Websites that promise to match crew with captains include www.floatplan.com/crew.htm which carries details of actual vacancies, usually a male skipper looking for a female crew, eg 'I'm a 58-year-old Dutch/Canadian sailor looking for a 45+-year-old female sailing partner to join me in the Med on my 28' Bristol Channel Cutter. I'm physically in good shape and speak four languages. Share cost.' Captains who look for crew through agencies (see below) may be less likely to have a lonely hearts motive.

USEFUL CREWING CONTACTS

Crewing agencies in Britain, France, Denmark, the West Indies, the USA and elsewhere match yacht captains and crew. These are mostly of use to experienced sailors. In the UK the Cruising Association (CA House, 1 Northey Street, Limehouse Basin, London E14 8BT; ☎ 020 7537 2828; office@cruising.org.uk; www.cruising.org.uk/cahouse/crewing.shtml) runs a crewing service to put skippers in touch with unpaid crew. Meetings are held on the first Wednesday of the month at 7pm between February and May for this purpose. They claim to offer a variety of sailing (including two or three week cruises to the Mediterranean and transatlantic passages) to suit virtually every level of experience. The fee to non-members for this service is £20.

Among the largest crewing registers in the UK is the Global Crew Network (☎ 0870 910 1888; www.globalcrewnetwork.com) which specialises in crew recruitment for tall ships, traditional boats and luxury yachts worldwide. Another matching service is operated by the Southampton-based Crewseekers Crew Introduction Agency (☎ 01489 578319; www.crewseekers.net). Their membership charges are £60 for six months, £85 for a year; joint members may be added for an extra £15. Alternatives include:

Crew Network Worldwide – www.crewnetwork.com. Crewing offices in Antibes, Palma de Mallorca, Fort Lauderdale, Auckland and others.
Reliance Yacht Management – First Floor Suite; www.reliance-yachts.com. One year registration fee of £38.

Concentrations of crewing agencies can be found in other yachting capitals too such as Antibes and Fort Lauderdale. The main crewing agencies in Antibes are housed in La Galerie du Port, 8 boulevard d'Aguillon, 06600 Antibes. For example, try contacting Peter Insull's Crew Agency (☎ +33 4 93 34 64 64; www.insull.com/crew.html).

RACING THE OCEANS

Sailors with the prospect of an extended career break might want to consider participating in one or more legs of a round-the-world race. This will require a huge commitment of time and money. A round-the-world race can be brutally demanding where you live from watch to watch, with no more than three hours at any one stretch to sleep, eat and wash. For all of the romance of sailing, it remains a dangerous and strenuous sport, wherein lies part of its enormous appeal. The lure of the sea draws many to try their luck. The boat becomes a sealed world of its own.

Whereas some yacht races such as the Volvo Ocean Race (formerly the Whitbread Round the World Race) are open only to professional sailors, others cater to novices as well as more experienced yachtsmen and women. However, if you're drawn to the notion of joining the crew of a racing boat, there are other opportunities such as the Challenge and Clipper races described below. It is possible to join a crew for one leg of a race or for an entire race. The costs are very steep but previous crew members see this as part of the general challenge.

Humphrey Walters lectures on inspirational leadership after deciding a few years ago to join the 'Global Challenge', a notoriously gruelling round-the-world yacht race which involved racing the 'wrong' way around the world (ie against the prevailing winds, currents and tides). His primary motivation was to increase his knowledge of team building and leadership. 'I wanted to know what makes the difference between average and high performance teams and the critical actions needed in hostile and unpredictable conditions.' Such a learning experience, he hoped, could be applied to developing his business. Humphrey also wanted to learn how to step away from his responsibilities and to delegate to others in the company. It would be a chance to re-focus and re-energise himself. However, he wanted to do something dramatic during a career break, to embark on a project with a purpose.

Sailing around the world proved to be as informative as he had hoped at the outset:

> *It was astonishing what I learned. Leadership is only one element in a successful organisation. I found that the most important thing is 'followership', how people follow a leader. Leaders can go through anything provided they know they are supported. Great leadership is born from great followership. Otherwise the leader won't take the risk.*

The environment of a yacht produced uncertainty, instability, turbulence and complexity, all features of the business world. What many have discovered before, the effectiveness of each team to work together, is what matters ultimately. The age of participants ranged from 21 to 60 and included many nationalities and professional backgrounds. Ocean Rover's team included an unemployed person, a student, doctor and scientist. Without the race, these individuals' paths would probably never have crossed but soon they had become an 'aquatic Coronation Street'. All were struck by how narrow one's life can become without realising it and how easy it is to experience life within a limited circle of professional colleagues and old friends and neighbours.

Because the conditions of the race were particularly demanding, an outstanding level of cooperation was necessary. Speed of progress is about a third as fast as in the opposite direction. Travelling against the winds produces waves of 45 degrees, so that every crew member had to be tethered to the boat while on deck. Shifts were exhausting too, with everyone working three hours on and three hours off. Their three hours off had to include eating and sleeping. Crews lose track of the normal calendar in a perpetual rhythm of working on deck and attending to the body's most basic physical needs. It was a dangerous journey. Humphrey seriously believed that the boat would sink the night that it was hit six times in a row by huge waves and knocked down.

Humphrey Walters is now an energetic advocate of taking a career break to test yourself. He sees many people in their 30s avoiding the opportunity to take on a major challenge outside work:

People around 35 and up should go on a career break. They need to find experiences which will allow them to find out that they can do things they never realised they could do and stretch themselves to limits they never thought possible. You are likely to come back notched up a gear in terms of your confidence, the way you operate and your ability to handle difficulty. It doesn't need to be yachting. You've just got to keep yourself in a learning environment especially nowadays in the competitive economy. It took me three times as long as a 25-year-old to learn new skills and I'm not stupid.

Unfortunately the Global Challenge, founded by Chay Blyth, went into administration a couple of years ago and no longer takes place. More accessible sailing opportunities exist, for example the Jubilee Sailing Trust operates two tall ships, the *Lord Nelson* and the *Tenacious*, which are crewed by disabled and able-bodied volunteers on short voyages costing from £399.

Ocean rowing is another way of pushing yourself to the limit. The progress of teams attempting this feat is recorded on the website of Woodvale Events (www.woodvale-events.com).

SAILING CONTACTS

Clipper Round the World Yacht Race – www.clipper-ventures.co.uk. Race balances short sprints and long tactical races. The company is looking for people from all ages and walks of life including those without sailing experience. The shortest leg is just six weeks. A berth for the whole 10 months costs about £30,000 and a single leg costs from £6,500 including about £3,000 for the compulsory 19-day training.

Flying Fish – see Directory entry.

International Academy – see Directory entry.

Jubilee Sailing Trust — Hazel Road, Woolston, Southampton SO19 7GB ☎ 023 8044 9138; www.jst.org.uk. The JST was created in 1978 to provide an environment which promotes the integration of physically disabled and able-bodied people on board two square-rigged tall ships the *Lord Nelson* and the *Tenacious*. Anyone can join the crew on short voyages lasting between five and 16 days at a cost starting at £399.

Plas Menai National Watersports Centre — Caernarfon, Gwynedd, Wales LL55 1UE ☎ 0845 846 0029; ☎ 01248 670964; www.plasmenai.co.uk.

Royal Yachting Association — RYA House, Ensign Way, Hamble, Southampton SO31 4YA; ☎ 0845 345 0400; ☎ 023 8060 4100; www.rya.org.uk. As the governing body for sailing and motor boating in the UK, the RYA is the best starting place for any information about courses at every level for sailing or power boating.

UK Sailing Academy — West Cowes, Isle of Wight PO31 7PQ; ☎ 01983 294941; www.uksa.org. A registered charity to promote yachting. £6,600 for 12-week Yachtmaster course, £875 for Kick Start (2 weeks in UK) and other options.

The Tall Ships People — Moorside, South Zeal Village, Okehampton, Devon EX20 2JX; ☎ 01837 840919; www.tallshipspeople.com. Offer berths for the annual Tall Ships Race (formerly the Cutty Sark Race) run by the charitable organisation Sail Training International and for other maritime events and races. The full daily cost of a berth is £70–£90. Although at least half the places are reserved for people 18–25, many older people are accepted too.

SPECIAL INTEREST HOLIDAYS

According to a BBC survey, swimming with dolphins was ranked top of the list of 50 things to do before you die. Many other dream trips on the list involve contact with wildlife, including whales and sharks, elephants, tigers and camels (see p. 125 for a case study of Neil Munro, a Scottish gent who spent time in Africa looking after lion cubs). Many wildlife charities and placement agencies listed in the *Directory* arrange for untrained volunteers to work with rangers and conservationists, and these are among the most popular ways to spend a grown-up gap year.

SKIING AND SNOWBOARDING

Just as life at sea or in the bush becomes an obsession for some, spending time on the snow slopes is the ambition of a whole community of initiates. Many were introduced to skiing or snowboarding at a young age and have returned to the mountains at every opportunity. But snatched holiday weeks do not satisfy the craving and taking a whole season out to ski can constitute a fantastic gap year at any age.

A growing number of companies specialise in running intensive instructors' courses; see Part 9, *New Skills and New Projects*. If you merely want to spend a season skiing, you might contact companies that rent out affordable accommodation to skiers and snowboarders for between one and six months in various European and Canadian resorts, for example, Planet SubZero (☎ +33 6 12 51 92 33; www.planetsubzero.com) and Seasonaires (☎ 0870 068 4545; www. seasonaires.com) with options in Les Arcs, Trois Vallées and Chamonix (France), Mammoth and Breckenridge (USA), Whistler and Fernie (Canada) and Wanaka (New Zealand). Accommodation in the British Columbia resort of Whistler costs about C$28,000 for a two-bedroom apartment for the whole season. Be warned that most people who want to spend a whole season in a ski resort are young party animals. To offset the expense of skiing, it may be possible to pick up work in ski resorts (see Part 6, *Working and Living Abroad*).

ADVENTURE SPORTS

Sailing and skiing are only two sporting activities among many that can form the basis of an adventure trip. Many tour operators specialise in delivering extraordinary experiences rafting, trekking, cycling, mountaineering or diving to name just a few. As well as checking adverts in the magazine *Wanderlust*, check the searchable listings of the Association of Independent Tour Operators (AITO, www.aito.co.uk).

The travel-quest site (www.travel-quest.co.uk) is a free online directory of specialist tour operators including activity and adventure holiday providers. It provides company profiles and gives information on activities from heli-skiing to hot air ballooning around the world. Also check Action-Outdoors (www.action-outdoors.co.uk; ☎ 0845 890 0362) which offers hundreds of activity and sports holidays in a range of destinations.

Operators in the field of adventure sports holidays often make a pitch for older people fed up with everyday routines and conventional holidays. The following publicity from a rafting company is typical and hard to resist:

Take a break from your modern, hectic work schedule. All too often now we are so caught up in the hustle and bustle of life that we forget the important things: good friends, lots of fun, a bit of sunshine and great food. A river journey for those who have yet to experience it offers complete escapism from your regular life – no hassles and no stress! If you need a real holiday, we have the perfect solution.

After his expedition with Raleigh in Sabah (Malaysia) came to an end, **Matt Heywood** relished the prospect of realising huge ambitions for the rest of his gap year, before returning to work as an engineer:

I intend to take my PADI Open Water diving course in Borneo, then do a six-day expedition up the East Ridge of Mount Kinabalu. I will then spend three weeks doing a lap of Sabah by bicycle. Following that I intend to get as many adrenaline fixes as possible as I mountain bike, climb and raft my way around Canada, USA, Central America and New Zealand. I may try to use my Raleigh experience to gain temporary employment as a mountain bike guide. The final part to my dream year is to use my Raleigh experience to gain managerial employment within Holden, Ford of Australia (however, my girlfriend still needs a little convincing).

Another ambition that some people have is to learn to fly, whether as a paraglider, hang glider or Microlight pilot, for example, with the Fly Gap Academy in the Swiss Alps which offers all types of paragliding holidays from introductory courses to instructor courses specially designed for British career breakers and gap year students. Closer to home you can join paragliding and microlight training courses at places such as Airways Airsports in Derbyshire (☎ 01335 344308; www.airways-airsports.com) with a sister airport in Ontur, Spain.

BIRDWATCHING HOLIDAYS

Anyone who pursues birdwatching as a hobby should be aware that trips organised by specialist ornithological tour operators are often over-subscribed. This has been attributed to the gathering anxiety in the developed world that unspoiled natural environments are being whittled away and species lost at an alarming rate. The media has in recent years made people in the developed world aware of all the threats to unspoiled natural environments, creating a feeling of urgency that these precious places should be visited before it is too late.

The Reverend **Brian Blackshaw** fitted in two birdwatching holidays during his 14-week sabbatical from his parish duties. He greatly enjoyed his trip with the eco-tourism operator Company of Whales (www.companyofwhales.co.uk) from England across the Bay of Biscay to the Picos Mountains of northern Spain, on which the group saw more than 104 species, including the exceedingly rare middle-spotted woodpecker. In the latter part of his sabbatical, Brian went to Scotland with Speyside Wildlife (www.speysidewildlife.co.uk) and felt mentally and spiritually renewed by his time spent in wilderness landscapes, away from the telephone and the pressures of work in a busy Hertfordshire parish.

PART 8

TAKING THE FAMILY

ADJUSTING THE WORK–LIFE BALANCE
TRAVELLING WITH YOUR KIDS
SCHOOLING

MY GROWN UP GAP YEAR:
BRYAN HAVENHAND

Bryan Havenhand from Australia spent one whole year in Cambodia with his wife Anna and 13-year-old daughter Bonny. Anna found work as a language teacher after arrival in Siem Reap, and her wages covered all local living expenses including the rent of a comfortable house. They had a fascinating year, though not without its challenges.

My wife Anna wanted to teach English overseas and had completed a CELTA to this end. (A native German speaker, she ended up mostly teaching German instead to tour guides at Angkor Wat in Cambodia.) Our daughter was in the early years of high school so if we were to go, this was the time. I took the idea on as a bit of an adventure. The family (siblings and parents) were not overwhelmed by the idea and both sets of parents were opposed to it. They did not say this outright, but constantly stressed the negative side of things. It was seen as dangerous, more so because of the spread of bird flu in Cambodia and nearby countries. It was seen as somewhat irresponsible taking our 13-year-old daughter as well. Our friends thought it was a great idea and especially encouraged our daughter, who was not looking forward to it as she thought she would miss her friends badly.

The year out was self-funded although my wife earned up to US$700 per month, which well and truly covered our basic costs in Cambodia including the rental of our house. We did not travel much (our daughter didn't want to travel around the country at all) though we went once to Thailand, once to Laos just before we left and two short trips around northern Cambodia. I also did some English teaching that came along plus I taught quite a few local kids (as did our daughter for a while). Otherwise I was still working on my business (a small publishing company called Global Exchange), attempting to help home school our daughter, run the household (we did have a housekeeper) and generally keep things on an even keel.

The highlights were the people who lived around us (we had much more contact with the locals than with other expats), the Angkor temple complex, people we met in villages and locals we befriended. We were also lucky to have quite a number of friends from both Australia and Germany visit us during the year. For me the hardest part was the constant heat (for much of the year it would be 35 degrees Celsius at 6.30am and it would only get hotter from there). I also had problems with the monotony, the barking dogs at night and the early morning (4.30am) chanting from nearby wats. Sometimes I got little sleep.

It was definitely worth the effort and I think it has given our daughter a useful perspective on life that she wouldn't have otherwise got from simply travelling to a place. She dropped her Paris Hilton look-a-like friends not long after she came back and took up with some new friends who have a healthier outlook on life. When our daughter has finished high school we might just do it again.

ADJUSTING THE WORK–LIFE BALANCE

Taking a sabbatical to spend more time with family is one of the major reasons that people take time out from work. Paid maternity leave can be viewed as a statutory career break. New family-friendly legislation ensures that either parent is allowed to take up to 13 weeks of leave (unpaid) to look after each pre-school child.

Once they return to full-time work, many parents harbour feelings of loss and guilt at the relatively small amount of time they can spend with their tiny children and resent being forced to delegate too much of the responsibility for rearing a child to a nanny or nursery. Obviously childcare is essential for anyone who wants to maintain and pursue a career, but any parents in a position to step off the professional treadmill for a time to spend time with their children might be tempted to read this chapter. And when the children get a little older, parents who work long hours often feel as if they are missing out on much of their offspring's childhood. It is a motivating factor in some parents' decisions to take time out from work to participate in a collective family activity. It might mean experimenting with living in a foreign country for several months, or it can involve a family adventure like overlanding, sailing or cycling.

Many parents decide to take a break from work to enjoy an expedition together or a family project. An extended family break allows the (increasingly rare) chance for a collection of individuals, sometimes with widely differing interests, to operate as a single unit. It affords a rare unbroken opportunity to experience unadulterated family life, undistracted by phones, meetings, deadlines, work and the demands of a social calendar. According to a recent article in the *New York Times* entitled 'A Long Weekend? How about a whole year?' a growing number of American families with school-age children are taking off on ambitious travels. A number of these families record their odysseys on blogs or even in newspaper columns such as the family gap year of the Tims family which lasted 17 months and was featured in a series in *The Times* up until the end of 2007. Anyone contemplating a gap year with their children might be a bit intimidated by the mind-boggling travels of the home schooling Escampette Family (www.escampette.net) or the Andrus family (www.sixintheworld.com) who with their four children ranging in age from high school to pre-school spent 11 months visiting six continents. The Flemingo published their Family Tale of a Global Adventure online (www.rfleming.net) after completing a round-the-world trip with their two daughters aged 8 and 4.

One problem about reading about these extraordinary family adventures is that in some cases the families must be wealthy. A comment added to the Timesonline website expressed scepticism about the value of reading about the 'incredibly privileged lives of this, presumably, ultra-rich family' (referring to the Tims). But plenty of more average families remove their children from the comfortable routines of home to create a memorable and bonding trip together and these too will pop up in Internet accounts.

Children will undoubtedly make a gap year more complicated, whatever their ages. In the first place, you will have more expenses and responsibilities than when you were childless (though if you are paying for full-time childcare, the saving of taking them out will be colossal). Certain things such as doing a round-the-world yacht race or spending time at a meditation centre in India will be out of the question unless you have a long-suffering partner willing to hold the fort during your absence. Sometimes a break away from family life as well as a job can be to the benefit of everyone, though you must make it clear to the children (and your partner!) that they are not being abandoned permanently.

This section is for those who have decided to spend a large chunk of time with their families on the road. Do not underestimate the number of people who will raise objections to a sabbatical *en famille* on grounds of risk to career, risk to health, irresponsibility to children's education, expense, etc. Mostly they are just envious. **Jen Moon** courageously decided to follow a promise she had made to herself that on her 40th birthday, she would be doing something completely different. As a single mother of two daughters aged 9 and 11, she faced even more opposition and describes the school yard reaction: '*Although other parents at the girls' school kept saying how they wished they could do it, all the while they were looking at me as if I belonged in a mental home*'. An account and assessment of her trip is included later in this chapter. She also maintains a website for family gappers (www.grownupgapyear.co.uk).

A sample objection is raised by someone on the www.bootsnall.com 'Travelling with Children' messageboard in reply to several families planning round-the-world trips with small children, though it seems clear that the killjoy did not himself have children. In any case it is best to be prepared for such negative attitudes:

> You do know the kids are not going to get much out of the experience. I always wonder about adults with small children who want to satisfy their travelling jones [Americanism for 'desires'] without taking into consideration the comfort of the children. Just do a favor and don't put them in danger like the Canadian woman I met while trekking in Nepal who had her 6-month-old baby on her back at 5,000m because she always dreamed of seeing the Himalayas. Small children should be in their neighborhood playing with their friends instead of being taken to museums, enduring long flights and car rides, and essentially being treated as an extra set of luggage when their parents have a travel agenda to satisfy. Sorry if this comes across as harsh and I am sure you will disagree, but I can't stand it when adults who have had children put their needs before the needs of their children.

The broadcaster Libby Purves looks back in wonder on the summer of 1988 when she and her husband took their two children (aged 3 and 5) on an adventurous and sometimes dangerous cruise around the British Isles recounted in her book *One Summer's Grace* (which could serve as a subtitle for any number of gap years *en famille*). Tragically the elder child, Nicholas, took his own life two years ago, aged 23. Not long afterwards, Libby Purves wrote movingly of how important it is for families to spend time together on holiday:

> Family holidays are great. Family holidays are indispensable. They are the stuff of life, they should go on as long as possible, and their blemishes do not matter. . . While routine memories are all very well, the ones that sustain us best through the darkness are the dozens of journeys, expeditions, skives, weekends, ferries, trains, planes, boats and adventures we somehow fitted in. . . We do get asked if there is any lesson the tragedy has taught us, and there is. Take family holidays! Take them now. Splash out. Forget the new car, sofa, autumn wardrobe – do a Grand Tour instead, together. And if you've any money left over, send it to the Family Holiday Association, which organises trips for the poorest and most hard-pressed of our fellow citizens, because they need the break and the memories just as much, and lasting joy can flow from a week in a caravan at Rhyl.

Libby Purves is still an advocate for the Family Holiday Association and her article is linked from its homepage (www.fhaonline.org.uk).

MATERNITY LEAVE

Maternity leave is the most common reason for female employees to take time out from work and it is now an accepted feature of modern working life. New mothers who have been in employment for at least half a year are paid at least 90% of their salary for the first six weeks after a birth and then £117.18 (2008) per week for the next 33 weeks. When that period is up, mothers are entitled to take a further 19 weeks of unpaid leave and still be guaranteed that their jobs will remain open for them (provided they have worked for that employer for a continuous 26 weeks before taking maternity leave). Provision has been substantially enhanced by the current Labour government and is indicative of its emphasis on improving the work–life balance. Significantly, a junior health minister, Yvette Cooper, set an example a few years ago by claiming her full entitlement to maternity leave and became the first government minister to do so. For more detailed advice, consult the admirably clear government website (www.direct.gov.uk) or the national Advisory, Conciliation and Arbitration Service (ACAS; see below).

For working mothers, a career break is a physical necessity in the period shortly before birth and in the baby's young life afterwards. Now that maternity leave is a commonly accepted feature of employment, companies have adopted strategies and set aside resources to cope with these temporary absences. The degree of generosity beyond the legal requirements varies among companies depending on such criteria as how eager a company is to encourage a female employee to return to her old job instead of remaining at home. The annual lists of the 50 or 100 best companies to work for produced by the *Financial Times* and *The Sunday Times* invariably include companies that are the most family-friendly and allow flexible working hours. Many allow mothers to take career breaks for child-rearing ranging from the statutory minimum to five years.

In order to motivate new mothers to return to work many top companies pay bonuses on return to work following maternity leave. For example, IBM gives female employees up to three years unpaid leave after eight weeks paid maternity leave, or the chance to go part time with a guarantee of full-time employment afterwards.

Booklets by the arbitration service ACAS on employment protection and rights are available from Jobcentres and via the website www.berr.gov.uk, formerly the DTI. Alternatively you can contact the Statutory Maternity Payment helpline (☎ 0845 302 1479) or Jobcentre Plus (☎ 0800 0556688). Other useful resources include:

Working Families – 1–3 Berry Street, London EC1V 0AA; ☎ 020 7253 7243; www.workingfamilies.org.uk. Lobby group, formerly Parents at Work and New Ways to Work. Information about sabbaticals on their site.

Work Foundation – www.theworkfoundation.com. Website has some information about work life balance issues.

PATERNITY LEAVE

Increasingly fathers are taking time out to help cope with the arrival of a new baby. Paid paternity leave of up to two weeks following the birth of a baby was introduced in 2003 and is paid at the same rate as maternity leave, i.e. £117.18 per week. Naturally, a two-week absence from work hardly qualifies as a gap year, but it indicates a growing acceptance that many fathers want to take time off from work to help with children or even become the proverbial 'house husband' for a period of time. Fathers are permitted to take up to a total of 13 weeks unpaid leave before a child turns five.

The government's benefits for parents have proved controversial with business (especially small business) though are now accepted practice. In fact many new fathers do not take up the entitlement because of the relatively low wage, preferring to take time out of their annual leave after the birth of their baby. Mothers with their own careers now expect their male partners to contribute more time to child-raising. An increasing number of fathers positively wish to do so, provided they can come to an arrangement with their employers.

GETTING EVERYBODY ON BOARD

In almost all cases, the idea of a gap year is the grand design of one person in a family who tends to be the prime mover, the one to initiate and orchestrate the break and who is prepared to bear the responsibility for uprooting the rest of the family. Whereas one parent might be enthusiastic about putting their professional life on hold, this may not be so welcome or manageable for the other. As 'the Dad' wrote in the De Jager Family blog (http://blogs.bootsnall.com/Dejags), several months before he and his wife and children aged 1 and 4 set off on their round-the-world trip: '*Well my wife's enthusiasm, courage and drive have finally paid off; she has drawn me out of the well called home renovating and into the world of travel, and I finally got down to the business of planning the first leg of our trip*'. Sometimes the instigator's enthusiasm is sufficient to carry all before it, but it is essential that the following partner should not bury his or her reservations since this can escalate quite quickly into resentment.

The Grant family embarked on a remarkable journey, to become the first to encircle the globe in a horse-drawn caravan, described in sometimes painful detail in David Grant's book *The Seven Year Hitch: A Family Odyssey*. On the tenth page of his narrative, after the family has had a trial run with a caravan in Ireland and before the Big Trip begins in earnest, he writes:

> *Unnoticed by me, Kate was beginning to have reservations but she did not say anything. She did not want to be the wet blanket who spoiled the fun. She had enjoyed Ireland as much as anyone but I think she foresaw, even then, that a prolonged sojourn in the confines of a caravan might not suit her. In her words, 'I really did have doubts about David and me travelling in such close confinement. The children I didn't doubt at all. Children are very adaptable, curious about new ideas and concepts. But I thought it was a trifle unfair to expect them at ages 5, 7 and 9 to appreciate what our proposed wee doddle round the world would really mean.' I was in no mood or state to notice. Fired by all I had learned during our travels, I was as eager to go as a horse in a starting-stall.*

By page 39 Kate has found the trip unbearable and flies home to her father's house. She rejoins the family at intervals and is with them as they trudge to their final destination, Halifax in Canada, seven years after setting off. The index is telling; of the several headings under David Grant, we can look up 'tensions of journey' not to mention 'horse collar accident' and 'sued for assault'.

Loved ones cannot always be expected to share our dreams, passions and grand schemes. If there is a great discrepancy in what partners want out of a gap year, accommodations must be reached, perhaps dividing the allotted time into two phases; the first an overland trip to the Andes or a sojourn in a Hebridean bothy for her sake, the second a cycling tour or cookery course in Tuscany for his. Of course most differences occur at the micro-level. **Marie Purdy** and long-term partner Howard went round the world when she was made redundant at age 50. He particularly wanted to stop over in Dubai (which she was sure she wouldn't enjoy) and the South Pacific Islands of Fiji and Cook Islands (which she knew would be too hot for her). All trips on this scale involve daily concessions.

If children are part of the picture, further compromises will be necessary. Children seldom welcome change and upheaval, especially as they get older. Whatever their ages, the children should be included in the planning and preparations, and their preferences taken into account. They could be allowed to choose the odd treat destination such as a theme park or a safari or even be given a chunk of the itinerary to arrange.

Apart from the challenge of persuading the children, you will be faced with daunting logistical complexities depending on your plan. Take the ambitious plans of **Ambrose Marsh** and **Leah Norgrove**, two physicians in Victoria, Canada who had long nurtured the dream of taking a year off with their sons aged 13 and 7. When struggling to rent out their house, Leah wrote: '*We are stuck at task number 46 (renting the house out) and there are moments of doubting the Great Adventure, because we will be so fried before we get there. It would be good to take two years off: one to prepare for the Great Adventure and one to do it.*' Their gap year plans are indeed remarkable and due to begin after this book went to press: six months of volunteering in palliative medicine in Tanzania, a couple of months of chilling out in eastern Turkey, and then cycling from Istanbul to Estonia, with Simon the younger boy on the back of a tandem.

Shorter stints of family volunteering present far fewer organisational problems. The Tubb family joined a 'mini-leap' project in Kenya organised by The Leap in the summer of 2007, as first **Rupert Tubbs** and then his son Felix describe:

The four of us (two desk-bound parents, a 10-year-old Felix and an 8-year-old Minna) stayed in Shimoni, the southern-most point on the coast of Kenya and 15km from the nearest tarmac. Just getting there feels like an adventure. The village scrapes by on fishing, and on trade with passing tourists on their way to the Kisite Marine Park. We went to help in some way towards conservation and communities in the area, to do something different, something that would broaden the children's horizons, and, it has to be said, for a holiday. In the forest, walking for up to five hours along narrow trails and through thick undergrowth, we jumped lines of soldier ants, removed animal snares, and logged the local fauna and flora. We were there to map the extent of deforestation and search for the endangered Colobus monkey; with this evidence to hand our hosts would be in a position to approach the World Wildlife Fund for support in protecting these fast disappearing forests. Every day a team also went to sea. This was the flag-ship project in Shimoni: recording the dolphin population in the Pemba Channel. . . This, like the forest, was real work whose results would add to the sum of human knowledge about the world, and would help protect our wildlife by presenting the locals with alternative livelihoods to the netting that decimates the dolphin population. From Shimoni, an hour's walk further into the forest is Mzizima. . . This is the isolated and desperately poor village where we took part in the schools project: building, plastering and painting, teaching in the schoolroom and on the undulating scrubland that passes for a games pitch. This is where we met coastal Africa at its most needy, and where we found the biggest smiles. If we learnt anything important on this trip, and I include the children, it was here: how to be happy when you have nothing.

Eleven-year-old Felix Tubbs's take on the trip is a little more focused on his encounters with the local fauna:

> On the first day of project work I was on the boat. We were looking for dolphins. In the first 20 minutes we saw two bottlenose dolphins, and that was it for the day! The next day we saw nothing, but I caught a king mackerel which we all ate for supper (20 of us – it was huge!) And on the third day we saw three more bottlenose dolphins; five dolphins altogether in three days, when my sister saw 80 dolphins in three days (ugh!) At 6 o'clock every evening I went to play volleyball at the local school – I loved it. After the marine project, I went to a school and I helped teach them about triangles. After teaching, we plastered a wall because we were building a library, or we painted the nursery walls. I painted the numbers. On the last day we could choose what we wanted to do, and I went on the boat. That day I saw 61 dolphins that included 33 spinner dolphins, two spinner babies, two indo-pacific dolphins and 24 bottlenose. And then we caught two fish!

THE IDEAL AGE

After children reach school age, disrupting their education becomes an issue. Some families prefer to take off just before their children start school declaring that this is the blessed age of innocence. In

Matthew Collins' book *Across America with the Boys in which the ex-BBC Travel Show* presenter describes his trans-America drive with his two sons aged 3 and nearly 5, he concludes that ages 3–4 is a perfect period to take children away for a long trip. Before that you will have to contend with nappies and toddler problems. And after they start school they begin to lose some of their innocence.

LOOKING BACK AT THE AMERICAN TRIP, MATTHEW COLLINS BELIEVES THAT IT WAS ONE OF THE BEST THINGS HE HAS EVER DONE:

A glorious experience, I'm so glad I did it. At the age of 3 and 4, the boys were so fresh. They had a pre-school innocence. Here was an opportunity to spend a large chunk of time with the children, watching their personalities develop. It was a time to enjoy my kids and they enabled me to appreciate new places through their eyes.

Matthew remembers that the children never got bored in the USA and there was no VCR for them in the motor home. 'One of the great things about travelling with kids is that you spend so much time talking. We talked about everything. The stimulation was so great for the children.' One tactic to avert any irritation with confinement on the road was to keep the driving light, reserving the heavy duty driving for the evening. The advantage of driving through the hot and humid southern states was that the boys had a siesta during the afternoons giving Matthew some time to catch up with chores or just to enjoy a period of silence. The family also enjoyed stopping in the campgrounds mostly equipped with swimming pools.

The other significant advantage of travelling with children was that they were fearless about talking to anyone and acted as an icebreaker between adults. Once they approached a Hell's Angel and asked why he had so many horrible tattoos. Instead of a hostile response, the tough biker was won over by their naïve charm.

Libby Purves' warts-and-all account of the coastal cruise in *One Summer's Grace* mentioned above includes the low as well as the high points. She describes how the children's moods swung wildly and on occasions they were overcome with rage or homesickness or anxiety that they would never see their friends and family at home again. The parents patiently tried to explain that 14 weeks might seem like a very long time but they would all return to their normal lives afterwards. Libby Purves writes: '*As we set off northward from Puffin Island Sound, crew morale was low, pulled down by this insistent infant undercurrent of discontent. . . Alone of the crew, I was relishing the whole adventure. I felt rather guilty about this because I had originated the whole thing, set the dates, organised the finance and the empty house for it, and effectively dragged my whole family off to sea. I realised that, as the only happy human being on board, I had a duty to improve our lot.*' And for the most part she was successful.

Other families argue that the ideal age for a big trip is the pre-adolescent years of 9–12. Every family will have to choose its moments according to its own circumstances.

TAKING THE CHILDREN OUT OF SCHOOL

If the children are in school, you will have to obtain the permission of the Local Education Authority to take them out of school for more than 10 days; the school office should have the form. Permission will be granted only if the authorities can be reassured that the child's education will not be damaged (see section below on Schooling). Try to avoid taking them away when they are scheduled to do special exams; in the UK, children sit Standard Assessment Tests (SATs) in the summer terms of Years 2, 6 and 9. Although an obvious time to take the children away is between finishing one school and starting another, it might make it harder for them to re-enter normal school life when all their peers have already made the transition.

An increasing number of parents are refusing to be deterred from taking the break they crave. They are finding ways that will be beneficial for their children while at the same time allowing them to spend a substantial amount of time together during the formative years of childhood. If there's a guaranteed way of maximising that ever elusive 'quality time,' a sabbatical expedition surely is one solution. Parents report that taking the kids away from television and videos teaches them to entertain themselves with reading, drawing and writing.

Transplanting teenagers from their natural habitat can be more problematic even if you are happy to interrupt their preparations for GCSEs, A levels or whatever other course they might have chosen. Most well adjusted adolescents will resent being removed from their social network and forced to spend more time with their parents and siblings than they would at home. If possible, try to give adolescents as much freedom as possible. One way of placating them might be to make sure they are allowed to spend plenty of time in Internet cafés so that they can maintain contact with their friends at home. You might consider arranging the exclusive use of a laptop for them.

Outsiders will often exclaim over the educational benefit of travel with children. But children have a way of subverting expectations and are more likely to remember the street urchin pestering them to buy a flower than the great Buddhist temple, or the time a wave knocked them over rather than the sea creatures on the beach. A career break with children should be organised at a time when the parents will most appreciate it, not the children. It doesn't matter if you go when they are too young to remember anything. It does matter that you communicate enthusiasm and demonstrate a zeal for travel, for nature, for history, for whatever it is you are zealous about, which they will emulate and someday apply to their own interests (you hope).

TRAVELLING WITH YOUR KIDS

The best opportunity for a joint family enterprise is an adventurous expedition abroad. This may involve backpacking in a developing country, sailing or off-road driving. For some parents a travel adventure is an ideal time for the family to spend a concentrated period of time together, finding ways to live harmoniously while also discovering new cultures and seeing some of the great natural and constructed wonders of the world.

RESISTING THE DOOM MERCHANTS

As mentioned, taking children on an extended trip overseas is not universally admired. While a few friends and family may question the legitimacy and wisdom of taking a sabbatical as an individual or in a couple, taking children abroad can be a source of friction. It may be deemed irresponsible, selfish, risky or unfair to uproot the children. Questions will be asked, perhaps with the best intentions. Will it be safe to take young children to extreme climates? How will their education suffer? Will they catch malaria or hepatitis? Won't it be very disruptive?

Every family sets its own priorities, rules and patterns of behaviour and they need not be dissuaded from a jointly desired project by the criticisms of outsiders. While some parents believe that keeping to a routine in the familiar environment of home is the best policy for keeping kids contented and attentive at school, others – especially those who have done some serious travelling in the past – concentrate on the positive potential of a Big Trip together.

Steps can be taken to minimise the unsettling effects of travel on children. Obviously they should carry a couple of their most beloved objects. A small photograph album of their friends and favourite places at home can serve to remind them that their old life still exists and can also be of interest to people met on the road. Whenever possible a routine should be established so that certainties such as a bedtime story are maintained. The key to minimising stress and fractiousness is to avoid constant movement. If possible, base yourself in one place long enough for the children to create a temporary network of familiar faces, if only the waiter or the greengrocer's son. And when you all need a break from each other, ask in your lodgings or contact a local student organisation about hiring a babysitter.

Cultural differences can result in incidents that can sometimes be upsetting, sometimes amusing. In many parts of Asia, children are considered almost public property. Local babies may be used to being prodded and cooed over and passed from hand to hand, but your Western children may not be so keen on these little acts of idolatry. Older children may well enjoy the attention and like to be in the photographs of umpteen Oriental matrons but may balk when they are squashed up beside the shy daughter to be in a photo. Be prepared to rescue your child from any situation that is making him or her uncomfortable.

Cultural clashes will be less apparent in Europe, though some parents have commented on the German penchant for intervention. While accompanying her children to a playground in Germany, Alison Hobbs, wife of a university physicist on sabbatical, was taken aback to be offered some money by a stranger in order to buy shoes for her (cheerfully shoeless) baby. Still on the subject of shoes, another mother was berated in German for wearing flip flops while balancing a two-year-old on her shoulders on a popular climb to the Dikteon Cave on Crete where Zeus was born.

THE INCALCULABLE BENEFITS

A family adventure can provide an educational stimulus that will exceed anything available in a classroom. Instead of merely looking at photographs of the Amazon or the Taj Mahal in a book from the school library, children can actually experience its beauty and scale, and glimpse the civilisation out of which it emerged. In terms of the geography field trip, driving across Europe or sailing round the Caribbean certainly outclasses a visit to the local wood. The world becomes a classroom for both parent and child. Just don't harbour inflated ideas of how rapt your children will be by the Himalayas or the Pyramids. From the time an infant is 24 hours old, parents learn that generalisations and advice about childcare are sometimes helpful, sometimes useless, depending on their child's nature. So the experiences of other parents on gap years may be of very limited use. While some will enthuse wildly about how their children learned Swahili/took up birdwatching/wrote poetry, you may be stuck with the kids for whom the highlight was the size of the billiard table in a faded old colonial hotel or how they mastered the art of building card houses. Your moment to enthuse wildly might come unexpectedly when you realise what little trojans your sturdy capable longsuffering children turned out to be, cheerfully wielding their chopsticks or stoically carrying their luggage through crowded sweltering bus stations.

SINGLE PARENTS MIGHT BE EVEN MORE RELUCTANT THAN OTHER PARENTS TO CONTEMPLATE A GAP YEAR WITH CHILDREN. JEN MOON IS AN EXCEPTION.

Convinced that it would be a wonderful learning experience for the children, she was determined to take 9-year-old Sarah and 11-year-old Lisa on a big trip. She successfully negotiated with her employer for a four-month break (which she decided in the end was just long enough) and also with the school. After years of saving by working at two jobs and writing a book (about working on yachts), she decided that her dream was affordable. Such a trip is inevitably expensive but she begrudged none of it: 'Seeing how happy I feel having achieved the dream and seeing how incredibly the children have come on, it would in my eyes be worth double what I paid. It's lovely to be home and I feel far more contented in my life having done what I did.' When asked about the high points, she says that out of 120 days at least 108 had high points. That conclusion with the benefit of hindsight displays a more confident attitude than she felt in the planning stages:

'One of the low points was the stress before actually going. It was incredibly tough, knowing that, as I was a single parent, the kids would have no one should something happen to me. I found that very scary.'

The trip to Australia, New Zealand and America was a resounding success for all three of them. However, Jen admits to odd moments of loneliness, especially when the young gappers headed off clubbing or wherever their fancy took them. She was surprised to encounter relatively few travellers in her age bracket, which is squarely between all the school and college-leavers and the retired folks. The kids would also have liked to meet more travelling kids.

With hindsight Jen would have stretched the budget to get a bigger camper van and two laptops. The children both did lots of homework during the trip and wrote journals, so that competition for laptop space was always intense and one or other was invariably behind.

But the experience was overwhelmingly positive:

'The rewards have been immense, not least of all spending concentrated quality time with the kids. Both of them have had their maths level improve significantly (Sarah by three grades), their geography means so much more to them and both generally feel "special" in that they have done something that most kids never even dream of doing. That makes them have a sort of inner confidence that many of my friends and family back home have noticed and approved of as it is not a brash precociousness.'

An extended family trip can be educational in another sense for fathers, many of whom have had less contact with young children than their partners. Author **Helena Drysdale** says that travelling around Europe in a motor home, while researching a book on tribal peoples, was instructive for her painter husband Richard. *'Having been working since their birth, he was aghast at how little time children left him to do his own thing. Like most men, he had no idea what bringing up children day in, day out, really means.'* Be prepared to experience occasional feelings of loss when you recall your travels pre-children. Some of the old carefree magic may be missing to be replaced by what might seem at times relentless domesticity. But parenthood at home or abroad encompasses highs and lows, and the lows always pass.

CROSSING THE SAHARA

The Allans of Paisley in Scotland undertook what might appear to be a heroic enterprise. Norman was a self-employed businessman and Judy was at home raising and educating the children when they decided to take their five children all under 11 overland across the Sahara to Zimbabwe where Judy had grown up. There they planned to work with a Christian charity called Youth With A Mission (☎ 01582 463216; www.ywam-england.com) which supports missionaries by organising building projects and working with children.

As all parents know, caring for young children at home is very time-consuming and tiring. To undertake all these chores on the road might seem, frankly, intimidating. Nevertheless, the Allans managed to achieve the trip without serious problems partly because of their ability to solve detailed logistical problems by sensible planning.

The most serious problem they encountered occurred long before they reached the wilds of Africa. Their Land Rover broke down on the notoriously Darwinian Peripherique, the orbital ring road around Paris, and they didn't trust it to carry them through Africa. Later in Gibraltar, they ditched the Land Rover in favour of a Toyota Land Cruiser, which they discovered to be more comfortable and spacious. They usually slept in the vehicle unless they were staying for three days or more in one spot. Then they would pitch a large tent. In north Africa there was no threat from wild animals, but in Zimbabwe, they were compelled to sleep in the vehicle and on the roof. Animals in southern Africa do pose a danger especially as they are often well camouflaged. Surprisingly, the wild buffalo presented one of the greatest hazards and not big cats as one might assume from umpteen television documentaries.

The principal difficulty they faced is one that other travellers complain of too: crossing borders. Bored and poorly paid border guards frequently ask for money. Crossing into Niger was particularly problematic and sometimes they encountered arbitrary roadblocks set up to extort money. One occasion was memorably menacing when the guards took their kettles. Judy and Norman's strategy was to refuse politely but firmly to pay any money but offered medicine or food instead. Travelling with the children helped ease their way because kids are very popular in Africa. Travelling with a young child in unlikely circumstances has been known to give travellers something akin to diplomatic immunity.

Despite their young age, the children learned to work together and to work hard. The boys learned to pitch the tent to help their parents with the task of setting up camp. The major challenge within the family was to keep the children occupied during the long hours of hot and dusty travel. Within the constraints of travel, they tried to keep to a daily routine, being on the road by 11am each morning. For the girls, Judy brought dolls and clothes and toy utensils, while for the boys she took toy figures, animals, cars and some Lego. She also brought board games and cards. Another helpful tool was a batch of story tapes including traditional fairy tales.

Averting boredom among the children was a challenge but maintaining their good health required much vigilance. Before leaving they were inoculated and began taking anti-malaria medication. The two youngest children took quinine in syrup form but they hated the taste so much that Judy was not sure whether they were receiving enough dosage to protect them. This was the reason why most of the family avoided driving through Equatorial Africa where malaria is most prevalent.

For medical supplies, the Allans took the excellent kit sold by MASTA (see Part 2 Nuts and Bolts), which includes a spoon that shows you how to measure out the right amounts of rehydration salts (one level teaspoon of salt and two tablespoons of sugar to a litre of water). Additionally, the kit included supplies for an emergency, which were in fact needed on the trip. The family doctor also supplied some basic antibiotics to take with them.

The main precaution the family took was to follow advice about food. They ate only canned or dried food from their stores towed in a trailer, and they always used purification tablets for water. The diet of canned chicken, beef, tuna, lentils and spaghetti might have become monotonous but it did the trick and none of them had serious stomach problems. Only once did they eat meat, when they knew it had been slaughtered that day. The other exceptions to the strict regimen of dried and canned food were fruit they had peeled themselves and local bread and porridge.

WORKING AND VOLUNTEERING ABROAD

Volunteering to work for a charity abroad is much trickier to organise for a family than an individual or couple. Companies that place volunteers in overseas conservation projects or as English teachers are simply not equipped to find housing for families. One organisation that does place families is VSO. However, VSO stresses that it can place families only in certain circumstances, for example if there are more requests for assistance than there are volunteers. In this case VSO can provide additional support for partners and/or dependant children, which would include housing and insurance. It stresses that each case is considered on its own merits and taking a partner and children may reduce the range of placement options. Sometimes it's possible for a parent to take children unsupported by VSO at additional cost to the family.

When **Bryony Close** and her husband turned 50 last year, they decided they wanted to go on a special holiday with their two teenage daughters that would not only be fun and adventurous, but also allow them to take action to improve the world around them. They signed up for a six-week volunteer expedition with Blue Ventures, diving through unexplored coral reefs in Madagascar, collecting data on marine species and helping conservation scientists develop plans to protect threatened coastal habitats. Blue Ventures' scientific research lab is located adjacent to the remote fishing village of Andavadoaka, population 1,200, where there is no electricity or running water and where people live on less than £1 a day. While Bryony and her husband went diving to collect data on marine health, their daughters (aged 14 and 16) spent their days snorkelling, tutoring village children how to speak English and exploring local coastal areas and baobab forests.

We're not into sitting on beaches and doing nothing. This was a holiday, but you're actually doing something, not just spending money. We felt we were really doing something great. It was good for the kids to learn about the Third World. I think what got us all was the fact that although they're poor, the people there are extremely happy. The kids learned that when you've got a strong community and a lot of support, you don't need money to be happy. We loved it. It was totally different from anything we've done before. I hope this trip will encourage our kids to do volunteer work in the future. This put it in their minds that it's something they can do. Meeting other volunteers on the trip from around the world and of all ages was also part of the fun. There were people who had just left university, people who were on career breaks, and one woman who was a little older than us. It was a complete cross-section of people but we all got along. It was quite eye-opening for us and the girls. You can make friends with all sorts.

It is possible to find volunteering opportunities with younger children as well. The **Battye Family** from New England were looking for a volunteer opportunity abroad that could incorporate their whole family for up to three months, a tall order with four children aged 3–13. After much research they chose Volunthai, a teaching programme in rural north-east Thailand (see entry) that arranged a homestay and an opportunity to teach English in the local school. While the father (a teacher) and boys taught older children, the mother and two little girls aged 3 and 7 worked with young children. The parents wrote on their blog of their motives before leaving (www.planetranger.com/battyefamily):

So why do all this? Why put our normal lives on hold, take the kids out of school, and travel so far from all that is familiar? Well, that's pretty much the point. It's so easy to stay in the same cycle for years at a time and we really wanted to take ourselves out of what we know and experience more of what is out there beyond our own small community. We also wanted the kids to see that there is more to the world than Portsmouth, New Hampshire and to realize their own potential to do good things for others. We felt it would be an incredible education for them.

And later looking back on the experience, they felt that their hopes for the trip had been more than realised:

The most meaningful thing by quantum leaps has been the homestay and volunteer teaching experience. I can only say that it has been a turning point in our lives. . . The experience in Thailand made an immense impact on our family and I would love to show others how easy and fulfilling that kind of travel can be. . . The benefits of making such a trip far outweigh the fears that might hold you back. There were so many moments that made it all worthwhile: My daughter, only there a week, proclaiming with conviction that we have way too much 'stuff' at home and could get along just fine with just a couple of toys; watching my sons bargain (respectfully, artfully, and successfully) in Thai at the local market, having the chance to watch the stars in an ink black sky from the back of a pickup, being part of daily life in a rural Thai village populated with the most generous people on earth, and, most importantly, seeing all of my kids pick up the custom of local Thai children who treat helping out and daily chores as an honour, not an obligation. Imagine that!

This kind of adventure is undoubtedly easier with two-parent families who also have the option of letting one parent take a paid or voluntary job while the other looks after the children. But what about single parents who want a break from home routines? Having spent long periods of her life living in Barcelona, Orlando and Australia, **Jacqueline Edwards** wanted to live abroad with her 2-year old son Corey after studying aromatherapy and massage. Ingeniously, she inserted notices in vegetarian and vegan magazines throughout Europe, and received a number of offers including an offer of a free house in Austria in exchange for helping to look after rescued animals, from an elderly couple near Paris and a natural therapies retreat centre west of Madrid. She chose to accept a live-in position as a cook/cleaner in Spain, though she returned home prematurely.

JACQUELINE EDWARDS THINKS THAT IT IS ALWAYS A GAMBLE WHEN YOU DECIDE TO LEAVE THE COMFORT AND SECURITY OF YOUR HOME ENVIRONMENT TO LOOK FOR A NEW LIFE ABROAD. SHE EXPLAINS THE SPECIAL PROBLEMS SHE ENCOUNTERED AS THE SINGLE MOTHER OF A YOUNG CHILD:

I felt that my son was too young (he was two) and still at an age when he needed my full attention, which severely limited my work options. Being a single parent meant spending 24 hours a day, every day with my son (who is borderline hyperactive) which I found exhausting. I didn't have the support network that I have in England with grandparents, family, friends, etc. to help with childcare and, as we were in a strange environment with a different language. I didn't feel comfortable leaving him with strangers. I moved around a lot, looking for a suitable place to live and this is very unsettling for a child of his age. He was too young to understand that he still had a home and family in England whom he would see again one day.

In general it was not a very positive experience for either of us. Having said that, we're back here in Spain again. Last year I met a family who were looking for an au pair (through an ad in a Spanish magazine) and we kept in touch. So I came here to look after their son and live in their house in exchange for room, board and a small wage. It seemed the ideal solution but unfortunately it wasn't. Living in someone else's house is always difficult but when you are bringing a small, active child with you the problems can multiply. We were all very optimistic because we had lots of things in common and similar lifestyles. But we hadn't considered such issues as whether the children would get on; they didn't and spent a lot of time fighting which put a lot of strain on all of us. Living as an au pair is fine for an 18-year-old but when you are a single mother aged 30 used to lots of freedom, it is almost impossible. So I moved out into a rented flat and continue to work for the family. I am earning the same wage as before so will have to look for another way of earning. I'm thinking of teaching English to children and doing massages in the evenings after my son has gone to bed.

Living and working on an organic farm, as described in the section about the international organisation WWOOF in Part 4 *Doing Something Worthwhile*, is something that families can do. For example one of the highlights of the Whitlock family's one year round-the-world tour was their short stay at an organic farm in Hungary which they arranged through WWOOF (Worldwide Opportunities on Organic Farms). Because of his interest in habitats and conservation projects, Nick Whitlock was especially looking forward to living and working alongside local people and fellow travellers on WWOOF farms. The family arranged to stay on a goat farm in a remote area about 25km from Kaposvar where they picked fruit and helped in the kitchen and where 10-year-old Tom helped look after the herd of goats, meanwhile all staying in an idyllic old farmhouse.

Opportunities like this are also open to solo parents, especially on communities. For example in South Africa, the travelling Rawlins family (www.rawlins.ws) met two British women, each travelling with her 11-year-old offspring and working at an eco-community near Durban.

RED TAPE

Children of British nationals need their own passports (unless they are already included on a parent's current passport). Always check that every member of the family has a current passport with enough validity to last for the whole trip plus a safety margin of six months which is demanded by some countries. Be aware that if a child is included on a parent's passport and that parent had to return (say, for a family emergency), the child could not travel separately with the other parent unless they were also included in that parent's passport. Note that some countries (eg Canada) have signed up to the Hague Convention on International Child Abduction to discourage unauthorised removal of children across borders, and a lone parent travelling with children can be asked to show a letter of permission from the absent parent.

ACCOMMODATION

If travelling with young children, take it slowly, allowing plenty of fun and relaxing interludes between the days of travel and sightseeing. Try to find accommodation which is not only child-friendly but where your children are likely to meet other children. Animals are always popular so you might try to stay on a farm or a campsite in the bush. Self-catering accommodation means that you don't have to worry about your little tearaways terrorising other diners in the hotel restaurant or other eating establishments. Out of season, villas in Italy and Spain can be vastly more affordable than during the school holidays.

Campsites and youth hostels are venues where children often feel most at home. Nature Friends International (www.naturfreunde-haeuser.net) with headquarters in Vienna run a network of 1,000 mountain, forest and city hostels, mostly on the continent, which welcome parents and children. This would be one way of keeping costs down in an expensive country such as Switzerland. Many have their own playgrounds and most are very inexpensive.

Agritourism is another appealing option where you spend a week or more on a working farm. One possibility for finding addresses of farms which might welcome families is to obtain one of the guides from ECEAT (European Centre for Eco-Agro Tourism, Postbox 10899, 1001 EW Amsterdam, Netherlands; www.eceat.nl). They publish separate English-language *Green Holiday Guides* for Bulgaria, Poland and the Baltics and many other countries in Dutch- or German language versions, most for €10–€15.

Renting a cottage or house for a few months and staying in one place is often a better way to organise a long family break. Everyone enjoys the chance to get to know (and to become known in) a new community but children especially like the security that familiarity imparts and the chance to develop relationships with local children or adults and perhaps even go to school.

CHILDREN'S HEALTH

As mentioned earlier, attention to hygiene and care about what children eat and drink in developing countries is critically important. Children tend to be conservative eaters so may be more content than adults with safe foods such as peanut butter and packet soups brought from home. But children get thirsty and care will have to be taken about purifying water in some countries. Purifying tablets and iodine make the water taste unpleasant, so you might want to invest in a piece of high-tech equipment which purifies water without changing the taste. General information on obtaining health advice can be found in Part 2 Nuts and Bolts. Most GPs nowadays have computer access to detailed information for patients heading for the tropics and will be able to advise on the recommended and necessary immunisations (including the correct dosage for children) for specific destinations. Malaria poses such a serious risk in some parts of the world that they are best avoided, and it would make sense to choose a route that minimises exposure to risk. Parents of children travelling through a malarial zone will soon come to dread the pill-taking ritual, since some, eg chloroquine, have an exceedingly bitter taste and most children find it difficult to swallow pills whole. Practising on something more palatable before departure might help. Mechanical precautions against malaria are easier to manage (eg wrist and ankle bands soaked in DEET); younger children might enjoy the experience of sleeping under a tent of mosquito netting.

Among the items in your medical kit, carry a disinfectant to treat even minor cuts and scrapes. In tropical climates, even minor wounds attract flies and can easily go septic. And be very disciplined in applying high factor sunblock at frequent intervals.

USEFUL BOOKS AND OTHER RESOURCES

Across America With The Boys and *Across Canada With the Boys and Three Grannies* (Matthew Collins, £7.99 each via www.matthewcollins.co.uk).

The Seven Year Hitch: A Family Odyssey (David R. Grant, Pocket Books, 2000, £7.99). The highlights of this epic journey by horse-drawn caravan seem few and far between, especially as the father and three children struggle to find enough to eat and keep warm as they cross Kazakhstan and then get bogged down in Mongolia. Hard to imagine anyone wanting to emulate this trip.

The Rough Guide to Travel with Babies and Young Children (Fawzia Rasheed de Francisco, Rough Guides Reference Titles, 2008, £9.99).

Are We Nearly There Yet? (Sheila Hayman, Hodder & Stoughton, 2003; second hand from amazon). Amusing book about travelling with children.

Family Travel: The Farther You Go, the Closer You Get (edited by Laura Manske, Travoloro' Tales, 1999, £10.99). Collection of 46 tales narrating the joys and trials of families finding their way abroad. The contributors include well-known personalities such as Michael Crichton and Tim Parks.

One Summer's Grace (Libby Purves, Coronet Books, 1997, £8.99). In the summer of 1988, Libby Purves and her husband Paul Heiney sailed with their children aged 3 and 5 on a voyage around the coastline of Britain.

Cadogan Take The Kids Series (www.cadoganguides.com). Destinations include Greece, Ireland and France.

Your Child Abroad: A Travel Health Guide (Dr. Jane Wilson-Howarth and others, Bradt Travel Guides, 2004, £10.95). Aims to help adventurous parents travel confidently with their kids, and explains how to diagnose any health problems.

As usual the web contains a wealth of useful and useless information. Start with www.travelwithyourkids.com, which has advice and suggestions from longtime expats and real parents on how to travel internationally (or just long distances) with your children. Try also www.travelforkids.com which lists kid-friendly sites worldwide. As mentioned earlier family blogs on the Internet can be both inspiring and instructive. Lonely Planet Thorntree has an online forum 'Kids to Go'. Bootsnall.com includes a travel forum about travelling with children which is worth surfing.

MY GROWN UP GAP YEAR:
THE WHITLOCK FAMILY

Lindsay Whitlock provides an honest and thoughtful account of her family's round-the-world travels. She was 28 and a full-time modern language teacher, her 39-year-old husband Nick was a tree surgeon, plus children Tom who was 9 and Esther who was 4 when they left home. Although they experienced a few problems on returning to the 'real world' in southern England, these have not cancelled out the thrills and benefits of a year away, all on a strict family budget of £42 a day. Their story is told in more detail on their website (www.thewhitlocks.org.uk).

The idea of travelling as a family came up, the opportunity arose, and it seemed to be a 'now-or-never' situation. Our aim was, of course, to see the world, and also to give our children the opportunity to experience life in a way that they cannot at home. We decided to live the dream, to exchange armchair for rucksack, and security for adventure!

Although my headteacher offered to keep my job open for me while I took a year's sabbatical, at the time I was feeling the need for a clean break, and opted to resign. We decided to go for one year, taking a full year out of teaching for me and a single full year out of school for the children. Once we had designed the route we wished to take, we divided the time fairly arbitrarily between the four continents we planned to visit. We booked the main flights beforehand, and treated each continent as a clean slate, arriving on our planned date, with our only constraint being the date and time of the onward flight at our overland destination.

The whole trip in fact fitted into our £25,000 overall budget, with the flights costing about £8,000. It is so hard to choose a single highlight, as our experiences were so diverse. Some that come to mind are:

- The WWOOF farm we visited in Hungary where we spent one week on a goat farm in a remote area picking fruit, helping in the kitchen, looking after the herd of goats (which our 10-year old took to) and staying in an idyllic old farmhouse.

- Matema beach at the northern tip of Lake Nyasa/Malawi in Tanzania which turned out to be one of the most inaccessible places we reached, and our experiences with the people there were some of the most beautiful memories we brought home.

- Christmas on Mount Mulanje, Malawi, hiking for three days through beautiful, unspoilt countryside with a guide and porter.

- Our stay with the Cocama community in the jungle near Iquitos, Peru.

- . . . and many, many more!!

Of course there were low points too like the night we spent at Keleti railway station in Budapest, having all been struck down with a severe tummy bug, to the point where we were unable to move and find accommodation, having arrived late at night Even worse was the boat journey across Lake Malawi. We had been given every reason to believe that a ferry was in operation. However this turned out not to be true and, stranded in the unimaginably remote village on Mbamba Bay on the Tanzanian lake shore, we were left with very few options for continuing. We ended up accepting passage on a small cargo boat, which was unsuitable. This was probably the only time I seriously feared for our lives. I didn't include a detailed account on the online journal as I honestly couldn't face reliving the experience to write one.

There were many surprises as to our differing reactions to experiences Perhaps the biggest surprise was that with all the thought we'd given to helping the children to adjust, they managed the upheaval in some ways far more effectively than we were able to! Coming home has not been easy at all which we were totally unprepared for! After a year of moving on every few days, of spending 24 hours a day together, of relying on each other for everything and of the biggest stress of each day being where the next meal/bed would come from, 'normality' was rather a distant memory.

For all of us, the feeling that we overcame difficulties and setbacks as a family to do something that some people at home thought impossible or impractical has been amazing. Our individual self-esteem, the children's problem-solving skills and self-belief, and a general bond between us of shared experience outside the norm have all been significant rewards and benefits. I think this is all the greater because we did our trip without the continued help or support of any outside agency. Of course, this also allowed us massive flexibility, opting in and out of different tours, activities and excursions as it suited us.

I'd say the main drawback of doing a trip in this way is the immense pressure it puts on relationships of individuals within the family. For us, getting a babysitter was only very rarely a possibility, due to the nature of our trip We were often staying in one room, very often with less than four beds, and getting 'space' was a very real issue on a day-to-day basis. I think I speak for all of us when I say that we've genuinely proud of the fact that we, as individuals and as a family, survived and grew as a result.

SCHOOLING

Most parents will feel anxious about removing their children from formal education for an extended period. Some lucky parents have managed to enrol their children in a school abroad which can be very worthwhile even for a relatively short time. The usual problem is language but most children would prefer to spend time interacting with children over a language barrier than being cooped up with their family. Sports, games, music, smiles and many other pleasures are still accessible to them.

In countries where English is spoken, it can be a wonderful eye-opener for children to experience a different school environment for a few months. Even if the school is ghastly, the children will learn to appreciate their old school instead of taking it for granted. People travelling on a tourist visa will not usually be permitted to put their children in the state education system free of charge but it is worth investigating the possibility both beforehand and locally. If one of the parents has a special visa (e.g. work permit, academic visitor visa), it may well be possible. If the children's visas are to be added to a parental visa, make sure they go on the one which has the permission to work/reside.

Lindsay and Nick Whitlock decided to spend an inheritance of £25,000 on something that would change their lives as a family for the better. They were not unduly worried about the schooling that Thomas (aged 10) and Esther (aged 4) would miss. With the benefit of hindsight on their year-long travels, their confidence was justified. It turned out that the academic disruption was less an issue than the social disruption:

Although both our children missed a year of school, and Tom even missed his SATs, this, offset against the experience they had gained, does not seem to have had a long-term effect. In fact, we never sought official permission from the LEA [local education authority], although I wrote to Thomas' headmaster, who was happy to give his full support! As a teacher myself, I felt that I would be able to provide a 'skeleton' curriculum as we travelled. This was not possible as I had envisaged it, as the conditions during the trip meant that it was impossible, and, even when we did do 'travel school' it was generally met with resistance by the children. However, my children are resourceful and have developed an immense ability to overcome difficulties, and catching up has posed no problem for either of them.

On our return, my son had grown unused to communicating with his peers. While he was brimming with enthusiasm and confidence talking to adults, and could happily entertain a hostel full of backpackers with eloquent travelling tales, he found it very hard to relate to others of his age group for whom the most interesting event of the year was (perhaps) Jade winning Big Brother. He quickly gained a reputation at his new school, where he tried so hard to settle in, for being a bit freaky. Fortunately, in some ways, circumstances forced us to move again four months after returning to the UK, and he had adjusted enough to cope better second time around.

For our daughter Esther, aged 5 on return, the adjustment was easiest. She had missed her 'reception' year at school, and, having shown no interest in being taught formally by me, was therefore behind academically. However she is a naturally sociable child, who had, if anything, developed quite exceptional social skills in play with children everywhere, language no obstacle, and she quickly fitted in and caught up. Now, at nearly 7, she's doing very well at school, and in all areas of her life.

HOME SCHOOLING

If you decide to take the children on a trip abroad, their formal education need not be completely suspended. Several sources of help are available from organisations that produce courses and reading material for parents who want to teach their children themselves. Not all children are susceptible to being taught formal lessons by their parents, and the project may not succeed with stubborn, wilful or rebellious children. But 'lessons' can be disguised: a child may be keen to keep a diary of the trip while being loath to do an exercise from a text book.

As mentioned earlier, **Jen Moon's** daughters did plenty of homework while they were on the road, mainly thanks to their mother's determination to keep them at it. Nine-year-old Sarah wrote in her journal after a 'really looonnnggg walk' to see giant redwoods in southern California: '*Although it was pouring with rain and it was really cold mum started to give Sarah a geology lesson! It just goes to show we do homework whatever the weather! I was glad to get home and have my nice hot chocolate.*' Writing a journal is of course an education in itself. Jen was fascinated to notice the progress they made, from the rough efforts at the beginning, especially of nine-year-old Sarah when she could barely write, to the 'very accomplished, laugh-out-loud, work' at the end. Much of the daily accounts concerned food, but the educational benefits often shine through, as in this extract from 11-year-old Lisa's journal, written in their campervan in northern New South Wales:

> *We walked down onto the beach where we splashed in the sea. Suddenly mum spotted something sparkly in the sand, it was called phosphorescence, it was so amazing. There were little sparks everywhere. It was so weird, like stars in the sand. It was really magical, almost fiction. We had a splash in the water, the sparkles were in the water too and it all got in my hair. Sadly we got cold so we had to go back. We had been there nearly two hours. It felt like twenty minutes! It had been a strange night that I will remember forever.*

The value of ticking curriculum boxes palls in comparison.

Bonny Havenhand was 13 when her parents decided to leave their comfortable ocean-side house in Newcastle, New South Wales, and spend a year in Siem Reap, Cambodia (see Personal Case Histories). Carrying on his publishing business remotely, her dad Bryan took on the role of home tutor which, he learned, requires serious commitment:

> *Home schooling is hard work and takes a lot more time than originally anticipated! Everything seems to be done with minimum effort, but maybe that's all you get from a 13-year-old. Bonny's going OK with it, but needs a lot of help with maths, so I've had to relearn fractions, algebra, the Pythagorean Theorem, etc., etc. She is keeping up with her schoolwork and is half way through her second term's work. Not, I might fairly add, without a great deal of hassling and patience from me. I'm not wanting to take anything away from her as she has spurts where she does a lot by herself without being hassled.*

Bonny's school in Australia sent material on a regular basis. As soon as it was returned it was marked and new work would be sent. This worked well until someone at home in charge of forwarding the post failed to do so which caused problems. Bonny was not just on the receiving end of education. Despite her young age, she started teaching English to the local kids each afternoon for an hour and the numbers grew so much that her father had to step in to lend a hand.

The Education Act in the UK makes specific provision for home schooling, stating that parents are responsible for their children's education, 'either by regular attendance at school or otherwise.' Children who are registered as being home schooled do not, by contrast with children who attend schools, need permission from the local education authority before departing.

Most travelling families latch on to technology. In fact Ray Fleming, the father of the travelling family mentioned above, wrote a series of articles for *The Times Education Supplement* on how to use ICT to educate your offspring (go to www.tes.co.uk and search for 'ICT on the Road'). A wealth of online courses and educational CD-ROMs is now available, though these materials can be expensive. Numerous options for online and open learning allow a child to study accredited courses and to acquire qualifications. Virtual schools have sprung up all over and mean that your child can study from a syllabus that suits him or her without having to be physically present. Usually, a child will be assigned to a teacher who monitors progress via email or less usually by the ordinary postal service. A good starting point for information about correspondence courses is to contact the Open and Distance Learning Quality Council, which maintains a database of all accredited correspondence courses.

The Home Education Advisory Service (HEAS) and Education Otherwise have good reputations for helping parents take on the formidable task of creating their own school. The HEAS Advice line can put you in touch with other subscribers who live abroad who might be able to offer practical advice. Some families may prefer to follow the British curriculum for Key Stages 1, 2, 3, GCSE, AS or A2 level by taking the syllabuses and textbooks with them. HEAS publishes a leaflet called 'Examinations and Qualifications' giving information about the different options available for taking formal qualifications.

HOME SCHOOLING RESOURCES

The two principal organisations in the field are Education Otherwise and HEAS:

Education Otherwise – PO Box 325, King's Lynn, Norfolk PE34 3XW; ☎ 0845 478 6345; www.education-otherwise.org. UK-based membership organisation which provides support and information for families whose children are being educated outside school and for those who wish to uphold the freedom of families to take responsibility for the education of their children. Membership costs £25 and includes a copy of 'School Is Not Compulsory' which sets out your rights and duties, and shares the experiences of home educating families. Other titles explain how to teach children at different stages of their education for example *Early Years*, a compilation of ideas and activities for the under-12s covering Maths, Art, History, Languages and so on (price £4).

Home Education Advisory Service (HEAS) – PO Box 98, Welwyn Garden, Hertfordshire AL8 6AN ☎ 01707 371854; enquiries@heas.org.uk; www.heas.org.uk. National organisation providing information, advice and support for home educating families. Subscription to HEAS is open to home educating families. Annual subscription is £15 (£21 overseas) and includes a quarterly bulletin, access to the Advice Line for curriculum information and a regional list of subscribers. The service produces several publications such as the *Introductory Pack*, the *Home Education Handbook*, and the Big Book of Resource Ideas for information on books, CDs, websites and clubs for most school subjects. Leaflets are available too covering exams, special educational needs and home education overseas.

RESOURCES FOR DISTANCE LEARNING

Cambridge International Exams (CIE) – 1 Hills Road, Cambridge CB1 2EU; ☎ 01223 553554; www.cie.org.uk. This examination board sets the International GCSE (IGCSE) among many exams. You can contact them for information about the syllabus, the location of examination centres abroad, past exam papers and suggested book lists to accompany the relevant syllabuses.

International Centre for Distance Learning (ICDL) – www-icdl.open.ac.uk. Database of 5,000 UK courses and programmes taught by distance learning, mainly post-secondary.

National Curriculum – http://curriculum.qca.org.uk. Information about the National Curriculum for England subject by subject. For the Scottish curriculum visit www.ltscotland.com. For Northern Ireland visit www.ccea.org.uk.

National Extension College (NEC) – Michael Young Centre, Purbeck Road, Cambridge CB2 8HN; ☎ 01223 400200; www.nec.ac.uk. E-learning primarily for learners in the UK who have missed out doing GCSEs and A levels in the conventional classroom.

Open and Distance Learning Quality Council (ODLQC) – www.odlqc.org.uk. This didn't seem to be maintained at the time of writing. For a list of distance learning centres accredited by the ODLQC, see www.accreditedcolleges.co.uk/accredited-dlp.php.

Schoolfriend – ☎ 0870 442 2287; www.schoolfriend.com. This website (accessible by subscription only) was set up to help children aged 4–13 practise online what they have learned at school. While not directly intended as a resource for distance learning, it can be used as an additional tool by parents teaching their children while they travel. Subscription charges from £2 a week.

Worldwide Education Service (WES) – Waverley House, Penton, Carlisle, Cumbria CA6 5QU; ☎ 01228 577123; www.weshome.demon.co.uk. WES supplies tutorial-based courses for children aged 4–14. All courses are based on the National Curriculum of England and Wales. WES Home School families live in more than 100 countries on every continent, or are travelling between them.

Exam revision sites proliferate on the web. For example the BBC has very good 'Bitesize' sites for Key Stages 2, 3 and GCSE (www.bbc.co.uk/schools/gcsebitesize).

PART 9

NEW SKILLS AND NEW PROJECTS

INTRODUCTION

Stepping back from the daily responsibilities of a career offers the unrivalled luxury of being able to enjoy time to pursue personal interests. Time is a precious commodity in the developed world and in short supply. Away from the hurly-burly of professional obligations, individuals can take stock of their lives and re-evaluate their personal ambitions. At least that's what they hope.

Having time for yourself allows you to define yourself as an individual rather than as a worker. Anyone who takes time off can use it, as many of the interviewees for this book have done, to develop new or under-used skills or simply to live in a manner of their own choosing. Literally and figuratively, it's a time to climb mountains, to set yourself challenges and learn how to accomplish them beyond the confining arena of the conventional workplace. All those avenues and byways for which a working schedule does not normally leave time can be explored, and opportunities grasped to participate in an activity for the sheer pleasure of it. Pursuing a new activity also expands your social horizons. It can prove remarkably stimulating to link up with a group of people totally unconnected with your professional experience.

Those whose working lives began immediately after finishing their education may never have deviated from the pre-ordained path of working life. Dutifully they proceed along their career path, assuming that most options are closed to them, that they will not have the chance to pursue other interests or hobbies in depth. But a career break can change all that, giving people a chance to take up further education, retrain or expand their skills.

The choices for further education are immense, ranging from weekly courses run by the local authority to a full-time university degree course. The Open University described later in this chapter is one of the most successful institutions to come out of the 1960s, enabling students to take degrees without having to become residential students.

A career break gives you time to stretch yourself in formal adult education or in learning new skills in or out of a classroom. Studies may be wholly for pleasure or they may be applicable to your career. Learning a foreign language often satisfies both requirements. Improving your knowledge of a language will give you access to a different culture while also enhancing your professional profile. Qualifying in TEFL (Teaching English as a Foreign Language) is popular and is discussed in Part 6 *Working and Living Abroad*.

Exploration of an entirely new field expands horizons and sometimes even prompts an unplanned-for career change. If you've only known one area of work, taking a career break might allow you to glimpse other professional worlds.

CREATING YOUR OWN PROJECT

A career break for study or leisure involves a serious commitment of money and time so should be used well. It deserves careful planning so that the time doesn't leak away. Many people will use the time to create their own project, to fulfil an ambition or simply to indulge a passion. You might have a general-ised desire to see the world, as described in Part 7 *Travel and Adventure*. On the other hand you may want to take the chance to fulfil a specific ambition such as perfect your watercolour technique, learn to parachute, join an archaeological dig, trace your family roots, row across the Pacific, concentrate on getting fit, write poetry or a book, make a pilgrimage, study circus skills or help to protect an endangered species. In those moments of disgruntlement at work, each person is likely to have a private fantasy of an alternative life, even if it involves just three months away.

It is not essential to go abroad to satisfy one's curiosity about different worlds or fulfil long-held ambitions outside one's sphere of employment. Among the favourite alternatives to the pressures of the corporate world are working on the land or in the country, eg gardening and animal care. Hadlow College in Kent (☎ 0500 551434; www.hadlow.ac.uk) offers a range of courses suitable for people who want a complete change; horticulture, equine studies, animal care, etc. can be studied full or part time. The Royal Horticultural Society (www.rhs.org.uk) offers a range of gardening courses for interest and career advancement. The English Gardening School is run by the Chelsea Physic Garden (66 Royal Hospital Road, London SW3 4HS; ☎ 020 7352 4347; www.englishgardeningschool.co.uk) and is a good place to turn a hobby into a job. One year diploma courses are available in garden design (£7,850) and practi-cal horticulture, plants and plantsmanship and botanical painting (all for £4,850). The school also offers courses by distance learning.

Domestic circumstances may make leaving home impossible or undesirable but that need not rule out a gap year. **Mike Bleazard** wanted to see how much fun he could have by staying in his home environment of Cambridge pursuing a personal project that he would never have had the time to pursue while working.

AS A SELF-EMPLOYED COMPUTER GEEK, MIKE BLEAZARD HAD SAVED UP ENOUGH PENNIES TO TAKE THREE MONTHS AWAY FROM WORK, THIS TIME TO PURSUE A NEW IDEA WHICH HE HAD DEVELOPED WITH A FRIEND.

They wanted to design and self-publish a series of themed walking tours of Cambridge and distribute them in pamphlet form through local shops and via their website (www.shortcutguides.co.uk). It proved to be great fun to research and design them, one on the old colleges, two on modern architecture, an-other on churches, with the possibility of adding one on punting. His aim was to break even though of course it will not be unwelcome if his venture ends up making a profit. By printing them in bulk, the production cost is just £0.13 plus £0.01 to the Ordnance Survey (for permission to adapt their map) while they retail at £1.20.

He ended up working harder than he did when he was in employment but found that he enjoyed the experience intensely. Through the project he met people from many different worlds, from architects to publicans. Not everyone was wildly enthusiastic about his take on the sights, for instance a senior member of St John's College strenuously objected to his description of the statue of King John in the gatehouse as 'effeminate'.

USING A GAP YEAR TO DEVELOP YOUR CAREER

One practical way of taking a gap year without creating too much distance between yourself and your work is to create a project that enhances your professional skills. Some bodies have established schemes whereby employees are temporarily assigned to another organisation to learn from a different environment. But you could also initiate such an exchange.

Often individuals will take a career break to pursue a particular goal within their own field. This is well established among university academics who (in theory if not always in practice) are given a break from their teaching duties one term in seven (the meaning of the word sabbatical) in order to engage in full time research. This time enables specialists to concentrate on their field and be productive, often resulting in an article or book. Some other employers have taken over the idea of sabbatical; for example newspapers such as the *Financial Times* bestow paid or unpaid leave on their columnists who want to write a book. School teachers, lawyers, doctors and other professionals occasionally organise an attachment to a different institution to work on a particular academic project.

After working in the same London law firm for five years, **Sara Ellis-Owen** was a valued member of staff. She came to a point where she felt she needed time out from work and from London, and so asked for unpaid leave for three months. She also asked the *pro bono* department (meaning working for the public good) whether they would be able to support her once she had found a short-term legal placement abroad in a developing country. They generously agreed to pay for her flight to Belize and her placement fees to the Edinburgh-based charity Challenges Worldwide with whom she had fixed up a legal placement in Belize City.

She wanted to make the most of her time off and use her legal skills in a different way. She had to choose between a placement reviewing the Fire Act (while living in the fire station!) or a placement reviewing the laws of Belize to determine their compliance with the UN Convention on the Rights of the Child. She chose the latter because it sounded interesting and completely different from what she had done before. She was working with a non-governmental organisation (NGO) that advocated for the rights of all children in Belize:

Within a day of arriving I got stuck in, printing off all the relevant legislation, reviewing each in turn, highlighting the gaps and suggesting improvements. In order to form a view, I had to get up to speed with the 49 separate Articles of the 700-page Convention, a daunting task. I remember thinking on my first day that this was such a big task that I might not get to finish it within three months. Once I was comfortable with the Convention, I met with various people in the community (Police, Family Court, Department of Human Services and Community Rehabilitation Department) all of whom had strong views on the shortcomings of the law. I discovered interesting gaps in the outdated laws, for instance Belize law permits the use of corporal punishment in schools, and the laws are slanted heavily in favour of girls (in terms of protection from violence and abuse). The most challenging part of my day was keeping up the motivation and not to become swamped by the wealth of information.

Although my placement was relatively short, I found myself able to accomplish a great deal and benefit the National Committee for Families and Children (NCFC) as well as myself. I hope that my report will be used by the various NGOs to push for much needed changes in the law. It was a slight shock to the system coming back to a busy environment in London, but I felt refreshed after my break and my perspective on life was different – I refused to get stressed.

Challenges Worldwide is experienced at placing volunteers in professionally relevant positions abroad from which they can gain new skills and different areas of expertise. Similarly Outreach International aims to match skills to placement. For example Helen Balazs, an orthotic technician in her early 30s, went to Cambodia for three months to train landmine victims and disabled young people to become commercial artists. It is often true that a change is as good as a rest.

Some career breakers who join volunteer projects in the developing world without much thought come back fired up to pursue international development more seriously. The Charities Advisory Trust (www. charitiesadvisorytrust.co.uk/development/index.html) runs a two- or four-week residential summer course called Development from the Inside in Mysore, India, which can serve as a taster of career-level work in development. It includes sessions led by Indian activists and visits and two work placements with local NGOs. The full course fee of £1,050 covers accommodation, food and transport within India.

A logical next step could be formal studies in international development. Some of the most well-established courses in the field are taught at the International Development Department of the University of Birmingham (Edgbaston, Birmingham B15 2TT; ☎ 0121 414 5009; www.idd.bham.ac.uk) where several MSc programmes in development are on offer which include overseas study visits.

ADULT EDUCATION

A prevailing theme of this book is that the modern economy demands an unprecedented degree of adaptability. While this can be stressful and even frightening, it also presents opportunities for reinvigoration and stimulation. Lifelong education has been one of the buzzwords of our era and can provide an exciting chance to move in a different direction, whether purely for pleasure, self-improvement or a combination.

The choices available in adult or continuing education are vast. It is possible to study any subject you can think of from Mandarin to massage, computing to archaeology.

- Are you interested in a part-time or full-time course?
- Do you want a vocational degree?
- Or are you keen to study a subject for pleasure?

Think about what it is you want to achieve by further study during a career break. You might want to take your undergraduate studies a stage further by gaining an MA, MSc or even a PhD. For example after taking early retirement at age 58 from a small importing business, **Howard Peters** signed up with Coral Cay Conservation (CCC) to do a volunteering stint helping to set up a marine environmental base in Fiji, and went on to do other CCC expeditions in Malaysia and the Philippines:

> *As for me, my years at CCC so motivated me that in 2007 I completed a full-time MSc university course in Marine Environmental Management at York University and will progress on to a PhD in the hope of adding the fruits of my research to the benefit of marine conservation.*

During the past 10 years the numbers attending postgraduate courses in the UK has quadrupled (including students from overseas). Most mature students prefer to study at their local university or college. Some elite institutions cater particularly for the needs of mature students. For example, Birkbeck College is a member of London University and specialises in teaching mature students. While it is possible to take a full-time postgraduate degree, most teaching takes place in the evenings so that mature students can continue working during the day. It is possible to enrol in first or higher degrees in the arts, sciences or social sciences. Most course details can be found on the college website (www.bbk.ac.uk) or you can write to the Registry, Birkbeck College, University of London, Malet Street, Bloomsbury, London WC1E 7HX; ☎ 0845 601 0174.

Ruskin College in Oxford specialises in providing educational opportunities for adults who want a second chance in education. For a variety of financial, personal or social reasons some adults have never had access to higher education. Ruskin seeks to redress this shortfall and has established a strong reputation for the quality of its adult education. The average age of students is 35 with a range from 22 to 74. Interestingly dyslexic students make up a significant proportion of the total student body of 300. Courses are residential although it's possible to take shorter courses too. For information call 01865 554331, check the website (www.ruskin.ac.uk) or write to Ruskin College, Walton Street, Oxford OX1 2HE. A fully funded residential programme at Ruskin called Ransackers is aimed at people over 55 who have never benefitted from higher education and who have a topic that they want to explore for a 10-week term.

At Cambridge University, Lucy Cavendish College (www.lucy-cav.cam.ac.uk) admits only women aged 21 and over, and encourages applications from women of all ages and backgrounds, including those with few or no academic qualifications. Many students at the college have returned to full-time study after a spell in the workplace or bringing up children, or are making career changes. Every July the University of Cambridge puts on a short summer school called 'Going Further' aimed at giving anyone thinking seriously of returning to education a taste of study at university level. Various other events take place to encourage mature students to consider Cambridge (see www.cam.ac.uk/admissions/under-graduate/events/femature.html).

According to UCAS (Universities and Colleges Admissions Service), the number of applicants over 25 years of age who are applying to universities and colleges keeps rising, so you are bound to find a peer group wherever you enrol. The UCAS website has links to Access to Higher Education courses throughout the UK (www.ucas.com/students/beforeyouapply/access_programmes). A lack of confidence inhibits many older potential students. Many mature students feel an extra burden of stress because often they have given up a lot to return to education and stand to lose more than a 19-year-old who drifts on from school. Most institutes of higher education have a mature student guidance officer who will be able to offer reassurance and practical advice on funding (see *Financial Support* section below).

LIFELONG LEARNING

Those who turned their backs on further or higher education at an earlier stage are now being encouraged to go back to college to acquire new skills and knowledge and an analytical training. A gap year might be the time, whatever your age, to pick up qualifications you never had the chance to study before or which you fluffed while being distracted by more entertaining youthful pursuits.

Formal adult education courses that award certificates and degrees can be roughly divided between further education, which takes place in local further education and tertiary colleges mainly offering vocational courses, and higher education which encompasses undergraduate and postgraduate study leading to a degree. Higher education includes degrees, Higher National Diplomas (HNDs) and Certificates, and Diplomas of Higher Education. It is possible to migrate from one to the other, as demonstrated in the case study later in this chapter of Sandra Murray, who took her first tentative steps back into education at her local college but continued her course at university in Edinburgh and went on to do an MBA.

Increasingly, universities run recreational courses for adults through departments variously called continuing education, extra mural departments or short course units. These courses do not offer the same academic challenges as the degree programmes, but they do give adult learners access to the same academic resources such as tutors and libraries without subjecting the students to the same pressure or commitments in terms of time and cost. If you already have a degree and professional qualifications you may not want to study towards another degree. If you want to study for pleasure, there may be little justification in putting yourself through another round of exams. Studying during an adult gap year should be pleasurable as well as enlightening, a period ideally free of anxiety and stress.

USEFUL CONTACTS AND RESOURCES FOR ADULT EDUCATION

Adult Residential Colleges Association (ARCA) – 6 Bath Road, Felixstowe, Suffolk IP11 7JW; ☎ 01394 278761; www.arca.uk.net. A group of small colleges specialising in short-stay residential adult education courses for the general public.

City & Guilds (C&G) – 1 Giltspur Street, London EC1A 9DD; ☎ 020 7294 2800; www.cityand-guilds.com. Set up in the 19th century to provide technical training for a variety of trades, C&G is now a leading provider of vocational qualifications in the UK suitable for anyone wishing to improve their skills or to retrain before returning to work. Subjects for study include agriculture, catering, clothing, construction, education, electronics, furniture, healthcare, IT, retail and distribution, sport and tourism.

Floodlight – www.floodlight.co.uk. Directories produced by the Association of London Government list 40,000 courses in London and are sold by newsagents and bookshops, or are available online in a searchable database of courses.

National Institute of Adult Continuing Education (NIACE) — Renaissance House, 20 Princess Road West, Leicester LE1 6TP; ☎ 0116 204 4200; www.niace.org.uk. Leading organisation for adult learning; publishes a range of booklets on topics related to lifelong learning and coordinates Adult Learners' Week each May.

UCAS – ☎ 0871 468 0468; www.ucas.com/students/maturestudents.

University of the Third Age – www.u3a.org.uk. Promotes lifelong learning mainly among retired people.

Second Chances (available from Trotman, 2005, £24.95). National guide to adult education and training opportunities.

BUSINESS STUDIES AND THE MBA

Mature students often consider embarking on a business degree to facilitate a career change or improve their prospects. Using a gap year to obtain a Master of Business Administration (MBA) is not uncommon among employees working in any form of financial or commercial administration. In recent years it has become almost *de rigeur* for advancement in certain professions like management consultancy. It's a trend that has taken its lead from the USA where this field of study was pioneered. Some of the major American business schools such as Harvard, Columbia and Wharton in Philadelphia are prestigious and expensive. But European business schools are catching up: the London Business School was ranked second, INSEAD in Paris sixth and the Judge Institute in Cambridge tenth by the *Financial Times* in their 2008 survey of global MBA programmes.

The MBA is an ideal degree for individuals who have spent some years in work following graduation. It offers the chance to study abroad in the USA or France, for example, while gaining a degree that is highly valued in business. Effectively, it almost guarantees a significant lift in professional salary and opportunities. Students tend to be aged between 26 and 35. Holders of MBAs are some of the best-paid employees in the workforce which is just as well since fees for one year's MBA study can easily rise to £20,000.

The Association of MBAs (www.mbaworld.com) is the internationally recognised authority on postgraduate business and management education. In the crowded and complex market, it provides impartial advice to potential MBA students. The association also runs a scheme with NatWest for financial assistance to prospective students wishing to take MBA courses. To qualify you must have a bachelor's degree or suitable professional qualification plus two years' relevant work experience; non-graduates must have five years' experience. It is possible to obtain two-thirds of present gross salary plus 80% of the tuition fees. Preferential interest rates apply.

OPEN LEARNING

Distance learning is often now referred to as open learning, replacing the old description of 'correspondence course'. It is a concept of keen interest to individuals who want to embark on adult education without leaving home. By definition, the concept allows any student to study from home with the assistance of the Internet supplemented by text and audio-visual materials. Tutorial help is provided by email, post, telephone and occasionally in face-to-face meetings. One-week residential courses are usually built in to the programme.

Many of the same qualifications are available by open learning as by attending courses on college campuses. Realistically, most adults in their 30s, 40s or 50s do not have the freedom (nor the inclination) to leave their comfortable homes to live in student digs or residential halls for extended periods. Parents at home caring for young children often find this a valuable option.

Flexibility is at the heart of open and distance learning, giving students the ability to learn at their own pace and in their own time from anywhere in the country or indeed the world. Computer skills are now compulsory. Course materials can be quite expensive although this can be mitigated by access to a good local library and the huge resources now available online. Generally speaking, distance courses are much cheaper than full-time residential ones. Learning any subject, especially practical ones, from books can be a challenge, as can disciplining yourself to stick to a self-imposed timetable. Be wary of extravagant claims by distance learning course providers since an element of practice may be considered essential for certain areas of endeavour (e.g. learning to teach English).

THE OPEN UNIVERSITY AND OTHER PROVIDERS

The Open University was established to teach mature students including those individuals without any formal qualifications. Now considered a great success, the OU has established a reputation for the quality of its teaching and research. All of this is a tremendous resource for aspirational adult students.

The large variety of courses ranges from short modules to PhDs. It is possible to construct your own degree programme by choosing from the 160 single nine-month courses or signing up for one of the 30 two-year diplomas listed in the *Undergraduate Prospectus*. Courses can be spread over many years with breaks and students can begin studying at any level appropriate for them. Most work is undertaken by distance learning, using interactive learning, audio-visual and printed materials, CD-ROMs, television and radio programmes on the BBC, and personal contact with tutors. Open2.net is the online learning portal from the Open University and the BBC.

Aside from first and higher degrees, Open University students can study a variety of non-degree courses such as computing, health and social welfare, management, the history of ideas and art history, among many others; log on to www.open.ac.uk/courses to conduct a search. Most courses from the undergraduate programmes are available too without proceeding to a full degree. For detailed information contact your nearest OU regional centre. (To find the nearest centre call the Course Information and Advice Centre on 01908 653231.)

Alternatives to the Open University take the form of specialist correspondence colleges, viz. the Open College of the Arts, National Extension College and Open Learning Centre. For information on accredited colleges, contact the Open and Distance Learning Quality Council (all listed below).

The Internet has revolutionised distance learning. To take just one example, Birkbeck College, the adult education arm of London University, has been running virtual screenwriting workshops for a number of years. One day a week, 10 students log on for a two-hour tutorial. One tutor claims that online learning gives students greater confidence to speak up and the students make great efforts to meet up socially.

People considering doing a distance course with a private institute should try to ascertain how widely recognised the qualification or 'diploma' will be. Certain fields attract the occasional cowboy operators, for example in the booming field of Teaching English as a Foreign Language (TEFL), a few companies in the field (often operating from a Post Office Box number) have a definite credibility gap. Try to find out if there is an accreditation council in the field and if so whether the institute is a member. Ask to be put in touch with past students and seek the opinion of respectable organisations or prospective employers in the field.

OPEN LEARNING CONTACTS

Association of British Correspondence Colleges (ABCC) – ☎ 020 8544 9559; www.homestudy. org.uk. A trade association representing correspondence colleges, offering advice and information for prospective students. Standards are regulated and a common code of ethics applied.

Learndirect – ☎ 0800 100 900; www.learndirect-advice.co.uk. Government information service on education at all levels including distance, open and flexible learning.

Open and Distance Learning Quality Council (ODLQC) – ☎ 020 7612 7090; www.odlqc.org.uk. Grants accreditation to private colleges offering distance learning. Accredited colleges range from the Kevala Centre in Devon which teaches alternative therapies such as Indian head massage to the Horticultural Correspondence College.

Open College of the Arts (OCA) – Registration Department, Freepost SF10678, Barnsley, Yorkshire S75 1BR; ☎ freephone 0800 731 2116; www.oca-uk.com. OCA offers home-study courses in art and design supported by tutors who are practising artists. There are 45 courses in painting, sculpture, textiles, interior design, photography, garden design, dance, music and singing. Students can begin their course at any time of the year. Most courses cost £580 and include either distance tuition or five hours of face-to-face tuition.

The Open University – Student Enquiry Service, PO Box 197, Milton Keynes MK7 6BJ; ☎ 0845 300 6090; www.open.ac.uk.

RDI (Resource Development International) – Midland Management Centre, 1A Brandon Lane, Coventry CV3 3RD; ☎ 024 765 15700; www.rdi.co.uk. Distance learning in Accounting, Finance, Management, Marketing, IT, Business Administration and Law via key partners such as the Universities of Sunderland, Leicester and Northumbria.

University of London External Programme – ☎ 020 7862 8398; www.londonexternal. ac.uk. 100 different degrees and diplomas are delivered externally to students in more than 140 countries.

FINANCIAL SUPPORT FOR RETURNING TO EDUCATION

Finding financial support for further education is undeniably difficult. At a time when the government has increased student fees in England and expects undergraduates to take out huge loans to fund themselves through college, it will be difficult to find financial aid as a mature or postgraduate student. The 1960s–1980s can now be viewed as a golden age for higher education in which studying was seen as an entitlement rather than a privilege.

Mature students over 21 are eligible to apply for the means-tested student loan like any other student. Recently the upper age limit was raised to 60. People over 19 who missed out on education when young and want to study full-time for GCSEs, NVQs or A levels may be eligible for the new means-test Adult Learning Grant of up to £30 a week. Full-time students who have dependent children may be eligible for a Childcare Grant and, depending on the household income, a Parents' Learning Allowance. Further information is available on the website (www.direct.gov.uk) which includes information about routes into higher education for mature students.

If you need help funding a training course, in anything from feng shui to TEFL teaching to ski instructing abroad, you may be eligible for a Career Development Loan. CDLs are bank loans covering up to 80% of the cost of a vocational course lasting less than two years followed by up to a year's practical experience. The Department for Innovation, Universities and Skills (DIUS) pays the interest until a month after your course finishes whereupon you must begin repayments at a favourable rate of interest. Details are available as always on www.direct.gov.uk or call 0800 585505.

Note that long-term unemployed people over 25 may be eligible for Job Seeker's Allowance even though they are doing a full-time training course (www.jobcentreplus.gov.uk). Some colleges are entitled to offer special dispensation to mature students. For example people over the age of 30 may be eligible for tax relief on vocational courses; see HMRC Leaflet IR119 which explains which payments and training qualify for Vocational Training Relief, who can claim it, and how the relief is given. In cases of hardship Learner Support Funds (www.support4learning.org.uk) may help with part of the fees and for books and travel.

Sometimes access bursaries are made available to eligible students. Colleges can make discretionary child care grants of up to £1,000 to help parents pay for care while they study. Similarly, colleges also run hardship funds from their respective social service departments.

When applying to a college or a university, enquire about the availability of financial support. Many educational institutions award scholarships and bursaries so it is always worth asking how to qualify for additional support. Sometimes paid research or teaching assistant positions are available in higher education which can partially offset the costs of your own study.

In order to encourage recruitment into nursing and teaching, the government has implemented a programme of inducements. For anyone considering an MBA course, special loans are available through the Association of MBAs at preferential rates provided you meet certain qualifying standards.

LEARNING FOR PLEASURE

Everyone has interests over the course of their lives that go into hibernation. Sometimes interests move on and change, but more often a shortage of time is to blame. Perhaps while at school or college you had a passion for football, art, photography, an allotment garden, chess, human rights campaigning, Thai cookery, mountaineering, creative writing, playing in an orchestra, pigeon racing or singing in a choir. Gradually this commitment may have dwindled as work has taken up more time and energy. This deficit may have been exacerbated by the onset of parenthood. A gap year can provide the leisure time to pursue an interest at a recreational level. Perhaps you have discovered an activity while on holiday such as riding, diving, art or cookery which you want to explore in more depth. A career break presents an ideal opportunity to immerse yourself for several months in a new interest. It is never too late to revive an old interest or introduce yourself to a new one. Throughout the UK literally hundreds of subjects can be studied in evening classes, for weekends or for longer periods. These courses tend to be listed under the rubric of 'adult education' and are often organised by the local education authority. Usually they are offered at an introductory level though advice can usually be offered about where to pursue an interest to a higher level. Courses are usually part time or take place outside regular working hours but there is never enough time to sign up for the courses you fancy. The bad news is that government policy favours 14–19 education and education for employment, at the expense of adult education. As a result fees have risen sharply which has led to the cancellation of many courses.

Fiona Carroll felt she had been neglecting her own life in favour of her job as a project manager for a software company in Switzerland and decided finally to take a full year's break to spend time with her family in Ireland and also to take painting courses in Switzerland. She believes her old company would have kept the job open for her but she wanted a change to decrease the amount of time she spent at work and obtain a better balance between her job and her private life. '*I didn't want to travel. I just wanted to be.*' Remaining at home gave her the opportunity to pursue her love of art. She started taking lessons in painting near her home, which she is able to continue still by working a four-day week. She takes every Tuesday off which she describes as 'wonderful'.

BRIAN BLACKSHAW HAD BEEN VICAR OF CHESHUNT IN HERTFORDSHIRE FOR EIGHT YEARS, WORKING IN A VERY LARGE AND CHALLENGING PARISH, WHEN HE INVESTIGATED THE POSSIBILITY OF A SABBATICAL:

The Church of England is an employer that allows its hard-working staff to take occasional sabbaticals and Brian's application for a three-month sabbatical was accepted when he was aged about 60. Such sabbaticals are not uncommon in the Church though only after at least 10 years of service. In the past, when Church of England sabbaticals tended to be longer, recipients were expected to pursue formal studies or do some writing. But three months is too short a time for that and, although it is necessary to demonstrate that one's time off will be spent in something worthwhile, a degree of latitude is given for pursuing personal interests.

Brian had been studying Italian on and off and one of his ambitions was to deepen his knowledge of the Italian language and culture. He had visited Florence before and had been encouraged to return by a Polish friend who loved the city. Like almost everybody else, he began his search on the Internet and his Google search for the British Council led him to the British Institute of Florence (see Directory entry) whose programmes sounded ideal. So he rented an apartment in Florence and attended Intensive Italian language classes for four hours a day. On arrival he noticed that the Institute also had places on a Baroque and Mannerist art course so he enrolled in that as well. This involved a one-hour lecture a day with some eminent art historians, both British and Italian, and visits to the Uffizi Gallery and other Florentine galleries as well as to Rome. He considered the standard of teaching to be superb and describes his art course as a joy. He felt that this intensive and enlightened exposure to some of the most magnificent examples of Renaissance art allowed him to break into a circle of knowledge which he had long found intimidating and from which he had felt excluded. He feels that many people are deterred by a perception of how difficult something will be, but that given the right circumstances it is possible to prick the bubble and enter the charmed circle.

He enjoyed the company of the 15 or 20 other people on his courses although most were much younger, including several post A level students, some interested in pursuing art history at university, and a sprinkling of more mature people including a couple of Americans temporarily resident in Florence. He was delighted with the facilities at the British Institute and now feels that he could make it a base for any future sojourns in Florence.

Altogether Brian was off work for 14 weeks and three days and felt that he made good use of his time. In addition to his month in Italy, he joined two birdwatching trips, one to the Picos Mountains of northern Spain and the other to Speyside, visited friends in Switzerland and his eldest daughter in America. He also luxuriated in having enough leisure time to read an average of two books a week. But the highlight remained his time in Florence when he felt in some ways he rediscovered his humanity. In his busy parish, 180 funerals must be conducted a year plus hospitals and prisons visited and countless other duties fulfilled. With the Church of England financially stretched, the vicar's workload can be gruelling, and time off all the more necessary.

RECREATIONAL COURSES ABROAD

A gap year allows you to contemplate studying something that interests you in a foreign country, like African drumming, flamenco dancing or skiing. Specialist travel companies can arrange special interest courses. For example the Association of Independent Tour Operators or AITO (☎ 020 8744 9280; www.aito.co.uk) lists a number of upmarket tour operators that can arrange watercolour courses in Italy, wine appreciation in Chile, birdwatching in China, and so on.

The American counterpart is the Specialty Travel Index (305 San Anselmo Ave, San Anselmo, California 94960; www.specialtytravel.com) which is a useful source of information about 400 specialist tour operators. Its website is searchable by destination and activity or you can purchase the twice-yearly directory for $10 ($25 abroad). Cultural tours and special interest programmes tend to be fairly upmarket and it is usually much cheaper to sign up with a local organisation abroad, something which is becoming easier with the help of the Internet.

American journalist and author, **Alice Steinbach**, seems to have made something of a career as a career breaker. After leaving her high-powered job as a journalist in Baltimore to spend six months in Europe, recorded in the recommended book *Without Reservations*, she went on to further travels but in this case to sign up for courses that appealed to her. In her follow up book *Educating Alice*, she records her impressions and encounters while studying dog training in Scotland, writing in Prague, gardening in Provence, calligraphy and flower arranging in Kyoto, music in Cuba, cooking in Paris and Jane Austen in Exeter. Others will want to focus on one or two interests on a career break. For example, inveterate traveller **Dave Sands**, who for years ran the International Association of Air Travel Couriers in the UK (until changes in the international system of document delivery virtually eliminated the business) has along with his wife become fascinated with tango.

The tango gives us an additional opportunity to travel to interesting places. Since we started tango we have travelled to Switzerland, France, Italy and Croatia just to attend classes in tango. The Cuba trip if we go is entirely for tango instruction, while the trip to China is mainly for a week of tango classes in Shanghai, but we will also travel around China whilst we are there.

Tango enthusiasts might want to look at http://festivals.tango.info for a calendar of forthcoming tango events worldwide or the organisation which (bizarrely) combines tango with Zen Buddhism (www.tangozen.com/workshopsUpcoming_new_en.htm).

COOKERY COURSES

Cookery is an important hobby for many and a passion for a few. Pursuing an interest in food in a foreign country can be one of the most satisfying courses to build into a career break. Furthermore a catering certificate opens up many appealing employment options in ski resorts, private villas or private yachts for those who are looking for a change of direction. Thirty-something **Steve Gale** was working as an e-commerce manager when he decided to travel around the world and then turned his experiences into a cookery book, *The Gap Year Gourmet* (www.gapyeargourmet.com). According to Steve, '*Travelling gives you the time and space to reflect on what's important.*'

Private certificate and diploma courses are expensive, especially if you splash out on one of the household names such as Cordon Bleu or Tante Marie. Here is a selection of courses in the UK and Europe:

Ashburton Cookery School & Wine School – 76 East Street, Ashburton, Devon TQ13 7AX; ☎ 01364 652784; www.ashburtoncookeryschool.co.uk. From £135 for one-day course to about £2,499 for four-week Basic Cookery Diploma course.

Ballymaloe Cookery School – Shanagarry, Midelton, Co. Cork, Ireland; ☎ 21 46 46 785; www.cookingisfun.ie. Situated on organic farm by the coast with access to excellent ingredients. 12-week Certificate in Cookery course plus range of short courses. €9,195 for Certificate course excluding accommodation.

Cookery at the Grange – The Grange, Whatley, Frome, Somerset BA11 3JU; ☎ 01373 836579; www.cookeryatthegrange.co.uk. Four-week course costs £3,090–£3,690.

Le Cordon Bleu Culinary Institute – 114 Marylebone Lane, London W1V 2HH; ☎ 020 7935 3503; www.cordonbleu.net. Also branches in Paris and many other cities. 10-week course costs £4,580.

Edinburgh School of Food & Wine – The Coach House, Newliston, Edinburgh EH29 9EB; ☎ 0131 333 5001; www.esfw.com. Diploma and certificate courses last six months, three months, four months, two weeks, one week and one day.

Food of Course Cookery School – Middle Farm House, Sutton, Shepton Mallet, Somerset BA4 6QF; ☎ 01749 860116; www.foodofcourse.co.uk. Four-week Foundation Cookery Course (£2,950) among others.

Gables School of Cookery – Bristol Road, Falfield, Gloucestershire GL12 8DF; ☎ 01454 260444; www.thegablesschoolofcookery.com. Specialists in training chalet hosts and yacht cooks. £2,950 inclusive for four-week course.

Leiths School of Food and Wine – 16–20 Wendell Road, London W12 9RT; www.leiths.com. Basic Certificate course lasts four weeks full-time in September. Beginners' Certificate lasts 10 weeks (Oct–Dec).

The Murray School of Cookery – Glenbervie House, Holt Pound, Farnham, Surrey GU10 4LE; ☎ 01420 23049; www.cookeryschool.net. £1,600 for a four-week course.

The Orchards School of Cookery – The Orchards, Salford Priors, Nr Evesham, Worcestershire WR11 8UU; ☎ 01789 490259; www.orchardscookery.co.uk. Five days to two weeks, year round.

Rosie Davies – Penny's Mill, Nunney, Frome, Somerset BA11 4NP; ☎ 01373 836210; www.rosiedavies.co.uk. Four-week certificate course for £3,050 including shared accommodation.

Tante Marie School of Cookery – Woodham House, Carlton Road, Woking, Surrey GU21 4HF; ☎ 01483 726957; www.tantemarie.co.uk. UK's largest independent cookery school.

CREATIVE WRITING AND ARTS

The working world is full of aspiring writers of fiction, poetry, travel journalism, plays and so on. A career break allows the leisure to pursue this aspiration a little more seriously. A course in creative writing might provide a useful fillip in this direction. You can't learn to write well without practice and without bouncing your attempts off a critical audience. Evening classes are available in most centres of population.

The Arvon Foundation (42a Buckingham Palace Road, London SW1W 0RE; www.arvonfoundation. org) runs five-day writing residential creative writing courses at its several locations in rural Britain (West Yorkshire, Devon, Inverness-shire and Shropshire). Courses are open to anyone keen to try their hand at writing poetry, fiction, stage drama or TV and radio scripts. The course tutors are professional writers, some of whom are well known from newspapers and bookstands. The current cost is £499–£550 inclusive of accommodation, food and tuition. Grants are available to those who can't afford the full cost (see their website).

Other courses, some abroad, are advertised in the literary pages of the quality press. For example writing courses are offered in the Writers' Lab between May and September on the Greek island of Skyros at the holistic holiday centre mentioned below in the section on Retreats. Past courses have been tutored by extremely well-known authors such as Margaret Drabble and Sue Townsend, author of the Adrian Mole series.

The dream of becoming a published travel writer is one that is chased by some career breakers. Because so many people are now blogging about their travels, some of them extremely entertainingly, it is becoming even harder for publishers to find a market for that kind of thing in print form. The cheapest way to acquire some practical wisdom is to look at Lonely Planet's *Guide to Travel Writing* (£10.99). Two companies in London offer short courses in travel writing: Travellers' Tales (www.travellerstales.org) and Travel Writing Workshops (www.travelworkshops.co.uk) are both taught by working journalists and well-known writers. As well as teaching participants ways to focus their observations, these courses also cover the essential topic of how to sell your work. A three-day Travellers' Tales course in London costs £375 while their occasional courses held abroad in Marrakesh, Seville or Tuscany cost about £750 for a few days including accommodation. You will have to be prepared to expose your writing to group criticism. Not long ago, the Radio 4 travel programme *Excess Baggage* featured one of these travel writing courses in Marrakesh, attended by Tessa Mills who runs thegapyearguru.com If you can 'Listen Again' on the BBC website, you will hear her contribution applauded by her fellow students.

Travel inevitably inspires artists. To take one example of a special interest holiday, Art Safari based in Suffolk leads tutored painting holidays worldwide, suitable for artists of all standards and experience. Destinations include Namibia, Malawi, Kenya, Zambia, Antarctica and India. Although the majority of clients treat such a trip as a one-off special interest holiday, some join as part of longer travels, for instance if they are doing voluntary work in the destination country and want a break or if they are about to start travelling and want to start their journey learning a new skill which they can develop throughout the rest of their trip. The director Mary-Anne Bartlett says that she can also help her guests who want to stay on to do placements with creative industries in the country.

Music is another of the arts that might be rediscovered in a career break, whether singing, playing an instrument or even joining a band. In the USA, there is a growing trend for professional adults to join a residential summer camp that specialises in their interest. A searchable database can be found at www.grownupcamps.com. The *New York Times* drew this resource to its readers' attention under the headline 'Taking a Break from Life to Live the Fantasy' which includes interviews with stressed doctors and lawyers become utterly absorbed in playing jazz or perfecting their cello technique or whatever else, and therefore rejuvenated.

LEARNING A LANGUAGE

A gap year is an ideal opportunity to brush up on a barely remembered GCSE (or perhaps even O level) language or start from scratch with a new language. Most current and future employers will view this as a commendably constructive allocation of time, and anyone with competence in another language has an advantage in many job hunts. Many older people might have in the back of their minds the possibility of buying property abroad or even retiring permanently and therefore have a straightforward motive in mastering a language.

Knowledge of a foreign language connects you to another culture and makes friendships with local people possible. Increasingly, UK residents are buying second homes in France, Spain, Italy, etc. Since the opening of the Channel Tunnel there has been a psychological shift in the British attitude to the continent and much of the nation is falling in love with aspects of foreign cultures.

British professionals are often put to shame by the linguistic superiority of their counterparts on the continent and feel that they were poorly taught at school with too much emphasis placed on grammar and literature. Even with a GCSE and A level in a language, many Britons arrive in France, Germany or Italy still tongue-tied through lack of confidence and a serious linguistic deficiency.

LANGUAGE LEARNING IN THE UK

Britons are notoriously slow to learn foreign languages. Yet the spirit is willing if a recent statistic is true claiming that 7% of the UK population are studying a language at any one time. Evening language classes offered by local authorities usually follow the academic year and are aimed at hobby learners. Intensive courses offered privately are much more expensive.

After stepping down from the post of Director General of the CBI and before becoming the country's pensions guru, **Adair Turner** (now Lord Turner) spent many months writing a book about the future of capitalism from his home in London. But he also exploited the time he took away from formal employment to improve his meagre French, which he felt was a serious gap in his education. Each week a tutor would visit him at home to develop his conversational ability:

> *I suspect that most people 15 years after leaving full-time education are aware that there are some things that they could have done but the choices they made or the education they were given didn't develop that. In my case it was languages. I made the right choices in education except that I wasn't taught languages very well. I wanted to fill that in.*

If you are really dedicated, consider using a self-study programme with books and CDs, or a distance learning course online. However strong discipline is required to make progress. Although many people have been turning to the web to teach them a language, many conventional teach-yourself courses are still on the market, for example from OUP (www.askoxford.com/languages), Berlitz, the BBC (www.bbc. co.uk/languages), Linguaphone (☎ 0800 282417; www.linguaphone.co.uk) and Audioforum (www.audioforum.com). All of them offer deluxe courses with refinements such as interactive DVDs and of course these cost more. Linguaphone recommends half an hour of study a day for three months to master the basics of a language. **Polly Botsford**, a lawyer in her early 30s, thinks that learning the language is the key to understanding a foreign country because that is the only way to communicate with the people. Although she made some progress in learning Khmer after joining her volunteer project in Cambodia, she regrets that she didn't study the language more seriously before leaving home:

It is arrogant to arrive somewhere and expect to hear and speak only English. I read quite a few books and talked to a lot of people, which is part of the fun and the build-up. For me the low point in Cambodia was a constant sense of frustration that I could not properly understand people. Often I felt like a complete uncultured idiot for not conversing with people in their native tongue. It has been the bane of my life that I cannot traverse linguistic borders.

If you are interested in an obscure language and don't know where to study it, contact the National Centre for Languages (CILT, ☎ 020 7379 5101; www.cilt.org.uk) which has a certain amount of documentation on courses, especially in London.

Hold out a carrot to yourself of a trip to a country where your target language is spoken. Even if you don't make much headway with the course at home, download some material onto your iPod and take books with you since you will have more incentive to learn once you are immersed in a language.

USEFUL CONTACTS

Alliance Française – www.alliancefrancaise.org.uk. Sponsored by the French government, the Alliance manages 770 teaching centres worldwide including 13 in the UK. Sample cost – £255 for 30 hours of tuition over two weeks.

CILT (Centre for Information on Language Teaching) – 3rd Floor, 111 Westminster Bridge Road, London SE1 7HR; ☎ 020 7379 5101; info@cilt.org.uk. The government's national centre for languages.

Goethe-Institute – 50 Princes Gate, London SW7 2PH; ☎ 020 7596 4004; german@london.goethe.org; www.goethe.de. German language courses at all levels in institutes around the world. UK branches in London, Glasgow and Manchester.

Instituto Cervantes (Spanish Cultural Institute) – 102 Eaton Square, London SW1W 9AN; ☎ 020 7235 0353; www.cervantes.es. The non profit Instituto Cervantes is the largest worldwide Spanish teaching organisation, with headquarters in Madrid and a network of centres around the world including London and Manchester.

Italian Cultural Institute – 39 Belgrave Square, London SW1X 8NX; ☎ 020 7823 1887; www.icilondon.esteri.it/IIC_Londra.

LEARNING A LANGUAGE ABROAD

A more enjoyable and successful way of learning a language is by doing it on location. While studying French or German at secondary school, you usually have two hours of classes a week, which works out at about 80 hours a year. While doing an eight-week intensive course, you might have 240 hours, the equivalent of three years of school instruction plus you will be speaking the language outside the classroom, so progress is usually much quicker. To give a very rough idea of the cost, a typical intensive French language course in a major European city might charge from €2,000 for eight weeks of 20 lessons per week; accommodation charges would be in addition to this.

Numerous British and international agencies represent a range of language schools abroad offering in-country language courses. The agents are very familiar with differences between schools, qualifications, locations, etc and what is most suitable for clients. CESA Languages Abroad, Caledonia, Cactus Language and Language Courses Abroad (see Directory entries), among some others listed below, all have wide-ranging programmes abroad in Europe and beyond. These agencies also provide a useful back-up service if the course does not fulfil your requirements in any way.

In her late middle years **Pamela Tincknell** began to toy with the idea of spending more time in Spain. Like so many others, Pamela has always hated the dark and gloomy British winter and fancied the idea of the Costa del Sol. She had been taking the regulation holidays in Spain since the 1960s and had dabbled in beginner Spanish evening classes but decided that the time had come to extend her linguistic aspirations. A chronic hoarder, Pamela fished out a cutting from a Sunday supplement she had squirreled away as many as 20 years earlier which was about language courses abroad. To her surprise she found that the company featured, CESA (see Directory entry), was still going strong and so she requested their brochure.

She knew that she wanted to be on the coast rather than inland and chose the civilised resort town of Nerja. She joined a fortnight-long course at the Escuela de Idiomas Nerja (www.idnerja. es) designed for the over-50s, consisting of three hours of language tuition a day plus plenty of excursions. That experience hooked her and she began to consider spending an entire year learning Spanish. She is thoroughly convinced that going off-season was a good move, not only because of the lovely weather but because the winter attracts older people, including what Pamela calls 'lifers'. Pamela recommends a small resort for an initial language course but now feels that she has outgrown living near an expat enclave and has grown tired of waiters who reply in English to questions in Spanish.

David Storey is another satisfied CESA customer. Because his job as a long-distance lorry driver takes him frequently to France, he wanted to improve his French, so signed up for a three-month course in Bordeaux last September:

I obviously improved my French but also I found the whole experience of meeting new people and noting the cultural differences to be very rewarding. I had taken up the course out of a desire to improve my French, which since A level had not been practised and just barely remembered. In my work for an international freight company I had travelled extensively throughout Europe working with many colleagues for whom English was not their first language. As I was reliant on people speaking my language I began to regret my inability to speak a second language myself so I decided to pick up again with my long-neglected French.

I found that many of the French people I met were very welcoming and friendly and were generally impressed that I was trying to speak their language. Whilst in Bordeaux I played at two small squash clubs and was welcomed, which was a great opportunity to chat and mingle. Also there was some good dressing room banter on the subject of football and I found myself on more than one occasion having to defend the football merits of Peter Crouch. I recommend going to watch the local football team in Bordeaux as well. The Saturday evening kick-off times really foster a family atmosphere.

I stayed in the home of a local man and found the experience to be delightful and informative in itself. For one thing his apartment was very near the school in a very beautiful part of the Centreville and he even invited me to spend time at his coastal home at Lacanau, which is a surfers' paradise, and in winter a wonderfully peaceful retreat from the madness of the city. It was a great introduction to the French 'esprit', as he would share his philosophies and outlook on life. As for Bordeaux, it's a fantastic city, with the Centreville being just the right size to retain a friendly and intimate atmosphere. I certainly plan to go back there next winter and settle a few squash match grudges.

It isn't necessary to book a language course via a mediating agency as **Annabel Iglehart** from Edinburgh discovered in her gap year after university when she signed up with a major Spanish language school with many branches:

After working in a variety of jobs at home, I went to Salamanca to do a three-month intensive Spanish language course with Mester. I planned and paid for my course and accommodation directly through Mester and this saved me a lot of money; it was by far the most economical way to organise the trip. The course was fantastic. The classes were fast-paced and the teachers excellent. I lived with a Spanish family for a while and then moved to a flat with other students. I met loads of people with whom I am still in touch.

Literally thousands of language schools around the world would like your business, so care needs to be taken in choosing one that suits individual needs. Possible sources of language school addresses on the web are www.languageschoolsguide.com (part of www.goabroad.com) and www.language-schools-directory.com. After considering obvious factors such as price and location when choosing a language school, also try to find out the average age and likely nationalities of your fellow learners, how experienced and qualified the staff are, whether there will be any one to-one tuition and whether the course concentrates on oral or written skills, whether extracurricular activities and excursions are included in the fee, and generally as much as you can. One key factor is whether or not a school prepares its students for exams. If they do and you are there only for the fun of it, you may find that lessons are not suitable. Yolande Blanchette from Canada was very pleased with the German course she did with Horizonte (affiliated to IALC in the *Directory*) located in the southern German city of Regensburg:

(translated from the French original)

The activities programme was interesting and relevant to the course, and was suitable for all age groups. I felt easily integrated despite the difference in age   Usually, when my courses in a school come to an end, I feel delighted, but not this time. In fact I regret not having registered for a full three months. The language courses I do abroad always have two objectives: to learn the language and to visit the country. I wanted to spend long enough to feel comfortable.

Whereas some language schools run purely recreational courses, others offer some kind of qualification. Some schools are instantly recognised such as the Alliance Française and the Goethe-Institut. At the other end of the spectrum, some schools offer nothing more than a certificate outlining the period of study and perhaps the level of language reached or work covered in the course, which may be of limited value if you ever need to show proof of language attainment.

However, the majority of adult learners are there not to gain a diploma but to have fun and learn more about a foreign culture to which they have been attracted. Recreational language courses are offered by virtually every school. Some programmes are more structured than others, so students need to look for flexible courses which allow them to progress at their own rate.

A recent innovation is language lessons on the street; instead of simulating a shopping situation in the classroom, instructors take their clients to the shops so that the language can be used in real situations. For instance Español Andando in Buenos Aires (www.espanol-andando.com.ar) offers Spanish tuition in this 'fun, budget and different way'.

Many people agree that the fastest way to improve fluency is to have one-to-one lessons, though of course these are more expensive than group classes. Usually a combination of the two works best.

RETIREMENT CAN PROVIDE THE PERFECT CATALYST FOR PLANNING NEW LANGUAGE LEARNING DEPARTURES, AS WAS THE CASE FOR ED MCFADD FROM SOUTHERN CALIFORNIA:

Retirement was to be a new adventure. In preparation for a vacation we had taken in France a couple of years previously, I had bought some language learning tapes, which I listened to on my suburban commute. Turned out I rather enjoyed my re-acquaintance with the language after three and a half decades. Even though I retained only a few rudimentary lessons from back then, the attraction was still there.

A highlight of my studies has been a three-week sojourn at a private language school in Montreal. I chose the winter in part because it was less expensive and also because I enjoy the change in seasons. Further, I stayed in a host family setting which was a treasured experience and I continue to correspond with the host as well as some other students from the school.

Studying with the younger generation as well as a few more mature students, walking about one of North America's premier cities in mid-winter, making new friends and learning to speak French all combined to reaffirm my decision to stick with this hobby.

Staying with a host family is obviously much better for language progress. Another possibility is to forgo structured lessons and simply live with a family. Several agencies arrange paying guest stays which are designed for people wishing to learn or improve language skills in the context of family life. Try En Famille Overseas (La Maison Jaune, avenue du Stade, 34210 Siran, France; ☎ +33 4 68 91 49 90; or in UK ☎ 01206 546741; www.enfamilleoverseas. co.uk) which specialises in France but also arranges homestays with or without language tuition in Germany, Italy and Spain. EIL, a non-profit cultural and educational organisation, offers short-term language exchange homestay programmes in a range of countries (287 Worcester Road, Malvern, Worcestershire WR14 1AB; ☎ 0800 018 4015; ☎ 01684 562577; www. eiluk.org). Of course you may prefer the most informal route of all, which is simply to use a phrasebook and interact with the locals. Round-the-world travellers **Stefan and Vanessa Aalten-Voogd** always made an effort but with varying degrees of success:

Stefan had grown up in a multi-lingual environment in Brussels and with his natural interest in languages and ability to pick them up, he rapidly outstripped my attempts to learn Spanish before we left. A few words in the local language, no matter how poorly executed, were always well received and often opened up the chance to make contact with local people rather than just other tourists. With English spoken widely in all but the most rural areas, our fudged linguistic attempts definitely gave us a richer experience than those who did not make the effort. Sign language, facial expressions, a bit of acting and a handy little book with pictures of everything from a chicken to a clothes peg created entertainment as well as aiding conversation.

Several years ago 30-something **Mike Bleazard** and his partner **Jane** took six months off to travel around the world. They were especially looking forward to the last leg of their travels since South America was the first completely non-English speaking region they visited. In preparation they had bought some 'Learn Spanish in no time at all' tapes and struggled through the first 90 minutes of lessons in six weeks. Once they landed of course they noticed a decided improvement, if only in motivation:

After seven weeks in Chile, we can now order a beer, a bus ticket and ask for a double room with private bathroom – fluently. We still can't understand a word that anyone says back to us. So we've taken to just nodding sagely and saying 'si' when anyone replies – which has got us into all kinds of trouble.

USEFUL CONTACTS FOR LEARNING A LANGUAGE ABROAD

The following companies represent language schools worldwide. Note that other key players (CESA, Caledonia, Cactus, IALC and Language Courses Abroad) all have more detailed entries in Part 5, *Directory of Specialist Programmes.*

Amerispan – PO Box 58129, Philadelphia, PA 19102, USA; ☎ +1 800 879 6640; ☎ 215 751 1100; www.amerispan.com. Specialist Spanish-language travel organisation with expertise in arranging language courses, voluntary placements and internships throughout South and Central America. Now offers 10 languages worldwide.

Don Quijote – 2–4 Stoneleigh Park Road, Epsom, Surrey KT19 0QT; ☎ 020 8786 8081; www. donquijote.org. Spanish specialist with courses in Spain (including Tenerife) and Latin America. £2,000+ for 12 weeks including student flat accommodation.

EF International Language Schools Emperors Gate, 114A Cromwell Road, London, SW7 4FS; ☎ 020 7341 8777; www.ef.com. Foreign language courses at privately owned and EF schools in France, Germany, Italy, Spain, Ecuador, China and Costa Rica.

Eurointerns – Gaztambide, 26, 2° – B, 28015 Madrid, Spain; ☎ 34 667 838 136; www.eurointerns.com. finds internships for about 100 candidates (average age 25) in Spanish, Belgian and Italian firms for practical language enhancement and work experience. Basic internship placement lasting two–six months costs £725.

Gap Year for Grown-ups – 1 Meadow Road, Tunbridge Wells TN1 2YG; ☎ 01892 701881; www. gapyearforgrownups.co.uk/Learn-a-Language. Spanish or Portuguese language courses integrated with volunteer placements in Latin America.

IALC (International Association of Language Centres) – Lombard House, 12/17 Upper Bridge Street, Canterbury, Kent CT1 2NF; ☎ 01227 769007; www.ialc.org. Language school association with more than 90 accredited members in 22 countries.

Journey Latin America – 12–13 Heathfield Terrace, Chiswick, London W4 4JE; ☎ 020 8747 3108; www.JourneyLatinAmerica.co.uk. Specialist travel agency and tour operator arranges Spanish and Portuguese courses throughout South and Central America. All programmes offer the opportunity to stay with a family. Prices range from £209 for one week in Antigua (Guatemala) to £915 for four weeks in Salvador (Brazil).

Lanacos – 64 London Road, Dunton Green, Sevenoaks, Kent TN13 2UG; ☎ 01732 462309; www.lanacos.com. Language agency run by linguists, offering courses in 200 destinations. From about £400 for a fortnight in Granada to £2,500 for 12 weeks in Paris.

OISE Intensive Language Schools – Binsey Lane, Oxford OX2 0EY; ☎ 01865 258333; info@oise.com/www.oise.com. Primarily an English language teaching organisation, OISE offers small class tuition of French in Paris, German in Heidelberg and Spanish in Madrid.

S.I.B.S. Ltd – Beech House, Commercial Road, Uffculme, Devon EX15 3EB; ☎ 01884 841330; www.sibs.co.uk. Language consultancy which arranges language courses abroad for clients.

Twin World Languages – 67–71 Lewisham High Street, London SE13 5JX; ☎ 0800 80 483 80; worldlanguages@twinuk.com; www.twinworldlanguages.com. French, Italian, German, Portuguese, Spanish, Russian, Chinese and Japanese.

Vis-à-vis – 2–4 Stoneleigh Park Road, Epsom KT19 0QT; ☎ 020 8786 8021; www. visavis.org. French courses for all levels at schools in France, Belgium and Canada.

LANGUAGE COURSES FOR NORTH AMERICANS

At a time when broad-minded Americans may find themselves wanting to try to dispel accusations of insularity and supremacy, going abroad in a gap year to learn or improve a foreign language may have special appeal. Programmes that combine structured study of a language or culture with volunteering are arguably a paradigm of the kind of foreign travel experience that can more than justify taking time out from work. Many organisations both international and local can arrange such placements, often in conjunction with a homestay to maximise exposure to the language. One of the cheapest options for Americans who want to study French is to head for Québec in Canada, for instance Language Studies Canada in Montréal (www.lsc-canada.com), the choice of Ed McFadd mentioned above.

As in the UK, agents in the USA and Canada make it easier for North Americans to find and book a suitable language course. An effective search engine for locating courses is provided by the Institute of International Education (www.iiepassport.org) which makes it easy to search by country and programme. Other recommended websites are: www.worldwide.edu, www.languagesabroad.com and www.studyabroad.com.

Here are some language course providers and agents of possible interest to North American grown-ups planning to spend time abroad learning a language.

Bridge-Linguatec – see entry in *Teaching English* chapter.

Center for Cultural Interchange – 746 N. LaSalle Drive, Chicago, IL 60610; ☎ +1 866 684 9675; www.cci-exchange.com. Language courses in Ecuador, France, Germany, Mexico, Italy and Spain. Independent homestay programme in 20 countries. High school semester or year abroad in Australia, France, Germany, Ireland, the Netherlands and South Africa.

Cultural Experiences Abroad – 1400 E Southern Ave, Suite B-108, Tempe, AZ 85282; ☎ +1 800 266 4441; info@gowithcea.com; www.gowithcea.com. Study abroad programmes for college students. Language courses (beginners to advanced) offered through European universities.

Eduvacations – 1431 21st St NW, Ste. 302, Washington, DC 20036–6930; ☎ +1 202 857 8384; info@eduvacations.com; www.eduvacations.com. Travel company specialising in customised language courses combined with sports, art instruction, etc. throughout Europe, Latin America, the Caribbean, Russia, the USA, etc.

Language Liaison – PO Box 1772, Pacific Palisades, CA 90272; ☎ +1800 284 4448; info@languageliaison.com/; www.languageliaison.com. Total immersion language/culture study programmes and leisure learning courses.

Language Link – PO Box 3006, Peoria, IL 61612 3006; ☎ +1 800 552 2051; info@langlink.com; www.langlink.com. Long-established agency (Director Kay Rafool) which represents dozens of language schools in Spain and Latin America.

Lingua Service Worldwide – 5 Prospect Street, Suite 4, Huntingdon, NY 11743; ☎ +1 800 394 5327; www.linguaserviceworldwide.com. Represents range of private language schools at all levels.

National Registration Center for Study Abroad – PO Box 1393, Milwaukee, Wisconsin 53201; ☎ +1 414 278 0631; info@nrcsa.com; www.nrsca.com. Full language and culture immersion and other courses offered at 125 language schools and universities in 43 countries.

Talking Traveler – 620 SW 5th Ave, Suite 625, Portland, OR 97204; ☎ +1 503 274 1776; ☎ +1 800 274 6007; info@talkingtraveler.org; www.talkingtraveler.org. Full immersion language and culture courses for adults worldwide. Links with schools in various Italian, Spanish, French, German, Mexican and Costa Rican cities.

We Study Abroad – 23786 Villena, Mission Veijo, CA 92692; ☎ +1 949 916 1096; travelstudy@yahoo.com; www.westu dyabroad.com. Travel Study Programmes in Spanish, French, Italian and English. Internships, jobs and volunteer projects can sometimes be provided.

SPORT AND LEADERSHIP COURSES

Few better ways exist of shaking out the cobwebs than to learn to sail, climb or lead trekkers during a gap year later in life. It is often difficult to master a sport or make significant improvements if you can only dabble in it during your free time and brief holidays. Concentrating over an extended period may allow you to gain useful qualifications for future use, such as a PADI diving certificate, a Yachtmaster sailing qualification or a Mountain Leadership course. Longer courses leading to a National Vocational Qualification (NVQ) are available in adventure tourism and expedition leadership which might be of interest if you are considering changing professional direction.

If you would like to do a sports course with a view to working abroad, you might be interested in courses offered by Flying Fish (www.flyingfishonline.com; see Directory entry) or one of the other training specialists. A gap year with Flying Fish starts with a course leading to a qualification as a sail, surf or windsurf instructor, yacht skipper, divemaster or dive instructor, ski or snowboard instructor, or even as galley chefs. A typical three-month course involves three or four weeks of sports training in Cowes on the Isle of Wight, followed by a work experience placement (eight weeks on average) in the UK, Australia or Greece. Trainees can seek advice from a Flying Fish careers adviser to find paid work too. The topic of sailing including crewing on yachts is covered in Part 7 *Travel and Adventure*.

SAIL AND DIVE TRAINING

Several training organisations specialise in preparing people for undertaking some serious sailing or watersports. For example one of the longest established recognised centres is Plas Menai National Watersports Centre in North Wales (between Snowdonia and the sea). As well as offering courses in sailing, kayaking and mountain sports at all levels, it also runs a fast track instructor training programme which would suit career breakers who are attracted by the worldwide employment opportunities for qualified yacht skippers and outdoor instructors. Plas Menai offers an 18-week Professional Yachtmaster course as well as 12- and 18-week dinghy, windsurfing, kayaking and mountain instructor courses. The RYA Yachtmaster qualifies you to charter a yacht from almost anywhere in the world or enter the yachting industry.

Another leader in the field is the UK Sailing Academy whose range of watersports courses extends to three and four months and which offers an on-site careers service used by more than 700 companies looking to recruit instructors. UKSA is also mentioned in Part 7 Travel and Adventure; course details are available from UKSA (West Cowes, Isle of Wight PO31 7PQ; ☎ 01983 294941; www.uksa.org). In fact, the marinas in Cowes are a good place to head if you are interested in sail training. See also Global Yacht Training (☎ 0845 634 1457; www.globalyachttraining.com) which offers tailored programmes lasting between five and 14 weeks, ocean expeditions and careers placement.

If you would like to do a watersports course abroad, see the entries for Flying Fish, Nonstop Adventure and the International Academy in the *Directory*.

Diving in an exotic location is another option that may appeal. Check www.divesitedirectory.co.uk for links to diving sites worldwide. A random sampling of possibilities includes:

Dive Indeep Co. Ltd – 162/8 Chaweng Beach Road, Koh Samui, Suratthani 84320, Thailand; ☎ +66 772 30155; www.diveindeep.com. PADI Scuba Diving Courses from beginner through Dive Master.

EcoSea Dive & Adventure Cambodia – Ekareach Street, Town Center, Sihanoukville, Cambodia; ☎ +855 12 654 104; www.ecosea.com. PADI Divemaster training.

Greenforce – 11–15 Betterton Street, Covent Garden, London WC2H 9BP; ☎ 020 7470 8888; www.greenforce.org/destinations/thailand. Learn-to-dive programmes in Gozo (Malta), the Red Sea and Thailand. Instructor programme for non-divers in Thailand costs £5,950 including accommodation for six months, and possibility of paid jobs in Fiji or the Bahamas at the end.

PJ Scuba – Mermaids Group, 75/124 Moo 12, Jomtien Beach Road Nongprue, Banglamung, Chonburi 20260, Thailand; www.learn-in-asia.com. Internship programme Learn in Asia Dive Internships Co. Ltd

Rich Coast Diving – Playas del Coco, Costa Rica; www.richcoastdiving.com. Dive training at all levels on the Pacific coast.

Scuba World Philippines – www.scubaworld.com.ph. Dive centres throughout the Philippines with scuba career training programmes.

Subway Watersports – Turquoise Bay Resort, Palmetto Bay Plantation and Barefoot Cay Re-sort, Roatan, Bay Islands, Honduras, Central America; www.subwaywatersports.com/Courses/internship.htm. Internship working in a dive shop while training towards a professional PADI Divemaster. Cost approximately $1,100 for four weeks; $1,550 for six weeks; $1,900 for eight weeks.

Ticket to Ride Ltd – ☎ 020 8788 8668, www.ttride.co.uk. Teams of 20 learn to surf along the coast of South Africa. Nine-week trip costs from £4,995.

Many dive shops operate an internship programme whereby dive trainees received subsidised or free accommodation and/or instruction in exchange for general help in the shop, filling tanks and so on. This is an excellent scheme for people who have obtained their PADI Open Water Certificate (which can be done in a week) and are aiming for the Divemaster qualification. **Holon Tirobuck** took advantage of such a scheme at one of the dive shops in Playas del Coco on the west coast of Costa Rica, at the end of 2007:

> *Leaving a good, secure, office job in the UK for a vague plan of becoming a dive master in Costa Rica certainly raised some eyebrows! I was determined to go to a Spanish-speaking country and wanted somewhere hot! I first started diving in 1998 but was basically a once-a-year holiday diver. I already had my qualification as an advanced open water diver but needed to gain my rescue qualification which I did within two weeks of arriving, then started my internship to get my Divemaster straight afterwards. The deal is I work for free for them for three months and in exchange I receive training and a scuba diving qualification which will allow me to work guiding scuba dives and assisting in courses.*

SNOW SPORTS

A surprising number of UK companies specialise in running intensive courses for aspiring ski and snowboard instructors, many of them for pre- and post-university gap year students. As in the case of many of the gap year agencies, some have recently started to target older clients; for example the Basecamp Group offers a course geared towards 'sabbatical' clients which is going strong and attracts dozens of career-break clients, mostly from the IT, financial, legal and medical professions. Nonstop Ski & Snowboard markets to career breakers more than the gap year market and claims that half of their clients are on sabbatical breaks or looking for a career change or time out.

Among the other companies listed in the Directory offering snow sports training for recreation or for qualifications, see Flying Fish, Global Sports Xperience, The International Academy, Peak Leaders and the

Warren Smith Ski Academy. As for the British Associaion of Snowsport Instructors or BASI; (Glenmore, Aviemore, Inverness-shire PH22 1QU (☎ 01479 861717; www.basi.org.uk). BASI runs training and grading courses throughout the year in alpine skiing, snowboarding, Telemark, Nordic and Adaptive. The most junior instructor's qualification is a Level 1 which is awarded by BASI after a five-day foundation course. Courses take place throughout the season and also on glaciers in the Alps in the summer.

At aged 34, **Wayne Beba** thought he was a bit young for a mid-life crisis but knew that he needed a new challenge:

> *After researching various companies NONSTOP came out as a clear winner for me, particularly as they were happy to accommodate my wife as well and they were the only one using all three Banff ski areas. As well as making great new friends, I gained my CSIA level 1 and 2 qualifications. Highlights were the snowmobiling trips and the many other extra activities enjoyed. Thanks to the course I'm now back in Banff working as an instructor.*

Meanwhile, Peakleaders also attracts older clients, one of whom was interviewed on You tube (linked from www.peakleaders.com/canadawhistlerskiandsnowboardcourse.asp and uploaded May 2008). **Dianne Freer** had worked in the insurance and re-insurance industry for 25 years and decided to take six months off, the first three months of which were with Peakleaders in the Canadian resort of Whistler. She chose Whistler because it is consistently ranked top 10 ski resort in the world, and after comparing hours of instruction, standard of accommodation, etc, she chose Peakleaders (at her age she definitely wanted her own room). The instruction in teaching skills as well as practical skiing skills was superb and her skiing improved 10-fold.

ADVENTURE TRAINING

Experience or training in adventure sports can open many doors. Even if a career change is not on the agenda, leadership training can be put to good use during vacation time. The website www.blue-dome.co.uk has information about useful outdoor qualifications including the Walking Group Leader and Mountain Leader Awards as overseen by Mountain Leader Training (www.mlte.org). A new all-round adventure instructor course lasting six weeks has been developed by Mountain Water Experience, Courtlands, Nr Kingsbridge, South Devon TQ7 4BN; ☎ 01548 550675; www.mountainwaterexperience.co.uk, which costs £2,000.

World Challenge Expeditions – Black Arrow House, 2 Chandos Road, London NW10 6NF; ☎ 08704 873 173; leaderinfo@world-challenge.co.uk. This long established schools expedition company takes on more than 400 overseas expedition leaders for at least a month of the summer to lead groups of young people to places like Bolivia, Zambia and Borneo. Leaders, who must be over 24 and have the MLTE (Mountain Leader Training) have their expenses covered for the duration of the expedition. Training courses are organised through WCE's Leadership and Development Centre in the Peaks (Manchester Road, Buxton, Derbyshire SK17 6ST; ☎ 01298 767900).

Opportunities exist closer to home as well. For example PGL Travel (www.pgl.co.uk/recruitment) offers training and work opportunities to people who want to work in the outdoors either in Spain or France especially as kayak, canoeing and sailing instructors; kayak and canoeing work (but not sailing) also available in the UK. The long-established charity HF Holidays (www.hfholidays.co.uk/leadersinfo) owns 17 country house hotels in scenic locations around the British Isles where guests enjoy a walking and social programme. Voluntary walks leaders are chosen after assessment courses held in the spring; call 01768 899988 in Cumbria for details.

PART 10

SPIRITUAL DEVELOPMENT

INTRODUCTION

Stress may not kill you, but it can stifle your inner life and shorten your actual life. Unfortunately, modern lifestyles don't allow much time for harmonising our minds and bodies or listening to our inner voices. The usual remedy of a relaxing holiday in the sun is often insufficient to recharge the batteries for the increasing strains to which people in full-time employment are constantly subjected.

Small wonder then, that there is a growing trend among people to take time out from their careers to 'find themselves'. Some prefer to be guided in the ways of self-improvement while others just seek the opportunity for the time and space to do their own thing. The growing demand for soul therapy, spiritual growth, personal development, or whatever you want to call it, has created a bewildering variety of options for the path to *nirvana*. As a measure of the rising demand, an increasing number of commercial travel companies are offering alternative holidays and spiritual enlightenment packages. The possibilities given here are intended to represent the more traditional and less commercialised possibilities, many of which you can arrange independently.

WHAT IS A RETREAT?

The main point about a retreat is that it springs from a conscious decision to step out of your normal daily life, away from ego and daily responsibilities to go on an inner spiritual journey. This does not necessarily mean having spiritual experiences (though many people do), but it is about refreshing yourself, re-ordering your priorities and making contact with your deeper self. It might be worth quoting here an iconoclastic view of retreats as expressed by *The Times* journalist Matthew Parris:

> *A vicar who came to stay told me he was shortly to go on a 'retreat'. I suggested he try an 'advance'. Why do people go on retreats? What is there to retreat from? Many of one's friends would benefit more from a rocket under them than from moping dreamily around in a meditation centre for a week.*

WHAT KINDS OF RETREAT ARE THERE?

The range of options that might once have been limited to convents, monasteries or *ashrams* is now much wider and can take you as near or as far from home as you wish. Retreats can involve anything from Buddhism to gardening and from communing with nature to timetabled lectures and seminars in a French convent or American religious foundation.

Many people's idea of a retreat is probably one where you stay in a convent or monastery for a period of reflection and meditation. This has long been practised by Christians, especially Roman Catholics, as well as Buddhists and other religious groups. But you don't have to be a devout adherent of the particular religion to take part. Ignatian retreats, based on the spiritual exercises of the founder of the Jesuits, can last 30 days (though shorter durations are also common). These are directed retreats on a one-to-one basis during which passages from the Gospels are chosen for daily contemplation and discussion. Seekers are led to review their life in the light of the Gospels. Despite their religious origins, Ignatian spiritual retreats are available to anyone, religious or not. For further information contact The Retreat Association (address below).

Among the best known Christian retreat communities in the UK are Ampleforth Abbey, home to Benedictine monks (www.ampleforth-hpo.org.uk), the Iona Community mentioned below and Mirfield, an Anglican monastic community in West Yorkshire (www.mirfield.org.uk). In France, the Taizé Community (www.taize.fr/en) invites adults over 30 and families with children to make Sunday-to-Sunday visits between March and October. Visitors may camp or stay in Taizé accommodation (€12–€25 a day) and participate in the three services a day plus Bible study.

Short retreats can be arranged in countless places. To take just one example L'Ermitage Sainte Thérèse is a convent in Lisieux, France, where a full board stay of five days and return coach travel from London costs £235. Mass is said daily and the teachings of St Theresa form the focus of the retreat. For details contact Tangney Tours (see below).

SECULAR RETREATS

A retreat does not have to be bound to the belief system of a particular religion such as Buddhism or Catholicism; it can be totally secular as in mind-body-spirit retreats which deal with awareness and self-discovery. A considerable revival of interest in Celtic spirituality has taken place in recent years. Celtic retreats tend to focus on a sense of God present everywhere in the natural world.

BUDDHIST CENTRES

Buddhism has wide appeal to Westerners and many Buddhist centres in Europe welcome individuals interested in learning the fundamentals. The Throssel Hole Buddhist Abbey in Northumberland offers introductory weekend retreats as well as longer guided Zen retreats. Guests make a voluntary contribution towards their keep which includes vegetarian meals. The association Buddhafield organises camping retreats in beautiful locations that cost £185 for a week.

Other Buddhist centres in the UK that welcome guests include the Losang Dragpa Buddhist Centre in West Yorkshire where the maximum stay is one week (two weeks for non-UK residents), the Madhyamaka Centre also in Yorkshire which accepts visitors for a week or longer, and the Manjushri Mahayana Buddist Centre in Cumbria with no limit on length of stay.

Sunnier climes can be even more life-enhancing and the Guhyaloka Buddhist Centre in the mountains near Alicante in Spain is a peaceful place for a break. This full-time community dedicated to study, meditation and work welcomes male visitors who want to spend a summer or winter retreat. Guests choose between a solitary retreat in one of the small chalets dotted around the nearby valley or a working retreat.

With the dramatic rise in tourism to Thailand, Sri Lanka and other Buddhist countries over the past decade, more and more Buddhist centres welcome Western seekers for short or longer stays. Some offer very challenging experiences such as the Vipassana meditation courses offered worldwide and especially throughout India. Followers follow a strict regimen of silence and focus on nothing but the physical sensations of remaining still. For a vivid and at times hilarious account of a Westerner who subjects herself to this discipline for 10 days, see Sarah Macdonald's book *Holy Cow: An Indian Adventure*.

ASHRAMS

The trend for foreigners to stay in ashrams or Gandhian communities in India and Nepal has continued ever since the Beatles made it fashionable in the 1960s. Ashrams offer teaching in *hatha* yoga, mantra, meditation, study of the scriptures or a combination. Ashrams vary greatly: rich and poor, modern and urbanised, humble and rustic. A few are even located in caves. Each ashram has a guru (leader) or ashram-in-charge whose personal style is crucial in determining the atmosphere of the ashram and whether or not you will find it sympathetic. Some have a fixed price for a stay; others request donations.

YOGA

Yoga can give you a whole new outlook on life as it works equally on the mind, body and spirit. Although many people use yoga simply as a way of staying fit instead of reaping its metaphysical benefits, others get interested in the spiritual aspect and want to explore more deeply. The obvious answer is to take a career break and book a place on a spiritual retreat at an ashram in India. Others get interested after they have travelled in a country where it is practised. Since discovering Sri Lanka on a turtle conservation project, **Sarah Spiller** became very interested in Buddhism and yoga. Practising both in Sri Lanka and London, she (almost) mastered standing on her head and will have plenty of opportunities to develop her practice since she has bought a holiday house in Sri Lanka.

Yoga teacher Ruth White of the Ruth White Yoga Centre in London has been running an annual yoga retreat (one to three weeks) in spring on the Aegean island of Lesbos for many years. The syllabus is validated by the yoga governing body in the UK, the British Wheel of Yoga.

HOW MUCH DOES IT COST?

The price of spiritual therapy can be very reasonable, but then a monastery or convent offers no frills or distractions. A typical charge for a week's full board is £200–£250. Commercially organised alternative holidays start at around £350 per week. Some organisations, particularly Buddhist ones, make no specified charge at all, but expect a voluntary contribution and help with the domestic chores. The time you can spend in such an arrangement should be negotiated with individual establishments. If you stay for several weeks and work for your keep you will still usually be expected to make a token contribution of, say, £30–£50 per week.

COMMUNITIES

Many communities (previously referred to as communes) welcome foreign visitors who share their values. Sometimes a small charge is made for a short stay or the opportunity given to work in exchange for hospitality. The details and possible fees must be established on a case-by-case basis.

Rob Abblett from Leicester is someone who has taken dozens of breaks on communities around the world:

> *I've visited, worked and had many varied experiences on over 30 communes around the world. I like them because they are so varied and full of interesting people, usually with alternative ideas, beliefs, but also because I almost always find someone that I can really connect with, for sometimes I need to be with like-minded folk.*

Before arranging a longish stay in a community, consider whether or not you will find such an environment congenial. Some are very radical or esoteric in their practices so find out as much as you can before planning to stay for any period of time. Most communards are non-smoking vegetarians and living conditions may be primitive by some people's standards.

Shorter stays in more distant places can be readily arranged. Many communities are engaged in special projects which may coincide with your interests. For example the long-established Corrymeela Community in County Antrim (www.corrymeela.org) works for reconciliation between Protestants and Catholics in Northern Ireland.

Many well-known communes in the world welcome visitors. For example Stifelsen Stjärnsund is located among the forests, lakes and hills of central Sweden. Founded in 1984, the community aims to encourage personal, social and spiritual development in an ecologically sustainable environment. It operates an international working guest programme throughout the year, but is at its busiest between May and September when most of the community's courses are offered. Carpenters, builders, trained gardeners and cooks are especially welcome. First time working guests pay SEK500 (about £42) for their first week of work and if the arrangement suits both sides it can be continued with a negotiable contribution according to hours worked and length of stay. Enquiries should be made well in advance of a proposed summer visit.

In Denmark the Svanholm Community consists of 120 people including lots of children. Numbers are swelled in the summer when more volunteers (EU nationals only) arrive to help with the harvest of the organic produce. Guests work 30–40 hours a week for food, lodging and (if no other income is available) pocket money.

One of the most famous utopian communities is Auroville near Pondicherry in the south Indian state of Tamil Nadu, whose ambition is nothing less than 'to realise human unity'. Unfortunately it became the subject of allegations of child abuse in 2008, which the community claims are unfounded. Volunteers participate in a variety of activities to reclaim land and produce food and are charged anything from $5 to $20+ a day for board and lodging according to their contribution.

USEFUL CONTACTS AND RESOURCES

Auroville Volunteering, Internships & Study (AVIS) Programme – Unity Pavilion, International Zone, Auroville 605101, Tamil Nadu, India; unity@auroville.org.in; www.auroville.org.

Communities – 138 Twin Oaks Road, Louisa, VA 23093, USA; ☎ +1 540 894 5798; http://directory.ic.org. Publish *Communities Directory: A Guide to Co-operative Living* (2007, US$30). It lists about 1,250 communities in the US and a few abroad including 'eco-villages, rural land trusts, co-housing groups, kibbutzim, student co-ops, organic farms, monasteries, urban artist collectives, rural communes and Catholic Worker houses'. Much of the information is available on its website.

Edge of Time – BCM Edge, London WC1N 3XX; ☎ 029 8133 1451; www.edgeoftime.co.uk. Publishes *Diggers and Dreamers: The Guide to Communal Living* (£14.50). The 2008/9 edition contains an updated listing of communities in the UK.

Eurotopia – www.eurotopia.de. *Directory of Intentional Communities and Ecovillages in Europe* (2005, £12.50). English version provides a comprehensive listing of 336 international communities in 23 countries (mainly Europe and the UK). It can be ordered from Edge of Time.

Global Ecovillage Network (GEN) – based at ZEGG Community in Germany and at Findhorn in Scotland; info@gen-europe.org; www.gen-europe.org; US contact: ecovillage@thefarm.org; Australasia information: http://genoa.ecovillage.org. GEN functions as the umbrella organisation for a wide range of intentional communities and eco-villages all over the world, many of whom welcome guests and volunteers.

Stifelsen Stjärnsund – Bruksallén 16, 77071 Stjärnsund, Sweden; ☎ +46 225 80001; www.frid.nu. Community that welcomes working guests who must contribute 500 kronor per week.

Svanholm Community – Visitors Group, Svanholm Allé 2, 4050 Skibby, Denmark; fax +45 4756 6670; www.svanholm.dk.

RELIGIOUS PILGRIMAGES

There are as many kinds of pilgrimages as there are faiths. Catholics, Protestants, Muslims, Hindus and others all have their sacred shrines to which their followers make pilgrimages. Whether it is to Lourdes, Knock or Mecca (the latter strictly Muslims on the Haj), Canterbury or Varanasi, the experience of being a pilgrim may clear a path to God or constitute a voyage of the inner self towards some kind of healing integration.

SANTIAGO DE COMPOSTELA

Probably the most publicised pilgrimage in western Europe takes place along a 500-mile route (El Camino de Santiago) through France and northern Spain to the purported grave of St James the Apostle (Sant Iago to the Spanish). The name 'Compostela' comes from *campus stellae* (field of stars), named after a hermit who was attracted to the site of Sant Iago's resting place by starry visions which reputedly preceded the rediscovery of his bones. A popular place of pilgrimage since the 9th century, it fell out of favour in recent, more secular times but was revived and was given a spectacular boost in 1994 when the Pope visited.

Pilgrims to Santiago are not all Catholic and many are not even religious, as the experience is individual and meaningful for those of all faiths or none. About a third of pilgrims are Spanish and the rest are foreigners. The true pilgrim covers the entire route on foot, which is a gruelling lesson in humility and blisters, and takes at least three weeks. But many people content themselves with doing just a section of the route or cover some of it by car or public transport which serves some of the towns en route.

Pilgrims can sleep out under the stars or stay in pilgrim hostels, many of which are in historic old buildings where cheap or even free simple accommodation is provided in dormitories. If you walk the route in autumn you may be able to sustain yourself in authentic pilgrim style on the bounty of nature garnered en route: walnuts, figs, chestnuts, apples and mushrooms are just part of the fare that can be picked wild. A classic modern account of the pilgrimage from Paris to Santiago, *The Pilgrimage to Santiago* by Edwin Mullins is essential reading as is a guide to the walk and refuges such as *Walking the Camino de Santiago* by Davies and Cole.

INDIA

Many Westerners are attracted by Eastern faiths, particularly in India where the Hindu religion dominates. Among the most sacred Hindu shrines are the cave at Amarnath in (terrorist-affected) Kashmir, the all-year shrines at Ayodhya, Gaya and Varanasi in Uttar Pradesh and the summer-only shrine at Badrinath. You can also visit Dwarka in Gujarat all year round. Kurukshetra in Haryana is a popular destination for viewing eclipses of the sun or moon and Gangasagar Mela in West Bengal can be visited in January or February. In Sri Lanka, April is the favourite time of year for climbing Adam's Peak which can easily be done in a day. The biggest spiritual festival on earth is said to be the Kumbh Mela which takes place every three years on the banks of the Ganges, attracting up to 60 million pilgrims.

Although these sites are sacred to Hindus, Westerners are seldom prohibited from making a pilgrimage alongside believers just for the spectacle and sense of occasion. The more serious seeker after enlightenment may want to find a teacher (guru) or holy man (*sadhu*) in the vicinity of a temple or shrine. Sadhus are often rather alarming in appearance: unwashed, ash-smeared, unshaven with matted dreadlocked hair, wearing only a loincloth and with coloured markings on their forehead and bodies. However, there are plenty of bogus ones so if they seem too keen to get their hands on your money or even your body, you should make excuses and leave. Genuine sadhus should be approached with respect and courtesy. Don't touch them any under no circumstances, as you will defile their purity.

MY GROWN UP GAP YEAR:
GEMMA WHITEHOUSE

Gemma had been working for KPMG, managing graduate recruitment marketing for the southern region for a few years and had just completed a part-time masters degree in marketing. Despite these achievements she felt that something was missing, and thought it was time to use her skills in a totally different way and take time out to reflect.

When I told KPMG that I wanted to take some months to do volunteer work in Africa they offered to keep my job open for me. Although I decided not to take them up on this offer I was pleasantly surprised that they had a policy that supported staff taking career breaks. My friends, parents and husband were all supportive and this made all the difference. I spent three months working with an African organisation which is responsible for the world's first lion breeding/release project in Zimbabwe. The project aims to address the massively decreasing number of lions on that continent and offer a solution to re-populate the National Parks and Game Reserves all over Africa. I offered to help them market this project in order to generate funds. I also got involved in looking at the marketing for other volunteer programmes they had initiated to help deprived communities throughout Africa.

As I was offering my marketing skills and not joining the programme for paying volunteers to work with the lions, all I had to pay for was my flight and personal expenses. I had the most amazing experience and feel it was one of the best decisions I have ever made. Working in a marketing capacity for something I felt passionately about was very motivating and I came home with some incredible memories. The highlight was meeting Amanzi, a lion cub born during the time I was there, who was rejected by his mother and would have certainly died if he had not been removed and hand reared. I was fortunate enough to be one of the people there to care for Amanzi. When I returned to the UK I set up an organisation offering other people incredible volunteer experiences in Africa. Helping on wildlife conservation projects throughout the continent, as well as teaching and medical placements. This company … is called Amanzi Travel.

SPIRITUAL TOURISM

Travel companies are never slow to exploit a demand and the hunger for spiritual enlightenment has already produced packaged products. One route to self-improvement might be with Skyros. Skyros offers a variety of courses for a self-improvement sabbatical. People over 21, preferably with experience of nursing, catering or maintenance, may be eligible to become 'work scholars' at the holistic holiday centre on the Greek island of Skyros in the northern Aegean. In exchange for basic duties, work scholars are given full board and accommodation and a weekly allowance of £50. The minimum stay is three months from April or July. The main perk is that workers are allowed to participate in one of the 250 courses and workshops on offer including windsurfing, music, ikon painting, feng shui and yoga. Details are available from Skyros (www.skyros.com). Skyros also has centres in Havana (Cuba) for salsa and Ko Samet (Thailand) where the courses include an introduction to Thai culture, meditation and herbal massage.

Religious organisations have often been canny when it comes to free enterprise. In the Middle Ages this usually took the form of selling indulgences. Nowadays you can go on a religious holiday which may or may not contribute to remission of your sins. The ecumenical Christian Iona Community maintains a resident community on the Isle of Iona in the Hebrides. Visitors can share in the common life, at the Abbey or in the more modern MacLeod Centre, with a week's programme costing £250 per person. There is an access fund for those on low incomes. The Iona community also accepts volunteers to help with many different duties, usually for periods of at least six weeks. The season runs from March to October. Details of all the above are available on its website (www.iona.org.uk).

If your requirements are for something older than Christianity, then you can search for enlightenment among the oldest sciences of ancient civilisations, which are mainly of the holistic and herbal medicine variety. These include *ayurveda* from India, *reiki* and *tui na* (a healing art of Chinese massage). Many other healing techniques can be used to minister to the mind-body-spirit. Neal's Yard Agency mails a free quarterly *Holiday & Events Guide* listing green and holistic holidays.

Cortijo Romero has been organising year-round, personal development holistic and creative holidays in Spain for more than a dozen years and offers a choice from holistic massage to the joy of communal singing. Many courses revolve around unlocking your hidden potential and finding your true self.

Emotional and even physical healing can come from sources other than retreats and holistic treatment. You could take a leaf out of St Francis of Assisi's book and find your ideal retreat communing with creatures. There are many who swear that swimming with dolphins is a cure-all especially for the emotionally dysfunctional and those suffering from depression. While you could test this claim by trying to arrange a sabbatical in a dolphinarium, most prefer to swim with dolphins in the wild, though even this has been arousing controversy. How the dolphins feel after charming the demons from humans is not recorded, though studies have shown that too much human interaction interferes with the ability of dolphins and their offspring to fend for themselves in the wild.

Living and working among less privileged people often has a spiritual dimension. Those who think that this might be their route to inner harmony should consider some of the voluntary opportunities canvassed throughout this book. **Nicholas Carbis**, a potter and deacon of the Russian Orthodox Church in Devon, spent six weeks at the Kitezh Community for orphans in western Russia through the Ecologia Trust (see Directory entry) and describes how the experience fed his inner self:

When I first arrived at Kitezh it was like a beautiful painting, peaceful under a blanket of snow. I walked through the frost-hard compacted snow to share in the meditation exercises as the red sun crept through the silhouetted forest. Together connecting with natural energy that warmed the circle of figures, flying without leaving the ground. Afterwards I would jog to the church to say some prayers, and I would pass the children in their circle preparing for the day. I have a picture of the Church alive with angels, waiting for the Easter procession lit by candles under paper wigwams. I would like to render down my thoughts of my time at Kitezh by giving two illustrations: while standing in the church of the monastery of Optina Pustyn, looking up at the beautiful icons and listening to the most lovely voices singing, I had a deep feeling of reverence. Later I had the same feeling of reverence standing in the middle of Kitezh, looking up at the most beautiful starlit night, listening to the nightingales sing. Life in Russia is hard, and the community of Kitezh is burdened with many pressures. However, I believe it is the way Kitezh incorporates beauty and reverence into everyday life that enables people to have hope.

RELIGIOUS RETREATS

Buddhafield Retreats – Trevince House, Hittisleigh, Exeter, Devon EX6 6LP; ☎ 01647 24539; www.buddhafield.com. Meditation and Buddhism taught at festivals, fairs and other events, as well as retreats in Devon and Somerset.

Guhyaloka Buddhist Retreat Centre – Finca El Morer, Sella, Alicante 03579, Spain; ☎ +34 647 240791; www. guhyaloka.com. Summer or winter retreats for men only at a centre in a remote valley of Spain.

Iona Community – Iona Abbey or MacLeod Centre, Isle of Iona, Argyll PA76 6SN; ☎ 01681 700404; ionacomm@iona.org.uk; www.iona.org.uk. £250 per person for a one-week stay but 130 volunteer positions available between March and October for a minimum of six weeks.

Kadampa Buddhist Centres – http://kadampa.org/en/center. Links to meditation and retreat centres worldwide.

Kagyu Samye Ling Tibetan Centre – ☎ 01387 373232; admin@samyeling.org; www. samyeling.org. Tibetan monastery retreat near the River Esk in the Scottish borders. Weekend workshops cost £62. Volunteers with maintenance skills sometimes needed.

Losang Dragpa Buddhist Centre – Dobroyd Castle, Pexwood Road, Todmorden, West Yorkshire OL14 7JJ; ☎ 01706 812247; www.losangdragpa.com. Working volunteers pay £40 per week.

Madhyamaka Buddhist Centre – Kilnwick Percy Hall, Pocklington, York YO42 1UF; ☎ 01759 304832; info@madhyamaka.org. Free meditation classes, three vegetarian meals a day and dormitory accommodation given in return for 35 hours of gardening, decorating, etc per week alongside community residents.

Manjushri Mahayana Buddhist Centre – Conishead Priory, Ulverston, Cumbria LA12 9QQ; ☎ 01229 584029; workingvisits@manjushri.org; www.manjushri.org.uk.

Tara Buddhist Centre – Ashe Hall, Ash Lane, Etwall, Derbyshire DE65 6HT; ☎ 01283 732338; www.taracentre.org.uk. Working visitors are charged £5 a day.

Throssel Hole Buddhist Abbey – Carrshield, Hexham, Northumberland NE47 8AL; ☎ 01434 345204; www.throssel.org.uk.

ALTERNATIVE HOLIDAYS AND TRAVEL COMPANIES

Circle of Light Spiritual Holidays & Retreats – PO Box 96, Kingsbridge, Devon TQ8 8WR; ☎ 0845 456 1007; info@spiritualholidays.com; www.spiritualholidays.com. Organises spiritual journeys to Bhutan, Nepal, India, the Holy Land, etc. Also organises Wellbeing Weekend Retreats in the UK (www.wellbeingretreats.com).

Cortijo Romero – 23 Cottage Offices, Latimer Park, Latimer, Chesham, Buckinghamshire HP5 1TU; ☎ 01494 765775; www.cortijo-romero.co.uk. Centre located in southern Spain offering interesting range of personal development courses; typical cost £485 per week.

Neal's Yard Agency – see below.

Pax Travel Ltd – 152–156 Kentish Town Road, London NW1 9QB; ☎ 020 7485 3003; www.paxtravel.co.uk. Organises pilgrimages for individuals to Rome, Santiago, Latvia, Mexico, etc.

Pilgrim Adventure – Culver Park, Tenby, Pembrokeshire SA70 7ED; ☎ 01834 844212; www.pilgrim-adventure.org uk. Christian walking pilgrimages around the British Isles, e.g. to the Hebrides, Scillies, etc. Walking through mountains, island hopping, traditional music and seashore worship.

Retreats Beyond Dover – c/o St Etheldreda's Church, 14 Ely Place, London EC1N 6RY; ☎ 02476 315520; www.retreats.dircon.co.uk. Organises time-out-with-God retreats in Spain, France and Italy. Sample price £985 for 12 days in Calabria.

Skyros – 9 Eastcliff Road, Shanklin, Isle of Wight PO37 6AA; ☎ 01983 865566; www.skyros.com.

Tangney Tours Pilgrimages – Pilgrim House, Station Court, Borough Green, Kent TN15 8AF; ☎ 0800 917 3572; 01732 886666; www.tangney-tours.com. Organises retreats and stays in convents and monasteries including the Convent of St Thérèse mentioned above.

USEFUL CONTACTS AND PUBLICATIONS

British Wheel of Yoga – 25 Jermyn Street, Sleaford, Lincolnshire NG34 7RU; ☎ 01529 306851; www.bwy.org.uk. Primarily deals with Yoga Centres in the UK but can help provide contacts for studying at yoga centres in India. Membership (£25) includes a subscription to the quarterly magazine *Spectrum* which deals with yoga issues worldwide.

Neal's Yard Agency – BCM Neal's Yard, London WC1N 3XX; ☎ 0844 888 5050; www.nealsyardagency.com. Gives independent advice on holistic, yoga and alternative holidays in the UK and worldwide. Agency operates a booking service.

The Retreat Association – The Central Hall, 256 Bermondsey Street, London SE1 3UJ; ☎ 0845 450 1429; info@retreats.org.uk. Group of Christian retreat centres which publishes *Retreats*, an annual guide to 200 retreats mostly in England, Scotland and Ireland, available from Christian Bookshops including SPCK, Wesley Owen and St Paul's Media or directly (£5.50). You do not have to be a committed Christian, but must respect the rules.

The Retreat Company – The Manor House, Kings Norton, Leicestershire LE7 9BA; ☎ 0116 259 9211; www.theretreatcompany.com. One-stop resource for all those seeking to take a retreat of any kind, at home or abroad. Holistic professionals and staff offer unbiased advice and support. Maintain a directory of holidays, getaways and courses that promote personal transformation and a healthy work/life balance.

Ruth White Yoga Centre – Church Farm House, Spring Close Lane, Cheam, Surrey SM3 8PU; ☎ 01993 831032; www.ruthwhiteyoga.com. Weekend yoga retreats around the UK plus annual yoga holiday in Greece for one, two or three weeks (£653, £1,144 and £1,714, excluding flights).

The Good Retreat Guide (Stafford Whiteaker, Rider Press, 2004, £12.99). Over 500 secular and religious places are listed, ranging from cottages to castles, in Britain, Ireland, Spain and France.

MY GROWN UP GAP YEAR:
MARGARET HOLLAMBY

Margaret Hollamby from Sussex spent last autumn volunteering in Ecuador. Despite some mild disappointments with her placement and accommodation, she made the most of her opportunities and overall had a great experience. Because she is diabetic she did not want to be in a remote non-English speaking placement so chose to work in the nursery of a women's prison in Quito.

In 2007 I decided to make changes to my life. After having thought about quitting my job as a learning support maths teacher for the previous two years, I finally decided to do it. My husband had died four years earlier and for the first couple of years after this it was good to stay in the job – 'Don't make life changes too quickly' people had advised me and I feel they were right. I have always been an adventurous type of person but having an ill husband and bringing up children puts all this somewhat on hold. However, with both my children at university there was an opportunity to have a bit of an adventure myself. After a bit of web searching I found Carol Carlisle's website about gap and career breaks for adults.

I didn't find Quito a particularly attractive place to be. It is noisy and very smelly with pollution, partly due to the low-grade fuel used and partly to its altitude of 2,800m. Street crime is common and there are constant reminders of this with armed guards outside big shops and banks. My voluntary work in the prison was enlightening, but if I'm honest, also a little disappointing. I was only expected to work for three hours, five days a week which was much less than I had anticipated. With some of my spare time, I booked one-to-one lessons in the Academia Latinoamericana de Espanol. The voluntary work wasn't giving me much opportunity for conversation so at least this way I could keep my Spanish improving. In addition I organised some more voluntary work teaching English at the 'Jovenes Contra Cancer Fundacion' for young cancer patients.

Living with the family also wasn't quite what I expected but it was OK. The family consisted of an elderly woman (also diabetic) and her daughter. The only conversation I had was at breakfast and dinner. It made me appreciate my home so much. My host 'Mum' certainly found it difficult to comprehend my lifestyle of regular runs in the park, in all weathers. Things I liked in Quito were the interesting museums, the botanical gardens, the park (for running and Sunday morning aerobics) and most surprising of all – free entry on Sunday to a performance of Taming of the Shrew by the Ecuadorian Ballet.

I'd dreamed of visiting the Galapagos ever since I learned about them as a teenager but didn't think I would really ever get there. The week's trip to the Galapagos Islands rounded off my adventure and it goes without saying that this was a big highlight. Overall my Ecuador experience was something I shall never forget and I hope to do something similar again in the future.

MY GROWN UP GAP YEAR:
GOSBERT CHAGULA

When an opportunity to go to Ghana came along to take up the first legal placement that Changing Worlds had arranged, Gosbert Chagula felt that this chance would come once, and then vanish leaving only regrets behind. However it did leave him with more questions than answers.

I had been to Africa previously, however, that experience had been very sheltered in Western-style hotels, and I didn't get a chance to experience Africa 'in the flesh'. I looked at a lot of gap year companies and the main factors which influenced my choice were cost and safety. I wanted reassurances that the organisations had people on the ground who knew the country. I feel that the presentation of the gap companies' websites also played a big role. Changing Worlds' website was accessible, easy to use and it projected an air of professionalism. A significant number of other gap year websites I visited were often confusing, cluttered and swamped the reader with a large amount of information. Furthermore, Changing Worlds placed an emphasis on meeting you in person rather than trying to supply you with everything over the net.

My gap year did allow me to experience life as an 'ordinary Ghanaian' which means catching the crowded minibus to work in the morning, eating at chop bars (small food stalls which sell traditional Ghanaian dishes), celebrating Independence Day in Kumasi, living with a Ghanaian family and even accompanying them to church services (which could last three hours). But most rewarding was meeting different types of people, from the self-proclaimed 'street hustlers' who are based outside Vic Baboo's Café in Adum in Kumasi, who are legendary. Every day for three months they would heckle me on my way to work, constantly shocked by my refusal to buy any of their overpriced art. They would shout at me 'Hey British boy, come over here!'... it was light-hearted banter, which on occasions was the highlight of my walk to and from work.

Having studied law at degree level I had a sterilised expectation of how the human rights law would operate in Africa. I was told before I arrived in Ghana that 'things work differently' and in Ghana you must have patience. I don't think that any amount of warning could have prepared me for the change in speed, as well as differing work ethic of the Ghanaian legal system. Workwise it was rewarding to work in the human rights field in Africa, and to have been at the forefront of the Ghanaian Human Rights Commission for a short period was a rewarding opportunity. However when taking an overview, my time in Ghana, in a legal sense did make me slightly cynical. The work of the Commission on human rights is slow-paced, with a huge amount of effort needing to be expended. I feel that I did help bring a fresh perspective to legal issues they faced; however long after I'm gone won't things just return to how they were before I arrived? Did I actually make a meaningful contribution to the development of Ghana?

PART 11

BACK TO NORMAL OR A CHANGE FOR LIFE?

INTRODUCTION

The thrill of a grand project or adventure during a gap year will ultimately run its course. Eventually the time off that has been negotiated will come to an end. With luck you will be anticipating many pleasures on re-entry. If you have been abroad for an extended period, you may have escaped homesickness but you might still be longing to see your loved ones, to visit your local pub for a pint and a bacon sandwich, to switch on Radio 4's *Today* programme or walk across green fields. These and many other compensations should help to alleviate the post-travel blues.

In some cases the prospect of returning to a former career is too dismal to contemplate. If the choice to take a career break has been of value it should have taught you that everyone has the ability to determine his or her own course. There is nothing shameful in changing direction in mid-life if you have discovered that your heart lies elsewhere. By the same token there is nothing shameful about returning to your old employer if that is what you choose to do. After all, that is what the majority of teachers, nurses, managers, computer geeks, etc., who take a gap year do.

Changing direction can take many forms. For four years **Helen Tirebuck** had enjoyed working for the Edinburgh charity Challenges Worldwide before deciding to move south, where she quickly realised that London was not for her:

> At the ripe old age of 29, I decided it was now or never so handed in my notice and started looking for my next challenge but this time somewhere overseas . . . Following completion of my divemaster qualification, the whole experience in Costa Rica has overall been extremely positive for me. Having never considered diving as a career before I am now contemplating going on to complete my instructor qualification. It's tempting to look at a job in the diving industry as a 'gap year' or beach bum lifestyle but having now worked in the industry for the last three months it has shown me that it is indeed a thriving industry to be a part of. Someone has to teach the thousands of wannabe divers, and why can't that job be a career?
>
> The experience so far though has definitely spurred me on to not go back to the life I had before. I have always had itchy feet and loved travelling, now I have a real opportunity to combine that with gainful employment in some of the most incredible places in the world. Even if I don't work in scuba diving in the future, the experience I have had taking a break from my life in the UK has inspired me beyond belief. Having successfully completed my internship and had a great time in the process I now feel even more passionate about staying true to that decision to make a shift in my life. I feel now, more than ever, that the world truly is my oyster.

RETURNING TO WORK

Returning to work after a career break, particularly one lasting a year or more, necessitates a period of adjustment that is bound to be challenging. Your time away should have energised you and given you inspiration to make changes in your personal life and in the way you work. In all probability, the experiences you had while your career was on hold will not only have enhanced your appreciation of life and added to your professional versatility, but also equipped you with new skills.

These skills may not seem to have an obvious application in your department or office, but your experiences are bound to have boosted your self-confidence, improved your ability to think on your feet, handle a crisis or persevere in the face of setbacks. If you have helped to build a medical centre in the Andes, taught English as a foreign language, trekked in the Himalayas or made a temporary home in a foreign city, you will have pushed yourself in difficult circumstances beyond the safety of your daily routine. To take just one example, computer training firm Happy Computers (www.happy-people.co.uk) believe that TEFL teachers make good IT trainers even if they lack an IT background.

Coping successfully with upheaval in leaving your job, town and friends behind should be valued in a society and economy in which willingness to change is often expected and usually rewarded. It is your job to sell this positive angle to your current and prospective employers.

Some people use a career break to sample alternative lifestyles, particularly if they aren't happy with the direction their professional life is taking. In some cases people discover a new or better vocation. In others, the fantasy idly entertained while commuting to work may prove impractical or unsuitable. Their gap year may have brought about a process of disillusionment, which is not a bad thing in itself, since no one wants to build a future on illusions. It is always worth getting such things out of your system if you can. The result might be that an unrealistic ambition can now be put aside, leaving you to move on and rededicate yourself to your profession.

AFTER SIX MONTHS OF TRAVELLING ROUND-THE-WORLD, JANE O'BEIRNE AND HER PARTNER MIKE BLEAZARD FLEW HOME FROM RIO, MILDLY DREADING THE PROSPECT OF RE-ESTABLISHING THEMSELVES.

Jane had wrestled with the idea of making her career break into a career change. While on the road she had considered many alternatives to the law, from care work to opening a pasta restaurant. After a couple of months of combing the ads in the newspaper it became clear that without going back to do extensive retraining (e.g. in physiotherapy), she would be eligible to apply only for ... administrative or care jobs paying a third of what she had earned as a solicitor. So she enlisted with a legal temp agency near Cambridge and enjoyed a series of locums of short duration, which is an efficient way of sampling the working environments of potential permanent employers. Jane soon found full-time employment in the probate department of a small laid-back law firm where hours were civilised, pressures few and where 'billable hours' were not the motive force.

Mike was also faced with having to find another job on his return. He had kept in touch with various potential employers by email. However while he was away, many high-level IT businesses had been forced to batten down the hatches in the current economic climate, and he could see no way in. He could have walked into a contract in London but was determined to find a job within cycling distance of home. After a few months he did so and was content to be once again earning a steady income since he and Jane have now got a young son.

At a more private level, a gap year can act simply as a time for personal development. Priorities change with age. The successful career that seemed such a glittering prize in your youth may not seem so important in later life. Some careers begin to feel insatiable in their demands, in which case returning to work may require careful deliberation. How are you going to avoid the problems that plagued you before the gap? It may be a question of working fewer hours to spend more time with family. You may now want more time to enjoy interests outside work or it may simply be a desire to take on less managerial responsibility to alleviate levels of stress. Before you return to work, evaluate the aspects of your working life that you might like to change. Have your career goals shifted?

The Battye family spent a marvellous six months volunteer teaching in a Thai village and exploring New Zealand together (see Part 8 Taking the Family). Re-integrating into life at home in the USA was not so easy:

> *The truth is our heads are still really whirling. Life will be different for us now as the result of our experiences during these travels. Part of the reason for this trip was to get out of the fishbowl, as it were, and think expansively about what we want our lives to be about. We explored the idea of John getting a teaching job overseas, Susan pursuing a career in writing (perhaps something relative to family travel) and moving our family to a community that we feel really great about. When I reflect on the impact of Thailand on our lives, I know that it was an important stepping stone, one that is continuing to propel us as we look at discovering who we are and how we can help.*

On returning they moved to a progressive school in Virginia for a year but decided New Hampshire was home after all and moved back in the summer of 2008.

RETURNING TO YOUR OLD JOB

It is advisable to keep up some contact with a workplace during a career break and to demonstrate your ongoing commitment to return, to allay understandable doubts on the part of your employer that you will actually return from your adventure. Keeping yourself informed of staff and organisational changes will also prove beneficial on your return. Particularly in fields where change occurs at a rapid pace, efforts to remain abreast of changes will assist the process of returning to work. After volunteering to refurbish a school in Granada, Nicaragua with her husband, Deby Hardy returned to her job as a nurse in the very busy emergency medical unit of her hospital in Devon. The job is stressful at the best of times but she had to relearn some of her skills, which are quickly lost. After joining an orangutan project in Borneo, **Jake Brumby** returned to his job in project and account management for a website development company:

> *It took me one month to get back up to speed at work. I was not very productive at first. It is important to remember the things you discovered about yourself and keep these alive. You can easily slip back into old/bad habits.*

Some organisations that offer formal career breaks stress the importance for absent staff of keeping informed of any changes to the organisation and their old department. Employees will probably want to stay in touch by email with colleagues or other freelancers in the field. Lots of companies and organisations produce staff newsletters which you should make an effort to obtain so that a connection to the workplace is maintained during the absence which will help the process of readjustment.

Likewise, the Training & Development Agency for Schools (www.tda.gov.uk/Recruit.aspx) produces a termly magazine *Return to Teaching* and information about free refresher or 'returner' courses for teachers taking a professional break. Details of the Returning to Teach Programme are available on 0845 6000 993 or by emailing info@returning2teach.co.uk.

Returning to work is bound to be a shock to the system even if you have been away for only a few months. Rarely do absentees return to find that their bosses or colleagues harbour any resentment, though your return to work may unsettle new working relationships or fiefdoms that have developed during the break. In your absence, you may have gained a new line manager or managing director who has made significant changes to a corporate culture. Old colleagues may have left and new technology introduced. Adapting to change is the principal challenge to returning to the workplace. Former travelling routines such as commuting by train will have to be revived and tolerated. Freelancers will have to relearn the discipline of organising their time according to the requirements of clients.

Sometimes individuals expect to be treated like conquering heroes but are in fact given a rather matter-of-fact or even frosty reception. A jocular 'you lucky thing' can disguise a modicum of resentment and jealousy. These feelings are not inevitable but they may surface as they did when Ceri Evans returned from a spell of living in Barcelona to take up her old job as a senior counsellor in a sexual health clinic. She hadn't expected to encounter hostility but that is what she sensed among some colleagues in her department.

The period of adjustment may be painful at first though it is bound to get easier. In all likelihood, the office or department has continued to function smoothly without you, as any organisation must. On your return you may even be a little irritated to see how well others have coped in your absence.

JOB-HUNTING AFTER A GAP YEAR

If you need to look for a new job after a gap year, the technique will be the same as for any job search. The difference is that a career break means an interlude from formal work and therefore a gap on your CV, which will not necessarily be viewed in a positive light. However, if you can demonstrate that you have developed and acquired new skills as a result of the experience, a gap year can be seen as a strength and an advantage.

If you have volunteered in a relevant field, you may find your employability much improved. For example **Phillip Elcombe** from Folkestone had finished a media degree but had not been able to find the kind of work he wanted in the UK. With the help of the volunteer travel agency i-to-i, he joined a privately owned and funded radio station in Accra, Ghana, which airs a variety of programmes including news, talk shows, music and interviews with celebrities and politicians. Volunteers were expected to take a lot of initiative, bringing new ideas, styles of reporting and giving a fresh perspective on local issues. He concluded at the end of his stint as a volunteer that his future career prospects had definitely been improved:

> *If you are passionate about what you have done and can show how your experiences as a volunteer have benefited you, then it always stands you in good stead. One of my co-volunteers in Ghana had an interview in London just after she got back, took her photos from the project with her and the employer was so impressed by the qualities she could offer from her experience in volunteering that she got the job.*

Leaving a chronological gap on your CV will inevitably attract attention so don't try to hide the fact that you've taken a gap year. There is no need to apologise or feel defensive about it. The time spent away will almost certainly have recharged your batteries and enhanced your employment prospects (unless you just sat at home and watched television). It might have also provided the impetus to attempt a step change.

After more than five years working as an engineer for Jaguar in the Midlands, **Matt Heywood** was ready for a long break. He also wanted to figure out whether to pursue a career in management on his return to normal paid life. Having chickened out of joining a Raleigh expedition before university he now was impressed with what he learned from its website and thought that becoming a staff member on a three-month Raleigh expedition to build a school in Borneo would give him a competitive edge on his CV:

> *Whilst on expedition I have realised that there is a lot of satisfaction to be gained from developing people, not just products. As a result, I will be applying for managerial positions when I return to employment.*

Career advisers and human resources people often say that a good CV can include some life experiences that may not relate directly to a job application. Often these unrelated activities demonstrate social skills, initiative and breadth of interests. This is partly why students are urged to fill their time at college with a range of activities outside their formal degree studies.

THE OLDER JOB-SEEKER

With the recent proposals to raise the state pension age to 68 (some time after 2024), we can all expect to work longer than our parents' generation did mainly because we are living longer. Since the Employment Equality (Age) Regulations came into force in 2006, it has been illegal for employers to discriminate on the basis of age, in line with EU legislation, which reinforces the idea that the average working life will be extended. Rachel Krys of the Employers Forum on Age (www.efa.org.uk), which campaigns for diversity of ages in the workforce, teased out a relevant implication of these changes:

> *As the Government makes these changes we must consider the impact they will have on employers and employees. Given our ageing population, raising the pension age should come as no surprise. It does mean that flexible working practices, career breaks, part time working and job sharing can no longer be the preserve of the most enlightened employer – they have to become a reality for everyone in order to make working for longer palatable.*

If our working lives are being extended why should a career break in our 40s or 50s present a problem for employers, particularly when skills are in short supply? Furthermore, a longer working life will save businesses millions in training and recruitment costs.

A return to work for women after raising a family may necessitate retraining or learning new skills. The major issues are childcare costs, loss of confidence and lack of skills. By going back to work part-time, many women lose out on training opportunities open to full-time staff.

Specialist recruitment agencies in the Greater London area target older job-seekers or those returning to work after a break. For example Thirty Plus Recruitment (92–93 Great Russell Street, London WC1B 3PS; ☎ 020 7323 4155; www.thirtyplus-recruitment.com) places people up to retirement age in administrative, secretarial and accounting jobs. Forties People (11–13 Dowgate Hill, London, EC4R 2ST; ☎ 020 7329 4044; www.fortiespeople.com) specialises in clerical and secretarial work for more mature candidates in London and Watford. Wiseowls in East London (www.wiseowls.co.uk) is a non-profit organisation providing an employment agency, educational website, and Business Start Up Initiative assistance for people over 45.

CHANGING EMPLOYMENT PRACTICES

As described in the first chapter of this book, the government and many companies are increasingly interested in promoting the work–life balance. This shift is bound to strengthen the employability of someone who has taken a career break. For promoting a healthy work–life balance, experts identify the importance of flexible working, including flexi-time, part-time work, job-sharing, shift-swapping, working from home and team-based self-rostering. Companies that favour work–life balance and family-friendly policies are enjoying reduced absenteeism and better employee retention. A recent winner of the Working Families American Express Best Boss Competition, Bruce Draper of Geotechnical Instruments in Leamington Spa, claims that staff turnover was running at a third each year before he introduced flexible working which brought that figure down to about zero.

If you are returning to the workplace after a break you might want to adjust your working life to suit new priorities, of which childcare is the most obvious example. One popular measure is the adoption of a shorter working week. Some companies have gone so far as to reduce the working week to four days, leaving an extra day for administration or domestic life. **Fiona Carroll**, a project manager in a software company located in Switzerland, asked for a four-day week when she found her new job after a career break. Her weekly pay has reduced by a fifth but she now has an extra day to devote to her outside interests. Subtle changes in work can dramatically improve one's quality of life, but you may need to be proactive in persuading an employer to grant flexibility.

Working life can be very demanding and so it pays for employers to encourage loyalty and create a supportive, friendly working environment. A positive experience at work is guaranteed to improve loyalty and performance. Obviously, only a few companies can be pioneers, but in a competitive environment for recruitment, those employers that lag behind will lose the most talented staff to their rivals. Beyond certain resistant professional niches, change seems more rapid in sectors such as IT and financial services. Employers are being prodded by competition to liberalise their policies on a range of issues from maternity leave to flexible working. Returning from a gap year need not be an intimidating experience. The public sector is similarly keen to promote flexible working and to recruit staff who might bring valuable skills from elsewhere. In tandem with the government's support for work–life balance, organisations such as the National Health Service, Britain's largest employer, are eagerly introducing employment policies that earn staff loyalty, particularly as the costs of training staff in areas like nursing are so high.

USEFUL CONTACTS AND RESOURCES

The annually updated *What Color is Your Parachute?* (Richard Nelson Bolles, Ten Speed Press, California, $28.95/£16.99) has become a classic in the job-search and career-change market. Its supportive advice encourages readers to evaluate their own personalities and strengths, and then to apply these insights to the job hunt.

Changing Direction (www.changingdirection.com) is a company dedicated to helping people to approach the workplace after a career break, especially women. As well as exploiting the resources of Job Centre Plus (the government job-finding service), you might be able to benefit from returning to the careers service of your old university. Institutions have different policies but they are usually happy for an alumnus to make use of their resources. An increasingly popular source of help is to consult a private career counsellor or life coach.

The ease with which recruitment websites can be updated and personalised makes them invaluable tools in providing up-to-date information which can be quickly sorted according to preference. These specialist websites allow the user to search updated listings, build and post an online CV and obtain email alerts. National newspapers such as the *Guardian* and *The Times* have also made a big pitch for the jobs market, with entire sub-sections of their websites dedicated to this area.

Besides the above, the Internet in general offers a bewildering array of job-finding resources. Everywhere you look on the Internet potentially useful links can be found. However, be aware that many seem to offer more than they can deliver and you may find that the number and range of jobs posted are disappointing. A surprising number of company home pages feature an icon you can click to find out about jobs with that company. Here is a brief selection of potentially useful websites.

- **www.brookstreet.co.uk** – Brook Street is a UK-wide employment agency. Type in your postcode and the site will point you to the nearest office. There's also advice on compiling a CV, interview techniques, etc.
- **www.cityjobs.com** – Contains thousands of jobs on behalf of clients who specialise in the finance, IT, accountancy and legal sectors.
- **www.JobsGoPublic.com** – Aimed at public sector workers looking for employment in a range of fields from museums and libraries to nursing and midwifery.
- **http://jobs.guardian.co.uk** – Guardian Unlimited runs impressive job listings online. Particularly strong on public service, charity and media jobs, the site also incorporates a special section for graduates.

- **www.manpower.co.uk** – Manpower is one of the UK's largest recruitment chains. On the site you can find current job listings, online training courses and office addresses. The international website is www.manpower.com.
- **www.monster.co.uk** – Lists thousands of jobs worldwide and publishes advice on job hunting and preparing a CV.
- **www.prospects.ac.uk** – UK's official career site for graduates maintained by the Higher Education Careers Services Unit (Prospects House, Booth Street E, Manchester M13 9EP). Publishes huge amount of information for graduates and students in the UK. Links to 'Jobs Abroad'.
- **www.realworldmagazine.com** – Mainly aimed at new graduates though information of use to 'mature graduates'. It carries articles about various professional fields including interviews with employees and advice on how to get hired.
- **www.rec.uk.com** – The Recruitment & Employment Confederation is the professional body representing recruitment agencies in the UK. Search the website for agencies in your field.
- **www.stepstone.co.uk** – Stepstone describes itself as the leading European jobs portal and carries thousands of searchable job vacancies in Europe and the UK. The site also offers careers advice and tips on how to market yourself.
- **www.workthing.com** – A free job website providing a searchable database of vacancies, editorial advice, information on training courses and employment news.

CHANGING DIRECTION

A year spent away from professional life may be the prelude to larger more permanent changes. You may have had an inkling that your old job was going nowhere or was causing dissatisfaction. A gap year may act as a stepping stone to leaving for good even if that was not the original plan. Another scenario is that a break spent in another activity may have been so rewarding that it compels a re-evaluation of one's career path, which had once been taken for granted.

The charms of office life may have palled with distance. A career breaker met by the *Daily Telegraph* journalist **Rosemary Behan** (who took a gap year herself to travel the world) reported her motives for taking off to rough it in China: '*I had bosses who made David Brent look competent. This has taught me that I have many options in life, and my time could be better used. I am going back to work as a freelance consultant, because I'm sick of working around people who sit behind a desk for eight hours a day, eat Mars bars for lunch and don't even have time to look in the mirror to see how ill they look.*' Some career breaks are consciously taken at the outset as a way of forcing the pace, as a springboard for changing career. You may literally be returning to the first rung of a ladder. Of course skills learned in a former occupation will never leave you, even though you may be starting afresh in a new field. In some cases, it will mean modifying a previous experience, for example applying a medical or legal qualification to a manufacturing, business or commercial service.

Changing direction in life is often fraught with anxiety. However, taking a risk is sometimes necessary before reaching a certain goal. Cultural commentator Michael Bracewell, writing in the *Guardian* of a widely held sense of entrapment in office life puts it well: '*Whatever might lie beyond the office, from goat farming in Snowdonia to having that one idea which will make you worth more than Ikea, there is always that membrane of fear which keeps the bulk of us at our desks.*'

Clodagh O'Brien's gap half-year in south-east Asia changed his outlook permanently:

Before I left I worked in London as a science journalist. I now work as Communications Officer for a charity that provides services to people affected by acquired brain injury (www.headway.ie). I found that my experiences in Asia, especially after visiting Cambodia, made me want to give back something to society while still remaining involved in science. I think the trip opened my eyes to the huge array of obstacles that people in third world countries face and made me realise I eventually want to work in a disadvantaged country to make life easier for those living in awful conditions

A NEW CAREER IN DEVELOPMENT?

Some career breakers return from their travels or volunteer work in far-flung impoverished countries all fired up to carry on working in the field of international aid and development. They dream of living in exotic places, helping disadvantaged people to improve their lives, and getting paid for it. Working in development aid or disaster relief offers all these things. However, while many dream of such a career, only a chosen few actually manage to get a foothold in what has become a highly competitive and increasingly professional business.

After a six-month stint as a volunteer with Outreach International in Cambodia, **Dale Hurd** had made so many contacts that she intended to return in a private capacity, having used the agency placement as a stepping stone into the world of international development and longer term humanitarian work. She says, '*Little did I know that my whole life would change in the most radical way.*'

Till Bruckner has a great deal of experience in pursuing this trail, having travelled the world after university funded by working in a bread factory in Wales, picking flowers in Cornwall and so on. Over the past few years, he has gradually gained enough relevant experience with non-governmental organisations (NGOs), in Sudan for example, to land contracts with aid agencies that saw him recently with a budget of $900,000 on a contract to design a project for refugees in Georgia. Here he debunks some of the myths:

*To understand why a few succeed where so many fail, it is best to look at what kind of people agencies like CARE, Oxfam and Save the Children do **not** need. These fall into three categories – heroes, unskilled idealists, and people with skills that are available locally.*

To take the first one, agencies do not need heroes. Many people believe that development work is in some way heroic, with Western aid workers battling desert storms to get medicine to a relief camp in the nick of time. The truth is far more prosaic. The vast majority of relief and development work done by foreigners involves answering emails, writing reports and attending boring meetings. The last thing a truck driver in a sandstorm needs is a foreigner giving smart advice, and the nightmare of every agency boss is an employee who jeopardises a whole programme by disregarding tight security restrictions. If you want to do heroic stuff, become a freelance journalist instead.

Secondly, agencies do not need unskilled idealists. Posters of aid agencies sometimes show good white people spoon-feeding starving African babies. In the real world, this never happens. Even if you offer to work for free, it makes much more sense for an agency to create much needed employment by paying a local to do unskilled work. If you are an idealist and want to help poor people, get in touch with an agency in your home country and offer your services as a fundraising volunteer there. Alternatively, if you are in a poor country, just walk into an orphanage or nature park and ask if they can use some unpaid help.

The third group that agencies do not need is people with skills that are available locally. Aid agencies exist to help poor people. Therefore, they will always hire car mechanics, forklift drivers, secretaries and translators from inside the poor countries where they operate. Taking on a foreigner – even without any pay – to drive a truck in an African country makes no sense. It is far better to lift one more local person out of unemployment and poverty by giving him or her a job.

So what sort of people are aid agencies looking for? The best way to find out is to look at some of the websites listed below and see what skills are in demand. Generally speaking, agencies hire people with considerable technical skills and a few years of professional experience, including doctors, logisticians, accountants, and microfinance specialists. Most advertised vacancies will draw dozens, if not hundreds, of applications from qualified and experienced people. With no prior experience, unless you are a doctor and willing to work for free, it is nearly impossible to find a job this way. Most people working in development today originally started off far more informally. For example many are former US Peace Corps volunteers or hardcore travellers who somehow got a foot in the door while they were in a developing country. The majority began their careers as unpaid interns or volunteers, proved that they were capable of doing a good job, and then after half a year or so started moving up the ladder and into administrative or managerial positions. However, even becoming an unpaid volunteer can be difficult. Volunteers create costs by taking up the time of their supervisors, and by requiring office space and computer access.

TILL BRUCKNER GOES ON TO SHARE HIS INSIGHTS INTO THE JOB HUNT:

So how do you find an international development organisation that suits you and convince it to give you a chance? Here's a step-by-step guide:

Think about what you can offer. *One skill that is severely in demand in most countries is the ability to write coherent texts in flawless English. Development organisations produce an amazing amount of paperwork, much of which is produced by local staff with shaky English and then has to be corrected or rewritten by a native speaker. If you have good writing and editing skills, and you volunteer to subject yourself to the tedium of proofreading documents for half a year, there should be demand for your services. Alternatively, you could offer to teach English for free for a few hours a week, or give a course in writing skills. Also, think about special skills that you can offer. Maybe you could revamp an agency's computer system or layout publicity materials for free? If you are unsure about what agencies are looking for, just drop in on one, or take part in a training course for relief and development workers.*

Identify organisations you want to work for. *In every poor country, there is some website directory listing most of the agencies working there with their activities in detail. If you cannot find this website, just ring the local office of any agency and ask them where to find the directory. Look for organisations whose work interests you. Do they work with children, farmers, refugees, or with the environment? Make a shortlist and then get the email address of the 'country director'. If necessary, phone the organisation to get it. An email to a general address is likely to get lost.*

Write a short email *to the country director of each organisation you have chosen. State that you are interested in helping his/her work, and write precisely identifying which problem you are proposing to solve for him/her, eg proofreading, training staff in specific software skills, language lessons, etc. If you have a professional-looking CV, attach it to your email. Make clear that you expect little or no pay, but that in return, you would appreciate being able to learn about how international development works. Ask for a chance to meet and discuss your possible contribution. If you are already in your target country, you have a huge advantage. If not, state in your email that you will be visiting the country during a certain week in the future, and ask for an interview date then. Once you get a couple of positive replies, pack your bags and go! People are unlikely to take you on without having met you in person. Without a lot of initiative, you will never get a foot in the door.*

Be professional at the interview. *If you get an interview, treat it like any job interview. Dress smart-casual (no tie). Have a copy of your CV with you. Make sure that you know in detail what the organisation does. Also remember that development aid has become big business. The person interviewing you is probably on a very good salary. If you save him/her time and money, it is perfectly acceptable to ask for what you will get in return, eg participation in training and workshops, remuneration for transport expenses or even free accommodation. If the country director seems hesitant to commit to taking you on for a long time, offer to start by doing a week of free work with no strings attached. Once you have a foot in the door, it becomes easy to walk in. As elsewhere, most people are hired through word of mouth, and if you are good at getting things done, word will spread. Working part-time for two or three organisations at once can accelerate this process.*

Welcome to one of the most exhilarating, frustrating and challenging careers in the world!

People returning from conservation projects abroad often have the same impulse to change direction as happened to **Richard Nimmo** in his early 30s:

For over 10 years I had been working in London in sales and marketing for television and radio. I needed a break in a hectic and pressurised work life and I also had a strong desire to take some time to see and work a new environment, challenge myself, as well as make a positive contribution through a conservation project. My friends, family and partner were all hugely supportive of the idea and my plans. This helped me make the decision to take a three-month break and join Blue Ventures' conservation expedition in Madagascar. Originally the break was intended to be two months – it turned into 16 months. My experiences as a volunteer in Andavadoaka with Blue Ventures and my travels in the rest of Madagascar were extraordinary. I decided that Madagascar was a place that I wanted to spend more time. On returning to the UK in late May I applied for the position of Expedition Leader in Madagascar and was back working there in July and since then I have been General Manager and now Managing Director of Blue Ventures in London. Living and working in a remote community with volunteers from many countries and local people gave me a huge sense of achievement as we all contributed to a successful and award-winning marine project. Working and living in Madagascar was a wonderful experience that has given me a new focus and an impetus to work in a new sector. Seeing and travelling in another culture is always interesting but to live in a different culture and work there gives you a deeper insight and understanding.

USEFUL WEBSITES FOR DEVELOPMENT WORK

Till Bruckner has provided this annotated list of resources on the web:

- **www.aidworkers.net** – Info for relief and aid workers.
- **www.bioforce.asso.fr** – French organisation that provides relief training and short courses with humanitarian experts.
- **www.bond.org.uk/classifieds/index.html** – BOND stands for British Overseas NGOs for Development.
- **www.charityjob.co.uk/seekers.htm** – Strong on administration jobs.
- **www.comminit.com/vacancies.html** – The Communication Initiative based in Victoria, Canada. Also information on relief training courses.
- **www.dotorgjobs.com** – vacancies mainly in the USA, primarily of interest to Americans.
- **www.eldis.org/news/jobs.htm** – Based at the Institute of Development Studies (IDS) in Brighton. Has useful links.
- **www.idealist.org** – Good for beginners.
- **www.interaction.org** – Job and volunteer newsletters for paying subscribers.
- **www.jobsincharities.co.uk** – Jobs in UK.
- **www.reliefweb.int/vacancies/index.html** – Lots of vacancies for professionals, good for checking out what is in demand.
- **www.sussex.ac.uk/cdec** – Search for 'International Development' on the careers site of the University of Sussex, which is a great place to start.
- **www.wse.org.uk** – World Service Enquiry offers information and advice. Its new booklet *Working in Development* (2008, £10.99) has been written specifically for career changers and new graduates. It also offers one-to-one consultations for £80, £150 or £290.

UNEXPECTEDLY DETAINED

A gap year may have an unavoidably life-changing effect, especially one which involves exposure to new cultures, lifestyles, ways of working and a different set of values. According to the 19th-century aphorist and Harvard professor, Oliver Wendell Holmes, '*a mind that is stretched by a new experience can never go back to its old dimensions*'.

In some cases the changes which a gap have brought about may be more than just psychological. Bachelors may have found partners, women may have found motherhood and so on. Or the reverse may have happened. An earlier relationship may not have survived a separation or diverging goals and you now find yourself free to form new attachments whether to a new lover, a new culture or a new pursuit. Perhaps you have fallen under the spell of Paris, Sydney, Rio or the African veld and have lost the urge to return to your roots (see the chapter 'Staying On' in Part 6 Working and Living Abroad).

The downside of an open-ended career break is the absence of security. Venturing through the game parks of Africa or learning to scuba dive on the Great Barrier reef is certainly more appealing to some if they know that they can return to normality by having a job to return to. For others, a clean break is the goal and any commitments back home would negate the mystique and catharsis of leaving old responsibilities behind.

Even when there is no intention of veering away from a known profession, events can dictate otherwise. **Rachel Pooley** decided not to go back to her former career working for a mental health charity on returning from a trans-Africa Land Rover trip with her partner Charlie. Having accidentally found themselves running a backpacking lodge on the edge of Lake Malawi, they learned to value work differently. Their experience of running the lodge without electricity or running water and managing the staff made them more practical and self-reliant. They are now much less preoccupied with a traditional career and are much choosier about the work they want to do. Malawi and the ubiquitous tragedy of Aids taught them to appreciate life more and to approach the challenge of each day as it arrives. The opportunity to be self-employed and to run their own business, albeit for just six months, made the idea of returning home to work in a big organisation much less appealing. Their break encouraged them to explore different ways of working and to hold out against opportunities that didn't feel right for them.

BECOMING SELF-EMPLOYED

For some people, being an employee suits their lifestyle and aspirations. They enjoy being part of a team in which the major decisions are taken by the boss. They feel that their contribution is sufficiently valued and financially rewarded and they appreciate being able to leave professional worries in the office at 5.30pm every day and during four weeks of paid holiday. Whereas many employees feel that this leaves enough free time to pursue outside interests, others feel constrained by this regimen.

One means of taking greater control of your working life is to become self-employed which, in the eyes of the tax office, is the same thing as setting up a business, even though you simply want to deliver a service or product yourself without the worry and hassle of employing other people. Being a self-employed freelancer or consultant can be an economically efficient way of working because many expenses such as office equipment and business travel can be set against tax.

Before deciding, it is advisable to speak to an accountant who specialises in working with the self-employed. Assess how your income is likely to change and whether you can expect to meet all your financial obligations. Above all, you will have maximum freedom to set your own working hours and holidays. The obvious drawback is that your income will vary, for example there may be seasonal variations in the demand for your work and there will be no perks traditionally provided by an employer such as a free telephone and envelopes and Christmas parties, let alone contributions to pensions, paid holidays and company cars.

When long-term employment with one company is declining and employment is increasingly available on short-term contracts only, it makes good sense to sell your skills and experience as a contractor, flexibly moving from one project to another. It will certainly provide variety and the stimulus of frequent change.

A useful reference book here is *Go It Alone: The Streetwise Secrets of Self-Employment* (Geoff Burch, Capstone, 2003) or there are other more recent books which canvas all kinds of economic activity that can be conducted from home, many of which are concerned with self-employed activities such as running a playgroup or bed and breakfast through to practising complementary therapies. This guide provides you with all the hints and tips you might need if you are to make a success of it.

In a few cases, a grown-up gap year has been so inspiring that it spurs the returning traveller to start a business based on their experiences. For this edition of this book, the stories of three have come to light: **Tara Leaver** gave up being a Montessori teacher to travel in Central America and came home with the idea of selling ethically produced handicrafts, so set up the online shop www.boutiko. co.uk. **Gemma Whitehouse** had such an amazing career break volunteering in animal conservation in Antelope National Park in northern Zimbabwe that on returning to Bristol she set up a business called Amanzi (named for one of the orphaned lion cubs she had cared for) that arranges volunteer placements like hers. She says, '*I found returning home exciting and very easy as I came back with a clear idea of what I wanted to do next – set up my own business offering others the same amazing opportunities to help in Africa.*' Finally, the round-the-world travels of **Tessa Mills** taken at a crossroads in her life persuaded her that too many people are held back by fear and diffidence. She felt that if they could turn to someone like her to advise on how to construct a gap year, their reluctance could be overcome and their lives enhanced. So she set up her advisory business The Gap Year Guru (www.thegapyearguru. com) to fill that hole in the market. When she set off, her main ambition had been simply to see the Taj Mahal. She could never have foreseen that nine months later she would return itching to start her own business on the back of her adventures.

REVERSE CULTURE SHOCK

Before worrying about re-adjusting to the working world, you should be prepared for a certain level of disorientation on a personal level. Not everybody can be as upbeat as **Barbara Schick**, an Austrian photographer whose gap year was spent in Brazil travelling and volunteering: '*It was beautiful to be away for half a year but just as beautiful to come back home to friends and work*' though she goes on to confess that a year on, she is ready to leave again for a while.

Coming home from a stay away can engender reverse culture shock, especially if your gap year has included extended travels in the developing world. You may feel suffocated by the commercialism all around. Life at home may seem dull and routine at first, while the outlook of your colleagues, friends and family can strike you as limited and parochial. You may find it difficult to bridge the gulf between you and your stay-at-home colleagues who (understandably) may feel a little threatened or belittled by your experiences.

Joni Hillman vividly recalls her case of reverse culture shock after returning from being a volunteer in India:

> *Reverse culture shock is always much worse than the acclimatisation process you go through when you first arrive in a foreign country because you're just not prepared to feel different about your old life. I think being aware that it might be difficult to return home is the key. Give yourself time, or throw yourself into something. I moved house and started my Masters within 10 days of arriving home. If you have seen horrific poverty or had conflict experiences it can sometimes be really difficult to engage in a conversation with your oldest friends about seemingly trivial things like Eastenders! It can also be difficult to sum up your experiences in a couple of sentences, which is generally all people have got time for when they ask 'How was it?'. Keeping a diary is a good idea because it can help you digest your experiences into manageable chunks for other people. And remember that they are invariably jealous of the wonderful experiences you have been gutsy enough to go out and find, while they waste their lives in offices.*

The process of shaking up your life is undoubtedly risky. The experience may leave you out of step with your social and professional circle at home. Even if you know that you are perfectly capable of settling back into your old life, you may not be willing, because too many of your views and values have changed to be comfortable. On the other hand you don't really have a choice and will simply have to stop looking agog at your Starbuck's bill and telling everyone that this would pay for a week's travelling in India or a fortnight in Laos.

After an exhilarating period of living and teaching in Vietnam, **Beth Buffam** returned home:

> *Coming back to the US, I felt like a different person, and I felt a bit like a stranger. I felt I had significantly changed during my five months in Vietnam. I had lost 15 pounds, and I think I carried myself straight up but with humility like a Vietnamese. The loudness and crassness and ugliness of the US bothered me.*

This telling extract describes re-entry to normal life. It is taken from the final chapter 'An English Alien' of Nigel Barley's *The Innocent Anthropologist*, a superbly amusing account of the author's time spent researching the Dowayo tribe of the Cameroons (Penguin, 1983):

> *It is positively insulting how well the world functions without one. While the traveller has been away questioning his most basic assumptions, life has continued sweetly unruffled. Friends continue to collect matching French saucepans. The acacia at the foot of the lawn continues to come along nicely. The return-ing anthropologist does not expect a hero's welcome, but the casualness of some friends seems excessive. An hour after my arrival, I was phoned by one friend who merely remarked tersely, 'Look, I don't know where you've been but you left a pullover at my place nearly two years ago. When are you coming to collect it?' In vain one feels that such questions are beneath the concern of a returning prophet.*

As Nigel Barley sees it, the sight of groaning supermarket shelves induces either revulsion or crippling indecisiveness. Polite conversation may seem temporarily impossible. But most returned field workers end up feeling overwhelming gratitude for having been born a Westerner. Generally the feelings of displacement and restlessness pass soon enough when the reverse culture shock wears off and you begin to feel reintegrated.

While at times it will seem that time has stood still during your absence, at others you may feel that you have missed important events while away: children are born, friends get married, couples part, neighbours move away, governments are voted out, radio presenters retire. Despite modern telecommu-nications making it much easier to keep abreast of these changes, there may be a feeling of alienation from your past.

One aspect that **Marcelle Salerno** found most difficult after one of her many adventures during her gap years was the naïve generalisations some of her fellow Americans were prone to make:

> *Already I find it difficult to speak to people when they discuss 'world news' if I know they haven't seen any-thing of the world first-hand. After living with Muslims for a month in Morocco I see the current political issues differently. After living with tribal Africans for six months I see race in a whole different light.*

Apart from social unease, you might have more immediate practical worries such as where you will live. If you have a house or flat to return to, that should be no trouble, assuming the tenants or housesitters have looked after it adequately. But if you gave up your rented or mortgaged accommodation to take a career break, finding a place to live will be of primary concern. You can only camp out with friends for so long, though you will probably be welcome to stay longer with parents or siblings at least to provide a base while you're house hunting. Depending on how much privacy you have and to what extent you feel yourself to be imposing, this arrangement will probably spur you on to find a place of your own as briskly as possible. Casting yourself at the mercy of your parents again can be viewed in a positive light as 30-something **Lucy Bailey** did after four wonderful months working at two different game lodges in Kenya with *The Leap*, although finding a stimulating job proved impossible in the short term:

> *I ended up going to live with my parents in Derbyshire (who I get on with fantastically and which was actually a really lovely opportunity to be with them for a little while and get to know them again!) for a few months and did some temping to keep the wolf from the door before moving back down to London. I was a secretary for a company that made bespoke generators located on an industrial estate on the out-skirts of a really grim ex-mining town in rural Derbyshire! There was nothing to do at lunchtime apart from drive to the local gravel pit where I'd sit in my car eating my ham butties, smoking cigarettes and watching the giant rats scuttle in and out of the piles of burnt out clothes and abandoned broken toilets. It was easily one of the worst jobs I've ever had, but certainly had comedy value, which is fortunate seeing as I do some comedy writing and performing and it's provided a great deal of material!*

If you have been away for a long time, consider throwing a party to let everyone know that you're home and available for a continuation of your former social life. But don't expect to slot back seamlessly. In some cases your interests and priorities may have changed and be prepared for it to take time before you find the common ground with friends and family. The physical trappings of your life may have changed too. The well-loved garden of a home you rented to strangers may have declined beyond recognition and years of hard work lost. On the other hand, you may find that nothing much has changed at all which can be equally alienating in its way. From having returned to her job in the law after six months spent in Cambodia, Japan and South America, **Polly Botsford** passes on what she learned about re-entry:

> *You just have to be realistic. If you think things are going to be different, then you are going to get very depressed. Time stands still – or so it seems. Your flat will look the same, your wardrobe will not have been revamped, and the tube strikes will still be going on. But in fact, much will have changed and happened without you, it just takes a bit longer to see the subtleties. If possible, plan to come back in the summer (always a little kinder). Get every photo into an album (or onto a webpage if that is how you are doing it) within a month or you'll never do it. Don't rely on staying in touch with fellow travellers as a way of keeping the experience alive. You have to move on. If you do develop fantastic new friendships then that's great but you can't force them.*

While change may be somewhat surprising and even shocking, it cannot negate or diminish the extraordinary phase of life you will have enjoyed during your gap year.

MY GROWN UP GAP YEAR:
BRADWELL JACKSON

American Bradwell Jackson's holiday travels throughout his 20s and 30s persuaded him to re-invent himself as a long-term world traveller. His dream is to wander the earth in a happy-go-lucky way, earning and paying as he goes, and his travels as a roving English teacher have taken him to some exotic corners of the globe.

After reading Work Your Way Around the World, I wondered if it was really possible to get a job teaching English so easily. Well I found out that it is.

I made the decision to quit my job, leave my home, give away most of my belongings to charity, and sell my car so that I could wander the earth freely. I was sitting at a metro stop in Mexico City, trying to figure out what school to go to for my first planned job enquiry. After I decided that the particular school I had in mind was too far away, I looked up and saw an English school right across the street. Providence, I thought. I was right. I sauntered on upstairs, cheerfully asked if they needed an English teacher, and about an hour and a half later, I was told when to start my training. It really was that easy.

After travelling round Britain and France, I went to west Africa. By a happy accident of fate, I found out about The English Language Center in Nouakchott, the capital of Mauritania... and I was hired to teach for a minimum of two months. I was given free accommodation in a home the owner had kept for teachers (a very good deal) and my monthly wages started at 50,000 ouguiyas ($190) which later increased to 68,000 ($259). There's not much to do in Nouakchott, so I spent most of my time reading and exploring the poorer parts of the city, experiencing a cultures very different from my own.

In March of 2008, I was offered a job with Aston in China on the basis of a telephone interview and I am very happy with this. Aston is good to me, and my co-workers scramble to help me whenever I have even a mild matter that needs attention. For example, when I told them I was looking for a kung-fu school, they took this as a very important issue and had many long discussions-cum-negotiations with each other in order to come up with the best option for me. I think it might be hard to convince a Westerner to come and stay in an out-of-the-way city like Tangshan.

Really, I'm living the life of Reilly here. I've got nothing to complain about. The school has given me a free apartment complete with cable TV, washing machine, toaster oven, microwave, and refrigerator. Whenever I'm hungry, I just mosey on down to the street vendors and get some proper Chinese food for a friendly budget price. Who can ask for more?

MY GROWN UP GAP YEAR:
TIM RHODES JONES

Tim found that openings for physiotherapists were few and far between in his native Isle of Man, so he decided to work abroad for six months. He felt that this would be killing two birds with one stone: the need to use his physiotherapy skills and his desire to see a new country and culture.

After deciding I would go to a hospital in Kumasi in Ghana, I was met with only encouragement from both my family and friends. Whereas my friends mainly focused on the travelling aspect of my decision (the wildlife, local rituals, living conditions, weather), my family were more aware of the professional implications of my break. They wanted to know about conditions in the hospital, standards of practice and the benefits this experience would have for my own practice. Both sets of conversations never failed to get me very excited, and also a little bit nervous about my impending trip.

When researching my trip I was surprised at how few sending agencies offer physiotherapy placements so was glad to find Changing Worlds which was offering just the placement I required, in a desirable location and whose feedback from previous clients was impressive. And when I needed to return to the UK for family reasons they were very helpful arranging a flight for me.

The main highlight of my experience was the amount of physiotherapy practice I was able to have. The very busy hospital environment provided a large range of conditions, some of which I had not had previous contact with. I feel the experience enhanced my skills as a therapist hugely. Another highlight was the speed at which I felt I became a part of the society at both the workplace and with my host family. The people accepted and included you in their routines very quickly, and at all times gave a sense of mutual respect for your beliefs and a compassion which I have found to be unrivalled. The final highlight was simply the beauty of Ghana, from the coastal 'paradise' beaches to the northern national park wildlife, various stunning waterfalls and lakes and mountains.

Returning to the UK was surprisingly tricky. You get immersed in the social rules of Ghana, the methods of communication, the haggling for everything you buy, the way you eat with your right hand, the method of washing your clothes, and these are hard to shake off. Slowly the urge to haggle decreases, the greeting you use for people returns to the normal handshake or nod, and you start to take things like washing machines for granted again. Obviously the weather is a big thing to get used to though. Step off that plane and you definitely know you're back in good old rainy England.

If you liked this book, you might also enjoy:

HANDS-ON HOLIDAYS

Hands-On Holidays is the definitive guide to finding the most rewarding short-term breaks around. For people who are dissatisfied with conventional holidays and want to make a difference, or just do something different.

The book collects a host of opportunities from monitoring the movements of elephants in a Kenyan wildlife sanctuary, to trekking through the Costa Rican rainforest for charity, or helping to rebuild homes that were destroyed in the Tsunami.

Vividly illustrated with first hand accounts, Hands-On Holidays proves you don't have to put your life on hold to pursue a dream.

Author: Guy Hobbs
Published: June 2007
ISBN: 978-1-85458-373-4

www.crimsonpublishing.co.uk